STUDY GUIDE
Volume II: From 1100

James Schmiechen
Central Michigan University

A History of World Societies

Third Edition

John P. McKay
University of Illinois at Urbana-Champaign

Bennett D. Hill
Georgetown University

John Buckler
University of Illinois at Urbana-Champaign

HOUGHTON MIFFLIN COMPANY   BOSTON   TORONTO
DALLAS   GENEVA, ILLINOIS   PALO ALTO   PRINCETON, NEW JERSEY

Sponsoring Editor: John Weingartner
Senior Development Editor: Lance Wickens
Ancillary Coordinator: Tracy Theriault
Manufacturing Coordinator: Priscilla Bailey
Marketing Manager: Diane Gifford

Printed in the U.S.A.

ISBN: 0-395-58908-8

BCDEFGHIJ-PO-998765432

Contents

To the Student   v

Chapter 14   Creativity and Crisis in the High and Later Middle Ages   1

PRIMARY SOURCES: Three Documents from the Thirteenth Century   27

Chapter 15   Africa Before European Intrusion, ca 400–1500   31

Chapter 16   The Americas Before European Intrusion, ca 400–1500   46

Chapter 17   European Society in the Age of the Renaissance and Reformation   61

PRIMARY SOURCES: Two Sixteenth-Century Thinkers   87

STUDYING EFFECTIVELY—EXERCISE 3: Learning How to Identify Main Points That Are Effects, Results, Consequences   91

Chapter 18   The Age of European Expansion and Religious Wars   94

Chapter 19   Absolutism and Constitutionalism in Europe, ca 1589–1725   116

Chapter 20   Toward a New World View in the West   143

STUDYING EFFECTIVELY—EXERCISE 4: Learning to Classify Information According to Sequence   159

Chapter 21   The Life of the People in Europe   162

Chapter 22   African Kingdoms and Societies, ca 1450–1800   176

PRIMARY SOURCES: The Transatlantic Slave Trade   189

Chapter 23   The Middle East and India, ca 1450–1800   194

Chapter 24   China and Japan, ca 1400–1800   210

PRIMARY SOURCES: Japan and China in the Early Seventeenth Century: Reaction to the West   227

Chapter 25   The Revolution in Western Politics, 1775–1815   231

PRIMARY SOURCES: The Rights of Man and of Woman   249

Chapter 26   The Industrial Revolution in Europe   254

PRIMARY SOURCES: Industrialization and Urban Life
for the Working Classes   271

STUDYING EFFECTIVELY—EXERCISE 5:   Learning to Identify Main Points
That Are Causes or Reasons   285

Chapter 27   Ideologies and Upheavals in Europe, 1815–1850   288

Chapter 28   Life in European Urban Society   307

Chapter 29   The Age of Nationalism in Europe, 1850–1914   323

PRIMARY SOURCES: Varieties of Socialism   341

Chapter 30   The World and the West   346

Chapter 31   Nation Building in the Western Hemisphere and in Australia   364

Chapter 32   The Great Break: War and Revolution   385

STUDYING EFFECTIVELY—EXERCISE 6:   Learning to Make
Historical Comparisons   405

Chapter 33   Nationalism in Asia, 1914–1939   407

Chapter 34   The Age of Anxiety in the West   427

Chapter 35   Dictatorships and the Second World War   445

Chapter 36   Recovery and Crisis in Europe and the Americas   463

PRIMARY SOURCES: The Vietnam War   483

Chapter 37   Asia and Africa in the Contemporary World   487

Chapter 38   Life in the Third World   511

Chapter 39   One Small Planet   526

Answers to Objective Questions   543

Duplicate Outline Maps   557

To the Student

How to Study History and Prepare for Exams

The study of history can be rewarding but also perplexing. Most history courses require you to read and understand large bodies of detailed information. The history student is expected to perform many tasks—memorize information, study the reasons for change, analyze the accomplishments and failures of various societies, understand new ideas, identify historical periods, pick out broad themes and generalizations in history, and so forth. These jobs often present difficulties. This guide will make your study easier and increase your efficiency. It has been developed to help you read, study, and review *A History of World Societies*, and regular and systematic use of it will improve your grade in this course. You may use the guide in a variety of ways, but for best results you might choose the following approach:

1. *Preview the entire chapter* by reading the "Chapter Questions" and "Chapter Summary"; then quickly read through the study outline, noting the reading with understanding exercises. All of this will take only a few minutes but is an important first step in reading. It is called *previewing*. By pointing out what the chapter is about and what to look for, previewing will make your reading easier and improve your reading comprehension.

2. *Now read your assignment in the textbook*. Pay attention to features that reveal the scope and major emphasis of a chapter or section, such as the chapter title, chapter and section introductions, questions, headings, conclusions, and illustrative material (e.g., maps and photographs). Note study hint 3 on page ix about underlining.

3. After reading, *review what you have read* and check your comprehension by going over the chapter outline once again—but this time make sure that you understand all the points and subpoints. If you do not fully understand a particular point or subpoint, then you need to return to the text and reread. It is not at all uncommon to need to read the text at least twice.

4. Continue your review. *Answer the review questions* that follow the study outline. It is best to write out or outline your answer on a sheet of paper or a note card. Be sure to include the supporting facts. Reread your answers periodically. This process will help you build a storehouse of information and understanding to use at the time of the exam.

5. Now work on the definitions, identifications, and explanations in the study-review exercises provided in each chapter of the *Study Guide*. This will help you to understand and recall both concepts and specific facts. Know not just who or what, but also why the term is significant. Does it illustrate or represent some fundamental change or process? Note that if a particular term appears in the text *and* in your lecture notes, it is of special importance. Do the geography exercises found in all appropriate chapters. This is important because they will enable you to visualize the subject matter and thus remember it better. It will take a few minutes, but the payoff is considerable. (Duplicate copies of all outline maps in the *Study Guide* can be found at the end of the book.)

6. Next, *complete the multiple-choice and fill-in exercises* for each *Study Guide* chapter. Some of these questions look for basic facts, while others test your understanding and ability to synthesize material. *The answers are at the end of the Guide.* If you miss more than two or three, you need to restudy the text or spend more time working on the *Guide*.

7. The section "Major Political Ideas" will help you understand some of the political concepts that are raised in the text. Keep a special section in your notebook where you write out the answers to these questions. By the time you take your exam you will have a good understanding of what these political concepts are and how and why they developed.

8. "Issues for Essay and Discussion" sets out one or two broad questions of the type you may be asked to answer in an essay exam or discuss in a classroom discussion. Answer these by writing a one to two page essay in which you address each part of the question with a well-organized answer based on material from the text. Remember, your instructor is looking for your ability to back up your argument with historical evidence.

9. Last, "Interpretation of Visual Primary Sources" is a way for you to expand your understanding of the chapter and to help you learn how to use prints, photographs, architectural artifacts and the like in assessing historical change. Keep a section in your notebook where you answer these questions—but also use your new skills in this area when you study the other visuals in the chapter. Don't be reluctant to make reference to these visual sources when you write your examination essays.

Additional Study Hints*

1. *Organize your study time effectively.* Many students fail to do well in courses because they do not organize their time effectively. In college, students are expected to read the

*For a complete text and workbook written to meet the needs of students who want to do their best in college, see James F. Shepherd, *RSVP, The Houghton Mifflin Reading, Study, and Vocabulary Program*, Fourth Edition (1992).

material before class, review, and do the homework on their own. Many history teachers give only two or three tests during the semester; therefore, assuming personal responsibility for learning the material is vital. Mark up a semester calendar to show scheduled test dates, when term projects are due, and blocks of time to be set aside for exam study and paper writing. Then, at the beginning of each week, check the calendar and your course outlines and notes to see what specific preparation is necessary for the coming week, and plan your time accordingly. Look at all the reading with understanding exercises in this *Study Guide* and try to estimate how much time you will need to master study skills. Set aside a block of time each day or once every several days for reading your text or studying your lecture notes and working in the *Study Guide*. Despite what one observes on college campuses, studying is not done most effectively late at night or with background music. Find a quiet place to study alone, one where you can tune out the world and tune into the past.

2. *Take good lecture notes*. Good notes are readable, clear, and above all reviewable. Write down as much of the lecture as you can without letting your pen get too far behind the lecturer. Use abbreviations and jot down key words. Leave spaces where appropriate and then go back and add to your notes as soon after the lecture as possible. You may find it helpful to leave a wide margin on the left side for writing in subject headings, important points, and questions, as well as for adding information and cross-references to the text and other readings. One way to use your notes effectively is by *reciting*. Reciting is the act of asking a question and then repeating the answer silently or aloud until you can recall it easily. Above all, do not wait until the night before an exam to use lecture notes you have not looked at for weeks or months. Review your lecture notes often and see how they complement and help you interpret your reading.

3. *Underline*. Too often students mark almost everything they read and end up with little else than an entire book highlighted in yellow. Underlining can be extremely helpful or simply a waste of time in preparing for exams; the key is to be selective in what you underline. Here are some suggestions:

    a. Underline major concepts, ideas, and conclusions. You will be expected to interpret and analyze the material you have read. In many cases the textbook authors themselves have done this, so you need to pinpoint their comments as you read. Is the author making a point of interpretation or coming to a conclusion? If so, underline the key part. Remember, learning to generalize is very important, for it is the process of making history make sense. The author does it and you must learn to identify his or her interpretation as well as conflicting interpretations; then to make your own. Here is where your study of history can pay big rewards. The historian, like a good detective, not only gathers facts but also analyzes, synthesizes, and generalizes from that basic information. This is the process of historical interpretation, which you must seek to master.

    b. Underline basic facts. You will be expected to know basic facts (names, events, dates, places) so that you can reconstruct the larger picture and back up your analysis and interpretations. Each chapter of this guide includes several lists of important items. Look over these lists before you begin to read, and then underline these words as you read.

c. Look at the review questions in the *Study Guide*—they will point to the major themes and questions to be answered. Then, as you read, underline the material that answers these questions. Making marginal notations can often complement your underlining.

4. *Work on your vocabulary.* The course lectures and each chapter in the text will probably include words that you do not know. Some of these will be historical terms or special concepts, such as *polis, feudalism,* or *bourgeoisie*—words that are not often used in ordinary American speech. Others are simply new to you but important for understanding readings and discussion. If you cannot determine the meaning of the word from the context in which it appears or from its word structure, then you will need to use a dictionary. *Keep a list of words* in your lecture notebook or use the pages in the back of this guide. Improving your historical and general vocabulary is an important part of reading history as well as furthering your college career. Most graduate-school entrance exams and many job applications, for instance, have sections to test vocabulary and reading comprehension.

5. *Benefit from taking essay exams.* Here is your chance to practice your skills in historical interpretation and synthesis. Essay exams demand that you express yourself through ideas, concepts, and generalizations as well as by reciting the bare facts. The key to taking an essay exam is preparation. Follow these suggestions:

a. *Try to anticipate the questions on the exam.* As you read the text, your notes, and this guide, jot down what seem to be logical essay questions. This will become easier as the course continues, partly because you will be familiar with the type of question your instructor asks. Some questions are fairly broad, such as the chapter questions at the beginning of each chapter in this guide; others have a more specific focus, such as the review questions. Take a good look at your lecture notes. Most professors organize their daily lectures around a particular theme or stage in history. You should be able to invent a question or two from each lecture. Then answer the question. Do the same with the textbook, using the *Study Guide* for direction. Remember, professors are often impressed when students include in their essay textbook material not covered in class.

b. *Aim for good content and organization.* Be prepared to answer questions that require historical interpretation and analysis of a particular event, series of events, movement, process, person's life, and so forth. You must also be prepared to provide specific information to back up and support your analysis. In some cases you will be expected to give either a chronological narrative of events or a topical narrative (for example, explaining a historical movement in terms of its social, political, and economic features). Historians often approach problems in terms of cause and effect, so spend some time thinking about events in these terms. Remember, not all causes are of equal importance, so you must be ready to make distinctions—and to back up these distinctions with evidence. This is all part of showing your skill at historical interpretation.

    When organizing your essay, you will usually want to sketch out your general thesis (argument) or point of interpretation first, in an introductory sentence or two. Next move to the substance. Here you will illustrate and develop your argument by weighing the evidence and marshaling reasons and factual data. After you have completed this stage (writing the body of your essay), go on to your conclusion, which most likely will be a restatement of your original thesis. It is often helpful to outline your major points before you begin to write. Be sure you answer all parts of the question. Write clearly and directly. All of this is hard to do, but you will get better at it as the course moves along.

6. *Enhance your understanding* of important historical questions by undertaking additional reading and/or a research project as suggested in the "Understanding History Through the Arts" and "Problems for Further Investigation" sections in the *Study Guide*. Note also that each textbook chapter has an excellent bibliography. Many of the books suggested are available in paperback editions, and all of the music suggested is available in most record-lending libraries and record stores. If your instructor requires a term paper, these sections are a good starting point.

7. *Know why you are studying history*. Nothing is worse than having to study a subject that appears to have no practical value. And indeed, it is unlikely that by itself this history course will land you a job. What, then, is its value, and how can it enrich your life? Although many students like history simply because it is interesting, there are a number of solid, old-fashioned reasons for studying it. It is often said that we need to understand our past in order to live in the present and build the future. This is true on a number of levels. On the psychological level, identification with the past gives us a badly needed sense of continuity and order in the face of ever more rapid change. We see how change has occurred in the past and are therefore better prepared to deal with it in our own lives. On another level, it is important for us to know how differing political, economic, and social systems work and what benefits and disadvantages accrue from them. As the good craftsperson uses a lifetime of experience to make a masterpiece, so an understanding of the accumulated experiences of the past enables us to construct a better society. Further, we need to understand how the historical experiences of peoples and nations have differed, and how these differences have shaped their respective visions. Only then can we come to understand how others view the world differently from the ways in which we do. Thus, history breaks down the barriers erected by provincialism and ignorance.

The strongest argument for the study of history, though, is that it re-creates the big picture at a time when it is fashionable and seemingly prudent to be highly specialized and narrowly focused. We live in the Age of Specialization. Even our universities often appear as giant trade schools, where we are asked to learn a lot about a little. As a result, it is easy to miss what is happening to the forest because we have become obsessed with a few of the trees. While specialization has undeniable benefits, both societies and individuals also need the generalist perspective and the ability to see how the entire system works. History is the queen of the generalist disciplines. Looking at change over time, history shows us how to take all the parts of the puzzle—politics, war, science, economics, architecture, sex, demography, music, philosophy, and much more—and put them together so that we can understand the whole. It is through a study of the interrelationships of the parts over a long expanse of time that we can develop a vision of society. By promoting the generalist perspective, history plays an important part on today's college campus.

Finally, the study of history has a personal and practical application. It is becoming increasingly apparent to many employers and educators that neglect of the liberal arts and humanities by well-meaning students has left them unable to think and reason analytically and to write and speak effectively. Overspecialized, narrowly focused education has left these students seriously deficient in basic skills, and an understanding of the meaning of Western culture, placing them at a serious disadvantage in the job market. Here is where this course can help. The study of the past enables us to solve today's problems. It is universally recognized that studying history is an excellent way to develop the ability to reason and write. And the moving pageant of centuries of human experience you are about to witness will surely spark your interest and develop your aptitude if you give it the chance.

Acknowledgments

The authors wish to thank the following people for their help and suggestions in the preparation of this edition of the *Study Guide:* Susan Conner, James Dealing, Susan Pyecroft, Pat Ranft, Gabriel Chien, John Robertson, and Nina Nash-Robertson.

CHAPTER 14
Creativity and Crisis in the High and Later Middle Ages

Chapter Questions

After reading and studying this chapter, you should be able to answer the following questions:

How did medieval rulers in England, France, and Germany solve their problems of government and lay the foundations of the modern state? How did medieval towns originate and how do they reflect radical change in medieval society? Why did towns become the center of religious heresy? How did universities develop and what needs of medieval society did they serve? What does the Gothic cathedral reveal about the ideals, attitudes, and interests of medieval people? How did economic difficulties, plague, and war affect Europeans socially, economically, and politically in the fourteenth century?

Chapter Summary

The High Middle Ages—roughly, the twelfth and thirteenth centuries—was an era of remarkable achievement in law, the arts, philosophy, and education. The modern idea of the sovereign nation-state took root in this period. By means of war, taxation, and control over justice, the kings of England and France were able to strengthen royal authority and establish a system of communication with all of their people.

The Normans were important in bringing a centralized feudal system to England by using the sheriff, the writ, and other devices to replace baronial rule with royal power. Out of this process emerged the concept of common law and, with the Magna Carta, the idea of supremacy of the law. The process, however, was not altogether smooth, as the conflict between Henry II and Becket illustrates. The evolution of the territorial state in France was not quite as rapid as in England. France was less of a geographical unit than England, and the creation of strong royal authority involved more armed conflict between king and barons. And in Germany, royal power failed to develop at all, despite a good start by Emperor Frederick Barbarossa. Part of the reason was the historic connection between Germany and

Italy. The church-state struggle was another major reason why royal authority in Germany was destined to remain weak.

The rise of the universities accompanied the emergence of the strong secular states because the new states needed educated administrators to staff their bureaucracies. The new universities became centers for the study of law and medicine.

Improvement in agriculture, coupled with a reopening of the Mediterranean to Christian traders, fostered the growth of towns and commerce. Flanders and Italy led the way in this urban revival. Towns meant a new culture and social order, increased economic opportunities, and the beginnings of modern capitalism.

Religious heresy grew as the traditional Christian religion was unable to meet the needs of urban dwellers. The result of the heretical crisis was the evolution of several new religious orders of Friars, which counteracted the heretical movement by putting emphasis on a nonmaterialistic clergy that could preach to the needs of the people and at the same time manage the process of reconversion.

Few periods in history can claim as many artistic achievements as the High Middle Ages. The Gothic cathedrals, shimmering in stone and glass, stand not only as spiritual and artistic testimony to the age but also as a reflection of the economic power and civic pride of the great cities. By 1300, the energy of the High Middle Ages had been spent.

The fourteenth century was a time of disease, war, crime, and violence. The art and literature of the period are full of the portrayal of death, just as the historical accounts are full of tales of conflict and violence. There were several major causes for this century of human suffering. Natural disaster—including changes in climate and horrible new diseases—attacked Europe. A long series of wars between France and England not only brought death and economic ruin but increased personal violence and crime as well.

Amid such violence the church lost power and prestige, partly because of the religious disillusionment that accompanied the plague. In short, the institutional church failed to fill the spiritual vacuum left by the series of disasters.

But the century of disaster was also a century of change, some of it for the good of ordinary people. It is in this light that the chapter examines some important changes in marriage practices, family relations, and the life of the people. The decline in population meant that those who survived had better food and higher wages. Peasants in western Europe used the labor-shortage problem to demand higher wages and freedom from serfdom. These demands often resulted in conflict with their lords. The disillusionment with the organized church also led to greater lay independence and, ultimately, ideas of social and political equality. The wars actually fostered the development of constitutionalism in England. All in all, it was a period of important changes.

Study Outline

Use this outline to preview the chapter before you read a particular section in your textbook and then as a self-check to test your reading comprehension after you have read the chapter section.

I. The medieval origins of the modern state
   A. For five hundred years after the fall of Rome, the state did not exist and political authority was completely decentralized.
      1. In their effort to strengthen royal authority, medieval kings laid the foundations for the modern national state.
      2. The modern state is an organized territory, with a body of law, which protects its citizens in return for their loyalty.
   B. Unification and communication
      1. The seven Anglo-Saxon kingdoms of England united under the Danish king Canute, giving England a political head start.
         a. All shires (counties) were under a royally appointed sheriff.
         b. All thegns (chieftains) recognized royal authority.
      2. William the Conqueror weakened the power of the feudal lords.
         a. He demanded military quotas and an oath of allegiance.
         b. He made local people, such as the sheriff, responsible for order, and he used the *writ* and the inquest (the results of which were compiled in the *Domesday Book*) as a way to tax and to centralize government.
      3. Henry II of England was able to claim half of France—the so-called "Angevin empire."
      4. France was an area of independent provinces wherein the king had little or no real power, except for his own royal domain, the Ile-de-France.
         a. The king used the cult of Saint-Denis to foster national loyalty.
         b. The unification of France began under Philip II (Augustus), who gained control of northern France from the English.
         c. By the end of the thirteenth century, his successors had come to control most of what is modern France.
      5. French royal government rested on the principle of royal interests superseding local interests—as with the royally appointed baillis and seneschals—and on a professional royal bureaucracy.
      6. By the twelfth century, Germany was split into hundreds of independent areas ruled by local lords.
         a. Strong central government was blocked because of the absence of a strong royal domain, the lack of royal succession, and dreams of imperial rule over Italy.
         b. Anarchy led to the election of Frederick Barbarossa as emperor in 1152.
         c. He gained the loyalty of his princes and churchmen and forbade private warfare, but his interests in Italy eventually led to failure and a decentralized power system in Germany.
   C. Finance
      1. In England, Henry I established a bureau of finance called the Exchequer.
         a. Royal income came from taxes, legal fees, feudal dues, and from scutage—money paid in lieu of military service.
         b. The Exchequer was the beginning of the English bureaucracy.

2. In France the ballis and seneschals were responsible for the collection of royal taxes.
    a. New sources of revenue were found in the tallage (or taille) and in merciless taxes on French Jews.
    b. But French localism retarded the growth of central (royal) finance until the establishment of the Chamber of Accounts.
3. Sicily had an advanced financial bureaucracy.
    a. Under Norman overlords it developed an efficient feudal system that used the Muslim record-keeping bureau, the *diwan*.
    b. Roger II secured a monopoly on the sale of lumber and salt, and he hired a mercenary army.
    c. In Sicily, Emperor Frederick II Hohenstaufen banned private warfare, made royal courts supreme, set forth royal law in the *Constitutions of Melfi*, taxed imports and exports, and obtained the right to levy regular taxes.
    d. All of this made Sicily into a modern state, although when Frederick died much of his bureaucracy collapsed.
    e. In Germany, Frederick gave so much to the princes and the church that he greatly weakened imperial authority.

D. Law and justice
    1. France and England led the way in building a system of uniform law.
    2. In France, Louis IX replaced local justice with a royal judicial system.
        a. This included the Parlement of Paris, a supreme court of appeal.
        b. Louis's royal judges were sent throughout the country, and laws were published for the entire kingdom.
    3. In England, Henry II advanced common law (law common to all) and annually sent royal judges throughout the land.
        a. He also instructed sheriffs to provide the royal judges with a list of suspected criminals—this is the forerunner of the modern grand jury.
        b. In the thirteenth century, the custom of trial by ordeal was replaced by trial by jury.
    4. Henry's rejection of the custom of "benefit of clergy" led to conflict with Archbishop Thomas Becket—and to Becket's murder.
    5. Henry's sons, Richard ("the Lion-Hearted") and John, were ineffectual kings; John lost Normandy and with it England's hopes in France.
        a. John so antagonized his feudal barons that they rebelled and forced him to sign the treaty called Magna Carta, which set forth the principle that all are protected by law and that all, including the king, must obey the law.
        b. Every English king in the Middle Ages reissued Magna Carta as a promise to obey the law.
    6. By 1272, English common law was universal.
        a. It relied on precedents, not fixed legal maxims.
        b. Under common law the courts were open to the public, and the accused had access to evidence used against them.
        c. Judges were to be impartial, and torture was prohibited.

7. Legal uniformity throughout Europe led to social conformity and hence rising hostility toward minorities, Jews, and homosexuals.
   a. In most of Europe, Jews could not own land; they were primarily tradesmen and moneylenders and lived in legally defined sections of towns.
   b. Economic and social changes in the later twelfth century led to ugly anti-Semitism, including expulsion from England and France.
   c. Despite the absence of prejudice against homosexuals in early Christian and medieval society, between 1250 and 1300 homosexual activity came to be regarded as illegal and evil.

II. Economic revival
   A. The rise of towns laid the foundation for the great transformation of Europe.
      1. Many towns began as boroughs, or fortifications, and expanded into faubourgs, or settlements outside the walls.
      2. Others began as settlements to service cathedrals and schools, or were old Roman camps or seaports.
      3. Most towns had a wall, a marketplace, a mint, and a court.
      4. Townspeople (burghers) did not fit into the traditional medieval social order, nor did the church have a theological justification for this new class.
   B. Town liberties
      1. Towns were a place for opportunities—and profit for landholders who sold liberties, or special privileges, to townspeople.
      2. The most important liberty was that of personal freedom, which meant citizenship.
      3. Many towns, like London and Norwich, gained extensive rights in the twelfth and thirteenth centuries and developed a new kind of law called "law merchant," as well as judicial independence.
      4. Merchant and trade guilds were formed, and craft guilds determined the quality, quantity, and price of goods as well as the number of workers in the craft.
      5. Women outnumbered men in the towns; many acted as head of household, and they predominated in many crafts but received lower wages than men.
      6. Merchant guilds became rich and powerful and came to constitute an urban oligarchy.
      7. Royal charters gave various liberties to towns, and local lords granted town self-government in return for cash.
   C. The revival of long-distance trade
      1. A great revival of trade occurred in the eleventh century.
      2. Investment risks were reduced by group investment.
      3. Geography and political stability allowed Flemish and Italian towns (particularly Venice) to predominate in long-distance trade.
      4. Availability of English wool stimulated Flemish and English textile industries.
      5. Unlike foodstuffs, the price of wool was determined by demand, not supply.

D. The commercial revolution
1. From the late eleventh through the thirteenth centuries, Europe went through a period of expansion and growth of trade and transportation firms, new types of commercial credit, and a new capitalistic spirit.
   a. The German Hanseatic League was an association of North Sea/Baltic towns, dominated by Lübeck, which carried on trade across all of Europe.
   b. The league traded in furs, wax, copper, fish, grain, timber, and wine, and developed new business techniques such as the business register.
2. This commercial revolution created new wealth and a higher standard of living, and gave greater power to the middle classes.
   a. It also provided new opportunities for many serfs, although local society still was under the control of the church and the feudal nobility.
   b. The commercial changes did, however, pave the way for the development of urban life and culture.

III. Medieval universities
A. The word *university* is from the Latin word meaning "corporation" or "guild"—hence the medieval university was an educational guild.
B. Origins
1. Universities grew out of cathederal schools and municipal schools, first in Bologna and Salerno in Italy.
   a. The University of Bologna grew out of a renewed interest in Roman law inspired by the great teacher Irnerius (d. 1125).
   b. Salerno's university grew out of an interest in medicine; it received the support of King Roger II of Sicily.
2. Peter Abelard was important in attracting students to the University at Paris.
   a. His book *Sic et Non* was a controversial philosophical work that argued that truth is perceived through systematic doubting.
   b. Abelard was censured by the church but remained a highly popular teacher.
3. Universities were organized and run by the professors.
C. Instruction and curriculum
1. Professors used the Scholastic method of teaching in which questions were raised in order to arrive at definitive answers; classical texts were used to unify faith and reason.
   a. Aristotle was reinterpreted, and his emphasis on direct observation and fact were used to understand Christian truths—although the conclusions were often wrong.
   b. Scholastics laid the foundation for later scientific work.
2. The Scholastics sought to organize all knowledge into summa, or reference books, the most famous of which was Aquinas's *Summa Theologica*.
   a. Aquinas argued that although reason can demonstrate many Christian principles, other truths cannot be proved by reason—but this does not mean that they are contrary to reason.
   b. He investigated epistemology, the branch of philosophy concerned with knowledge, and maintained that the mind understands everything

through the senses; hence all knowledge comes through reason, including knowledge of the existence of God.

3. The method of teaching at the universities was the lecture, followed by interpretation, called the gloss, which students wrote down.
   a. Exams were given only after the three to five years of study.
   b. The degree certified competence in a given subject.

IV. Creative outburst
   A. From Romanesque gloom to "uninterrupted light"
      1. The medieval Gothic style was innovative and reflected the wealth, creativity, pride, and energy of society.
         a. Peace in the eleventh century encouraged church building.
         b. The old Romanesque churches had thick walls and were very dark.
         c. The Gothic style originated with the monk Suger and featured the pointed arch, the ribbed vault, the flying buttress, and interior lightness.
      2. Gothic architecture spread from France to all of Europe.
   B. Community expression
      1. Cathederals were a symbol of civic pride and served many purposes.
         a. They were used for feast days, local guild meetings, and political meetings.
         b. Most important, they were a means of religious instruction—all of the building's architecture and decoration had religious or social significance.
      2. Drama, derived from the church's liturgy, emerged as a distinct art form.
   C. Vernacular literature
      1. The emergence of national consciousness is seen in the rise of literature written in national languages—the vernacular.
      2. Three literary masterpieces illustrate this new national pride.
         a. Dante's *Divine Comedy*, a symbolic pilgrimage to the City of God, embodies the psychological tensions of the age and contains bitter criticism of some church authorities.
         b. Chaucer, in his *Canterbury Tales*, uses a religious setting to depict the materialistic and worldly interests of a variety of English people.
         c. Villon used the language of the lower classes to speak of the reality, beauty, and hardships of life here on earth in the *Grand Testament*.
         d. Christine de Pisan wrote a variety of books on women and society, as well as on religion, love, and morality.

V. Heresy and the friars
   A. Heresy flourished most in the most economically advanced and urbanized areas.
      1. Neither traditional Christian theology nor the isolated monastic orders addressed the problems of mercantile society.
      2. Townspeople desired a pious clergy who would meet their needs.
   B. Heresy, originally meaning "individual choosing," was seen as a threat to social cohesion and religious unity.

1. The Gregorian injunction against clerical marriage made many priests vulnerable to the Donatist heresy, which held that sacraments given by an immoral priest were useless.
2. Various heretics, such as Arnold of Brescia, Peter Waldo, the Albigensians, and others denounced wealth, the sacraments, and material things.
   a. The Albigensian heresy grew strong in southern France and was the subject of a political-religious crusade.
   b. Heretical beliefs became fused with feudal rebellion against the French crown.
3. The Cathars, or Albigensians, rejected the Roman church and adhered to a belief in dualism—that is, God created spiritual things and the Devil created material things.
C. As a response to heretical cults, two new religious orders were founded.
   1. Saint Dominic's mission to win back the Albigensians led to the founding of a new religious order of "Preaching Friars" (the Dominicans).
   2. Saint Francis of Assisi founded an order (the Franciscans) based on preaching and absolute poverty of the clergy.
   3. These new orders of friars were urban, based on the idea of poverty, and their members were drawn from the burgher class.
D. The friars met the spiritual and intellectual needs of the thirteenth century.
   1. They stressed education and intellectual pursuit.
   2. Their emphasis on an educated and nonmaterialistic clergy won them the respect of the bourgeoisie.
   3. The friars successfully directed the Inquisition, and heresy was virtually extinguished.

VI. The Black Death
A. The plague, or Black Death, had its roots in economic problems and terrible famine due to climate changes and population growth.
   1. It entered Europe via Sicily in 1347 and then spread northward.
   2. All Europe felt its effects.
B. Pathology
   1. The plague was caused by a bubonic bacillus that lived in fleas that infested black rats.
      a. Unsanitary and overcrowded cities were ideal breeding grounds for the black rats.
      b. Standards of personal hygiene were low and invited disease.
      c. The disease started with a boil, or buba, which led to several stages of illness and then death.
   2. Medieval people had no rational explanation for the disease and hence turned to explanations based on ignorance and bigotry.
   3. Between a quarter and two-thirds of the population died; the disease recurred many times up to 1700.
C. Social and psychological consequences
   1. The plague hit the poor harder than the rich, but all classes suffered.

      2. The decline in population meant labor shortages; thus wages went up and social mobility increased.

      3. The psychological consequences of the plague were enormous: depression, gross sensuality, flagellantism, and obsession with death.

VII. The Hundred Years' War (ca 1337–1453)
  A. Causes of the war
    1. Edward III of England, the grandson of the French king Philip the Fair, claimed the French crown, and French barons used Edward's claim as a way to check their king.
    2. Flemish wool merchants supported the English claim to the crown.
    3. Both the French and the English saw military adventure as an excuse to avoid domestic problems.
    4. Royal propaganda for war and plunder was strong on both sides; the war provided great opportunities for individual wealth and advancement.
  B. The course of the war to 1419
    1. The battles took place in France and the Low Countries.
    2. At the Battle of Crécy (1346), the English disregarded the chivalric code and used new military tactics: the longbow and cannon.
  C. Joan of Arc and France's victory
    1. Joan of Arc's campaigns meant a turning point and victory for France.
    2. Joan was turned over to the English, and a French church court burned her as a heretic.
  D. Costs and consequences
    1. The war meant economic and population decline for France and England.
    2. War financing caused a slump in the English wool trade.
    3. In England, returning soldiers caused social problems.
    4. The war encouraged the growth of parliamentary government, particularly in England.
    5. The war generated feelings of nationalism in England and France.

VIII. The decline of the church's prestige
  A. The leaders of the fourteenth-century church added to the sorrow and misery of the times.
    1. The kings of England and France (Edward I and Philip the Fair) insisted on the right to tax the clergy, while Pope Boniface VIII denied this right and defended clerical diplomatic immunity; the result was a church-state conflict.
      a. Philip the Fair declared the pope to be a heretic, and the pope responded with the *Unam Sanctam* (1302), which claimed that all Christians are subject to the pope.
      b. French troops arrested the pope, who died shortly thereafter.
    2. Pope Clement V was pressured to move the papacy to France (Avignon) in 1305.
  B. The Babylonian Captivity (1309–1377)
    1. The Babylonian Captivity, during which the popes lived in France, damaged papal power and prestige.

2. Pope Gregory XI brought the papacy back to Rome in 1377, but then a split occurred when the newly elected Urban VI alienated the church hierarchy in his zeal to reform the church.
3. A new pope, Clement VII, was elected, and the two popes both claimed to be legitimate (the Great Schism).

C. The Great Schism lasted until 1417.
1. England and Germany recognized Pope Urban VI.
2. France and others recognized Pope Clement VII.

D. The conciliar movement was based on the idea of reform through a council of church leaders.
1. Marsiglio of Padua claimed that authority within the church should rest with a church council and not the pope.
2. The English teacher John Wyclif and his Lollard followers attacked papal authority and called for even more radical reform of the church.
3. Wyclif's ideas were spread to Bohemia by John Hus.
4. Finally, the council at Constance (1414–1418) ended the schism with the election of Pope Martin V and condemned Hus to death.

IX. The life of the people in the fourteenth and fifteenth centuries
A. Marriage
1. Marriage usually came very early for women and later for men; divorce did not exist.
2. Postponement of marriage meant other socially acceptable sexual outlets.
   a. Houses of prostitution were allowed and regulated by the town government.
   b. Some prostitutes grew wealthy, but overall prostitutes were scorned.
3. Until the nineteenth century, economic factors, not romantic love or physical attraction, determined whom and when a person married.

B. Life in the parish
1. The land and the religion were the centers of life.
2. Mobility within guilds declined in the fourteenth century, and strikes and riots within guilds became frequent.
3. Cruel sports, such as bullbaiting, and drunkenness reflect the violence and frustrations of the age.
4. In the fourteenth and fifteenth centuries, many nobles turned to crime as a way of raising money—the so-called "fur-collar crime."
5. Lay people increasingly participated in church management as criticism of churchmen grew more common.

C. Peasant revolts
1. Peasants revolted in France in 1358 and in England in 1381.
2. One cause was the lords' attempt to freeze wages.
3. In general, the revolts were due to rising expectations.
4. The 1381 revolt in England began as a protest against taxes.
5. Workers in Italy, Germany, and Spain also revolted.

Review Questions

Check your understanding of this chapter by answering the following questions.

1. Define the modern state. What are its characteristics and goals?

2. Describe the unification and centralization of royal power in England. Who were the participants, and what methods did they use?

3. What problems did the French kings face in unifying France under royal authority? What techniques did they use?

4. Why was unification in Germany so much more difficult than in England or France? What factors weakened and divided Germany?

5. Evaluate the work of Frederick Barbarossa. In what did he succeed, and why, in the end, did he fail?

6. Why was Frederick II Hohenstaufen called the "Transformer of the World"? What was so modern about him? What effect did he have on Germany? On Sicily?

7. Describe the evolution of common law and royal justice in England. Who were the important participants, and what were their methods and accomplishments?

8. What were the principal reasons for the rise of urban society in the eleventh century?

9. How did the new townspeople manage to gain political status and liberty for their towns?

10. What were the purpose and origins of the medieval university?

11. Who were the Scholastics? What were their basic beliefs about knowledge and education, and what were their methods of acquiring knowledge?

12. What were the chief features of the Gothic style of architecture?

13. What were the reasons for the rise of the heretical cults? Why and how were they extinguished?

14. What was the source of the bubonic plague, and why did it spread so rapidly in Europe?

15. What impact did the plague have on wages and demand for labor? What happened to land values?

16. Describe the psychological effects of the plague. How did people explain this disaster?

17. What were the immediate and other causes of the Hundred Years' War?

18. How did the Babylonian Captivity greatly weaken the power and prestige of the church?

19. What was the conciliar movement, and who were its advocates? Was this a revolutionary idea?

20. What was fur-collar crime, and why did it become a central feature of life in the fourteenth and fifteenth centuries?

21. Did peasants' lives improve or deteriorate in the fourteenth and fifteenth centuries? In what ways?

22. What were the reasons for the French Jacquerie of 1358 and the English peasants' revolt of 1381?

23. Why did a great amount of conflict and frustration among guild members develop during the fourteenth century?

Study-Review Exercises

Define the following key concepts and terms.

thegn

Gothic

scholasticism

universitas

common law

Hanseatic League

burgher

Pasteurella pestis

fur-collar crime

conciliar movement

vernacular literature

craft guild

Define each of the following terms and explain how it contributed to the evolution of the modern state.
writ

sheriff

baillis and seneschals

Exchequer

tallage

Identify and explain the significance of the following people and terms.
merchant guild

heresy

Frederick II Hohenstaufen

Philip II of France

Saint Thomas Aquinas

Suger, abbot of Saint-Denis

Henry II of England

Peter Abelard

Summa Theologica

Louis IX of France

Saint Dominic

Saint Francis of Assisi

Queen Isabella of England

Hundred Years' War

Battle of Crécy (1346)

Martin V

Joan of Arc

Babylonian Captivity

Edward III

John Wyclif

Jacquerie

Explain what the following events were and why they are important in understanding the High Middle Ages.

Domesday survey

crusade against the Albigensians

Frederick Barbarossa's Italian wars

William of Normandy's conquest of England

conflict between Pope Boniface VIII and King Philip the Fair of France

Test your understanding of the chapter by providing the correct answers.

1. This letter declared that everyone must submit to the papacy. _____

2. The English royal bureau of finance. _____

3. The emperor of Germany who tried to unify Germany. _____

4. William the Conqueror's survey of English wealth. _____

5. The European country best known for its common law. _____

6. The area that underwent development by Frederick II Hohenstaufen.

   _____

7. This document implied that in English society the law is above the king.

   _____

8. The method of teaching at medieval universities. _____

9. The architectural style that reflects Roman and early Christian models.

   _____

10. Medieval reference books. _____

11. A league of German cities with its center at Lübeck. _____

12. Author of *Sic et Non*. _____

13. The bishop who was murdered as the result of a church-state struggle.

    _____

14. In reaction to the calls for reform in the fourteenth century, the church *did/did not* enter into a period of reform and rejuvenation.

15. Prior to the plague in 1348, Europe experienced a period of unusually *good/bad* harvests.

16. The Hundred Years' War was between the kings of _____ and

    _____ .

17. Up to the nineteenth century, *economic/romantic* factors usually determined whom and when a person married.

Place the following events in correct chronological order.

First instance of the bubonic plague in Europe   1. _____

Babylonian Captivity   2. _____

Start of the Hundred Years' War   3. _____

Council of Constance   4. _____

Battle of Crécy   5. _____

Jacquerie   6. _____

Dante's *Divine Comedy*   7. _____

Great Schism   8. _____

Multiple-Choice Questions

1. By origin and definition, a burgher, or bourgeois, was
   a. a person involved in trade or commerce.
   b. a person who lived within town walls.
   c. a resident of Hamburg, Germany.
   d. a person who lived on hamburgers.

2. Artisans and craftspeople in medieval towns formed
   a. courts to try corrupt businessmen.
   b. craft guilds.
   c. merchant guilds.
   d. the scutage.

3. The French government, as conceived by Philip Augustus, was characterized by
   a. centralization at the local level and diversity at the top.
   b. diversity at the local level and centralization at the top.
   c. complete local government.
   d. a system identical to England's.

4. Frederick Barbarossa's success in restoring order to the Holy Roman Empire was spoiled by his involvement in
   a. France
   b. Germany
   c. England.
   d. Italy.

5. The principle implied in the Magna Carta was
   a. democracy.
   b. that all people, even the king, are subject to the law.
   c. that the king is above the law.
   d. that the people rule the monarch.

6. Which of the following is *not* a characteristic of a Gothic cathedral?
   a. Pointed arches
   b. Ribbed vaults
   c. Thick walls
   d. Flying buttresses

7. The surge of cathedral building in the twelfth and thirteenth centuries was closely associated with
   a. the increase of university-trained architects.
   b. financial hard times, which caused people to turn to religion.
   c. the low cost of building materials.
   d. the growth of towns and the increase of commercial wealth.

8. Heresy flourished
   a. in the most economically advanced and urbanized areas.
   b. in the backward rural areas.
   c. only in southern France.
   d. in urban areas suffering from plague and economic depression.

9. The two European states that first developed efficient bureaucracies were
   a. England and Sicily.
   b. England and France.
   c. England and Italy.
   d. Sicily and France.

10. The first European universities were located in
    a. England.
    b. France.
    c. Italy.
    d. Germany.

11. Prior to the systemization of law in the thirteenth century, homosexuality was
    a. socially accepted.
    b. outlawed.
    c. uncommon.
    d. unknown.

12. One forerunner of the Western university was the
    a. manor school.
    b. monastery.
    c. cathedral school.
    d. medieval public school.

13. The standard method of teaching in medieval universities was
    a. *summa*.
    b. a gloss.
    c. reading assignments in books.
    d. the lecture.

14. Common law differed from the system of Roman law in that it
    a. applied only to the peasant class.
    b. was more permanent and static.
    c. relied on precedents.
    d. relied heavily on torture.

15. By the end of the twelfth century, the general European attitude toward Jews
    a. became increasingly intolerant.
    b. moved in the direction of greater acceptance.
    c. led to political emancipation of the Jews.
    d. had not changed over that of previous generations.

16. The *Summa Theologica* was written by
    a. John of Salisbury.
    b. Peter Abelard.
    c. Thomas Aquinas.
    d. William of Sens.

17. The Waldensians were
    a. a heretical group that attacked the sacraments and church hierarchy.
    b. the political and financial supporters of the German princes.
    c. the merchant bankers of Hamburg.
    d. the religious order that built the abbey church at Saint-Denis.

18. The conciliar movement was
    a. an effort to give the pope the power to use councils to wipe out heresy.
    b. the effort by the French lords to establish a parliament.
    c. a new monastic order vowing poverty.
    d. an attempt to place ultimate church authority in a general council.

19. The plague was probably brought into Europe by
    a. Chinese soldiers.
    b. Spanish warriors returning from South America.
    c. English soldiers pushing into France.
    d. Genoese ships from the Crimea.

20. Generally, the plague disaster of the fourteenth century resulted in all of the following
    except
    a. higher wages for most workers.
    b. a severe decline in the number of German clergymen.
    c. a decline in flagellantism.
    d. an obsession with death.

21. The author of *Defensor Pacis* and proponent of the idea that authority in the Christian
    church rested in a general council rather than in the papacy was
    a. Cardinal Robert of Geneva.
    b. Pope Urban V.
    c. John Wyclif.
    d. Marsiglio of Padua.

22. *Fur-collar crime* is a term used to describe
    a. the robbery and extortion inflicted on the poor by the rich.
    b. the criminal activity carried out by bandits like Robin Hood.
    c. crimes committed by churchmen.
    d. the illegal activities of noblewomen.

23. English military innovation(s) during the Hundred Years' War included
    a. the crossbow.
    b. the cannon and longbow.
    c. the calvary.
    d. the pike.

24. For the French, the turning point of the Hundred Years' War was
    a. the relief of Paris.
    b. the defeat of the English fleet in the English Channel.
    c. the relief of Orléans.
    d. the Battle of Poitiers.

25. Prostitution in late medieval society
    a. did not exist.
    b. existed only among the lower classes.
    c. was not respected but was legalized and widespread.
    d. existed in the countryside but not the city.

26. In the fourteenth century, craft guilds began to change in that
    a. master and journeyman distinctions began to disappear.
    b. the guilds lost control over the production process.
    c. apprenticeship was abandoned.
    d. membership became more restrictive and master-journeyman relations
       deteriorated.

27. The effect of the Hundred Years' War on England was that it
    a. brought great wealth in the form of cash reserves to England.
    b. caused a great increase in wool exports.
    c. allowed many English knights to become very rich.
    d. resulted in a net loss in cash.

Major Political Ideas

1. Define and describe the concept of the sovereign nation-state. How does it compare to
   the early medieval idea of government?

2. What is meant by common law? How and why did it evolve?

3. The history of towns is also the history of merchants' efforts to acquire liberties. What does *liberties* mean, and what role did the merchant and craft guilds and their members play in its evolution?

4. Define nationalism. How did the Hundred Years' War encourage nationalism? What is the purpose and function of a national assembly? Why did a national representative assembly emerge in England but not in France?

5. What were the ideas set forth by Marsiglio of Padua in *Defensor Pacis*? What were the political implications of these ideas?

Issues for Essays and Discussion

The High Middle Ages witnessed remarkable achievements in the areas of political organization, law and justice, the evolution of the town, and art. What were the major developments in these areas? How did they differ in England, France, Germany, and elsewhere? What were the reasons for these developments and were there any negative effects?

Interpretation of Visual Sources

1. Study the section of the Bayeaux Tapestry reproduced on page 405 of the textbook. What is the subject of this tapestry? What information about medieval life does it provide? What is the political significance of the event depicted?

2. Study the reproduction of the painting *The Plague-Stricken* on page 438 of the textbook. How did people respond to this mysterious disease? Look carefully at the figures in this painting. Who seems to be in control of the situation? Does the group of figures in the upper left-hand corner provide any information as to what was thought to be the origins of the disease?

Geography

On Outline Map 14.2 provided and using Map 14.2 in the textbook as a reference, mark the following:

1. The royal domain, or crown lands, of France as they existed in 1180, the names of the territories added by Philip Augustus, the territories added from 1223 to 1270, and the territories added from 1270 to 1314.

2. Using Map 14.4 and the text discussion as your sources, describe the various trade routes used by the Italians, the Flemish, and the Hanseatic League.

_____

_____

_____

3. Use Maps 14.7 and 14.8 in the textbook to complete the following:
   a. Locate the extent of the English posessions in France. What were the origins of English claims to the throne?
   b. Why was it unlikely that England could have held these territories permanently?
   c. Locate the main centers of popular revolt in France and England.
   d. Why were so many of the English revolts in the highly populated and advanced areas of the country?

Remember that duplicate maps for class use are at the back of this book.

Outline Map 14.2

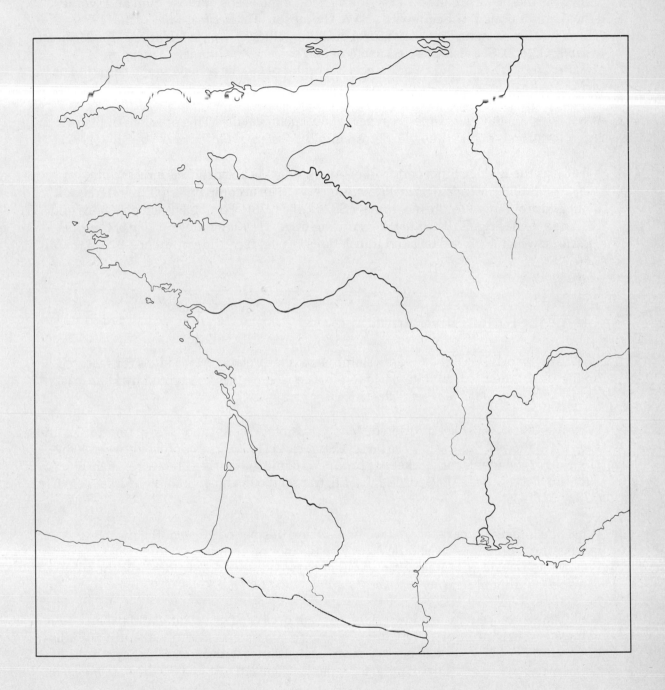

Understanding History Through the Arts

1. How was medieval architectural style affected by the needs of those men and women who commissioned it? Begin with M. W. Thompson, *The Decline of the Castle* (1988). Those interested in medieval cathedral building will want to see J. Harvey, *The Medieval Architect* (1972). See also Chaps. 3 and 4 of N. Pevsner, *An Outline of European Architecture* (7th ed., 1963). For France, the center of Gothic achievement, see J. Evans, *Art in Medieval France, 987–1498* (1969).

2. What does the Bayeaux Tapestry reveal about medieval life? This problem of historical interpretation is dealt with in D. Bernstein, *The Mystery of the Bayeaux Tapestry* (1987).

3. What was the music of this period like? An excellent introduction is a recording, *Instruments of the Middle Ages and Renaissance,* with an accompanying illustrated book by D. Munro (Angel recording number SB2-3810 [1976]). For the French chansons and the English madrigals, listen to the recording titled *The King's Singers Sing of Courtly Pleasures,* which includes text and translations (Angel recording number s-37025 [1974]).

Problems for Further Investigation

1. What are the origins of the modern state? New interpretations and ideas for research on the rise of the modern state are found in a collection of essays edited by H. Lubasz, *The Development of the Modern State* (1964).

2. Why was Thomas Becket murdered? Many possible research and term-paper topics are suggested in T. M. Jones, ed., *The Becket Controversy* (1970). The conflict between King Henry II and Archbishop Becket has produced some interesting literature, such as Jean Anouilh, *Becket; or the Honor of God,* L. Hill, trans. (1960), and T. S. Eliot, *Murder in the Cathedral* (1935).

3. What was life like for aristocratic women during this period? One of the most fascinating women of the Middle Ages was Eleanor of Aquitaine, wife to the king of France and the king of England and mother to two kings of England. She is the subject of a spellbinding biography, *Eleanor of Aquitaine and the Four Kings* (1950), by A. Kelly.

4. Did the emergence of urban life result in a clash between Christianity and urban values? Did urbanization force Christianity to re-evaluate its traditional antimaterialistic position? A good place to begin your investigation is with an excellent synthesis of the new urban life and Christianity: L. Little, *Religion, Poverty, and the Profit Economy in Medieval Europe* (1978).

*Available in paperback.

5. How can a single disease affect the course of history? Students interested in the plague should begin with G. C. Coulton, *The Black Death* (1929); P. Zeigler, *The Black Death: A Study of the Plague in Fourteenth Century Europe* (1969); and W. McNeill, *Plagues and Peoples* (1976).

6. Why did the peasant revolts start? Those interested in popular protest during this age should consult M. Mullett, *Popular Culture and Protest in Medieval and Early Modern Europe* (1987). The fourteenth century is analyzed in the interesting book *A Distant Mirror: The Calamitous Fourteenth Century* (1978) by B. W. Tuchman.

7. What was the cause of the conflict between Philip the Fair of France and the pope? Was the French king out to destroy the power of the papacy? These and other questions are debated by a number of historians in C. T. Wood, ed., *Philip the Fair and Boniface VIII** (1967).

*Available in paperback.

PRIMARY SOURCES

Three Documents from the Thirteenth Century

The thirteenth century was a century of progress and change. Each of the following documents represents a particular aspect of that change.

Although its initial purpose was to protect the interests of the barons under King John of England (1199–1216), the Magna Carta eventually came to protect the interests of other social classes as well. As a result, the document was regarded as a guarantee of certain rights. Sections 6, 7, 8, included below, were interpreted to allow women some powers. What were these? Sections 13, 20, and 35 afforded merchants of the towns a greater degree of freedom. What were these? Sections 39 and 40 contain the germ of the modern legal idea of due process of law for all people. On the other hand, Articles 10 and 11 reflect anti-Semitic attitudes deep in medieval society. In what ways do they indicate discrimination?

Magna Carta, 1215*

6. Heirs shall be married with disparagement; yet so that, before the marriage is contracted, it shall be announced to the blood-relatives of the said heir.

7. A widow shall have her marriage portion and inheritance immediately after the death of her husband and without difficulty; nor shall she give anything for her dowry or for her marriage portion or for her inheritance—which inheritance she and her husband were holding on the day of that husband's death. And after his death she shall remain in the house of her husband for forty days, within which her dowry shall be assigned to her.

*Source: Carl Stephenson and Frederick G. Morcham, Sources of English Constitutional History (New York: Harper & Brothers, 1937).

8. No widow shall be forced to marry so long as she wishes to live without a husband; yet so that she shall give security against marrying without our consent if she holds of us, or without the consent of her lord if she holds of another.

10. If any one has taken anything, whether much or little, by way of loan from Jews, and if he dies before that debt is paid, the debt shall not carry usury so long as the heir is under age, from whomsoever he may hold. And if that debt falls into our hands, we will take only the principal contained in the note.

11. And if any one dies owing a debt to Jews, his wife shall have her dowry and shall pay nothing on that debt. And if the said deceased is survived by children who are under age, necessities shall be provided for them in proportion to the tenement that belonged to the deceased; and the debt shall be paid from the remained, saving the service of the lords. In the same way let action be taken with regard to debts owed to others besides Jews.

13. And the city of London shall have all its ancient liberties and free customs, both by land and by water. Besides we will and grant that all the other cities, boroughs, towns, and ports shall have all their liberties and free customs.

20. A freeman shall be amerced [punished] for a small offence only according to the degree of the offence; and for a grave offence he shall be amerced according to the gravity of the offence, saving his contentment. And a merchant shall be amerced in the same way, saving his merchandise; and a villein in the same way, saving his wainage [agricultural implements]—should they fall into our mercy. And none of the aforesaid amercements shall be imposed except by the oaths of good men from the neighbourhood.

35. There shall be one measure of wine throughout our entire kingdom, and one measure of ale; also one measure of grain, namely the quarter of London; and one width of dyed cloth, russet [cloth], and hauberk [cloth], namely, two yards between the borders. With weights, moreover, it shall be as with measures.

39. No freeman shall be captured or imprisoned or disseised [unlawfully removed] or outlawed or exiled or in any way destroyed, nor will we go against him or send against him, except by the lawful judgement of his peers or by the law of the land.

40. To no one will we sell, to no one will we deny or delay right or justice.

The medicants, or orders of begging friars, were founded as a response to the spiritual needs of a growing urban society. Chief among these orders was the order of friars founded by Saint Francis of Assisi. Can you tell what the goals and practices of the Franciscans were? How did they differ from the older monastic orders like the Benedictines and Cistercians? What in these rules indicates that the Franciscans are involved in an urban as opposed to a monastic society?

The Rule of Saint Francis, 1223*

This is the rule and life of the Minor Brothers, namely, to observe the holy gospel of our Lord Jesus Christ by living in obedience, in poverty, and in chastity. Brother Francis promises obedience and reverence to Pope Honorius and to his successors who shall be canonically elected, and to the Roman Church. The other brothers are bound to obey brother Francis, and his successors . . .

I counsel, warn, and exhort my brothers in the Lord Jesus Christ that when they go out into the world they shall not be quarrelsome or contentious, nor judge others. But they shall be gentle, peaceable, and kind, mild and humble, and virtuous in speech, as is becoming to all. They shall not ride on horseback unless compelled in manifest necessity or infirmity to do so. When they enter a house they shall say, "Peace be to this house." According to the holy gospel, they may eat of whatever food is set before them.

I strictly forbid all the brothers to accept money or property either in person or through another. Nevertheless, for the needs of the sick, and for clothing the other brothers, the ministers and guardians may, as they see that necessity requires, provide through spiritual friends, according to the locality, season, and the degree of cold which may be expected in the region where they live. But, as has been said, they shall never receive money or property.

Those brothers to whom the Lord has given the ability to work shall work faithfully and devotedly, so that idleness, which is the enemy of the soul, may be excluded and not extinguish the spirit of prayer and devotion to which all temporal things should be subservient. As the price of their labors they may receive things that are necessary for themselves and the brothers, but not money or property. And they shall humbly receive what is given them, as is becoming to the servants of God and to those who practise the most holy poverty.

The brothers shall have nothing of their own, neither house, nor land, nor anything, but as pilgrims and strangers in this world, serving the Lord in poverty and humility, let them confidently go asking alms. Nor let them be ashamed of this, for the Lord made himself poor for us in this world. This is that highest pitch of poverty which has made you, my dearest brothers, heirs and kings of the kingdom of heaven, which has made you poor in goods, and exalted you in virtues . . . .

I strictly forbid all the brothers to have any association or conversation with women that may cause suspicion. And let them not enter nunneries, except those which the pope has given them special permission to enter. Let them not be intimate friends of men or women, lest on this account scandal arise among the brothers or about brothers.

*Source: Oliver J. Thatcher and Edgar H. McNeal, eds. and trans., *A Source Book for Medieval History* (New York: Scribner's, 1905), 499–507.

The following ordinance of the silk merchants' guild in the mid-thirteenth century tells us a great deal about women in industry in the High Middle Ages. How did women control their trade? Consider how the ordinance seeks to regulate the size of particular establishments and the number of workers in them, sets the number of years of training, prevents "raiding" of businesses, sets standards for the quality of the silk cloth, and seeks to build loyalty to the silk manufacturer's guild.

Ordinance of the Silk Spinsters in Paris, 1254–1271*

Any woman who wishes to be a silk spinster on large spindles in the city of Paris—i.e., reeling, spinning, doubling and retwisting—may freely do so, provided she observe the following customs and usages of the craft:

No spinster on large spindles may have more than three apprentices, unless they be her own or her husband's children born in true wedlock; nor may she contract with them for an apprenticeship of less than seven years or for a fee of less than 20 Parisian sols to be paid to her, their mistress. The apprenticeship shall be for eight years if there is no fee, but she may accept more years and money if she can get them. . . .

No woman of the said craft may hire an apprentice or workgirl who has not completed her years of service with the mistress to whom she was apprenticed. If a spinster has assumed an apprentice, she may not take on another before the first has completed her seven years unless the apprentice die or forswear the craft forever. If an apprentice spinster buy her freedom before serving the said seven years, she may not herself take on an apprentice until she has practiced the craft for seven years. If any spinster sell her apprentice, she shall owe six deniers to the guardians appointed in the King's name to guard the [standards of the] craft. The buyer shall also owe six deniers. . . .

If a working woman comes from outside Paris and wishes to practice the said craft in the city, she must swear before two guardians of the craft that she will practice it well and loyally and conform to its customs and usages.

If anyone gives a woman of the said craft silk to be spun and the women pawn it and the owner complain, the fine shall be 5 sols.

No workwoman shall farm out another's silk to be worked upon outside her own house.

The said craft has as guardians two men of integrity sworn in the King's name but appointed and changed at the will of the provost of Paris. Taking an oath in the provost's presence, they shall swear to guard the craft truly, loyally, and to their utmost, and to inform him or his agents of all malpractices discovered therein.

Any spinster who shall infringe any of the above rules shall pay the King a fine of 5 sols for each offense . . . [from which the craft guardians deduct their own expense].

*Source: Merry E. Wiesner, trans., unpublished ordinance in Memmingen Stadtarchiv, Zünfte, 471-1.

CHAPTER 15

Africa Before European Intrusion, ca 400–1500

Chapter Questions

After reading and studying this chapter, you should be able to answer the following questions:

What patterns of social and political organization prevailed among the peoples of Africa? What types of agriculture and commerce did Africans engage in? What values do Africans' art, architecture, and religions express?

Chapter Summary

The peoples and typography of Africa are diverse. The continent, which is the world's second largest, is divided into five climate zones, ranging from the fertile coastal lands to dry and vast deserts and dense, humid rain forests. The peoples of North Africa are a mix of native Berber and Mediterranean people, while black Africans were the dominant group that inhabited the regions south of the Sahara.

Africa is one of the places where knowledge of cultivation began. Gradually, agriculture and a settled way of life spread over the continent. Over the course of the centuries, Africa supported a variety of very different societies and civilizations. A network of caravan routes connected the Mediterranean coast with the Sudan, bringing Islam to West Africa and stimulating gold mining, trade in slaves, and urbanization. The kingdom of Ghana emerged as one of Africa's richest and most powerful states by virtue of its control of the southern end of the caravan route and its strong agricultural base. Another powerful state, Mali, had for centuries carried on a brisk trade in salt, gold, and slaves; significantly, as in much of Africa, this trade introduced the Africans to Islam, which in turn led to the conversion of rulers, the growth of intellectual centers such as Timbuktu, and the strong influence of Muslim *ulemas*.

By far, the most important foreign influence on Africa was Islam. In Ethiopia, however, the city of Axum became the capital of an important civilization that held to a distinctive brand of Christianity called Coptic Christianity. In South Africa a society evolved that was based on new farming techniques gained from Bantu peoples and the mining of gold.

Study Outline

Use this outline to preview the chapter before you read a particular section in your textbook and then as a self-check to test your reading comprehension after you have read the chapter section.

I. The land and peoples of Africa
   A. The geography of Africa
      1. Five geographical zones divide this continent, which covers 20 percent of the earth's land surface.
         a. The Mediterranean and southwestern coasts have fertile land, good rainfall, and dense vegetation.
         b. The dry steppe country of the inland in the north, the Sahel, has little plant life.
         c. From here stretch the great deserts—the Sahara in the north and the Namib and Kalahari in the south.
         d. The equatorial regions of central Africa have dense, humid, tropical rain forest.
         e. The savanna lands that extend from west to east across the widest part of Africa make up one of the richest habitats in the world.
      2. The climate of Africa is tropical; rainfall is seasonal and is sparse in the desert and semidesert areas.
      3. Five peoples inhabited Africa by 3000 B.C.
         a. The Berbers inhabited North Africa.
         b. The Egyptians were a cultural rather than a racial group.
         c. Black Africans inhabited the region south of the Sahara.
         d. Pygmies inhabited the equatorial rain forests.
         e. The Khoisan lived south of the equatorial rain forests.
   B. Early African societies
      1. Africa was one of the sites where agriculture began.
         a. It spread down the Nile Valley and then west to West Africa and south from Ethiopia.
         b. Agricultural development led to the establishment of settled societies and to population increase.
      2. Ironworking was introduced about 600 B.C., probably by the Phoenicians.
      3. The Bantu, a migratory group with ironworking skills, moved to central Africa and on to the southeast coast, absorbing the Pygmy and Khoisan people.

C. Western kingdoms in the Sudan (ca 1000 B.C.–A.D. 200)
1. A series of kingdoms emerged in the area bounded by Egypt, the Red Sea, Ethiopia, Uganda, Zaire, Chad, and Libya.
2. The Mande and Chadic peoples of western Sudan grew and prospered as a result of settled agriculture.
3. A strong sense of community was a key feature of early African society.
4. Religions were largely animistic and centered around the extended family and its ritual cults.

D. The trans-Saharan trade
1. The introduction of the camel had a profound economic and social impact on West Africa.
   a. Between A.D. 700 and 900, a network of caravan trade routes developed between the Mediterranean and the Sudan.
   b. Manufactured goods and food products were exchanged for raw materials and slaves.
   c. Caravan trade stimulated gold mining, slavery and the slave trade, and the development of strong urban centers in West Africa.
2. The most influential consequence of the trans-Saharan trade was the introduction of Islam to West African society.
   a. Conversion to Islam brought a rich and sophisticated culture, legal traditions and governing skills, and scientific knowledge.
   b. The arrival of Islam in West Africa also marked the advent of written documents.

II. African kingdoms and empires (ca 800–1450)
A. The medieval kingdom of Ghana (ca 900–1100) was a wealthy state that served as a model for other rulers.
1. The Soninke people called their ruler *ghana*, or war chief.
2. Skillful farming and efficient irrigation supported a large population.
3. The war chief captured the southern portion of the caravan route in 992.
4. The king was considered semisacred, his power was absolute, and he attained the crown through matrilineal heredity.
B. The court, influenced by Muslim ideas and run by a bureaucracy, was situated at Kumbi.
1. Muslims lived in their own quarter, or town, with their own religious-political authority.
2. The king resided in another town.
3. The royal court was extravagant and rich.
C. Ghana's juridical system was based on appeal to the supernatural, but the king could also be appealed to.
D. The royal estates, the tribute from chiefs, gold mining, and trade duties enabled the king to support a lavish court.
E. Ghanaian society consisted of several ranks.
1. The governing aristocracy (king, court, officials) occupied the highest rank.
2. Next were merchants, followed by the middle classes: farmers, miners, craftsmen, and weavers.

3. At the bottom was a small slave class.
4. Apart from these classes was the army.
F. The kingdom of Mali (ca 1200–1450)
   1. The kingdom of Ghana split into smaller kingdoms, one of which was Kangaba, which became Mali.
   2. Mali owed its greatness to its agricultural and commercial base and to its two great military rulers, Sundiata and Mansa Musa.
      a. The Mandinke people were successful at agriculture, and they profited from the West African salt and gold trade.
      b. Sundiata encouraged trade and expanded the kingdom.
      c. He transformed his capital, Niani, into an important financial and trading center.
      d. He conquered former Ghanaian territories and established hegemony over Gao, Jenne, and Walata.
   3. Mansa Musa continued these expansionist policies.
      a. He extended his influence northward to Berber cities in the Sahara, east to Timbuktu and Gao, and west to the Atlantic.
      b. Royal control over the trans-Saharan trade brought great wealth; the empire grew to 8 million people.
      c. Musa appointed members of the royal family as governors to rule provinces and dependent kingdoms.
      d. He embraced the Muslim religion, and Islamic practices and influence multiplied.
      e. Musa's visit to Egypt illustrated his great wealth, but his spending and gifts caused inflation.
      f. His pilgrimage to Mecca furthered relations among Mali, the Mediterranean states, and Islamic culture.
      g. Timbuktu was transformed into a commercial, intellectual, and artistic center; it became known as the "Queen of the Sudan."
   4. The mix between Arabic trade, Muslim culture, and African peoples encouraged a high degree of cosmopolitanism and racial toleration.
G. The East African city-states
   1. Commercial activity fostered the establishment of great city-states along the East African coast.
      a. Many of the natives were called "Ethiopian," or black.
      b. The relationship between Arab traders and native black people is unclear, although Islam did not supplant native African religions.
      c. Arab, Persian, and Indonesian immigrants to Africa intermarried with Africans, resulting in a society that combined Asian, African, and Islamic traits.
      d. This East African coastal culture was called "Swahili."
      e. Ibn-Battuta, a traveler, has left a written account of the great cities of Mombasa, Kilwa, and Mogadishu.

    2. By 1300 a ruler, or *sheik*, had arisen, and Kilwa was the most powerful city on the coast.

       a. Kilwa's prosperity rested on the gold trade and on the export of animal products.

       b. Swahili cities traded these products for pottery, beads, glassware, and cloth.

    3. Slaves were exported from East Africa for military, agricultural, maritime, and other purposes, including domestic work.

  H. Ethiopia: the Christian kingdom of Axum

    1. The kingdom of Ethiopia had close ties with the early Christian rulers of Nobatia, a Nubian state, and the Roman and Byzantine worlds.

       a. The Ethiopian city of Axum, the center of this civilization, adopted Monophysitic Christianity, which held that Christ was divine only, not divine and human.

       b. Axum was the major military and political power in East Africa.

       c. Economic contact with the Muslim world, along with the Abyssinian mountain range, caused Axum to sever ties with the Byzantine Empire.

    2. The distinctive brand of Christianity (Coptic Christianity) that developed in Ethiopia is the most striking feature of this culture between 500 and 1500.

  I. South Africa

    1. This region is bordered on the northeast by the Zambesi River, has a Mediterranean-type climate, and varies from desert to temperate grasslands.

    2. Until the arrival of the Portuguese (late fifteenth century), South Africa, unlike the rest of Africa, remained isolated from the outside world.

       a. Only the Bantus, with their ironworking and farming skills, reached South Africa (in the eighth century).

       b. In the west were Khosian-speaking farmers and in the east Bantu-speaking farmers who practiced polygamy.

       c. The city of Great Zimbabwe, built entirely of granite between the eleventh and fifteenth centuries, was over sixty acres in area, with elaborate decoration, a temple, and an encircling wall.

       d. This city was the capital of a vast empire in the Zambezi-Limpopo region, and its wealth rested largely on gold mining.

       e. Great Zimbabwe declined in the fifteenth century, and a new empire, also based on gold trade, was built in the Mazoe Valley under the Mwene Mutapa rulers.

Review Questions

1. Name and briefly describe the five groups of people who had inhabited Africa by 8000 B.C.

2. What have been the sources of our knowledge of Africa?

3. Describe the Bantu agricultural achievements. Why did the Bantu adopt the practice of migratory agriculture?

4. What does *anima* mean? Describe African animistic religions.

5. What were slaves used for, and how extensive was the trans-Saharan slave trade? What did race have to do with slavery?

6. What were the cultural and religious features of life in the western Sudan, and how did the introduction of the camel affect West African life?

7. What was the economic base of the Ghanaian state, and what sort of political organization did it exhibit?

8. Describe the reigns of Sundiata and Mansa Musa in Mali. What did they accomplish?

9. Why can East Africa be described as highly cosmopolitan, rich, and racially tolerant? Describe the economic, intellectual, and artistic features of the East African states.

10. Where was the location of the kingdom of Axum, and in what way did its form of Christianity differ from that of the orthodox West?

11. Why was South Africa "far removed" from the outside world, and how was it influenced by Bantu-speaking peoples?

12. Describe the city of Great Zimbabwe. What was its economic base?

Study-Review Exercises

Define the following key concepts and terms.

animistic religion

Guinea

trans-Saharan trade

ulemas

ghana

Swahili

Identify and explain the significance of the following people and terms.

Berbers

North African saddle

West African slave trade

kingdom of Ghana

kingdom of Mali

Coptic Christianity

Mansa Musa

Timbuktu

Ibn-Battuta

kingdom of Axum

Kilwa

Great Zimbabwe

Mwene Mutapa

Explain the main features and characteristics (social, political, economic, and religious) of the following civilizations.

Ghana

Mali

early South Africa

Test your understanding of the chapter by providing the correct answers.

1. Black Africans inhabited the region *north/south* of the Sahara.

2. *Seven/Five* peoples inhabited Africa by 3000 B.C.

3. Ironworking was probably introduced by the _____ .

4. *Sundiata/Mansa Musa* transformed his capital, Niani, into an important financial and trading center.

5. *Sundiata/Mansa Musa* appointed members of the royal family as governors.

6. *Axum/Timbuktu* became known as the "Queen of the Sudan."

7. Until the arrival of the *Portuguese/British* (late fifteenth century), South Africa, unlike the rest of Africa, remained isolated from the outside world.

Multiple-Choice Questions

1. The Berbers inhabited
    a. South Africa.
    b. the Congo region.
    c. North Africa.
    d. the Gold Coast.

2. Most of Africa's interior was not explored by Europeans until the
    a. 1800s.
    b. 1700s.
    c. 1500s.
    d. 1900s.

3. The Bantu people originally inhabited
   a. South Africa.
   b. Rhodesia.
   c. Nigeria.
   d. Ethiopia.

4. By A.D. 400, the western Sudan's population had increased dramatically as the result of
   a. changes in climate.
   b. increased concern for hygiene.
   c. increased food production.
   d. the practice of polygamy.

5. The religious beliefs of animism center on the
   a. worship of animals.
   b. sacredness of cows.
   c. idea that anima, or spirits, reside in almost everything.
   d. idea that the gods assume animal forms.

6. Trans-Saharan trade was made possible by
   a. the canteen.
   b. the camel.
   c. coined money.
   d. caravans.

7. The slave population of West Africa was composed of
   a. those guilty of civil or religious offenses.
   b. persons of certain ethnic groups.
   c. peoples captured in war.
   d. debtors who sold themselves into slavery.

8. The line of succession in the kingdom of Ghana was
   a. elective.
   b. matrilineal.
   c. patrilineal.
   d. none of the above.

9. The Ghanaian king's top officials were
   a. eunuchs.
   b. Muslims.
   c. Europeans.
   d. Arabs.

10. Mansa Musa created a stir in Egypt with his
    a. enormous armies.
    b. generosity.
    c. fabulous wealth in gold.
    d. both b and c.

11. At its peak, Timbuktu was
    a. a trade center.
    b. an intellectual center.
    c. a cosmopolitan, tolerant city.
    d. all of the above.

12. The Swahili language blends both Bantu and
    a. Indonesian.
    b. Mali.
    c. Malagasy.
    d. Arabic.

13. Arab influence in eastern Africa
    a. extended deep into the interior.
    b. spelled the end for animistic religion.
    c. was mostly confined to coastal ports.
    d. left few permanent traces.

14. The Coptic Christianity adopted by the Ethiopians holds that Christ's nature is
    a. both divine and human.
    b. unknown.
    c. divine only.
    d. human only.

15. People of the East African coastal towns who practiced various animistic religions
    were eventually converted to
    a. Islam.
    b. Christianity.
    c. the worship of anima.
    d. indigenous African religions.

16. South Africa remained far removed from the outside world until the arrival of the
    a. British.
    b. Egyptians.
    c. Muslim traders.
    d. Portuguese.

17. The city that was built from local granite, was highly decorated in gold and copper, and is today the most important archeological monument in Africa south of the Nile is
    a. Kilwa.
    b. Timbuktu.
    c. Kumbi.
    d. Great Zimbabwe.

18. The East African coastal culture was called
    a. anima.
    b. Mansa Musa.
    c. Swahili.
    d. Awkar.

19. In the eleventh century, the city of Kumbi consisted of two towns, one inhabited by the king and the other inhabited by
    a. the king's guards and priests.
    b. African artisans and tradespeople.
    c. Muslims.
    d. prisoners.

20. The kingdom of Mali owed its greatness to two fundamental assets, its exceptional rulers and its
    a. agricultural and commercial base.
    b. slave trade.
    c. rejection of Muslim traders and Muslim culture.
    d. ability to refrain from the West Africa trade and to stick to agriculture.

21. The book *Periplus of the Erythraean Sea* is
    a. the basis for Mansa Musa's religious conversion.
    b. the early history of Timbuktu.
    c. a Portuguese justification for the slave trade.
    d. the earliest surviving literary evidence of the city-states of the East African coast.

22. The most powerful of the East African city-states was
    a. Kilwa.
    b. Great Zimbabwe.
    c. Al Ghana.
    d. Kumbi.

23. For West Africa, an important consequence of the trans-Saharan trade was
    a. the end of the slave trade.
    b. economic depression.
    c. the decline of urban life.
    d. the conversion to Islam.

24. The introduction of the camel saddle into North Africa
   a. had little effect on commerce.
   b. allowed merchants to transport more goods.
   c. reduced the military advantage of the North Africans.
   d. meant an increase in the slave trade.

25. The region bounded on the north by the Sahara, on the south by the Gulf of Guinea, on the west by the Atlantic, and on the east by the mountains of Ethiopia is known as
   a. the Gold Coast.
   b. Madagascar.
   c. Ethiopia.
   d. the Sudan.

26. The great Malian emperor whose lavish spending during a visit to Egypt caused terrible inflation as well as world recognition was
   a. Mansa Musa.
   b. Sundiata.
   c. Al-Bakri.
   d. Taghaza.

Major Political Ideas

What sort of juridical system did Ghana have? How was it similar to that system used in western Europe? Could one describe the political/social organization of Ghana as "feudal"?

Issues for Essays and Discussion

1. Between about 400 and 1500, the African continent contained a number of very different societies and civilizations. Discuss political, social, and economic developments in West, East, and South Africa. What were the differences and the similarities? Why were some of these societies highly sophisticated while others were more simply organized?

2. What were the origins of the African slave trade, and how extensive was it? Was slavery a result of race distinctions, or was it the result of economic or other factors?

3. Why is the history of South Africa very different from the history of West Africa?

Geography

Using Outline Map 15.1 provided and referring to Maps 15.1 and 15.2 in the textbook, mark the following:

1. The geographic features that define the five distinct geographical zones in Africa. In the space below describe the climatic features of these zones and explain how geography has shaped the lives of African peoples.

2. The location and chief characteristics of the following early African societies: kingdom of Ghana, western Sudan, kingdom of Mali, East African city-states, kingdom of Axum, South Africa.

3. The location of the trans-Saharan trade routes. What was the economic basis of this trade and the importance of these routes to the history of Africa?

Remember that duplicate maps for class use are at the back of this book.

Outline Map 15.1

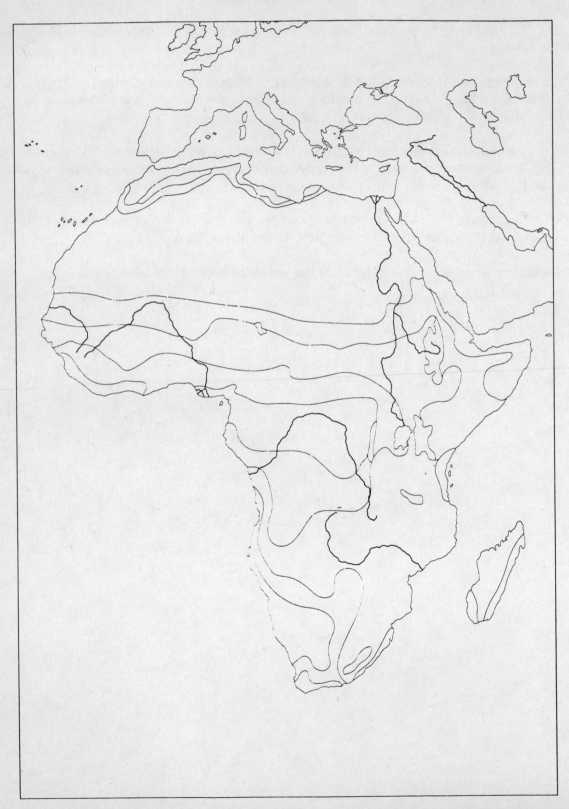

Problems for Further Investigation

1. The slave trade and its impact on both Africa and the West has been a highly controversial topic for historians. What questions do historians consider to be the most important, and how have these questions been answered? Begin your study with the American Historical Association pamphlet by Philip Curtin, *The Tropical Atlantic and the Age of the Slave Trade* (1991).

2. How did Islam help shape African society? Begin your research with J. Trimingham, *A History of Islam in West Africa** (1962) and *Islam in East Africa* (1964). An excellent way to begin research on this subject is to look at what historians have deemed the key issues as set forth in the American Historical Association pamphlet by Richard Eaton, *Islamic History as Global History** (1990).

*Available in paperback.

CHAPTER 16

The Americas Before European Intrusion, ca 400–1500

Chapter Questions

After reading and studying this chapter, you should be able to answer the following questions:

What is the geography of the Americas, and how did it shape the lives of the peoples? What patterns of social and political organization did Amerindian peoples display before the European intrusion? What are the significant cultural achievements of the Mayas, Aztecs, and Incas?

Chapter Summary

In America before European intrusion the Aztec, Maya, and Inca societies provide several of the most interesting (and puzzling) chapters in human history. Between 400 and 1500, three major Amerindian cultures flourished. The Maya are renowned for their art and their accomplishments in abstract thought; the Aztecs built a unified civilization based on Toltec heritage and distinguished by achievements in architecture, engineering, and scuplture. The Incas revealed a genius for organization, and their state was virtually unique in its time in assuming responsibility for the social welfare of all its people.

The climate and geography of the Americas is extremely varied. Mesoamerica, meaning Mexico and Central America, is dominated by high plateaus divided by great valleys and bounded by coastal plains. South America is characterized by great plains and the tropical lowlands of the Amazon River. The dominant peoples of these areas are the American Indians, or Amerindians, who discovered how to domesticate plants, particularly corn and potatoes. Development of the chinampas, or floating gardens, and terracing of slopes became ways to support a huge population. Agricultural skill had social and political benefits as well, in that labor was then available for activities besides agriculture.

The first distinct Mesoamerican culture was the Olmec society, which centered on a priestly elite and peasant farmers and succeeded in producing a large food supply and great stone

46

buildings. The highest level of Amerindian civilization came with the Maya peoples, whose intensive agriculture made huge populations and a thousand years of advancement possible. In central Mexico the Teotihuacán peoples built an enormous and rich city, but its collapse around A.D. 700 led to a "Time of Troubles" during which a Toltec confederation dominated central Mexico.

The Aztecs inherited the Toltec society and by 1428 embarked on a policy of territorial expansion—and a state based on war and human sacrifice. A number of possible reasons for the Aztec "rule by holocaust" are discussed. The most plausible is that human sacrifice was an instrument of state terrorism. Later Aztec society was highly stratified, the most numerous and the lowest classes being the workers, the landless workers, and the slaves. The center of this society was Tenochtitlán (Mexico City), whose layout, buildings, engineering accomplishments, and wealth were, according to eyewitness accounts, spectacular.

In the Andean regions of Peru an older civilization, that of the Incas, flourished. It too developed an excellent food supply and by 1200 was on a path of conquest that lasted until the Incas were overthrown by the Spanish in 1532. The Inca method of control was not terrorism but imperial unification, which included an excellent system of roads, an effective bureaucracy, and an enforced religion of state gods. Inca society was highly regimented, but the state took care of the poor and the aged.

Study Outline

Use this outline to preview the chapter before you read a particular section in your textbook and then as a self-check to test your reading comprehension after you have read the chapter section.

I. The geography and peoples of the Americas
   A. The combined total length of the continents of North and South America is about 11,000 miles. They are crossed by a mountain range that stretches from Alaska to the tip of South America and provides rugged terrain along the west coast of both continents.
      1. Mesoamerica (Mexico and Central America) is dominated by high plateaus bounded by coastal plains.
      2. The Central American coast is characterized by jungle, heavy rainfall, and heat; the uplands are better for agriculture and habitation.
      3. South America contains twelve nations and is a continent of extremely varied terrain.
         a. The western coast is edged by the Andes Mountains.
         b. On the east coast is the range called the Brazilian Highlands.
         c. Three-quarters of the continent is plains.
         d. The Amazon River bisects the north-central part of the continent and creates dense and humid jungle lands.

B. Immigrants—including Amurians and Mongoloids—crossed the Bering Straits as long as 20,000 years ago.
   1. Amerindians, or the American Indians, were a hybrid of these two groups.
   2. They practiced migratory agriculture, but some settled in villages.
   3. These newcomers spread out to form diverse linguistic and cultural groups.
   4. By about 2500 B.C., they had learned how to domesticate plants and became skilled in agriculture.
      a. The Mexicans built chinampas (floating gardens), whereas the land was terraced in Peru.
      b. Because the main Amerindian crops of corn and potatoes require less labor than grain, Amerindian civilizations were able to use their large labor forces for other things besides just agriculture.

II. Mesoamerican civilizations from the Olmec to the Toltec
   A. The Olmec civilization (ca 1500 B.C.–A.D. 300) was the first Mesoamerican civilization.
      1. All subsequent Mesoamerican cultures built on the Olmec.
         a. Olmec society revolved around groups of large stone buildings that housed the political and religious elite.
         b. Peasants inhabited the surrounding countryside.
         c. A hereditary elite governed the mass of workers.
      2. Around 900 B.C., power shifted from San Lorenzo to La Venta.
         a. The Great Pyramid at La Venta was the center of the Olmec religious cult.
         b. When La Venta fell around 300 B.C., Tres Zapotes became the leading Olmec site.
   B. The Maya of Central America
      1. Between A.D. 300 and 900 (the Classic period, or golden age of Mesoamerican civilization) the Maya of Central America built one of the world's most advanced cultures.
         a. The first Maya emigrated from North America.
         b. The Cholan-speaking Maya apparently created the Maya culture.
         c. Its economic base was agriculture, which supported a large population, and trade between cities evolved.
         d. Sharply defined social classes characterize the Maya culture.
         e. No distinct mercantile class existed.
         f. The hereditary nobility possessed the land and acted as warriors, merchants, and priests.
         g. The rest were free workers, serfs, and slaves.
      2. Maya hieroglyphic writing has been deciphered, allowing us to understand the history and art of the Maya.
         a. The Maya invented a calendar and devised a form of mathematics.
         b. They also made advances in astronomy and wrote books of history.
      3. Maya civilization collapsed between the eighth and tenth centuries.

C. Teotihuacán and Toltec civilizations also flourished during the Classic period.
   1. New people from the Mexico Valley built the city of Teotihuacán, which reached a population of over 200,000.
      a. Its inhabitants were stratified into the powerful elite and ordinary workers.
      b. It was the center for Mesoamerican trade and culture as well as its ceremonial center.
      c. At its middle were the Pyramids of the Sun and Moon, while other gods were worshiped at lesser temples.
   2. In the valley of Oaxaca, the Zapotecan peoples established a great religious center.
   3. Teotihuacán society collapsed before invaders around A.D. 700.
   4. This was followed by the "Time of Troubles"—a period of disorder, militarism, and emphasis on militant gods and warriors.
D. The Toltec confederation gained strength during this period.
   1. The Toltecs assimilated with the Teotihuacán people and sought to preserve their culture.
   2. Under Toliptzin, or Quetzalcoatl, the Toltecs came to control most of central Mexico from coast to coast.
   3. According to legend, the rich and powerful Quetzalcoatl went into exile when the god Tezcatlipoca won the battle over human sacrifice.
      a. Quetzalcoatl's promise to return became part of Aztec legend and was remembered when the Spanish conquerors arrived.
      b. Drought, weak rulers, and northern invasions brought trouble to the Toltecs.
      c. In 1224 the Chichimec peoples of the north captured the Toltec capital of Tula.
      d. The last of these Chichimec were the Aztecs, who absorbed the Olmec-Teotihuacán-Toltec culture.

III. Aztec society: religion and war
   A. The early Aztecs founded a meager city on the swamps of Lake Texcoco in 1325.
      1. By the time of Cortés in 1519, the Aztecs controlled all of central Mexico.
      2. The Aztecs attributed their success to their god Huitzilopochtli and to their own will power; equally important, the Aztec state was geared for war.
   B. War and human sacrifice in Aztec society
      1. War was the dominant cultural institution in Aztec society.
         a. The Aztecs believed that the sun needed human blood as its fuel.
         b. Victim-gladiators were sacrificed to the sun god.
         c. At times thousands of victims were sacrificed and then eaten.
      2. Anthropologists have proposed a variety of explanations for these practices.
         a. Human sacrifice served to regulate population growth.
         b. Protein deficiency made the Aztecs turn to cannibalism.
         c. Most plausible, human sacrifice was used as an instrument of state terrorism to control the people.

C. The life of the people
  1. The early Aztecs made no sharp social distinctions.
  2. By the early sixteenth century, however, a stratified social structure existed.
     a. Legend claims that the first king, a Toltec, fathered a noble class.
     b. At the time of the Spanish intrusion, warriors dominated the state.
     c. The great lords, or *tecuhtli*, were appointed by the emperor from among the war heroes; they became the provincial governors, judges, and generals.
     d. Provincial governors functioned much like the feudal lords in medieval Europe.
     e. Beneath the nobility of soldiers and great lords were the common warriors.
     f. Male children were instructed in the art of war and sought to become *tequiua* (nobility).
  3. The *maceualti*, or working class, made up the backbone of society.
     a. Members of this class were assigned work, but some of them enjoyed certain rights.
     b. Members of this group paid taxes.
  4. The next class was the *thalmaitl*, which was made up of the landless workers or serfs.
     a. They were bound to the soil.
     b. They had some rights and often performed military service.
  5. The lowest social class was the slaves.
     a. Most were prisoners of war, thieves, or debtors.
     b. They could own goods and property and purchase their freedom.
  6. Alongside all of these secular classes were the temple priests, who performed the sacrifice rituals and predicted the future.
  7. At the very top was the emperor, who was selected by a small group of priests, warriors, and officials.
     a. He lived in great luxury and with great ceremony.
     b. He was expected to be a great warrior and the lord of men (*tlacatecuhtli*).
D. The cities of the Aztecs
  1. Tenochtitlán, or Mexico City, was one of the largest and greatest cities in the world at the time of Díaz.
     a. Built on salt marshes and connected to the mainland by four highways, it had a population of half a million.
     b. Streets and canals crisscrossed the city and were lined with stucco houses.
  2. The Spaniards marveled at the city's aqueduct, public squares, and marketplace with its variety of goods.
  3. The pyramid-shaped temple of Huitzilopochtli dominated the city's skyline; it was surrounded by a wall and many towers.

IV. The Incas of Peru
A. The Inca civilization was established in the six fertile valleys of highland Peru.
  1. The Incas built terraces along the mountain slopes to cultivate white potatoes and produced bumper crops.

       a. They learned how to preserve them by a process of freeze-drying.

       b. They also cultivated corn.

  2. By the fifteenth century, the farms could support a large number of warriors and industrial workers.

B. Inca imperialism

  1. The Incas ascribed divine origin to their earliest king, Manco Capac (ca 1200).

  2. The king Pachacuti Inca and his son, Topa Inca, launched the imperialistic phase of Inca civilization.

       a. They extended Inca domination north to modern Ecuador and Colombia and to the Maule River in the south.

       b. Pachacuti made Quechua the official language, and it spread the Inca way of life throughout the Andes.

       c. The Incas ruled by imperial unification, imposing their language, religion, and bureaucracy, and by using a policy of colonization called *mitima* that involved forced relocation of the inhabitants of newly conquered territories.

C. Inca society

  1. The *ayllu,* or clan, was the central unit of early Inca society.

       a. The chief, or *curacas,* of the clan conducted relations with outsiders.

       b. The Inca kings superimposed imperial institutions on top of these kinship ties and formed new ayllus.

       c. Peasants were required to work for the lords and for the state.

  2. Marriage was required of all and mates were sometimes selected by the state; polygamy was common.

  3. Daily life was regimented, but all people were cared for.

       a. Although it had some socialist characteristics, Inca society was not based on equal distribution of wealth.

       b. The great nobles (*Orejones*) were exempt from work and lived luxuriously.

Review Questions

Check your understanding of this chapter by answering the following questions.

1. What role did religion play in the Olmec civilization? How did architecture complement this?

2. What was the class structure and religion of the Teotihuacán-Toltec civilization?

3. What was the legend of Quetzalcoatl's exile, and what role may it have played in later Mexican history?

4. To what features of Aztec culture do you attribute its success in building a great empire?

5. Why was human sacrifice an integral part of Aztec culture? What explanation is most plausible to you?

6. Describe the social structure of Aztec society. Who were the *tecuhtli*, the *maceualtin*, and the *thalmaitl*? Who was the *tlacatecuhtli*?

7. Who were the Maya, and how was their society organized?

8. What did the Maya accomplish?

9. What are the similarities between the Maya and the Inca agricultural-economic and political systems? The differences?

10. In what sense was the Inca emperor a benevolent despot? Was Inca society an early socialist state?

11. How do the Maya and Aztec military systems and methods of warfare compare?

12. What was the food production system and diet of the Amerindians of Mesoamerica? What were the political and social consequences of this development?

13. Why did the Maya peoples abandon their cultural and ceremonial centers?

14. What questions are raised by the discovery of Cardal and other settlements in Peru? What facts are known about these communities?

Study-Review Exercises

Define the following key concepts and terms.

chinampas

Mesoamerica

mitima

tecuhtli

ayllu

Identify and explain the significance of the following people and terms.

Maya calendar

Cardal

Pampa de las Llamas Moxeke

Tenochtitlán

Amerigo Vespucci

Toliptzin-Quetzalcoatl

Huitzilopochtli

Pachacuti Inca and Topa Inca

Manco Capac

Montezuma II

Aztec "gladiator"

maceualti

thalmaitl

Quechua

Orejones

Explain the main features and characteristics (social, political, economic, and religious) of the following civilizations.

Olmec

Teotihuacán-Toltec

Aztec

Incan

Mayan

Test your understanding of the chapter by providing the correct answers.

1. The western coast of South America is edged by the _____ Mountains.

2. The north-central part of the continent is bisected by the *Niger/Amazon* River.

3. The Aztecs attributed their success to the god *Teotihuacán/Huitzilopochtli*.

4. The *Mayans/Aztecs* believed that the sun needed human blood as its fuel.

5. Legend claims that the first king, a *Toltec/Olmec*, fathered a noble class.

6. The Incas ascribed divine origin to the earliest king *Manco Capac/Topa Inca*.

Multiple-Choice Questions

1. The Indians of Mexico used *chinampas* in
   a. human sacrifice.
   b. the growing of corn.
   c. military campaigns.
   d. religious observances.

2. The secret of Inca imperial power seems to have been
   a. its military might.
   b. its religion.
   c. its use of terror and human sacrifice.
   d. its language, religion, and administrative system.

3. The great temple that dominated the skyline of Tenochtitlán was the temple of
   a. Mali
   b. Quechua.
   c. Huitzilopochtli.
   d. Toltec.

4. *Milpa* refers to the Maya technique of
   a. growing maize.
   b. religious sacrifice.
   c. tax-gathering.
   d. apartment living.

5. The Mesoamerican society that demonstrated mastery of abstract thinking, particularly in the areas of astronomy, mathematics, history, and calendric development, was
   a. the Inca civilization.
   b. the Aztec civilization.
   c. the Maya civilization.
   d. the Olmec civilization.

6. Under Toliptzin—also known as Quetzalcoatl—the Toltecs extended most of their hegemony over
   a. Peru.
   b. northern Mexico and California.
   c. South America.
   d. central Mexico.

7. The early Aztecs founded their city of Tenochtitlán on the swamps of
   a. Lake Texcoco.
   b. Ethiopia.
   c. Thalmaitl.
   d. Orejones.

8. The potato originated in
   a. West Africa.
   b. South America.
   c. eastern Europe.
   d. India.

9. The earliest American civilization was the
   a. Aztec.
   b. Inca.
   c. Maya.
   d. Olmec.

10. The central institution of the Aztec state was the
    a. priesthood.
    b. army.
    c. peasantry.
    d. great landed estates.

11. The Aztecs believed that without human sacrifice the
    a. corn would not grow.
    b. rain would cease.
    c. gods would take revenge.
    d. sun's orbit would stop.

12. The text suggests that the social purpose of human sacrifice and cannibalism was to
    a. control population.
    b. alleviate a scarcity of meat.
    c. terrorize and subdue the population.
    d. control bloodthirsty impulses.

13. The Maya were most advanced in their
    a. mathematics.
    b. literature.
    c. agriculture.
    d. architecture.

14. In the Inca empire, *mitima* was the
    a. colonization of conquered areas.
    b. paying of tribute to the king.
    c. cult of the sun-god.
    d. system of roads.

15. An Inca man courted a girl by
    a. sending her gifts.
    b. getting permission from the governor to marry.
    c. hanging around her house and sharing in the work.
    d. formally asking her father for permission to marry.

16. The fundamental unit of early Inca society was the
    a. curacas.
    b. ayllu.
    c. mitima.
    d. mizquitl.

17. The Teotihuacán civilization developed in
    a. central Mexico.
    b. the Panamanian isthmus.
    c. southern Florida.
    d. Peru.

Major Political Ideas

This chapter emphasizes the relationships between food and the political-social organization of society. What impact did food production in Mesoamerica have on political and social organization? Is food supply the key variable in understanding Mesoamerica politics between about 400 and 1500?

Issues for Essays and Discussion

1. Compare and contrast the Aztec, Maya, and Inca societies in terms of agriculture, social organization, and accomplishments. What are the common threads that connect these societies, and what are the principal differences?

2. The Aztec society is described in the text as a culture ruled by holocaust. What does this mean? Did a holocaust occur? Why?

3. How were the early Mesoamerican cities organized? What was their economic/agricultural base, and what were their accomplishments? Why did these great cities fall?

Interpretation of Visual Sources

Study the photo that shows the reconstruction of Tenochititlán on page 498 of your text. What do the scene and the accompanying buildings tell us about Aztec society?

Geography

Using Outline Map 16.4 provided and referring to Maps 16.1, 16.2, and 16.3 in the text, answer the following questions about South America.

1. Identify the major South American mountain range and river.

2. Describe the geography of Inca Peru in terms of (a) its impact on Inca contact with the outside world, (b) its agriculture, and (c) the Inca imperial road system.

3. Describe the variety of Central American geography. In which of these areas did the Aztec and Maya civilizations evolve?

Remember that duplicate maps for class use are at the back of this book.

Outline Map 16.4

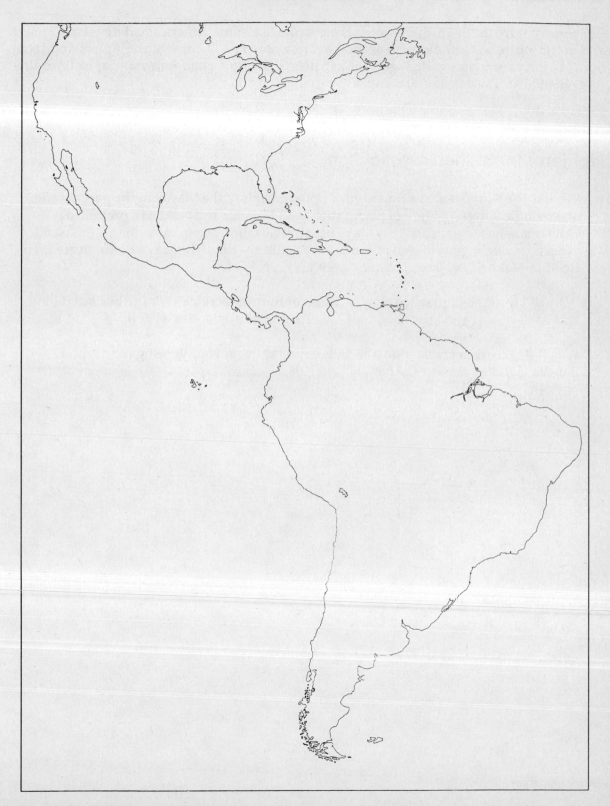

Understanding History Through the Arts

Centuries before the Spanish conquest, the peoples of Central America had developed an art and architecture of their own. How and why were the fabled cities of the Aztecs and Incas built? Begin your investigation with L. Castedo's *A History of Latin American Art and Architecture** (1969).

Problems for Further Investigation

1. What is the significance of the cultural achievements of the Maya? In the past decade, archeological investigation of places such as El Mirador and Nakbe in present-day Guatemala has established that Maya urban civilization began more than a thousand years ago. Begin your investigation of Maya culture with "The Maya Rediscovered: The Road to Nakbe," in *Natural History*, May 1991, pp. 8–14.

2. Why did the Aztecs practice bloody rituals of human sacrifice? For further insight into this issue of war and terrorism, see G. Vaillant, *Aztecs of Mexico** (1979).

3. Was the early Inca civilization a socialist society? Begin your investigation with L. Baudin, *Socialist Empire: The Incas of Peru* (1961).

*Available in paperback.

CHAPTER 17

European Society in the Age of the Renaissance and Reformation

Chapter Questions

After reading and studying this chapter, you should be able to answer the following questions:

What does the term *Renaissance* mean? How did the Renaissance manifest itself in politics, government, and social organization? Why did the theological ideas of Martin Luther trigger political, social, and economic reactions? What response did the Catholic church make to movements for reform?

Chapter Summary

The Renaissance was an era of intellectual and artistic brilliance unsurpassed in European history. It is clear that some thinking people in this era, largely a mercantile elite, saw themselves living in an age more akin to that of the bright and creative ancient world than that of the recent dark and gloomy Middle Ages. Although many of the supposedly "new" Renaissance ideas are actually found in the Middle Ages, scholars generally agree that the Renaissance was characterized by a number of distinctive ideas about life and humanity—individualism, secularism, humanism, materialism, and hedonism.

The Renaissance began in Florence, Italy, in the late thirteenth century. It subsequently spread to the rest of Italy—particularly Rome—and then to northern Europe, where it developed somewhat differently. The best-known expressions of the bold new Renaissance spirit can be seen in the painting, sculpture, and architecture of the period. New attitudes were also found in education, politics, and philosophy; in northern Europe new ideas of social reform developed. Although the Renaissance brought some benefits to the masses of people, such as the printing press, it was basically an elitist movement. A negative development of the age was a deterioration in the power and position of women in society.

In politics, the Renaissance produced an approach to power and the state that historians often call the "new monarchy." The best-known and most popular theoretician of this school was the Florentine Niccolò Machiavelli. Its most able practitioners are the fifteenth- and sixteenth-century monarchs of France, England, and Spain. In Italy, the city-state system led to wealthy and independent cities that were marvelously creative but also vulnerable to invasion and control from the outside by powerful Spanish and French kings.

A religious upheaval called the Protestant Reformation ended the centuries-long religious unity of Europe and resulted in a number of important political changes. In the sixteenth century, cries for reform were nothing new, but this time they resulted in revolution. There were a number of signs of disorder within the church, pointing to the need for moral and administrative reform. For example, it was the granting of indulgences that propelled Martin Luther into the movement for doctrinal change in the church. Luther had come to the conclusion that salvation could not come by good works or indulgences, but only through faith. This was to be one of the fundamental tenets of Protestantism and one of the ideas that pushed Luther and the German nobility to revolt against not only Rome but Rome's secular ally, the Holy Roman emperor.

It is important to recognize that Luther's challenge to the authority of the church and to Catholic unity in Europe invited and supported an attack on the emperor by the German nobility. The pope and the emperor, as separate powers and allies, represented religious and political unity and conformity in Germany. Thus, the victory of Luther and the nobility was a victory for decentralized authority. It meant the collapse of Germany as a unified power in Europe. This is one reason Catholic France usually supported the German Protestants in their quarrel with Rome.

Outside of Germany, the Protestant reformer John Calvin had a greater impact on Europe than Luther. Calvin's harsh and dogmatic religion spread from Geneva into northern Europe and England. It was England, in fact, that eventually became the political center of Protestantism. Initiated by Henry VIII, the English Protestant Reformation was at first motivated by the personal and political interests of the king himself.

With the Council of Trent of 1545–1563, the Catholic church, finding the Habsburgs unable to destroy the heretical Protestantism, launched a massive and partly successful Counter-Reformation to convince dissidents to return to the church.

All in all, Protestantism developed and spread for economic and political reasons as well as religious ones. In the end, Protestantism meant greater spiritual freedom for some individuals, but spiritual disunity and disorganization for Europe as a whole. In England, the Scandinavian countries, and elsewhere, it contributed to the power of the nation and thus meant a further political division of Europe, while in Germany it slowed down the movement toward nationhood.

Study Outline

Use this outline to preview the chapter before you read a particular section in your textbook and then as a self-check to test your reading comprehension after you have read the chapter section.

I. The evolution of the Italian Renaissance
   A. Beginnings
      1. The Renaissance was a period of commercial, financial, political, and cultural achievement in two phases, from about 1050 to 1300 and from about 1300 to about 1600.
      2. The northern Italian cities led the commercial revival, especially Venice, Genoa, and Milan.
      3 The first artistic and literary flowerings of the Renaissance appeared in Florence.
         a. Florentine mercantile families dominated European banking.
         b. The wool industry was the major factor in the city's financial expansion and population increase.
   B. Communes and republics
      1. Northern Italian cities were communes—associations of free men seeking independence from the local lords.
         a. The nobles, attracted by the opportunities in the cities, often settled there and married members of the mercantile class, forming an urban nobility.
         b. The pòpolo, or middle class, was excluded from power.
         c. Pòpolo-led republican governments failed, which led to the rule of despots (signori) or oligarchies.
      2. In the fifteenth century, the princely courts of the rulers were centers of wealth and art.
   C. The balance of power among the Italian city-states
      1. Italy had no political unity; it was divided into city-states such as Milan, Venice, and Florence, the Papal States, and the kingdom of Naples in the south.
      2. The political and economic competition among the city-states prevented centralization of power.
      3. Shifting alliances among the city-states led to the creation of permanent ambassadors.
      4. After 1494 a divided Italy became a European battleground.

II. Intellectual hallmarks of the Renaissance
   A. Many, like the poet and humanist Petrarch, saw the fourteenth century as a new golden age and a revival of ancient Roman culture.
   B. Individualism
      1. Literature specifically concerned with the nature of individuality emerged.
      2. Renaissance people believed in individual will and genius.
   C. The revival of antiquity
      1. Italians copied the ancient Roman lifestyle.
      2. The study of the classics led to humanism, an emphasis on human beings.
         a. Humanists sought to understand human nature through a study of pagan and classical authors and Christian thought.
         b. The humanist writer Pico della Mirandola believed that there were no limits to what human beings could accomplish.
      3. Ancient Latin style was considered superior to medieval Latin.

  D. A new secular spirit
   1. Secularism means a concern with materialism rather than religion.
   2. Unlike medieval people, Renaissance people were concerned with money and pleasure.
    a. In *On Pleasure*, Valla defended the pleasure of the senses as the highest good.
    b. In the *Decameron*, Boccaccio portrayed an acquisitive and worldly society.
   3. The church did little to combat secularism; in fact, many popes were Renaissance patrons and participants.

III. Art and the artist
  A. Florence was the first center of the Renaissance, but other cities, such as Rome, followed its artistic lead.
  B. Art and power
   1. In the early Renaissance, powerful urban groups commissioned works of art, which remained overwhelmingly religious.
   2. In the later fifteenth century, individuals and oligarchs began to sponsor works of art as a means of self-glorification.
   3. As the century advanced, art became more and more secular, and classical subjects became popular.
   4. The style of art changed in the fifteenth century.
    a. The individual portrait emerged as a distinct genre.
    b. Painting and sculpture became more naturalistic and realistic, and the human body was glorified, as in the work of the sculptors Donatello and Michelangelo.
    c. A new "international style" emphasized color, decorative detail, and curvilinear rhythms.
    d. In painting, the use of perspective was pioneered by Brunelleschi and della Francesca.
  C. The status of the artist
   1. The status of the artist improved during the Renaissance; most work was done by commission from a prince.
   2. The creative genius of the artist was recognized and rewarded.
   3. The Renaissance was largely an elitist movement; Renaissance culture did not directly affect the middle classes.

IV. Social change during the Renaissance
  A. Education and political thought
   1. Vergerio wrote a treatise on education that stressed the teaching of history, ethics, and rhetoric (public speaking).
   2. Castiglione's *The Courtier*, which was widely read, describes the model Renaissance gentleman as a man of many talents, including intellectual and artistic skills.

   3. Machiavelli's *The Prince* describes how to acquire, maintain, and increase
      political power.
      a. Machiavelli believed that the politician should manipulate people and
         use any means to gain power.
      b. Machiavelli did not advocate amoral behavior but believed that political
         action cannot be governed by moral considerations.
B. The printed word
   1. The invention in 1455 of movable type by Gutenberg, Fust, and Schöffer
      made possible the printing of a wide variety of texts.
   2. Printing transformed the lives of Europeans by making propaganda possible,
      encouraging a wider common identity, and improving literacy.
C. Women in Renaissance society
   1. Compared to women in the previous age, the status of upper-class women
      declined during the Renaissance.
   2. Although the Renaissance brought improved educational opportunities for
      women, they were expected to use their education solely to run a household,
      and male resentment toward female learning was considerable.
   3. Women's status declined with regard to sex and love.
      a. Renaissance humanists laid the foundations for the bourgeois double
         standard.
      b. The rape of women by upper-class men was frequent and not considered
         serious.
   4. Because of poverty, infanticide and abandonment of children were frequent
      and eventually led to the establishment of foundling hospitals.
D. Blacks in Renaissance society
   1. Beginning in the fifteenth century, black slaves were brought into Europe in
      large numbers.
   2. Blacks as slaves and freemen filled a variety of positions, from laborers to
      dancers and actors and musicians.
   3. The European attitude toward blacks was ambivalent—blackness symbolized
      both evil and humility.
   4. During the Renaissance, blacks were displayed as signs of wealth.

V. The Renaissance in the north began in the last quarter of the fifteenth century.
   A. It was more Christian than the Renaissance in Italy, and it stressed social reform
      based on Christian ideals.
   B. Christian humanists sought to create a more perfect world by combining the best
      elements of classical and Christian cultures.
      1. Humanists like Lefèvre believed in the use of the Bible by common people.
      2. Thomas More, the author of *Utopia*, believed that society, not people, needed
         improving.
      3. The Dutch monk Erasmus best represents Christian humanism in his
         emphasis on education as the key to a moral and intellectual improvement
         and inner Christianity.

C. The stories of the French humanist Rabelais were distinctly secular but still had a serious purpose.
   1. Like More, Rabelais believed that institutions molded individuals and education was the key to moral life.
   2. He combined a Renaissance zest for life with a classical insistence on the cultivation of body and mind.
D. Northern art and architecture were more religious than in Italy and less influenced by classical themes and motifs.
   1. Van Eyck painted realistic, incredibly detailed works.
   2. Bosch used religion and folk legends as themes.

VI. Politics and the state in the Renaissance (ca 1450–1521)
   A. The rise of the "new" monarchs
      1. The fifteenth century saw the rise of many powerful and ruthless rulers interested in the centralization of power and the elimination of disorder and violence.
      2. Many of them, such as Louis XI of France, Henry VII of England, and Ferdinand and Isabella of Spain, seemed to be acting according to Machiavelli's principles.
      3. These monarchs invested kingship with a strong sense of royal authority and national purpose.
      4. The ideas of the new monarchs were not entirely original—some of them had their roots in the Middle Ages.
   B. France after the Hundred Years' War
      1. Charles VII ushered in an age of recovery and ended civil war.
         a. He expelled the English, reorganized the royal council, strengthened royal finances, reformed the justice system, and remodeled the army.
         b. He made the church subject to the state.
      2. Louis XI expanded the French state and laid the foundations of later French absolutism.
   C. England
      1. Feudal lords controlled the royal council and Parliament in the fifteenth century.
      2. Between 1455 and 1471, the houses of York and Lancaster fought a civil war called the Wars of the Roses that hurt trade, agriculture, and domestic industry.
      3. Edward IV and his followers began to restore royal power.
      4. The English Parliament had become a power center for the aristocracy but was manipulated by Henry VII into becoming a tool of the king.
      5. Henry VII used the royal council and the court of Star Chamber to check aristocratic power.
      6. Henry and his successors won the support of the upper middle class by linking government policy with their interests.

D. Spain
1. The central theme in medieval Spanish history was disunity and plurality.
2. The marriage of Ferdinand and Isabella was the first major step in the unification and Christianization of Spain.
   a. Under their reign, however, Spain remained a loose confederation of separate states.
   b. They used the hermandades, or local police forces, to administer royal justice.
3. They restructured the royal council to curb aristocratic power.
4. The church was also used to strengthen royal authority.
5. Ferdinand and Isabella completed the reconquista in 1492, but many Jews remained.
   a. Jews were often financiers and professionals; many (called conversos) had converted but were still disliked and distrusted.
   b. Ferdinand and Isabella revived the Inquisition and used its cruel methods to unify Spain and expel the Jews.

VII. Germany and the Protestant Reformation
A. The Holy Roman Empire in the fourteenth and fifteenth centuries
1. The Golden Bull of 1356 gave each of the seven electors virtual sovereignty.
2. Localism and chronic disorder allowed the nobility to strengthen their territories and reduced the authority of the emperor.
B. The rise of the Habsburg dynasty
1. The Habsburgs gave unity to much of Europe, especially with the marriage of Maximilian I of Austria and Mary of Burgundy in 1477.
2. Charles V, their grandson, inherited much of Europe and was committed to the idea of its religious and political unity.

VIII. The condition of the church (ca 1400–1517)
A. The declining prestige of the church
1. The Babylonian Captivity and the Great Schism damaged the church's prestige.
2. Secular humanists satirized and denounced moral corruption within the church.
B. Signs of disorder in the early sixteenth century
1. Clerical immorality (neglect of celibacy, drunkenness, gambling) created a scandal among the faithful.
   a. The lack of education of the clergy and low standards of ordination were condemned by Christian humanists.
   b. The absenteeism, pluralism (holding of several benefices, or offices), and wealth of the greater clergy bore little resemblance to Christian gospel.
2. The prelates and popes of the period, often members of the nobility, lived in splendor and moral corruption.
C. Signs of vitality in the late fifteenth and early sixteenth centuries
1. Sixteenth-century Europe remained deeply religious, and calls for reform testify to the spiritual vitality of the church.

2. New organizations were formed to educate and minister to the poor.
   a. The Brethren of the Common Life in Holland lived simply and sought to make religion a personal, inner experience based on following the Scriptures.
   b. *The Imitation of Christ* by Thomas à Kempis urged Christians to seek perfection in a simple way of life.
   c. The Oratories of Divine Love in Italy were groups of priests who worked to revive the church through prayer and preaching.
3. Pope Julius II summoned an ecumenical council on reform in the church called the Lateran Council (1512–1527).

IX. Martin Luther and the birth of Protestantism
   A. Luther's early years
      1. Luther was a German monk and professor of religion whose search for salvation led him to the letters of St. Paul.
      2. He concluded that faith was central to Christianity and the only means of salvation.
   B. Luther's Ninety-five Theses (October 1517)
      1. Luther's opposition to the sale of indulgences (remissions of penalties for sin) prompted his fight with Rome.
         a. Luther rejected the idea that salvation could be achieved by good works, such as indulgences.
         b. He also criticized papal wealth.
      2. At Leipzig in 1519 Luther denied the authority of the pope and was excommunicated and declared an outlaw by Charles V at Worms in 1521.
   C. Protestant thought
      1. "Protestant" at first meant Lutheran, but it later became a general term applied to all non-Catholic Christians; it means a modification of Catholicism.
      2. Luther provided new answers to four basic theological issues.
         a. He believed that salvation was achieved through faith alone, not faith and good works.
         b. He stated that religious authority rests with the Bible, not the pope.
         c. He believed that the church consists of the entire community of Christian believers.
         d. And he believed that all work is sacred and everyone should serve God in his or her individual vocation.
      3. Protestantism, therefore, was a reformulation of Christian beliefs and practices.

X. The social impact of Luther's beliefs
   A. By 1521 Luther's religious ideas had a vast following among all social classes.
      1. Luther's ideas were popular because of widespread resentment of clerical privileges and wealth.
      2. Luther's ideas attracted many preachers, and they became Protestant leaders.

3. Peasants cited Luther's theology as part of their demands for economic reforms.
   a. Luther did not support the peasant revolts; he believed in obedience to civil authority.
   b. Widespread peasant revolts in 1525 were brutally crushed, but some land was returned to common use.
4. Luther's greatest weapon was his mastery of the language, and his words were spread by the advent of printing.
   a. Zwingli and Calvin were greatly influenced by his writings.
   b. The publication of Luther's German translation of the New Testament in 1523 democratized religion.
5. Luther believed that marriage was a woman's career, and he stressed the idea of marriage.

B. The political impact of Luther's beliefs
1. The Protestant Reformation stirred nationalistic feelings in Germany against the wealthy Italian papacy.
2. Luther's appeal to patriotism earned him the support of the princes, who used religion as a means of gaining more political independence and preventing the flow of German money to Rome.
3. The Protestant movement proved to be a political disaster for Germany.
   a. The dynastic Habsburg-Valois wars advanced the cause of Protestantism and promoted the political fragmentation of Germany.
   b. By the Peace of Augsburg of 1555, Charles recognized Lutheranism as a legal religion, and each prince was permitted to determine the religion of his territory.

XI. The growth of the Protestant Reformation
A. Calvinism
1. Calvin believed that God selects certain people to do his work and that he was selected to reform the church.
2. Under Calvin, Geneva became a theocracy, in which the state was subordinate to the church.
3. Calvin's central ideas, expressed in *The Institutes of Christian Religion*, were his belief in the omnipotence of God, the insignificance of humanity, and predestination.
   a. These ideas were expressed in the *Genevan Catechism*.
4. Austere living and intolerance of dissenters characterized Calvin's Geneva.
   a. The Genevan Consistory monitored the private morals of citizens.
   b. Michael Servetus was burned at the stake for denying the Christian dogma of the Trinity and rejecting child baptism.
5. The city of Geneva was the model for international Protestantism, and Calvinism, with its emphasis on the work ethic, became the most dynamic and influential form of Protestantism.

B. The Anabaptists
1. This Protestant sect believed in adult baptism, literal interpretation of the Bible, religious tolerance, pacifism, and the separation of church and state.
   a. They allowed women to be priests.
   b. They shared property and appealed to the poor.
2. Their beliefs and practices were too radical for the times, and they were bitterly persecuted.

C. The English Reformation
1. The Lollards, although driven underground in the fifteenth century, survived and stressed the idea of a direct relationship between the individual and God.
2. The English humanist William Tyndale began printing an English translation of the New Testament in 1525.
3. The wealth and corruption of the clergy, as exemplified by Thomas Wolsey, stirred much resentment.
4. Henry VIII desired a divorce from his queen, Catherine, daughter of Ferdinand and Isabella of Spain, so he could marry Anne Boleyn.
5. Pope Clement VII (who did not wish to admit papal error) refused to annul Henry's marriage to Catherine.
6. Archbishop Cranmer, however, engineered the divorce.
7. The result was the nationalization of the English church and a break with Rome as Henry used Parliament to legalize the Reformation.
   a. Henry needed money so he dissolved the monasteries and confiscated their lands, but this did not lead to more equal land distribution.
   b. Some traditional Catholic practices, such as confession and the doctrine of transubstantiation, were maintained.
   c. Nationalization of the church led to changes in governmental administration, resulting in greater efficiency and economy.
8. Under Edward VI, Henry's heir, England shifted closer to Protestantism.
9. Mary Tudor attempted to bring Catholicism back to England.
10. Under Elizabeth I a religious settlement requiring outward conformity to the Church of England was made.

XII. The Catholic Reformation and the Counter-Reformation
A. There were two types of reform within the Catholic church in the sixteenth and seventeenth centuries.
1. The Catholic Reformation sought to stimulate a new religious fervor.
2. The Counter-Reformation started in the 1540s as a reaction to Protestantism and progressed simultaneously with the Catholic Reformation.
B. The slowness of institutional reform
1. Too often the popes were preoccupied with politics or sensual pleasures.
2. Popes resisted calls for the formation of a general council because it would limit their authority.
C. The Council of Trent
1. Pope Paul III called the Council of Trent (1545–1563).
   a. An attempt to reconcile with the Protestants failed.
   b. International politics hindered the theological debates.

2. Nonetheless, the principle of papal authority was maintained, considerable reform was undertaken, and the spiritual renewal of the church was begun.
    a. Tridentine decrees forbade the sale of indulgences and outlawed pluralism and simony.
    b. Attempts were made to curb clerical immorality and to encourage education.
    c. Great emphasis was placed on preaching.
D. New religious orders
    1. The Ursuline order of nuns gained enormous prestige for the education of women.
        a. The Ursulines sought to re-Christianize society by training future wives and mothers.
        b. The Ursulines spread to France and North America.
    2. The Society of Jesus played a strong international role in resisting Protestantism.
        a. Obedience was the foundation of the Jesuit tradition.
        b. With their schools, political influence, and missionary work, they brought many people into the Catholic fold.
E. The Sacred Congregation of the Holy Office
    1. This group, established by Pope Paul III in 1542, carried out the Roman Inquisition as a way to combat heresy.
    2. It had the power to arrest, imprison, and execute, but its influence was confined to papal territories.

Review Questions

Check your understanding of this chapter by answering the following questions.

1. What new social class developed in twelfth-century Italy? How did this social class affect the movement toward republican government?

2. How does the concept of individualism help explain the Renaissance?

3. How do Valla and Boccaccio illustrate and represent what Renaissance people were like?

4. What is humanism? What do humanists emphasize?

5. According to Vergerio, what is the purpose of education? Was he a humanist?

6. How does Castiglione's *The Courtier* define the "perfect Renaissance man"? How does this book serve as an example of humanism?

7. How did the invention of movable type revolutionize European life?

8. How did the Renaissance in northern Europe differ from that of Italy?

9. How do the works and ideas of Thomas More and Desiderius Erasmus exemplify Christian humanism?

10. Why did Italy became a battleground for the European superpowers after 1494?

11. What devices did Henry VII of England use to check the power of the aristocracy and strengthen the monarchy?

12. Why is the reign of Ferdinand and Isabella one of the most important in Spanish history? What were their achievements in the areas of national power and national expansion?

13. Why were blacks valued in Renaissance society? What roles did they play in the economic and social life of the times?

14. In what ways did life for upper-class women change during the Renaissance?

15. How was Renaissance art different from medieval art? How did the status of the artist change?

16. What was the condition of the church in 1517? Were the village clergy useless and corrupt?

17. What were some of the signs of religious vitality in fifteenth- and early sixteenth-century society?

18. What circumstances prompted Luther to post his Ninety-five Theses?

19. Describe the practice of indulgence selling. What authority did Luther question, and on what argument did he base his position?

20. What were Luther's answers to the four basic theological issues?

21. What effect did Luther's concept of state authority over church authority have on German society and German history?

22. Why was Calvin's Geneva called "the city that was a church"? What is a theocracy?

23. In what ways were the Anabaptists radical for their time? Why did many of their beliefs cause them to be bitterly persecuted?

24. What were the causes and results of the English Reformation?

25. What was the Elizabethan Settlement?

26. What were the repercussions of the marriage of Maximilian and Mary? What impact did this marriage have on France?

27. Charles V has been considered a medieval emperor. In what respects is this true? What were the origins of his empire?

28. Why was reform within the Catholic church often unwelcome and slow in coming?

29. What were the achievements of the Council of Trent?

30. What was the Inquisition? How extensive was its power?

Study-Review Exercises

Define the following key concepts and terms.

Renaissance

oligarchy

signori

communes

pòpolo

humanism

secularism

individualism

materialism

Identify and explain the significance of the following people and terms.

English Royal Council and Court of Star Chamber

conquest of Granada

Habsburg-Valois wars

Pico della Mirandola

Desiderius Erasmus

Jan van Eyck

Thomas More

Donatello

Baldassare Castiglione

Niccolò Machiavelli

Johan Gutenberg

Saint John Chrysostom

Lorenzo Valla

Savonarola

Jerome Bosch

François Rabelais

Brethren of the Common Life

Pope Paul III

Archbishop Cranmer

John Tetzel

Martin Luther

Angela Merici

Henry VIII

Charles V

Mary Tudor

Pope Alexander VI

Council of Trent

Counter-Reformation

Elizabethan Settlement

pluralism

benefices

Peace of Augsburg

Ninety-five Theses

Explain why each of the following is considered a "new monarch."
Louis XI of France

Henry VII of England

Ferdinand and Isabella of Spain

Charles VII of France

Cesare Borgia

Define the basic beliefs of the following Christian religions and churches.
Roman Catholicism

Lutheranism

Calvinism

Anabaptism

Church of England

Test your understanding of the chapter by providing the correct answers.

1. The author of a best-selling political critique called *The Prince.* _____

2. Renaissance humanists tended to be *more/less* concerned about religion than about people.

3. In the fifteenth century, infanticide *increased/decreased*.

4. An important English humanist and the author of *Utopia*. _____

5. Generally, the legal status of upper-class women *improved/declined* during the Renaissance.

6. It *is/is not* clear that the economic growth and material wealth of the Italian cities were direct causes of the Renaissance.

7. The Council of Trent *did/did not* reaffirm the seven sacraments, the validity of tradition, and transubstantiation.

8. The English Supremacy Act of 1534 declared the _____ to be the supreme head of the Church of England.

9. For the most part, the English Reformation under Henry VIII dealt with *political/theological* issues.

10. This pope's name became a synonym for moral corruption. _____

Multiple-Choice Questions

1. The Renaissance began in
   a. the Low Countries.
   b. Rome.
   c. France.
   d. Florence.

2. It appears that in Renaissance society blacks were
   a. valued as soldiers.
   b. valued as servants and entertainers.
   c. considered undesirable and not allowed in society.
   d. not much in demand.

3. A major difference between northern and Italian humanism is that northern humanism stressed
   a. economic gain and materialism.
   b. social reform based on Christian ideals.
   c. pagan virtues.
   d. scholastic dogma over reason.

4. The court of Star Chamber in England was
   a. a common-law court.
   b. under the control of the barons in the House of Lords.
   c. done away with by the powerful Tudors.
   d. used to check aristocratic power.

5. Most of the northern Renaissance thinkers agreed that
   a. democracy, not monarchy, was the only workable political system.
   b. humanity is basically sinful.
   c. Christianity is unacceptable.
   d. society is perfectible.

6. The dome of St. Peter's in Rome is considered to be the greatest work of
   a. Brunelleschi.
   b. Donatello.
   c. Michelangelo.
   d. Ghiberti.

7. The term *Renaissance* means
   a. a rise in the average standard of living among the masses.
   b. a resurgence of art and culture in the fourteenth through sixteenth centuries.
   c. an increase in the population after the ravaging effects of the "Four Horsemen of the Apocalypse."
   d. the recovery of the church from economic and moral decline.

8. The financial and military strength of the towns of northern Italy was directly related to
   a. their wealth, which enabled them to hire mercenary soldiers to protect their commercial interests.
   b. their contractual and marital alliances with the rural nobility.
   c. protections provided them by the Holy Roman emperor.
   d. their alliance with the papacy.

9. Erasmus advocated
   a. paganism.
   b. Christian education for moral and intellectual improvement.
   c. a monastic life of contemplation and divorce from the material world.
   d. obedience to church doctrine and ritual.

10. The Renaissance artist of talent and ability often lived a life
    a. of economic desperation.
    b. of economic security through patronage.
    c. of luxury, but without social status.
    d. like that of the masses.

11. The most influential book on Renaissance court life and behavior was
    a. Castiglione's *The Courtier*.
    b. Machiavelli's *The Prince*.
    c. Augustine's *City of God*.
    d. Boccaccio's *Decameron*.

12. The best description of Machiavelli's *The Prince* is that it is
    a. a description of how government should be organized and implemented.
    b. a satire on sixteenth-century politics.
    c. a call for Italian nationalism.
    d. an accurate description of politics as practiced in Renaissance Italy.

13. The Wars of the Roses were
    a. civil wars between the English ducal houses of York and Lancaster.
    b. between England and France.
    c. civil wars between the English king, Henry VI, and the aristocracy.
    d. minor disputes among English gentry.

14. Just before the advent of Ferdinand and Isabella, the Iberian Peninsula could best be described as
    a. a homogeneous region sharing a common language and cultural tradition.
    b. a heterogeneous region consisting of several ethnic groups with a diversity of linguistic and cultural characteristics.
    c. tolerant of religious and ethnic traditions different from Christianity.
    d. a region dominated equally by Arabs and Jews.

15. Thomas More's ideas, as best expressed in his book *Utopia*, centered on the belief that
    a. evil exists because men and women are basically corrupt.
    b. political leaders must learn how to manipulate their subjects.
    c. social order is only an unattainable ideal.
    d. corruption and war are due to acquisitiveness and private property.

16. According to Luther, salvation comes through
    a. good works.
    b. faith.
    c. indulgences.
    d. a saintly life.

17. The cornerstone of Calvin's theology was his belief in
    a. predestination.
    b. indulgences.
    c. the basic goodness of man.
    d. religious tolerance and freedom.

18. Overall, Henry VIII's religious reformation in England occurred
    a. strictly for economic reasons.
    b. for religious reasons.
    c. mostly for political reasons.
    d. mostly for diplomatic reasons.

19. The Reformation in Germany resulted in
    a. a politically weaker Germany.
    b. a politically stronger Germany.
    c. no political changes of importance.
    d. a victory for imperial centralization.

20. The great Christian humanists of the fifteenth and sixteenth centuries believed that reform could be achieved through
    a. the use of violent revolution.
    b. education and social change.
    c. mass support of the church hierarchy.
    d. the election of a new pope.

21. The Holy Roman emperor who tried to suppress the Lutheran revolt was
    a. Christian III.
    b. Charles V.
    c. Adrian VI.
    d. Henry VII.

22. By 1555, the Protestant Reformation had spread to all of the following countries *except*
    a. England.
    b. Scandinavia.
    c. Spain.
    d. Scotland.

23. The chief center of the Protestant reformers in the sixteenth century was
    a. Paris.
    b. Geneva.
    c. Zurich.
    d. Cologne.

24. Luther's German translation of the New Testament
    a. proved that the state was supreme over the church.
    b. convinced women that they had no constructive role in life.
    c. democratized religion.
    d. turned the common people away from the church.

25. The divorce of Henry VIII of England from his wife Catherine was complicated by the fact that Catherine's nephew was
   a. the pope.
   b. the emperor, Charles V.
   c. the king of France.
   d. the leader of the English Parliament.

Major Political Ideas

1. What were the political ideas behind the concept of the "new monarch"?

2. In what ways was Protestantism a political idea? Did it help or hinder the development of the nation-state? Compare and contrast the religious settlements made in the German states, England, Scotland, and Ireland. Why was Protestantism on the one hand a source of national strength and on the other a source of national weakness?

Issues for Essays and Discussion

1. The Renaissance was a period during which many people began to think and act in different ways. Sometimes this is referred to as a "self-conscious awareness," a stress on "humanism," and a "secular spirit." What do these phrases mean? Answer by making specific reference to developments in literature, political thought, and art.

2. Was the Reformation a blessing or a disaster for the people of Europe? Support your argument by making specific reference to Germany, England, and Scotland. What impact did the Reformation have on the power of the monarchs, the well-being of the common man and woman, and the overall balance of European power?

Interpretation of Visual Sources

Study the reproduction of the painting entitled *Death and the Miser* by Jerome Bosch on page 528 of the textbook. Describe how this painting reflects the religious orientation of the Renaissance in the north of Europe. What is happening in this scene? Account for as many symbolic references as you can. What do you believe to be Bosch's message?

Geography

1. On Outline Map 17.1 provided, and using Map 17.1 in the textbook as a reference, mark the following: the names of the Italian city-states and their principal cities (underline the five major powers of Venice, Milan, Florence, the Papal States, and the kingdom of Naples).

2. On Outline Map 17.4 provided, and using Maps 17.3 and 17.4 in the textbook as a reference, mark the following: the boundary of the Holy Roman Empire, the territory under the control of Charles V, the approximate areas of Lutheran influence, the approximate areas of Calvinist influence.

Remember that duplicate maps for class use are at the back of this book.

Outline Map 17.1

Outline Map 17.4

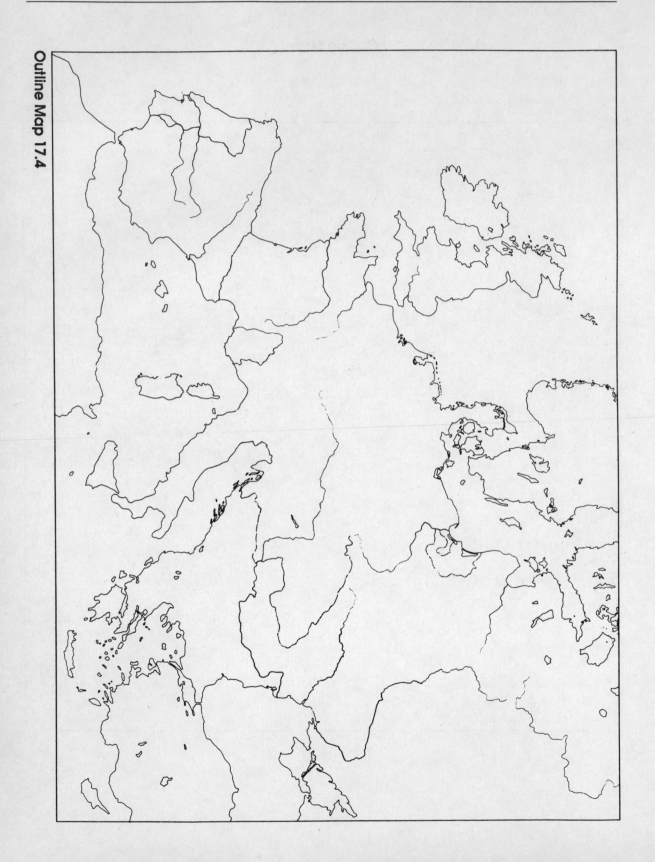

Understanding History Through the Arts

1. What does the music of the Renaissance tell us about the period? The music of the Renaissance is introduced in two recordings, *From the Renaissance* (STL-150) and *From the Renaissance—Concert* (STL-160), in the Time-Life series *The Story of Great Music* (1967), which also includes a book with a good introduction to the period and its musical styles, art, and history. Good written introductions to Renaissance music are H. Brown, *Music in the Renaissance** (1976), and G. Reese, *Music in the Renaissance* (1954).

2. How does the music of the Reformation express the spirit of the age? The church was the only place where music was regularly available to the public. Some of the most important baroque music evolved from the Protestant cities of north and central Germany. The leading composers of organ music in Germany were Dietrich Buxtehude in Lübeck, Johann Pachebell in Nuremberg, George Bohm in Luneburg, and Johann Sebastian Bach. For a written account of the baroque style, see M. Bukofzer, *Music in the Baroque Era: From Monteverdi to Bach* (1947). Numerous recordings of baroque organ music are available; one of the best is Dietrich Buxtehude, *Organ Works*, vol. 1, performed by Michel Chapuis on Das Alte Werke, Telefunken. 6.42001.AF., and vol. 2. as 6.35307.EK.

3. How did the art of Rome and Florence differ? What characteristics did they share? Begin your study with R. Goldthwaite, *The Building of Renaissance Florence** (1983); M. Andres, et al., *The Art of Florence*, 2 vols. (1989); and J. Andreae, *The Art of Rome* (1989). For the northern Renaissance, see O. Benesch, *The Art of the Renaissance in Northern Europe* (1965). Two of the finest Renaissance artists are the subjects of M. Kemp and J. Roberts, *Leonardo Da Vinci, Artist, Scientist, Inventor* (1989), and M. Levey, *Giambattista Tiepolo* (1987).

Problems for Further Investigation

1. Was the Renaissance an age of progress and advancement? Urban and rural life, court life, war, and witchcraft are among the many aspects of Renaissance life covered in E. R. Chamberlin, *Everyday Life in Renaissance Times** (1967).

2. How did the Renaissance alter the status of women? Begin your study by reading J. Kelly-Gadol, "Did Women Have a Renaissance?" in R. Bridenthal, C. Koontz, and S. Stuard, eds., *Becoming Visible: Women in European History* (1977), and M. Rose, et al., *Women in the Middle Ages and the Renaissance: Literary and Historical Perspectives* (1986).

3. What led Martin Luther to launch the Protestant Reformation? Few men in history have been the subject of more biographies than Martin Luther. One of the most important is

*Available in paperback.

a psychological study by E. Erikson entitled *Young Man Luther: A Study in Psychoanalysis and History** (1962). Other books about Luther include R. Bainton, *Here I Stand** (1950); E. Schwiebert, *Luther and His Times* (1952); G. Forel, *Faith Active in Love* (1954); and J. Atkinson, *Martin Luther and the Birth of Protestantism** (1968).

4. What motivated Henry VIII's break with Rome? King Henry VIII of England is the subject of a number of interesting biographies. Three of the best are L. B. Smith, *Henry VIII* (1971); A. F. Pollard, *Henry VIII** (1905); and J. Scarisbrick, *Henry VIII* (1968). Henry's marital problems, as seen from his wife's side, are the subject of the fascinating *Catherine of Aragon** (1941) by G. Mattingly.

*Available in paperback.

PRIMARY SOURCES

Two Sixteenth-Century Thinkers

Niccolò Machiavelli and Martin Luther were both mirrors of the sixteenth century, and both contributed to a new view of the relationship between man, God, and the state. However, Machiavelli is viewed as a man of the Renaissance, while Luther is largely associated with the Reformation. The following selections illustrate some of the similarities and some of the differences in their thought.

Machiavelli was a political analyist, not a theoretician. He based his observations on politics and government and on practical reality, not an ideal state. What does he say here about effective political leadership? How could this be misconstrued to support authoritarian rule?

Niccolò Machiavelli, *The Prince**

Here the question arises: is it better to be loved than feared, or vice versa? I don't doubt that every prince would like to have both; but since it is hard to accommodate these qualities, if you have to make a choice, to be feared is much safer than to be loved. For it is a good general rule about men, that they are ungrateful, fickle, liars, and deceivers, fearful of danger and greedy for gain. While you serve their welfare, they are all yours, offering their blood, their belongings, their lives, and their children's lives, as we noted above—so long as the danger is remote. But when the danger is close at hand, they turn against you. Then, any prince who has relied on their words and has made no other preparations will come to grief; because friendships that are bought at a price, and not with greatness and nobility of soul, may be paid for but they are not acquired, and they cannot be used in time of need. People are less concerned with offending a man who makes himself loved than one who makes himself

*Source: Reprinted from *The Prince* by Niccolò Machiavelli, Translated and Edited by Robert M. Adams, A Norton Critical Edition. With the permission of W. W. Norton & Company, Inc. Copyright © 1977 by W. W. Norton & Company, Inc.

feared: the reason is that love is a link of obligation which men, because they are rotten, will break any time they think doing so serves their advantage; but fear involves dread of punishment, from which they can never escape.

Still, a prince should make himself feared in such a way that, even if he gets no love, he gets no hate either; because it is perfectly possible to be feared and not hated, and this will be the result if only the prince will keep his hands off the property of his subjects or citizens, and off their women. When he does have to shed blood, he should be sure to have a strong justification and manifest cause; but above all, he should not confiscate people's property, because men are quicker to forget the death of a father than the loss of a patrimony. Besides, pretexts for confiscation are always plentiful; it never fails that a prince who starts living by plunder can find reasons to rob someone else. Excuses for proceeding against someone's life are much rarer and more quickly exhausted.

But a prince at the head of his armies and commanding a multitude of soldiers should not care a bit if he is considered cruel; without such a reputation, he could never hold his army together and ready for action. Among the marvelous deeds of Hannibal, this was prime: that, having an immense army, which included men of many different races and nations, and which he led to battle in distant countries, he never allowed them to fight among themselves or to rise against him, whether his fortune was good or bad. The reason for this could only be his inhuman cruelty, which, along with his countless other talents, [virtù], made him an object of awe and terror to his soldiers; and without the cruelty, his other qualities [le altre sua virtù] would never have sufficed. The historians who pass snap judgements on these matters admire his accomplishments and at the same time condemn the cruelty which was their main cause.

When I say, "His other qualities would never have sufficed," we can see that this is true from the example of Scipio, an outstanding man not only among those of his own time, but in all recorded history; yet his armies revolted in Spain, for no other reason than his excessive leniency in allowing his soldiers more freedom than military discipline permits. Fabius Maximus rebuked him in the senate for his failing, calling him the corrupter of the Roman armies. When a lieutenant of Scipio's plundered the Locrians, he took no action in behalf of the people; and did nothing to discipline that insolent lieutenant; again, this was the result of his easygoing nature. Indeed, when someone in the senate wanted to excuse him on this occasion, he said there are many men who knew better how to avoid error themselves than how to correct error in others. Such a soft temper would in time have tarnished the fame and glory of Scipio, had he brought it to the office of emperor; but as he lived under the control of the senate, this harmful quality of his not only remained hidden but was considered creditable.

Returning to the question of being feared or loved, I conclude that since men love at their own inclination but can be made to fear at the inclination of the prince, a shrewd prince will lay his foundations on what is under his own control, not on what is controlled by others. He should simply take pains not to be hated, as I said.

On his way to the Diet of Worms in 1521, Martin Luther preached the following sermon to the citizens of Erfurt. What teachings of the Roman church did he criticize? What ideas of his own did he emphasize? And how did Luther think salvation was to be achieved? If you did not know who had written this sermon, how would you describe its author's mind and education?

Sermon Preached by Martin Luther in Erfurt, Germany, 1521*

Now it is clear and manifest that every person likes to think that he will be saved and attain to eternal salvation. This is what I propose to discuss now.

You also know that all philosophers, doctors and writers have studiously endeavored to teach and write what attitude man should take to piety. They have gone to great trouble, but, as is evident, to little avail. Now genuine and true piety consists of two kinds of work: those done for others, which are the right kind, and those done for ourselves, which are unimportant. In order to find a foundation, one man builds churches; another goes on a pilgrimage to St. James' or St. Peter's; a third fasts or prays, wears a cowl, goes barefoot, or does something else of the kind. Such works are nothing whatever and must be completely destroyed. Mark these words: none of our works have any power whatsoever. For God has chosen a man, the Lord Christ Jesus, to crush death, destroy sin, and shatter hell, since there was no one before he came who did not inevitably belong to the devil. The devil therefore thought he would get a hold upon the Lord when he hung between the two thieves and was suffering the most contemptible and disgraceful of deaths, which was cursed both by God and by men [cf. Deut. 21:23; Gal. 3:13]. But the Godhead was so strong that death, sin, and even hell were destroyed.

Therefore you should note well the words which Paul writes to the Romans [Rom. 5:12–21]. Our sins have their sources in Adam, and because Adam ate the apple, we have inherited sin from him. But Christ has shattered death for our sake, in order that we might be saved by his works, which are alien to us, and not by our works.

But the papal dominion treats us altogether differently. It makes rules about fasting, praying, and butter-eating, so that whoever keeps the commandments of the pope will be saved and whoever does not keep them belongs to the devil. It thus seduces the people with the delusion that goodness and salvation lies in their own works. But I say that none of the saints, no matter how holy they were, attained salvation by their works. Even the holy mother of God did not become good, was not saved, by her virginity or her motherhood, but rather by the will of faith and the works of God, and not by her purity, or her own works. Therefore, mark me well: this is the reason why salvation does not lie in our own works, no matter what they are; it cannot and will not be effected without faith.

Now, someone may say: Look, my friend, you are saying a lot about faith, and claiming that our salvation depends solely upon it; now, I ask you, how does one come to faith? I will tell you. Our Lord Christ said, "Peace be with you. Behold my hands, etc." [John 20:26–27]. [In other words, he is saying:] Look, man, I am the only one who has taken away your sins

*Source: From *Luther's Works: Sermons I, Vol. 51*, edited by Helmut T. Lehmann and John W. Doberstein, translated by John W. Doberstein, copyright © 1959 Fortress Press. Used by permission of Augsburg Fortress.

and redeemed you, etc.; now be at peace. Just as you inherited sin from Adam—not that you committed it, for I did not eat the apple, any more than you did, and yet this is how we came to be in sin—so we have not suffered [as Christ did], and therefore we were made free from death and sin by God's work, not by our works. Therefore God says: Behold, man, I am your redemption [cf. Isa. 43:3]; just as Paul said to the Corinthians: Christ is our justification and redemption, etc. [I Cor. 1:30]. Christ is our justification and redemption, as Paul says in this passage. And here our [Roman] masters say: Yes, Redemptor, Redeemer; this is true, but it is not enough.

Therefore, I say again: Alien works, these made us good! Our Lord Christ says: I am your justification. I have destroyed the sins you have upon you. Therefore only believe in me; believe that I am he who has done this; then you will be justified. For it is written, Justicia est fides, righteousness is identical with faith and comes through faith. Therefore, if we want to have faith, we should believe the gospel, Paul, etc., and not the papal breves, or the decretals, but rather guard ourselves against them as against fire. For everything that comes from the pope cries out: Give, give; and if you refuse, you are of the devil. It would be a small matter if they were only exploiting the people. But, unfortunately, it is the greatest evil in the world to lead the people to believe that outward works can save or make a man good.

In conclusion, then, every single person should reflect and remember that we cannot help ourselves, but only God, and also that our works are utterly worthless. So shall we have the peace of God. And every person should so perform his work that it benefits not only himself alone, but also another, his neighbor. If he is rich, his wealth should benefit the poor. If he is poor, his service should benefit the rich. When persons are servants or maidservants, their work should benefit their master. Thus no one's work should benefit him alone; for when you note that you are serving only your own advantage, then your service is false. I am not troubled; I know very well what man-made laws are. Let the pope issue as many laws as he likes, I will keep them all so far as I please.

Therefore, dear friends, remember that God has risen up for our sakes. Therefore let us also arise to be helpful to the weak in faith, and so direct our work that God may be pleased with it. So shall we receive the peace he has given to us today. May God grant us this every day. Amen.

Studying Effectively—Exercise 3

Learning How to Identify Main Points That Are Effects, Results, Consequences

In the introduction to this *Study Guide* and in the "Studying Effectively" exercises 1 and 2, we noted that learning to underline properly plays an important part in college work. Underlining (or highlighting with a felt-tipped pen) provides a permanent record of what you study and learn. It helps you review, synthesize, and do your best on exams.

We suggested three simple guidelines for effective underlining or highlighting:*

1. Be selective; do not underline or highlight too much.
2. Underline or highlight the main points.
3. Consider numbering the main points.

These guidelines will help you in courses in many different subjects.

Cause and Effect in History

The study of history also requires learning to recognize special kinds of main points. These points are *explanatory* in nature. *They answer why and how questions*, thereby helping you to interpret and make sense of the historical record.

Two particularly important types of why and how questions focus on *cause* and *effect* in history. You are already familiar with questions of this nature, questions that provide much of history's fascination and excitement. "Why did the Roman Empire decline and fall?" That is, what *causes* explain the decline and fall of the Roman Empire? "What were the *effects* of the Black Death?" You should pay particular attention to questions of cause and effect. They give history meaning. They help you increase your ability to think and reason in historical terms.

Two other insights will help you greatly in identifying main points involving cause and effect. First, historians use a number of different words and verbal constructions to express

*The guidelines for underlining are from *RSVP: The Houghton Mifflin Reading, Study, & Vocabulary Program*, fourth edition, by James F. Shepherd (Houghton Mifflin, 1992). We urge students to consult this very valuable book for additional help in improving their reading and study skills.

these concepts. Thus "causes" often become "reasons" or "factors," or things that "account for," "contribute to," or "play a role in" a given development. "Effects" often become "results" or "consequences," or are "the product of an impact." In most cases students can consider such expressions as substitutes for cause and effect, although they should be aware that historians are not of one mind on these matters.

Second, cause and effect are constantly interrelated in the historical process. Yesterday's results become today's causes, which will in turn help bring tomorrow's results. To take examples you have studied, the *causes* of the fall of the Roman Empire (such as increasing economic difficulties) brought *results* (such as the self-sufficient agrarian economy) that contributed to—helped *cause*—the rise of Benedictine monasticism. In short, *a historical development can usually be viewed as a cause or an effect, depending on what question is being answered.*

Exercise A

Read the following passage once as a whole. Read it a second time to underline or highlight it in terms of main points identified as effects or results. Consider numbering the effects in the margin. Then do Exercise B at the end of the passage.

The effects of the invention of movable-type printing were not felt overnight. Nevertheless, within a half-century of the publication of Gutenberg's Bible of 1456, movable type brought about radical changes. Printing transformed both the private and the public lives of Europeans. Governments that "had employed the cumbersome methods of manuscripts to communicate with their subjects switched quickly to print to announce declarations of war, publish battle accounts, promulgate treaties or argue disputed points in pamphlet form. Theirs was an effort 'to win the psychological war.' " Printing made propaganda possible, emphasizing differences between various groups, such as Crown and nobility, church and state. These differences laid the basis for the formation of distinct political parties. Printed materials reached an invisible public, allowing silent individuals to join causes and groups of individuals widely separated by geography to form a common identity; this new group consciousness could compete with older, localized loyalties.

Printing also stimulated the literacy of lay people and eventually came to have a deep effect on their private lives. Although most of the earliest books and pamphlets dealt with religious subjects, students, housewives, businessmen, and upper- and middle-class people sought books on all subjects. Printers responded with moralizing, medical, practical, and travel manuals. Pornography as well as piety assumed new forms. Broadsides and flysheets allowed great public festivals, religious ceremonies, and political events to be experienced vicariously by the stay-at-home. Since books and printed materials were read aloud to the illiterate, print bridged the gap between written and oral cultures.

Exercise B

Study the last paragraph again. Can you see how it is a good example of the historical interaction of cause and effect? Do you see how a given development is an effect or a cause *depending on what historical question is being asked?* Be prepared for such "reversals" in the text, in lecture and class discussion, and on exams.

Hint: In the last paragraph, what is an *effect* of the invention of the printing press? (Ideas could be spread more rapidly.) What "stimulated"—helped *cause*—the spread of literacy? (The invention of the printing press. The authors develop this point further in Chapter 14.)

CHAPTER 18

The Age of European Expansion and Religious Wars

Chapter Questions

After reading and studying this chapter, you should be able to answer the following questions:

Why and how did Europeans gain control over distant continents? How did the Spanish overcome the powerful Aztec and Inca empires in America? What effect did overseas expansion have on Europe and on conquered societies? What were the causes of religious wars in France, the Netherlands, and Germany? How did the religious wars affect the status of women? How and why did African slave labor become the dominant form of labor organization in the New World? What religious and intellectual developments led to the growth of skepticism? What literary masterpieces did this period produce?

Chapter Summary

In this chapter we see how the trends in the High Middle Ages toward centralized nations ruled by powerful kings and toward European territorial expansion were revitalized. The growth of royal power and the consolidation of the state in Spain, France, and England accompanied and supported world exploration and a long period of European war.

The Portuguese were the first to push out into the Atlantic, but it was Spain, following close behind, that built a New World empire that provided the economic basis for a period of Spanish supremacy in European affairs. In the short run, Spanish gold and silver from the New World made the Spanish Netherlands the financial and manufacturing center of Europe, and Spain became Europe's greatest military power. In the long run, however, overseas expansion ruined the Spanish economy, created massive European inflation, and brought the end of Spain's empire in Europe.

The Aztec and Inca nations fell to the Spanish for a variety of reasons, including internal struggle, legendary beliefs, and technological and military backwardness. The takeover of the Americas led to the great seaborne trading empires, established first by the Portuguese and the Spanish and then by the Dutch. The Spanish concentrated in the Philippines, the Portuguese in the Indian Ocean, and the Dutch in Indonesia.

The major motive in Europeans' overseas expansion was the desire to Christianize pagan peoples. Jesuit Matteo Ricci tried to present Christianity to the Chinese in Chinese terms. Most Chinese were hostile to Western faiths, accusing Christians of corrupting Chinese morals. Regardless of their religious differences, the Christian West and the Chinese world learned a great deal from one another.

The attempts by Catholic monarchs to re-establish European religious unity and by both Catholic and Protestant monarchs to establish strong, centralized states led to many wars among the European states. Spain's attempt to maintain religious and political unity within its empire led to a long war in the Netherlands—a war that pulled England over to the side of the Protestant Dutch. There was bitter civil war in France, which finally came to an end with the reign of Henry of Navarre and the Edict of Nantes in 1598. The Thirty Years' War in Germany from 1618 to 1648 left that area a political and economic shambles.

The sixteenth century also saw a vast increase in witch-hunting and the emergence of modern racism, sexism, and skepticism. Generally, the power and status of women in this period did not change. Protestantism meant a more positive attitude toward marriage, but the revival of the idea that women were the source of evil and the end of the religious orders for women caused them to become increasingly powerless in society. North American slavery and racism had their origins in the labor problems in America and in Christian and Muslim racial attitudes. Skepticism was an intellectual reaction to the fanaticism of both Protestants and Catholics and a sign of things to come, while the Renaissance tradition was carried on by Shakespeare's work in late-sixteenth-century England.

Study Outline

Use this outline to preview the chapter before you read a particular section in your textbook and then as a self-check to test your reading comprehension after you have read the chapter section.

I. Discovery, reconnaissance, and expansion (1450–1650)
   A. Overseas exploration and conquest
      1. The outward expansion of Europe began with the Viking voyages, then the Crusades, but the presence of the Ottoman Turks in the East frightened the Europeans and forced their attention westward.
      2. Political centralization in Spain, France, and England prepared the way for expansion.
      3. The Portuguese, under the leadership of Prince Henry the Navigator, pushed south from North Africa.
         a. By 1500, Portugal controlled the flow of gold to Europe.
         b. Diaz, da Gama, and Cabral established trading routes to India.
         c. The Portuguese gained control of the Indian trade by overpowering Muslim forts in India.

4. Spain began to play a leading role in exploration and exploitation.
   a. Columbus sailed under the Spanish flag and opened the Caribbean for trade and conversion of the Indians.
   b. Spanish exploitation in the Caribbean led to the destruction of the Indian population.
   c. In 1519, Magellan sailed southwest across the Atlantic for Charles V of Spain; his expedition circumnavigated the earth.
   d. Cortez conquered the Aztec Empire and founded Mexico City as the capital of New Spain.
   e. Pizarro crushed the Inca Empire in Peru and opened the Potosí mines, which became the richest silver mines in the New World.
5. The Low Countries, particularly the cities of Antwerp and Amsterdam, had been since medieval times the center of European trade.
   a. The Dutch East India Company became the major organ of Dutch imperialism.
   b. The Dutch West India Company gained control of much of the African and American trade.
6. France and England made sporadic efforts at exploration and settlement.

B. The explorers' motives
1. The desire to Christianize the Muslims and pagan peoples played a central role in European expansion.
2. Limited economic and political opportunity for upper-class men in Spain led to emigration.
3. Government encouragement was also important.
4. Renaissance curiosity caused people to seek out new worlds.
5. Spices were another important incentive.
6. The economic motive—the quest for material profit—was the basic reason for European exploration and expansion.

C. Technological stimuli to exploration
1. The development of the cannon aided European expansion.
2. New sailing and navigational developments, such as the caravel ship, the magnetic compass, and the astrolabe, also aided the expansion.

D. The conquest of Aztec Mexico and Incan Peru
1. The strange end of the Aztec nation at the hands of the Spanish is one of history's most fascinating events.
   a. Cortez gained control of the capital in less than two years.
   b. One reason was that the Aztecs were preoccupied with harvesting their crops at the time of the invasion.
   c. A comet raised the specter of the return of Quetzalcoatl.
   d. Many people under Aztec rule welcomed the Spanish as liberators.
   e. The emperor Montezuma's vacillation led to his being taken hostage by Cortez.
   f. The major reason for the collapse of the empire lies in the Aztec notion of warfare and their low level of technology.

2. The Incan Empire, whose emperor was a benevolent despot, fell easily to the Spanish under Pizarro.
   a. Isolation and legendary beliefs kept the Incas from taking prompt action.
   b. Pizarro came at a time of civil war.
   c. Pizarro wisely captured the emperor, Atahualpa.
E. The South American Holocaust
   1. The Spanish settlers in the New World established encomiendas.
      a. The Spanish needed laborers to work their mines and agricultural estates.
      b. The encomienda system was a legalized form of slavery
      c. Millions of Indians died as a result of this system.
   2. Scholars have debated the causes of this devastating slump in population.
      a. The long isolation of the Indians made them susceptible to diseases brought from Europe, such as smallpox.
      b. The Spanish murdered thousands of others.
      c. Some argue that much death was due to mass suicide and infanticide.
F. Colonial administration
   1. The Spanish monarch divided his new world into four viceroyalties, each with a viceroy and audiencia, or board of judges, that served as an advisory council and judicial body.
   2. The intendants were royal officials responsible directly to the monarch.
   3. The Spanish acted on the mercantilist principle that the colonies existed for the financial benefit of the mother country.
      a. The Crown claimed the quinto, one-fifth of all precious metals mined in South America.
      b. The development of native industries was discouraged.
   4. Portuguese administration in Brazil was similar to Spain's, although one unique feature was the thorough mixture of the races.
G. The economic effects of Spain's discoveries in the New World
   1. Enormous amounts of American gold and silver poured into Spain in the sixteenth century.
   2. It is probable that population growth and not the flood of American bullion caused inflation in Spain.
   3. European inflation hurt the poor the most.
H. Seaborne trading empires
   1. The first global seaborne trade was the result of the linking of the newly discovered Americas and the Pacific with the rest of the world.
      a. The sea route to India came under Portuguese control; their major bases were at Goa and Malacca.
      b. The Portuguese traded in a variety of goods, including slaves and sugar.
      c. The Spanish built a seaborne empire that stretched across the Pacific, with Manila its center.
      d. Manila became rich from the Spanish silk trade.
   2. In the later seventeenth century the Dutch overtook the Spanish to gain dominance in world trade.
      a. The new Dutch East India Company led the Dutch to Indonesia, where they established a huge trading empire.

      b. The Dutch, Portuguese, and Spanish all paved the way for the French and the British.

II. The Chinese and Japanese discovery of the West
    A. A major motive for European expansion was Christianization.
        1. The Jesuit missionary Matteo Ricci found favor at the imperial court of China in the seventeenth and eighteenth centuries.
        2. Christianity was rejected for a variety of reasons, including its stress on absolutes and its corruption of Chinese morals.
        3. A dispute between the Jesuits and other Catholic orders weakened the influence of the missionaries.
    B. Christian missionaries (Jesuits) initiated a renewed interest in mathematics and science in China, while Europeans took home ideas on bridge building, electrostatics, and magnetism.
    C. Japanese contacts with the West were similar to those experienced by China.
        1. Portuguese, Dutch, and English trade was accompanied by Christian missionary activity.
        2. Saint Francis Xavier landed at Kasoshima in 1547; the government responded with a decree to close Japan to foreign influences.
        3. The Dutch were allowed to remain and used the island of Deshima as their trade center.
        4. Japan cut itself off from Western ideas and science; its view of the West was uncomplimentary and limited.

III. Politics, religion, and war
    A. The Spanish-French wars ended in 1559 with a Spanish victory, leading to a variety of wars centering on religious and national issues.
        1. These wars used bigger armies and gunpowder, and led to the need for administrative reorganization.
        2. Governments had to use various propaganda devices, including the printing press, to arouse public opinion.
        3. The Peace of Westphalia (1648) ended religious wars but also ended the idea of a unified Christian society.
    B. The origins of difficulties in France (1515–1559)
        1. By 1500, France was recovering from plague and disorder, and the nobility began to lose power.
        2. The French kings, such as Francis I and Henry II, continued the policies of centralization and were great patrons of Renaissance art but spent more money than they raised.
        3. The wars between France and Emperor Charles V—the Habsburg-Valois wars—were also costly.
        4. To raise money, Francis sold public offices and signed the Concordat of Bologna (1516), in which he recognized the supremacy of the papacy in return for the right to appoint French bishops.
            a. This settlement established Catholicism as the state religion in France.
            b. It also perpetuated corruption within the French church.

    c. The corruption made Calvinism attractive to Christians eager for reform, including some clergy and members of the middle and artisan classes.

C. Religious riots and civil war in France (1559–1589)

  1. The French nobility, many of them Calvinist, attempted to regain power over a series of weak monarchs.

  2. Frequent religious riots symbolized the struggle for power in the upper classes and serious religious concerns among the lower classes.

  3. The Saint Bartholomew's Day massacre of Calvinists in 1572 led to the War of the Three Henrys, a damaging conflict for secular power.

  4. King Henry IV's Edict of Nantes (1598) saved France from further civil war by allowing Protestants to worship.

D. The Netherlands under Charles V

  1. The Low Countries were part of the Habsburg empire and enjoyed commercial success and relative autonomy.

  2. In 1556, Charles V abdicated and divided his empire between his brother, Ferdinand, and his son, King Philip of Spain.

E. The revolt of the Netherlands (1556–1587)

  1. Calvinism took deep root among the merchants and financiers.

  2. Regent Margaret attempted to destroy Protestantism by establishing the Inquisition in the Netherlands.

  3. She also raised taxes, causing those who opposed the repression of Calvinism to unite with those who opposed the taxes.

  4. Popular support for Protestantism led to the destruction of many Catholic churches.

  5. The duke of Alva and his Spanish troops were sent by Philip II to crush the disturbances in the Low Countries.

  6. Alva's brutal actions only inflamed the religious war, which raged from 1568 to 1578.

  7. The Low Countries were finally split into the Spanish Netherlands in the south, under the control of the Spanish Habsburgs, and the independent United Provinces of the Netherlands in the north.

    a. The north was Protestant and ruled by the commercial aristocracy.

    b. The south was Catholic and ruled by the landed nobility.

  8. Elizabeth I of England supported the northern, or Protestant, cause as a safeguard against Spain attacking England.

    a. The wars in the Low Countries badly hurt the English economy.

    b. Elizabeth had her rival Mary, Queen of Scots, beheaded.

F. Philip II and the Spanish Armada

  1. Philip II planned war on England for several reasons.

    a. He wanted to keep England in the Catholic fold.

    b. He believed he would never conquer the Dutch unless he defeated England first.

  2. The destruction of the Spanish Armada of 1588 did not mean the end of the war, but it did prevent Philip from forcibly unifying western Europe.

  3. In 1609, Philip III agreed to a truce, recognizing the independence of the United Provinces.

G. The Thirty Years' War (1618–1648)
   1. Protestant Bohemian revolt over religious freedom led to war in Germany.
   2. The Bohemian phase (1618–1625) was characterized by civil war in Bohemia between the Catholic League and the Protestant Union.
      a. The Bohemians fought for religious liberty and independence from Habsburg rule.
      b. Ferdinand II wiped out Protestantism in Bohemia.
   3. The Danish phase of the war (1625–1629) led to further Catholic victory.
   4. The Swedish phase of the war (1630–1635) ended the Habsburg plan to unite Germany.
   5. The French phase (1635–1648) ended with a destroyed Germany and an independent Netherlands.
      a. The Peace of Westphalia recognized the independent authority of the German princes.
      b. The treaties allowed France to intervene at will in German affairs.
      c. They also denied the pope the right to participate in German religious affairs.
H. Germany after the Thirty Years' War
   1. The war was economically disastrous for Germany.
   2. The war led to agricultural depression in Germany, which in turn encouraged a return to serfdom for many peasants.

IV. Changing attitudes
   A. The status of women
      1. Literature on women and marriage called for a subservient wife, whose household was her first priority, and a protective, firm-ruling, and loyal husband.
         a. Catholic marriages could not be dissolved, while Protestants held that divorce and remarriage were possible.
         b. Women did not lose their identity or meaningful work, but their subordinate status did not change.
      2. Prostitution was common, and brothels were licensed.
      3. Protestant reformers believed that convents were antifeminist and that women would find freedom in marriage.
      4. With the closing of convents, marriage became virtually the only occupation for upper-class Protestant women.
   B. The great European witch-hunt
      1. Growth in religion and the advent of religious struggle led to a rise in the belief in the evil power of witches.
      2. The thousands of people executed as witches represent society's drift toward social and intellectual conformity.
      3. Witch-hunting reflects widespread misogyny and a misunderstanding of women.

C. European slavery and the origins of American racism
   1. Black slavery originated with the end of white slavery (1453) and the widespread need for labor, particularly in the new sugar-producing settlements.
   2. Africans were brought to America to replace the Indians beginning in 1518.
   3. Settlers brought to the Americas the racial attitudes they had absorbed in Europe from Christianity and Islam, which by and large depicted blacks as primitive and inferior.

V. Literature and art
   A. The origins of modern skepticism in the essays of Montaigne
      1. Skeptics doubt whether definitive knowledge is ever attainable.
      2. Montaigne is the best representative of early modern skepticism and a forerunner of modern attitudes.
         a. In the *Essays* he advocated open-mindedness, tolerance, and rejection of dogmatism.
         b. He rejected the claim that one culture may be superior to another, and he inaugurated an era of doubt.
   B. Elizabethan and Jacobean literature
      1. Shakespeare reflects the Renaissance appreciation of classical culture, individualism, and humanism.
         a. His history plays reflect national consciousness.
         b. His tragedies explore human problems—*Hamlet* is popular because through it people have seen themselves.
      2. The Authorized Bible of King James I (King James Bible) is a masterpiece of English vernacular writing.
   C. Baroque art and music
      1. In the late sixteenth century, the papacy and the Jesuits encouraged the growth of an emotional, exuberant art intended to appeal to the senses and kindle the faith of ordinary churchgoers.
      2. The baroque style took definite shape in Italy after 1600 and developed with exceptional vigor in Catholic countries.
         a. Rubens developed a sensuous, colorful style of painting characterized by animated figures and monumental size.
         b. In music the baroque style reached its culmination with Bach.

Review Questions

Check your understanding of this chapter by answering the following questions.

1. Describe the Portuguese explorations. Who were the participants, and what were their motives?

2. What role did Antwerp and Amsterdam play in international commerce?

3. Why was there such severe inflation in the sixteenth century?

4. What role did technology play in European expansion?

5. What were the major reasons for European expansion in the fifteenth and sixteenth centuries?

6. What were the motives of the Christian missionaries in China and Japan? How were they treated? Did they have a negative or positive impact on Japanese and Chinese societies?

7. What were the causes and consequences of the French civil war of 1559–1589? Was the war chiefly a religious or a political event?

8. What were the origins and the outcome of the war between the Netherlands and Spain in the late sixteenth and early seventeenth centuries?

9. What were the circumstances surrounding Elizabeth's decision to aid the United Provinces in their war against Spain? What was the Spanish reaction?

10. Why did Catholic France side with the Protestants in the Thirty Years' War?

11. What were the political, religious, and economic consequences of the Thirty Years' War in Europe?

12. What was the social status of women between 1560 and 1648?

13. What do the witch-hunts tell us about social attitudes toward women?

14. What were the origins of North American racism?

15. What is skepticism? Why did faith and religious certainty begin to come to an end in the first part of the seventeenth century?

16. What were the major literary masterpieces of this age? In what ways can Shakespeare be regarded as a true Renaissance man?

17. What was the baroque style?

Study-Review Exercises

Define the following key concepts and terms.

mercantilism

inflation

sexism

racism

skepticism

misogyny

baroque

South American Holocaust

Identify and explain the significance of the following people and terms.

Saint Francis Xavier

Low Countries

duke of Alva

politiques

Elizabeth I of England

Huguenots

Philip II of Spain

Prince Henry the Navigator

Michel de Montaigne

William Shakespeare

Globe Theater

Christopher Columbus

Bartholomew Diaz

Montezuma

Pizarro

Hernando Cortez

Habsburg-Valois wars

encomiendas

quinto

audiencia

corregidores

Deshima

Thirty Years' War

defeat of the Spanish Armada

Concordat of Bologna

Peace of Westphalia

Saint Bartholomew's Day massacre

War of the Three Henrys

Edict of Nantes

King James Bible

Test your understanding of the chapter by providing the correct answers.

1. The war that brought destruction and political fragmentation to Germany.

    _____

2. The Spanish explorer who conquered the Aztecs. _____

3. The law of 1598 that granted religious freedom to French Protestants.

    _____

4. Spain's golden century. _____

5. The king of Sweden who intervened in the Thirty Years' War. _____

6. After 1551, the seven northern provinces of the Netherlands were called

    _____ .

7. The city that became the financial capital of Europe by 1600. _____

8. The monarch of Britain at the time of the Spanish Armada. _____

9. The idea that nothing is completely knowable. _____

10. The emperor who divided the Habsburg empire into two parts. _____

11. The 1516 compromise between church and state in France. _____

12. The first European country to establish sea routes to the East. _____

Multiple-Choice Questions

1. Which of the following was a motive for Portuguese exploration in the late fifteenth and sixteenth centuries?
   a. The search for gold
   b. The conversion of peoples to the Islamic religion
   c. The discovery of sea routes to North America
   d. The conquest of Constantinople

2. Beginning in 1581, the northern Netherlands revolted against its political overlord, which was
   a. France.
   b. Spain.
   c. Elizabeth I of England.
   d. Florence.

3. North American racist attitudes toward African blacks originated in
   a. South America.
   b. Spain.
   c. France.
   d. England.

4. In the Thirty Years' War, France supported
   a. the German Catholics.
   b. the Holy Roman emperor.
   c. Spain.
   d. the German Protestants.

5. Which of the following statements about the Spanish Armada of 1588 is *false*?
   a. It was the beginning of a long war with England.
   b. It failed in its objective.
   c. It prevented Philip II from reimposing unity on western Europe by force.
   d. It made possible Spanish conquest of the Netherlands.

6. The nation that considered itself the international defender of Catholicism was
   a. France.
   b. Spain.
   c. Italy.
   d. England.

7. Columbus, like many of his fellow explorers, was principally motivated by
   a. a desire to discover India.
   b. a desire to Christianize the Americans.
   c. the desire of Spain to control the New World.
   d. the Spanish need to control the Mediterranean.

8. The earliest known explorers of North America were
   a. the Spanish.
   b. the Vikings.
   c. the Italians.
   d. the English.

9. Which of the following statements describes a feature of Spanish colonial policy?
   a. The New World was divided into four viceroyalties.
   b. Native industries were established.
   c. Each territory had local officials, or *corregidores*, who held judicial and military powers.
   d. The Spanish crown had only indirect and limited control over colonies.

10. To gain control of the spice trade of the Indian Ocean, the Portuguese had to defeat
    a. Spain.
    b. England.
    c. the Muslims.
    d. France.

11. The main contribution of Cortez and Pizarro to Spain was
    a. the tapping of the rich silver resources of Mexico and Peru.
    b. the Christianizing of the New World peoples.
    c. the further exploration of the Pacific Ocean.
    d. the discovery of South Africa.

12. The flow of huge amounts of gold and silver from the New World caused
    a. serious inflation in Spain and the rest of Europe.
    b. the Spanish economy to become dependent on New World gold and silver.
    c. the suffering of the poor because of the dramatic rise in food prices.
    d. Spain's economic strength and dominance in Europe.

13. By which treaty did the king of France, Francis I, recognize the supremacy of the papacy?
    a. The Treaty of Westphalia
    b. The Treaty of Cateau-Cambrésis
    c. The Concordat of Bologna
    d. The Edict of Nantes

14. France was saved from religious anarchy when religious principles were set aside for political necessity by King
    a. Henry III.
    b. Francis I.
    c. Henry IV of Navarre.
    d. Charles IX.

15. Calvinism was appealing to the middle classes for each of the following reasons *except*
    a. its heavy moral emphasis.
    b. its stress on leisure and ostentatious living.
    c. its intellectual emphasis.
    d. its approval of any job well done, hard work, and success.

16. The vast palace of the Spanish monarchs, built under the direction of Philip II, was called
    a. Versailles.
    b. the Escorial.
    c. Tournai.
    d. Hampton Court.

17. The Treaty of Westphalia, which ended the Thirty Years' War
    a. further strengthened the Holy Roman Empire.
    b. completely undermined the Holy Roman Empire as a viable state.
    c. maintained that only Catholicism and Lutheranism were legitimate religions.
    d. refused to recognize the independence of the United Provinces of the Netherlands.

18. Who among the following best represents early modern skepticism?
    a. Las Casas
    b. James I
    c. Calvin
    d. Montaigne

19. The Spanish missionary Las Casas convinced Charles V to import Africans to Brazil for all the following reasons *except*
    a. the enslavement of Africans seemed more acceptable to the church.
    b. he believed they could endure better than the Indians.
    c. the native Indians were not durable enough under such harsh conditions.
    d. the native Indians revolted and refused to work as slave labor.

20. The Portuguese explorer who first reached India was
    a. Bartholomew Diaz.
    b. Prince Henry the Navigator.
    c. Vasco da Gama.
    d. Hernando Cortez.

21. The style of art popular in late-eighteenth-century Europe was called
    a. Elizabethan.
    b. Jacobean.
    c. skepticism.
    d. baroque.

22. The appearance of gunpowder in Europe
    a. made the common soldier inferior to the gentleman soldier.
    b. changed the popular belief that warfare bettered the individual.
    c. eliminated the need for governments to use propaganda to convince their people
       to support war.
    d. had little effect on the nature of war.

23. The ten southern provinces of the Netherlands, known as the Spanish Netherlands,
    became the future
    a. Netherlands.
    b. Bohemia.
    c. Belgium.
    d. Schleswig.

24. The Thirty Years' War was fought primarily
    a. on German soil.
    b. in France.
    c. in eastern Europe.
    d. in Spain.

25. The Ottoman capture of Constantinople in 1453 was significant in the history of
    slavery and racism in that it
    a. introduced the concept of slavery to the Christian European world.
    b. ended the transport of black slaves to Europe.
    c. caused Europeans to turn to sub-Saharan Africa for their slaves.
    d. ushered in a flow of slaves from the Indies.

26. The Western traders who were allowed to remain in Japan and trade on a limited
    basis were the
    a. Portuguese.
    b. Spanish.
    c. Americans.
    d. Dutch.

27. The ecomienda system established by the Spanish in South America was
    a. a legalized form of slavery.
    b. a church law that gave Amerindians their freedom.
    c. an alternative to forced labor.
    d. a series of military outposts.

28. The Christian West was influenced by China in all of the following ways *except*
    a. the building of bridges suspended with chains.
    b. the use of new farming techniques.
    c. providing models for experiments in electrostatics and magnetism.
    d. making Europeans more sensitive to the beautiful diversity of peoples and manners.

Major Political Ideas

1. This chapter emphasizes how the medieval concept of a unified Christian society under one political ruler and one church began to break down. What was the cause of this breakdown?

2. *Misogyny* and *racism* are political terms in that they help to explain the distribution of power within society. Discuss each of these terms in the context of the sixteenth and seventeenth centuries.

3. It is suggested in this chapter (see pages 585–586) that Calvinism contributed to Dutch ideas of national independence. Explain the connection. Do you agree?

Issues for Essays and Discussion

The age of European expansion and religious wars was a period of both the breakdown and the reconstruction of society. Describe this process of breakdown and reconstruction by discussing civil war, international war, and overseas expansion from about 1450 to about 1560. What were the causes of these events? What country (or countries) emerged from this era as the most powerful?

Interpretation of Visual Sources

Study the sixteenth-century print that has been reproduced on page 586 of your textbook. Describe the scene by identifying the precise actions of the participants. What specific types of offensive references are being destroyed? What are the ideas behind this "purification"?

Geography

1. On Outline Map 18.1 provided, and using Maps 18.1 and 18.2 in the textbook as a reference, mark the following: the exploration routes of da Gama, Columbus, and Magellan, Cueta, the Cape of Good Hope, Amsterdam, Guinea, Calicut, Cape Horn, London, Lisbon, Goa, Antwerp, Mexico City, Moluccas.

2. Using Map 18.5 in the textbook as a reference, identify the areas that were the main sources of African slaves and the main areas of slave importation into the New World. Do the latter areas illustrate the economic origins of the slave trade?

3. On Outline Map 18.4 provided, and using Map 18.4 in the textbook as a reference, mark the following: the areas under Spanish Habsburg control, the areas under Austrian Habsburg control, Prussian lands, the United Netherlands, the German states, the boundary of the old Holy Roman Empire, Swedish possessions, Madrid, Lisbon, Vienna, Amsterdam.

Remember that duplicate maps for class use are at the back of this book.

Outline Map 18.1

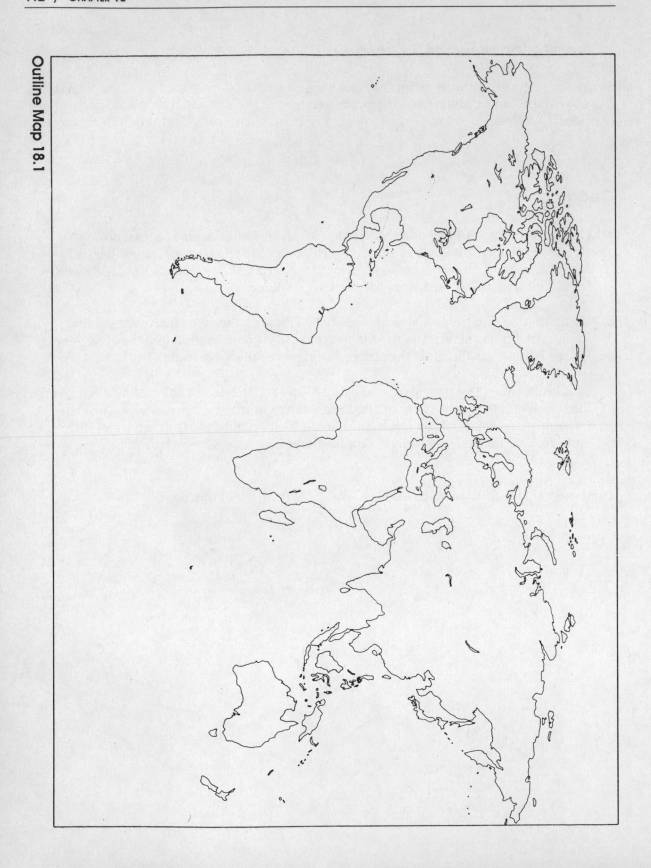

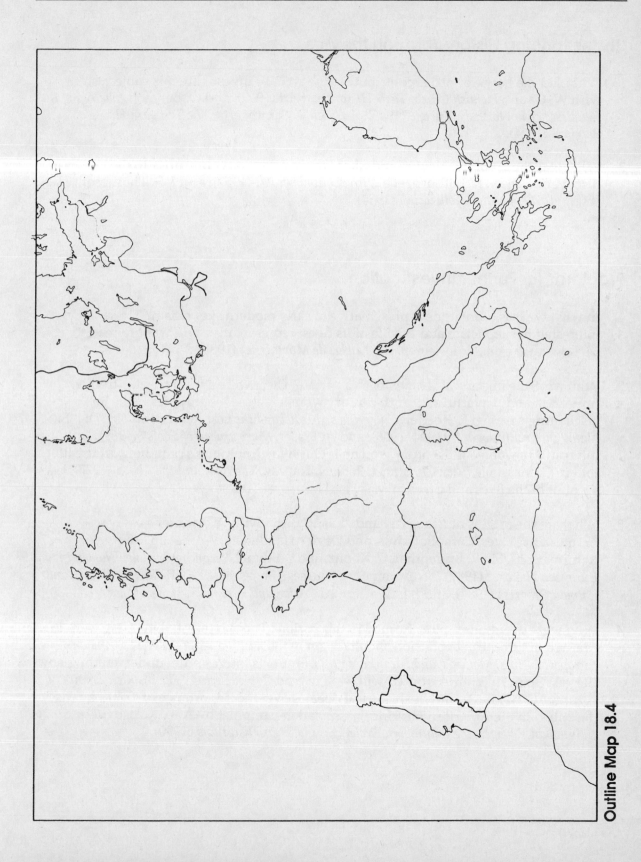

Outline Map 18.4

Understanding History Through the Arts

1. What did the Low Countries contribute to the arts? To investigate this subject, start with W. Gaunt, *Flemish Cities, Their History and Art* (1969), and O. Benesch, *The Art of the Renaissance in Northern Europe* (1945). See also E. Cammaerts, *The Treasure-House of Belgium* (1924).

2. What was the art of the New World like? For the arts of America prior to the European discoveries, see S. K. Lothorp, et al., *Pre-Columbian Art* (1957), and J. E. Thompson, *The Rise and Fall of Maya Civilization* (1954).

Problems for Further Investigation

1. In what ways is Montaigne representative of early modern skepticism? Those interested in skepticism and the life of its finest representative will want to read M. Lowenthal, ed., *Autobiography of Michel de Montaigne** (1935).

2. Who were the important women of this period? There were a number of extremely important and powerful sixteenth-century women whose biographies make for fascinating reading: R. Roeder, *Catherine de Medici and the Lost Revolution** (1937); J. E. Neal, *Queen Elizabeth I** (1934, 1966); and A. Fraser, *Mary Queen of Scots** (1969). An interesting seventeenth-century woman is Gustavus Adolphus's daughter, whose life is told in G. Masson, *Queen Christina* (1968). N. Harvey, *The Rose and the Thorn* (1977), is an account of the lives and times of Mary and Margaret Tudor.

3. What are the origins of misogyny and racism? Begin with W. Monter's essay, "Protestant Wives, Catholic Saints, and Devil's Handmaid: Women in the Age of Reformations," in R. Bridenthal, C. Koonz, and S. Stuard, *Becoming Visible: Women in European History** (1987). To examine the sources of racism, see D. B. Davis, *Slavery and Human Progress* (1984), and J. L. Watson, ed., *Asian and African Systems of Slavery* (1980).

4. Why were overseas empires formed in this period? Those interested in doing work in the area of European expansion should begin with D. L. Jensen, ed., *The Expansion of Europe: Motives, Methods, and Meaning* (1967). Students interested in understanding how the vast Spanish Empire worked will want to read C. H. Haring, *The Spanish Empire in America** (1947, 1963), and the historical debates over the importance of Columbus are described in the American Historical Association pamphlet by A. W. Crosby, *The Columbian Voyages, the Columbian Exchange, and Their Historians* (1990).

*Available in paperback.

5. Why were such severe religious wars fought in this era? Some of the problems faced in studying the religious conflict in France are discussed in J. H. M. Sahnon, *The French Wars of Religion** (1967). Anyone interested in research on the Thirty Years' War should begin with S. H. Steinberg, *The Thirty Years' War and the Conflict for European Hegemony, 1600–1660** (1966), and T. K. Rabb, *The Thirty Years' War** (1964).

*Available in paperback.

CHAPTER 19

Absolutism and Constitutionalism in Europe, ca 1589–1725

Chapter Questions

After reading and studying this chapter, you should be able to answer the following questions:

How did absolute monarchy and constitutionalism differ from the feudal and dynastic monarchies of earlier centuries? Why did the basic structure of society in eastern Europe move away from that in western Europe? How and why did the rulers of Austria, Prussia, and Russia manage to build more durable absolute monarchies than that of Louis XIV of France? How did the absolute monarchs' interactions with artists and architects contribute to the achievements of both western and eastern Europe? What were the characteristics of the constitutional state, and why did it rather than absolutism triumph in Holland and England?

Chapter Summary

The seventeenth century marks the development of two patterns of government in Europe: absolute monarchy and the constitutional state. This chapter examines how the political system of absolutism succeeded gloriously in France and failed dismally in England in the seventeenth century. Few kings have been as successful in establishing complete monarchial sovereignty as France's Louis XIV. Louis gave Europe a masterful lesson on how to collaborate with the nobility to strengthen the monarchy and to reinforce the ancient aristocracy. He was a superb actor and propagandist who built on the earlier achievements of Henry IV and Richelieu and used his magnificent palace of Versailles to imprison the French nobility in a beautiful golden cage. He succeeded in expanding France at the expense of the Habsburgs, and his patronage of the arts helped form the great age of French classicism.

While the France of Louis was the classic model of absolutism as the last phase of an historic feudal society, Spain was the classic case of imperial decline. By 1600 Spain was in trouble, and by 1700 it was no longer a major European power. Not only did the silver and labor of

America run out, but this great American wealth ruined the Spanish economic and social structure.

England and the United Provinces of the Netherlands provide a picture of constitutionalism triumphing over absolutism. For England, the seventeenth century was a long period of political conflict, complete with a bitter civil war and a radical experiment with republicanism. The causes of this era of conflict were varied, but it is clear that by 1689 the English army and Parliament had destroyed the Stuart quest for divine-right absolutism. The Netherlands was important not only because it became the financial and commercial center of Europe, but also because it provided the period's third model of political development—a loosely federated, middle-class constitutional state.

The rulers of Eastern Europe also struggled to build strong absolutist states in the seventeenth century. Gains made by the peasantry during the High Middle Ages were rolled back as the princes and landed nobility reimposed serfdom. The drop in population and prices in the fourteenth and fifteenth centuries caused severe labor shortages and hard times for the nobles. In attempts to remedy this, nobles steadily took more and more of their peasants' land and made their kings and princes issue laws that restricted or eliminated the peasants' right to free movement. Even as the economy improved, the serfs' position continued to deteriorate. Scholars offer both political as well as economic explanations for the rise of serfdoms in Eastern Europe as a similar economic climate led to the decline of serfdom in the West.

Despite the strength of the nobility and the weakness of many monarchs before 1600, strong kings did emerge in many eastern European lands in the course of the seventeenth century. Under constant threat of war, monarchs reduced the political power of the landlord nobility. Cautiously leaving the nobles the unchallenged masters of their peasants, the absolutist monarchs of eastern Europe gradually gained and monopolized political power in three key areas. They imposed and collected taxes without consent. They maintained standing armies. And they conducted relations with other states as they pleased.

Study Outline

Use this outline to preview the chapter before you read a particular section in the textbook and then as a self-check to test your reading comprehension after you have read the chapter section.

I. Absolutism: an overview
   A. In the absolutist state, sovereignty resided in the king, not the nobility or the parliament.
      1. Absolute kings considered themselves responsible to God alone.
      2. They created new state bureaucracies to control the economy, maintained permanent standing armies, regulated all the institutions of government, and secured the cooperation of the nobility.
   B. The absolutist state foreshadowed the modern totalitarian state but lacked its total control over all aspects of its citizens' lives.

II. France: the model of absolute monarchy
    A. The foundations of French absolutism: Henry IV and Richelieu
        1. Henry IV achieved peace and curtailed the power of the nobility.
        2. His minister, Sully, brought about financial stability and economic growth.
        3. Cardinal Richelieu, the ruler of France under King Louis XIII, broke the power of the French nobility.
            a. His policy was total subordination of all groups and institutions to the French monarchy.
            b. He leveled castles and crushed aristocratic conspiracies.
            c. He established an efficient administrative system using intendants, who further weakened the local nobility.
            d. The Huguenot revolt of 1625 led to the destruction of fortified cities in France, eliminating another source of aristocratic power.
        4. Under Richelieu, France sought to break Habsburg power.
            a. He supported the struggle of the Swedish king, Gustavus Adolphus, against the Habsburgs.
            b. He acquired land and influence in Germany.
        5. The French government's ability to tax was severely limited by local rights and the tax-exempt status of much of the nobility and the middle class.
    B. Mazarin continued Richelieu's centralizing policies, but these policies gave rise to a period of civil wars known as the Fronde.
    C. The Fronde had three significant results for the future.
        1. It became clear that the goverment would have to compromise with the state bureaucracy.
        2. The French economy was badly damaged.
        3. It convinced the new king, Louis XIV, that civil war was destructive of social order and that absolute monarchy was the only alternative to anarchy.

III. The absolute monarchy of Louis XIV
    A. Louis XIV, the "Sun King," was a devout Catholic who believed that God had established kings as his rulers on earth.
    B. He successfully collaborated with the nobility to enhance both aristocratic prestige and royal power.
    C. He made the court at Versailles a fixed institution and used it as a means of preserving royal power and as the center of French absolutism.
        1. The architecture and art of Versailles were a means of carrying out state policy—a way to overawe Louis's subjects and foreign visitors and reinforce his power.
        2. The French language and culture became the international style.
        3. The court at Versailles was a device to undermine the power of the aristocracy by separating power from status.
        4. A centralized state, administered by a professional class taken from the "nobility of the robe," was formed.
    D. Financial and economic management under Louis XIV: Colbert
        1. Mercantilism is a collection of government policies for the regulation of economic activities by and for the state.

2. Louis XIV's finance minister, Colbert, tried to achieve a favorable balance of trade and make France self-sufficient so the flow of gold to other countries would be halted.
    a. Colbert encouraged French industry, enacted high foreign tariffs, and created a strong merchant marine.
    b. Though France's industries grew and the commercial classes prospered, its agricultural economy suffered under the burdens of heavy taxation, population decline, and poor harvests.

E. The revocation of the Edict of Nantes
1. In 1685, Louis revoked the Edict of Nantes, which had given religious freedom to French Protestants.
2. This revocation caused many Protestants to flee the country, but it had little effect on the economy.

IV. French classicism in art and literature
A. French classicism imitated and resembled the arts of the ancients and the Renaissance.
B. Louis XIV was a patron of the composers Lully, Couperin, and Charpentier.
C. The comedies of Molière and the tragedies of Racine best illustrate the classicism in French theater.

V. Louis XIV's wars
A. The French army under Louis XIV was modern because the state, rather than the nobles, employed the soldiers.
1. He appointed Louvois to create a professional army.
2. Louis himself took personal command of the army.
B. Louis continued Richelieu's expansionist policy.
1. In 1667, he invaded Flanders and gained twelve towns; by the treaty of Nijmegen (1678) he gained some Flemish towns and all of Franche-Comté.
2. Strasbourg was taken in 1681 and Lorraine in 1684, but the limits of his expansion had been met.
3. Louis fought the new Dutch king of England, William III, and the League of Augsburg in a war.
    a. Louis's heavy taxes fell on the peasants, who revolted.
    b. Poor harvests, rising grain prices, and higher taxes brought great suffering to the French people.
4. The War of the Spanish Succession (1701–1713) was fought over the issue of the succession to the Spanish throne: Louis claimed Spain but was opposed by the Dutch, English, Austrians, and Prussians.
    a. The war was also an attempt to preserve the balance of power in Europe and to check France's commercial power overseas.
    b. A Grand Alliance of the English, Dutch, Austrians, and Prussians was formed in 1701 to fight the French.
    c. The war was concluded by the Peace of Utrecht in 1713, which forbade the union of France and Spain.

       d. The war ended French expansionism and left France with widespread misery and revolts.

VI. The decline of absolutist Spain in the seventeenth century
    A. Factors contributing to Spain's decline
       1. Fiscal disorder, political incompetence, the lack of a strong middle class, population decline, lack of investment, intellectual isolation, and psychological malaise contributed to its decline.
       2. The defeat of the "Invincible Armada" in 1588 was a crushing blow to Spain's morale.
       3. Spain's economy began to decline by 1600.
          a. Royal expenditures increased, but income from the Americas decreased.
          b. Business and agriculture suffered.
          c. South American silver mines started to run dry; slave workers suffered greatly.
          d. Spain was held back because of lack of a middle class.
       4. Spanish kings lacked force of character and could not deal with all these problems.
    B. The Treaty of the Pyrenees of 1659, which ended the French-Spanish wars, marked the end of Spain as a great power.

VII. Lords and peasants in eastern Europe (ca 1050–1650)
    A. The medieval background
       1. Personal and economic freedom for peasants increased between 1050 and 1300.
          a. Serfdom nearly disappeared.
          b. Peasants bargained freely with their landlords and moved about as they pleased.
       2. After 1300, powerful lords in eastern Europe revived serfdom to combat their economic problems.
          a. Laws that restricted the peasants' right of free movement were passed.
          b. Lords took more and more of the peasants' land and imposed heavier labor obligations.
    B. The consolidation of serfdom
       1. The re-establishment of hereditary serfdom took place in Poland, Prussia, and Russia between 1500 and 1650.
       2. The consolidation of serfdom was accompanied by the growth of estate agriculture.
          a. Lords seized peasant lands for their own estates.
          b. They then demanded unpaid serf labor on those estates.
    C. Political reasons for changes in serfdom in eastern Europe
       1. Serfdom increased for political, not economic, reasons.
       2. Weak monarchs could not resist the demands of the powerful noble landlords.
       3. The absence of the Western concept of sovereignty meant that the king did not think in terms of protecting the people of the nation.

4. Overall, the peasants had less political power in eastern Europe and less solidarity.
5. The landlords systematically undermined the medieval privileges of the towns.
   a. The lords sold directly to foreign capitalists instead of to local merchants.
   b. Eastern towns lost their medieval right of refuge.

VIII. The rise of Austria and Prussia (1650–1750)
   A. Austria and the Ottoman Turks
      1. After the Thirty Years' War, the Austrian Habsburgs turned inward and eastward to unify their holdings.
         a. The Habsburgs replaced the Bohemian Czech (Protestant) nobility with their own warriors.
         b. Serfdom increased, Protestantism was wiped out, and absolutism was achieved.
         c. Ferdinand III created a standing army, centralized the government in Austria, and turned toward Hungary for land.
      2. This eastward turn led Austria to become absorbed in a war against the Ottoman Turks over Hungary and Transylvania.
      3. Under Suleiman the Magnificent the Turks had built the most powerful empire in the world, which included parts of central Europe.
      4. The Turkish attack on Austria in 1683 was turned back, and the Habsburgs conquered all of Hungary and Transylvania by 1699.
      5. The Habsburg possessions consisted of Austria, Bohemia, and Hungary, which were joined in a fragile union.
         a. The Pragmatic Sanction (1713) stated that the possessions should never be divided.
         b. The Protestant Hungarian nobility thwarted the full development of Habsburg absolutism, and Charles VI had to restore many of their traditional privileges after the rebellion led by Rákóczy in 1703.
   B. Prussia in the seventeenth century
      1. The Hohenzollern family ruled the electorate of Brandenburg but had little real power.
      2. The Thirty Years' War weakened the representative assemblies of the realm and allowed the Hohenzollerns to consolidate their absolute rule.
      3. Frederick William (the Great Elector) used military force and taxation to unify his Rhine holdings, Prussia, and Brandenburg into a strong state.
         a. The traditional parliaments, or estates, which were controlled by the Junkers (the nobles and the landowners), were weakened.
         b. War strengthened the elector, as did the Junkers' unwillingness to join with the towns to block absolutism.
   C. The consolidation of Prussian absolutism
      1. Frederick William I encouraged Prussian militarism and created the best army in Europe plus an efficient bureaucracy.
      2. The Junker class became the military elite and Prussia a militarist state.

IX. The development of Russia

    A. The Vikings and the Kievan principality

        1. Eastern Slavs moved into Russia between the fifth and ninth centuries.

        2. Slavic-Viking settlements grew up in the ninth century.

        3. The Vikings, or Varangians, unified the eastern Slavs politically and religiously, creating a ruling dynasty and accepting Eastern Orthodox Christianity for themselves and the Slavs.

            a. The united Slavic territory was known as the Kievan state.

            b. After Iaroslav's death in 1054 this state disintegrated into competing units.

        4. A strong aristocracy (the boyars) and a free peasantry made it difficult to strengthen the state.

    B. The Mongol yoke and the rise of Moscow

        1. The Mongols conquered the Kievan state in the thirteenth century and unified it under their harsh rule.

        2. The Mongols used Russian aristocrats, such as Alexander Nevsky, as their servants and tax collectors.

            a. The princes of Moscow served the Mongols well and became the hereditary great princes.

            b. Ivan I served the Mongols while using his wealth and power to strengthen the principality of Moscow.

            c. Ivan III stopped acknowledging the Mongol khan as the supreme ruler and assumed the headship of Orthodox Christianity.

    C. Tsar and people to 1689

        1. By 1505, the prince of Moscow—the tsar—had emerged as the single hereditary ruler of the eastern Slavs.

        2. The tsars and the boyars struggled over who would rule the state; the tsars won and created a new "service nobility," who held the tsar's land on the condition that they serve in his army.

        3. Ivan IV, "the Terrible," was an autocratic tsar who expanded Muscovy and further reduced the power of the boyars.

            a. He murdered leading boyars and confiscated their estates.

            b. Many peasants fled his rule to the newly conquered territories, forming groups called Cossacks.

            c. Businessmen and artisans were bound to their towns and jobs; the middle class did not develop.

        4. The Time of Troubles (1598–1613) was a period characterized by internal struggles and invasions.

            a. There was no heir, and relatives of the tsar fought against each other.

            b. Swedish and Polish armies invaded.

            c. Cossack bands slaughtered many nobles and officials.

            d. Their defeat led to greater serfdom.

    D. The reforms of Peter the Great

        1. Peter wished to create a strong army for protection and expansion.

            a. He forced the nobility to serve in the army or in the civil service.

            b. He created schools to train technicians for his army.

2. Army and government became more efficient and powerful as an interlocking military-civilian bureaucracy was created and staffed by talented people.
3. Russian peasant life under Peter became more harsh.
   a. People replaced land as the primary unit of taxation.
   b. Serfs were arbitrarily assigned to work in the factories and mines.
4. Modest territorial expansion took place under Peter, and Russia became a European Great Power.
   a. Russia defeated Sweden in 1709 at Poltava to gain control of the Baltic Sea.
   b. Peter borrowed many Western ideas.

X. Absolutism and the baroque
   A. Royal cities and urban planning
      1. Absolute monarchs and baroque architects remodeled capital cities or built new ones, such as Karlsruhe in Germany in 1715.
         a. These cities had broad avenues, imposing government buildings, mathematical layouts, townhouses, and shopping arcades.
         b. The arrival of the carriage widened the social gap between rich and poor.
      2. The new St. Petersburg is an excellent example of the ties among architecture, politics, and urban development.
         a. Peter the Great wanted to create a modern, baroque city from which to rule Russia.
         b. The city was built by the forced labor of the peasants.
         c. The nobility was ordered to build costly stone houses; nobles and merchants were ordered to pay for the city's avenues, parks, and bridges.
      3. During the eighteenth century, St. Petersburg became one of the world's largest and most influential cities.

XI. Constitutionalism in England and the Netherlands
   A. Constitutionalism defined
      1. Under constitutionalism, the state must be governed according to law, not royal decree.
         a. It implies a balance between the power of the government and the rights of the subjects.
         b. A nation's constitution may be written or unwritten, but the government must respect it.
         c. Constitutional governments may be either republics or monarchies.
      2. Constitutional government is not the same as full democracy because not all of the people have the right to participate.
   B. England: the triumph of constitutional monarchy
      1. The Stuart kings of England lacked the political wisdom of Elizabeth I.
      2. James I was devoted to the ideal of rule by divine right.
      3. His absolutism ran counter to English belief.
      4. The House of Commons wanted a greater say in the government of the state.
         a. Increased wealth had produced a better-educated House of Commons.

    b. Between 1603 and 1640, bitter squabbles erupted between the Crown and the Commons over taxation.

5. Many English men and women were attracted by the values of hard work, thrift, and self-denial implied by Calvinism and wanted to purify the Church of England.

6. Charles I and his archbishop, Laud, appeared to be pro-Catholic.

7. Charles I had ruled without Parliament for eleven years.
    a. A revolt in Scotland over the religious issue forced him to call a new Parliament into session to finance an army.
    b. The Commons passed an act compelling the king to summon Parliament every three years; it impeached Archbishop Laud and abolished the House of Lords.
    c. Religious differences in Ireland led to a revolt there, but Parliament would not trust Charles with an army.

8. Charles initiated military action against Parliament.
    a. The civil war (1642–1649) revolved around the issue of whether sovereignty should reside in the king or in Parliament; the problem was not resolved, but Charles was beheaded in 1649.

C. Puritanical absolutism in England: Cromwell and the Protectorate

1. Hobbes set set forth the theory that power is derived from the people, not God.

2. Kingship was abolished in 1649 and a commonwealth proclaimed.
    a. A commonwealth is a government without a king whose power rests in Parliament and a council of state.
    b. In fact, the army controlled the government.

3. Cromwell, leader of the "New Model Army" that defeated the royalists, came from the gentry class that dominated the House of Commons.
    a. He became a military dictator, absolutist and puritanical.
    b. He allowed religious toleration for all Christians, except Roman Catholics, and savagely crushed the revolt in Ireland.
    c. The mercantilist navigation act that required English goods to be transported on English ships was a boon to the economy and led to a commercial war with the Dutch.

D. The restoration of the English monarchy

1. The restoration of the Stuart kings in 1660 failed to solve the problems of religion and the relationship between king and Parliament.
    a. According to the Test Act of 1673, those who refused to join the Church of England could not vote, hold office, preach, teach, attend the universities, or assemble, but these restrictions could not be upheld.
    b. Charles II appointed a council of five men to serve as both his major advisers and as members of Parliament; this was the forerunner of the cabinet system.

2. Charles's pro-French policies led to anti-Catholic fear.

3. James II, an avowed Catholic, violated the Test Act by appointing Catholics to government and university positions.

      4. Fear of a Catholic monarchy led to the expulsion of James II and the Glorious Revolution.
- E. Constitutional monarchy and cabinet government
  1. The "Glorious Revolution" that expelled James II and installed William and Mary on the throne ended the idea of divine-right monarchy.
  2. The Bill of Rights of 1689 established the principle of Parliament's sovereignty.
     a. Locke maintained that people set up government to protect life, liberty, and property.
     b. Locke's ideas that there are natural, or universal, rights played a strong role in eighteenth-century Enlightenment thought.
  3. In the cabinet system, which developed in the eighteenth century, both legislative and executive power are held by the leading ministers, who form the government.
- F. The Dutch republic in the seventeenth century
  1. The Dutch republic emerged from the sixteenth-century struggle against Spain and flowered in the seventeenth century.
  2. Power in the republic resided in the local Estates.
     a. The republic was a confederation: a weak union of strong provinces.
     b. The republic was based on middle-class ideas and values.
  3. Thrift, frugality, and religious toleration fostered economic growth.
  4. The province of Holland became the commercial and financial center of Europe—much of it based on transport of goods from all over the world.
     a. The Dutch East India Company was formed in 1602; it cut heavily into Portuguese trading in East Asia.
     b. The Dutch West India Company, founded in 1621, traded extensively in Latin America and Africa.
  5. War with France and England in the 1670s hurt the United Provinces.

Review Questions

Check your understanding of this chapter by answering the following questions.

1. In what way does the French minister Richelieu symbolize absolutism? What were his achievements?

2. Why can it be said that the palace of Versailles was used as a device to ruin the nobility of France? Was Versailles a palace or a prison?

3. Define mercantilism. What were the mercantilist policies of the French minister Colbert?

4. Was the revocation of the Edict of Nantes a great error on the part of Louis XIV?

5. What were the reasons for the fall of the Spanish Empire?

6. Discuss the foreign policy goals of Louis XIV. Was he successful?

7. Define absolutism. How does it differ from totalitarianism?

8. What was the impact of Louis XIV's wars on the French economy and French society?

9. What were the causes of the War of the Spanish Succession? What impact did William III of England have on European events after about 1689?

10. What is constitutionalism? How does it differ from the democratic form of government? From absolutism?

11. What were the attitudes and policies of James I that made him so unpopular with his subjects?

12. What were the immediate and the long-range causes of the English Civil War of 1642–1649? What were the results?

13. Were the events of 1688–89 a victory for English democracy? Explain.

14. Why is it said that Locke was the spokesman for the liberal English Revolution of 1689 and for representative government?

15. What accounts for the phenomenal economic success and political stability of the Dutch republic?

16. What were the reasons for the re-emergence of serfdom in eastern Europe in the early modern period?

17. Why would the reign of the Great Elector be regarded as "the most crucial constitutional struggle in Prussian history for hundreds of years"? What did he do to increase royal authority? Who were the losers?

18. Prussia has traditionally been considered one of the most militaristic states in Europe. How do you explain this development? Who or what was responsible?

19. How did the Thirty Years' War and invasion by the Ottoman Turks help the Habsburgs consolidate power?

20. What was the Pragmatic Sanction, and why were the Hungarian and Bohemian princes opposed to it?

21. What was the relationship between baroque architecture and European absolutism? Give examples.

22. It has been said that the common man benefited from the magnificent medieval cathedrals a much as the princes. Can the same be said about the common man and the building projects of the absolute kings and princes? Explain.

23. How did the Vikings influence Russian history?

24. What role did Ivan the Terrible play in the rise of absolutism? Peter the Great?

Study-Review Exercises

Define the following key concepts and terms.

sovereign

totalitarianism

autocracy

absolutism

mercantilism

republicanism

constitutionalism

cabinet government

French classicism

baroque

Pragmatic Sanction

Identify and explain the significance of each of the following people and terms.

Sully

Russian boyars

Prussian Junkers

Romanovs

Hohenzollerns

Habsburgs

paulette

Fronde

Cardinal Richelieu

French Academy

Louis XIV of France

Versailles

Molière

Racine

Dutch Estates General

intendants

Peace of Utrecht

cabal of Charles II

Puritans

Oliver Cromwell

James II of England

English Bill of Rights

John Churchill

Philip II of Spain

Suleiman the Magnificent

Frederick the Great

Charles VI of Austria

Prince Francis Rákóczy

Jenghiz Khan

Ivan the Terrible

Frederick William the Great Elector

Frederick William I

Great Prince Iaroslav the Wise

Ivan III

Peter the Great

Prince Eugene of Savoy

Explain what each of these men believed about the placement of authority within society.
Cardinal Richelieu

James I of England

Thomas Hobbes

Louis XIV of France

John Locke

Peter the Great

Explain what the following events were and why they were important.
revocation of the Edict of Nantes

siege of Vienna, 1683

War of the Austrian Succession

Time of Troubles in Russia

Battle of Poltava

Scottish revolt of 1640

War of the Spanish Succession

Glorious Revolution

English Civil War of 1642–1649

Test your understanding of the chapter by providing the correct answers.

1. The highest executive office of the Dutch republic. _____

2. Louis XIV's able minister of finance. _____

3. During the age of economic growth in Spain, a vast number of Spaniards *entered/left* religious orders.

4. For Louis XIV of France the War of the Spanish Succession was a *success/disaster*.

5. The Englishman who inflicted defeat on Louis XIV at Blenheim. _____

6. The archbishop whose goal was to enforce Anglican unity in England and Scotland.

   _____

7. He said, "From where do the merchant's profits come except from his own diligence

   and industry?" _____

8. The founder of the new Russian city on the coast of the Baltic Sea.

   _____

9. After 1500, serfdom in eastern Europe *increased/decreased*.

10. The Ottoman Turkish leader who captured Vienna in 1529. _____

11. In the struggle between the Hungarian aristocrats and the Austrian Habsburgs, the Hungarian aristocrats *maintained/lost* their aristocratic privileges.

12. This Prussian monarch doubled the size of Prussia in 1740 by taking Silesia from

    Austria. _____

Place the following events in correct chronological order.

Election of the first Romanov tsar   1. _____

Establishment of the Kievan state   2. _____

Time of Troubles   3. _____

Invasion by the Mongols   4. _____

Building of St. Petersburg   5. _____

Battle of Poltava   6. _____

Multiple-Choice Questions

1. Mercantilism
   a. was a military system.
   b. insisted on a favorable balance of trade.
   c. was adopted in England but not in France.
   d. claimed that state power was based on land armies.

2. French Protestants tended to be
   a. poor peasants.
   b. the power behind the throne of Louis XIV.
   c. a financial burden for France.
   d. clever business people.

3. The War of the Spanish Succession began when Charles II of Spain left his territories to
   a. the French heir.
   b. the Spanish heir.
   c. Eugene of Savoy.
   d. the archduke of Austria.

4. Which of the following cities was the commercial and financial capital of Europe in the seventeenth century?
   a. London
   b. Hamburg
   c. Paris
   d. Amsterdam

5. Of the following, the country most centered on middle-class interests was
   a. England.
   b. Spain.
   c. France.
   d. the Netherlands.

6. Which of the following is a characteristic of an absolute state?
   a. Sovereignty embodied in the representative assembly
   b. Bureaucracies solely accountable to the middle classes
   c. A strong voice expressed by the nobility
   d. Permanent standing armies

7. Cardinal Richelieu's most notable accomplishment was
   a. the creation of a strong financial system for France.
   b. the creation of a highly effective administrative system.
   c. winning the total support of the Huguenots.
   d. allying the Catholic church with the government.

8. Cromwell's government is best described as a
   a. constitutional state.
   b. democratic state.
   c. military dictatorship.
   d. monarchy.

9. Cardinal Richelieu consolidated the power of the French monarchy by doing all of the following *except*
   a. destroying the castles of the nobility.
   b. ruthlessly punishing conspirators who threatened the monarchy.
   c. keeping nobles from gaining high government offices.
   d. eliminating the intendant system of local government.

10. One way in which Louis XIV controlled the French nobility was by
   a. maintaining standing armies in the countryside to crush noble uprisings.
   b. requiring the presence of the major noble families at Versailles for at least part of the year.
   c. periodically visiting the nobility in order to check on their activities.
   d. forcing them to participate in a parliamentary assembly.

11. The Peace of Utrecht in 1713
    a. shrunk the size of the British Empire significantly.
    b. represented the balance-of-power principle in action.
    c. enhanced Spain's position as a major power in Europe.
    d. marked the beginning of French expansionist policy.

12. The downfall of Spain in the seventeenth century can be blamed on
    a. weak and ineffective monarchs.
    b. an overexpansion of industry and trade.
    c. the growth of slave labor in America.
    d. the rise of a large middle class.

13. When Archbishop Laud tried to make the Presbyterian Scots accept the Anglican Book of Common Prayer, the Scots
    a. revolted.
    b. reluctantly accepted the archbishop's directive.
    c. ignored the directive.
    d. heartily adopted the new prayerbook.

14. Which of the following men was a proponent of the idea that the purpose of government is to protect life, liberty, and property?
    a. Thomas Hobbes
    b. William of Orange
    c. John Locke
    d. Edmund Burke

15. After the United Provinces of the Netherlands won independence from Spain, its government could best be described as
    a. a strong monarchy.
    b. a centralized parliamentary system.
    c. a weak union of strong provinces.
    d. a democracy.

16. The Dutch economy was based on
    a. fishing, world trade, and banking.
    b. silver mining in Peru.
    c. export of textiles.
    d. a moral and religious disdain of wealth.

17. The unifiers and first rulers of the Russians were the
    a. Mongols.
    b. Turks.
    c. Romanovs.
    d. Vikings.

18. In eastern Europe the courts were largely controlled by
    a. the peasants.
    b. the monarchs.
    c. the church.
    d. the landlords.

19. The principality called the "sandbox of the Holy Roman Empire" was
    a. Brandenburg-Prussia.
    b. Hungary.
    c. Sweden.
    d. Austria.

20. Ivan the Terrible
    a. failed to conquer the khan.
    b. was afraid to call himself tsar.
    c. monopolized most mining and business activity.
    d. abolished the system of compulsory service for noble landlords.

21. Peter the Great's reforms included
    a. compulsory education away from home for the higher classes.
    b. a lessening of the burdens of serfdom for Russian peasants.
    c. an elimination of the merit-system bureaucracy.
    d. the creation of an independent parliament.

22. The noble landowners of Prussia were known as
    a. boyars.
    b. Junkers.
    c. Vikings.
    d. Electors.

23. Apparently the most important reason for the return to serfdom in eastern Europe from about 1500 to 1650 was
    a. political.
    b. economic.
    c. military.
    d. religious.

24. After the disastrous defeat of the Czech nobility by the Habsburgs at the battle of White Mountain in 1618, the
    a. old Czech nobility accepted Catholicism in great numbers.
    b. majority of the Czech nobles' land was given to soldiers who had fought for the Habsburgs.
    c. conditions of the enserfed peasantry improved.
    d. Czech nobles continued their struggle effectively for many years.

25. The result of the struggle of the Hungarian nobles against Habsburg oppression was that
    a. they suffered a fate similar to the Czech nobility.
    b. they gained a great deal of autonomy compared with the Austrian and Bohemian nobility.
    c. they won their independence.
    d. their efforts were inconclusive.

26. The rise of the Russian monarchy was largely a response to the external threat of the
    a. French monarchy.
    b. Asiatic Mongols.
    c. Prussian monarchy.
    d. English monarchy.

27. The Time of Troubles was caused by
    a. a dispute in the line of succession.
    b. Turkish invasions.
    c. Mongol invasions.
    d. severe crop failures resulting in starvation and disease.

28. The real losers in the growth of absolutism in eastern Europe were the
    a. peasants.
    b. peasants and middle classes.
    c. nobility.
    d. nobility and clergy.

29. The Battle of Poltava marks a Russian victory over
    a. Sweden.
    b. Turkey.
    c. Prussia.
    d. Austria.

Major Political Ideas

1. What are the major characteristics of absolutism, and how does it, as a political system, differ from totalitarianism?

2. What is constitutionalism? What is the source of power within a constitutional state? How does constitutionalism differ from absolutism?

3. In 1649 England declared itself to be a commonwealth, or republican form of government. What is a republican state? Where does power reside in such a state?

4. Why is the history of Russia more a history of servitude than of freedom? Was the major reason for the reinstatement of serfdom political or economic? Explain.

5. Is architecture and urban planning a political language? Discuss this with reference to the development of the baroque form. Provide examples.

Issues for Essays and Discussion

1. The seventeenth century saw great political instability and change, during which some modern forms of political organization emerged. Why did political turmoil exist, what new concepts of politics and power emerged, who were the most important participants in this process, and how was stability achieved?

2. Compare and contrast the political development of France, the Netherlands, Russia, and England in the seventeenth century. Of these four states, which is the most "modern"?

3. Peter the Great of Russia and Frederick William the Great Elector of Prussia are often viewed as heroes and reformers in the histories of their own countries. How valid is this assessment?

Interpretation of Visual Sources

1. Study the reproduction of the woodcut entitled *The Spider and the Fly* on page 615 of the textbook. What message does the artist seek to convey? Does the woodcut make a political statement? In your opinion, is there any historical evidence set forth in this chapter to suggest that this woodcut represents historical truth?

2. Study the print entitled *Molding the Prussian Spirit* on page 630 of the textbook. Describe the scene. Why would this print have been included in a book for children? What were the reasons for Prussia's "obsessive bent for military organization and military scales of value"?

Geography

On Outline Map 19.1 provided, and using Map 19.1 in the textbook as a reference, mark the following:

1. The territory added to France as a result of the wars and foreign policy of King Louis XIV.

2. Explain how each of the territories was acquired and from whom.

3. What changes in the balance of power occurred as a result of the Treaty of Utrecht in 1713?

4. On Outline Map 19.4 provided, and using Map 19.4 in the textbook for reference, mark the following: the area covered by the principality of Moscow in 1300, the territories acquired by the principality of Moscow from 1300 to 1689, the acquisitions of Peter the Great.

5. Looking at Map 19.3 in the textbook, identify the three territorial parts of the Habsburg (Austrian) state and explain how they came to be united.

Remember that duplicate maps for class use are at the back of this book.

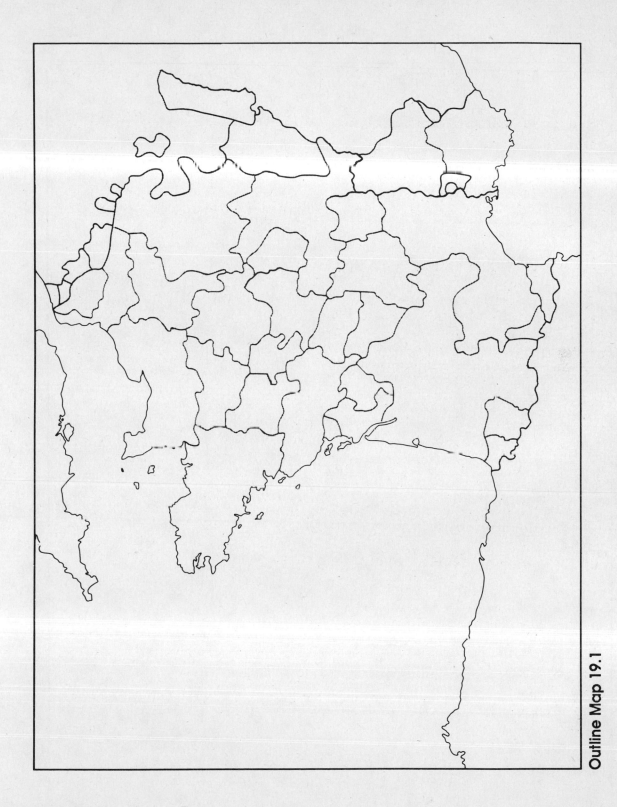

Outline Map 19.1

Outline Map 19.4

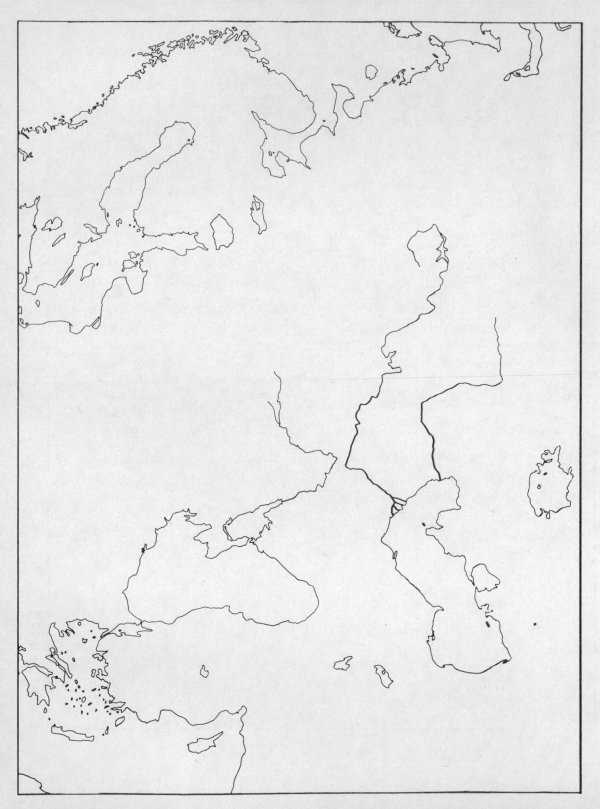

Understanding History Through the Arts

1. What was life at Versailles like? At the great English estates? Louis XIV and the magnificence of his court at Versailles are re-created with color and spirit in W. H. Lewis, *The Splendid Century** (1953). The splendor of Versailles and French and British baroque painting and architecture are the subjects of Chap. 7, "The Baroque in France and England," in H. W. Janson, *History of Art* (1962). See also G. Walton, *Louis XIV's Versailles** (1986). A vivid picture of life of the English upper classes—how they ran their estates, entertained, and influenced politics—is found in M. Girouard, *Life in the English Country House: A Social and Architectural History* (1979).

2. What can we learn from the great literature of the period? Much good reading is found in the literature of the seventeenth century. The great comic writer of the age was Molière, whose *Tartuffe* is still a source of entertainment. LaFontaine's fables are a lively reworking of tales from antiquity, and Cervantes's *Don Quixote* continues to inspire its readers. The greatest writer to emerge from the Puritan age in England was John Milton, whose *Paradise Lost* is a classic.

3. What forms did Russian art take? For centuries the Kremlin in Moscow was the axis of Russian culture—the place where works of great historical and artistic significance were amassed. Many examples of painting and applied art of the Kremlin are discussed and illustrated in *Treasures of the Kremlin** (1979), published by the Metropolitan Museum of Art, New York. See also, T. Froncek, ed., *The Horizon Book of the Arts of Russia* (1970), and G. Hamilton, *The Art and Architecture of Russia* (1975).

4. How does baroque music reflect the age? Baroque music, the dominant musical style in the age of absolutism, was often written for a particular monarch or princely court. The mathematical and harmonic emphasis of baroque music and its aristocratic patronage are illustrated in the six Brandenburg Concertos by Johann Sebastian Bach, written for the margrave of Brandenburg in the early eighteenth century, and in George F. Handel's *Water Music*, written for George I of England at about the same time. Both of these are available on numerous recordings. For the history of baroque music, see M. F. Bukofzer, *Music in the Baroque Era* (1947).

Problems for Further Investigation

1. What were the origins of the civil war in England? Some of the problems in interpretation of the crucial period 1642 to 1649 are considered in P. A. M. Taylor, ed., *The Origins of the English Civil War** (1960); L. Stone, ed., *Social Change and Revolution in England, 1540–1640** (1965); and B. Manning, *The English People and the English Revolution* (1976).

*Available in paperback.

2. How did the Sun King create an absolutist state? Students interested in research on absolutism and Louis XIV in France will want to consider H. G. Judge, ed., *Louis XIV* (1965); William F. Church, ed., *The Greatness of Louis XIV: Myth or Reality?** (rev. ed., 1972); and R. F. Kierstead, ed., *State and Society in Seventeenth-Century France** (1975). The best biography of Louis XIV is *Louis XIV* (1968) by J. Wolf.

3. What were the traditional patterns of military organization and strategy in this age of absolutism? In what ways did warfare change to reflect the political ambitions of Europe's monarchs and economic and social developments? Begin your investigation with M. van Creveld, *Technology and War, from 2000 B.C. to the Present* (1988). A helpful reference for the scholar of military history is R. Dupuy and T. Dupuy, *The Encyclopedia of Military History, from 3500 B.C. to the Present* (1982, 1990).

4. What Western ideas influenced Peter the Great? His personality and reign have generated considerable controversy for many years. Ideas for research in this and related subjects in Russian history can be found in M. Raeff, *Peter the Great* (rev. ed., 1972); V. Klyuchevsky and N. Riasanovsky, *Images of Peter the Great in Russian History and Thought* (1985); and L. J. Oliva, ed., *Russia and the West from Peter to Khrushchev* (1965).

*Available in paperback.

CHAPTER 20

Toward a New World View in the West

Chapter Questions

After reading and studying this chapter, you should be able to answer the following questions:

Why did the world-view of the educated classes change from a primarily religious one to one that was primarily secular and scientific? How did this new outlook on life affect society and politics?

Chapter Summary

In the course of the seventeenth and eighteenth centuries, the educated classes of Europe moved from a world-view that was basically religious to one that was primarily secular. The development of scientific knowledge was the key cause of this intellectual change. Until about 1500, scientific thought reflected the Aristotelian-medieval world-view, which taught that a motionless earth lay at the center of a universe made up of planets and stars in ten crystal spheres. These and many other beliefs showed that science was primarily a branch of religion. Beginning with Copernicus, who taught that the earth revolved around the sun, Europeans slowly began to reject Aristotelian-medieval scientific thought. They developed a new conception of a universe based on natural laws, not on a personal God. Isaac Newton formulated the great scientific synthesis: the law of universal gravitation. This was the culminating point of the scientific revolution.

The new science was more important for intellectual development than for economic activity or everyday life, for above all it promoted critical thinking. Nothing was to be accepted on faith; everything was to be submitted to the rational, scientific way of thinking. This critical examination of everything, from religion and education to war and politics, was the program of the Enlightenment and the accomplishment of the philosophes, a group of thinkers who propagandized the new world-view across Europe and the North American colonies. These writers and thinkers, among them Voltaire, Montesquieu, and Diderot, produced books and articles that influenced all classes and whose primary intent was teaching people how to think critically and objectively about all matters.

The philosophes were reformers, not revolutionaries. Their "enlightened" ideas were adopted by a number of monarchs who sought to promote the advancement of knowledge and improve the lives of their subjects. Most important in this group were Frederick II of Prussia and Catherine II of Russia and the Habsburgs, Maria Theresa and Joseph II. Despite some reforms, particularly in the area of law, Frederick and Catherine's role in the Enlightenment lay in the abstract rather than the practical. The Habsburgs were more successful in legal and tax reform, control of the church, and improvement of the lot of the serfs, although much of Joseph's spectacular peasant reform was later undone. Yet reform of society from the top down, that is, by the absolute monarchs through "enlightened absolutism," proved to be impossible because the enlightened monarchs could not ignore the demands of their conservative nobilities. In the end, it was revolution, not enlightened absolutism, that changed and reformed society.

The chapter closes with a discussion of how the middle class of France used the Parlement of Paris and its judgeships as a counterweight to absolutism and the revival of aristocratic power. This opposition was crushed by Louis XV's chancellor, Maupéou, only to reappear with the new King Louis XVI.

Study Outline

Use this outline to preview the chapter before you read a particular section and then as a self-check to test your reading comprehension after you have read the chapter section.

I. The scientific revolution: the origin of the modern world
   A. The scientific revolution of the seventeenth century was the major cause of the change in world-view and one of the key developments in the evolution of Western society.
   B. Scientific thought in the early 1500s
      1. European ideas about the universe were based on Aristotelian-medieval ideas.
         a. Central to this view was the belief in a motionless earth fixed at the center of the universe.
         b. Around the earth moved ten crystal spheres, and beyond the spheres was heaven.
      2. Aristotle's scheme suited Christianity because it positioned human beings at the center of the universe and established a home for God.
      3. Science in this period was primarily a branch of theology.
   C. The Copernican hypothesis
      1. Copernicus, a Polish clergyman and astronomer, claimed that the earth revolved around the sun and that the sun was the center of the universe.
      2. This heliocentric theory was a departure from medieval thought and created doubts about traditional Christianity.

D. From Tycho Brahe to Galileo
   1. Brahe set the stage for the modern study of astronomy by building an observatory and collecting data.
   2. His assistant, Kepler, formulated three laws of planetary motion that proved the precise relationships among planets in a sun-centered universe.
   3. Galileo discovered the laws of motion using the experimental method—the cornerstone of modern science.
      a. He also applied the experimental method to astronomy, using the newly invented telescope.
      b. Galileo was tried by the Inquisition for heresy in 1633 and forced to recant his views.

E. Newton's synthesis
   1. Newton integrated the astronomy of Copernicus and Kepler with the physics of Galileo.
      a. He formulated a set of mathematical laws to explain motion and mechanics.
      b. The key feature in his synthesis was the law of universal gravitation.
   2. Henceforth, the universe could be explained through mathematics.

F. Causes of the scientific revolution
   1. Medieval universities provided the framework for the new science.
   2. The Renaissance stimulated science by rediscovering ancient mathematics and supporting scientific investigations.
   3. The navigational problems of sea voyages generated scientific research and new instruments.
   4. Better ways of obtaining knowledge about the world improved scientific methods.
      a. Bacon advocated empirical, experimental research.
      b. Descartes stressed mathematics and deductive reasoning.
   5. After about 1630 the Catholic church discouraged science while Protestantism tended to favor it.

G. Some consequences of the scientific revolution
   1. A scientific community emerged whose primary goal was the expansion of knowledge.
   2. A modern scientific method arose that was both theoretical and experimental and refused to base its conclusions on tradition and established sources.
   3. Because the link between pure science and applied technology was weak, the scientific revolution had little effect on daily life before the nineteenth century.

II. The Enlightenment
   A. Enlightenment ideas made up a new world-view.
      1. Natural science and reason can explain all aspects of life.
      2. The scientific method can explain the laws of human society.
      3. Progress—the creation of better societies and better people—is possible.

B. The emergence of the Enlightenment
    1. Many writers made scientific thought understandable to a large nonscientific audience.
        a. Fontenelle stressed the idea of progress.
        b. He was also cynical about organized religion and absolute religious truth.
    2. Skeptics such as Bayle concluded that nothing can be known beyond all doubt and stressed open-mindedness.
    3. The growth of world travel led Europeans to look at truth and morality in relative, not absolute, terms.
    4. In his *Essay Concerning Human Understanding,* Locke insisted that all ideas are derived from experience—the human mind at birth is like a blank tablet (tabula rasa).
C. The philosophes and their ideas
    1. The philosophes asked fundamental philosophical questions and were committed to the reformation of society and humanity, although they often had to cloak attacks on church and state in satire.
        a. Montesquieu's theory of the separation of powers was extremely influential.
        b. Voltaire challenged traditional Catholic theology and exhibited a characteristic philosophe belief in a distant God who let human affairs take their own course.
        c. Diderot and d'Alembert edited the *Encyclopedia,* which examined all of human knowledge and attempted to teach people how to think critically and rationally.
    2. The later Enlightenment writers built rigid and dogmatic systems.
        a. D'Holbach argued that humans were completely controlled by outside forces.
        b. Hume argued that the mind is nothing but a bundle of impressions that originate in sense experiences.
        c. Rousseau attacked rationalism and civilization; he claimed that children must develop naturally and spontaneously, and in *The Social Contract* argued that the general will of the people is sacred and absolute.
D. The social setting of the Enlightenment
    1. Enlightenment ideas—including new ideas about women's rights—were spread by salons of the upper classes.
    2. The salons were often presided over by women.
    3. These salons seemed to have functioned as informal "schools" for women.

III. The development of absolutism
    A. Many philosophes believed that "enlightened" reform would come by way of "enlightened" monarchs.
        1. The philosophes believed that a benevolent absolutism offered the best chance for improving society.
        2. The rulers seemed to seek the philosophes' advice.
        3. The philosophes distrusted the masses and felt that change had to come from above.

B. The "Greats": Frederick II of Prussia and Catherine II of Russia
  1. Frederick II used the War of the Austrian Succession (1740–1748) to expand Prussia into a great power by seizing Silesia.
  2. The Seven Years' War (1756–1763) saw an attempt by Maria Theresa, with the help of France and Russia, to regain Silesia, but it failed.
  3. Frederick allowed religious freedom and promoted education, legal reform, and economic growth but never tried to change Prussia's social structure.
  4. Catherine II imported Western culture to Russia, supported the philosophes, and began a program of domestic reform.
  5. The Pugachev uprising in 1773 led her to reverse the trend toward reform of serfdom and give nobles absolute control of their serfs.
  6. She engaged in a policy of territorial expansion and, with Prussia and Austria, carved up Poland.
C. Absolutism in France and Austria
  1. Favored by the duke of Orléans, who governed as a regent until 1723, the French nobility regained much of the power it had lost under Louis XIV.
     a. The Parlement of Paris won two decisive victories against taxation.
     b. It then asserted that the king could not levy taxes without its consent.
  2. Under Louis XV the French minister Maupéou began the restoration of royal absolutism by abolishing the Parlement of Paris.
  3. Louis XVI reinstated the Parlement of Paris, and the country drifted toward renewed financial and political crises.
  4. Maria Theresa of Austria introduced reforms that limited church power, revised the tax system and the bureaucracy, and reduced the power of the lords over the serfs.
  5. Her successor, Joseph II, was a dedicated reformer who abolished serfdom, taxed all equally, and granted religious freedom.
  6. Because of opposition from both the nobles and the peasants, Joseph's reforms were short-lived.
D. An overall evaluation of absolutism and the influence of the Enlightenment
  1. In France, the rise of judicial and aristocratic opposition combined with liberalism put absolutism on the defensive.
  2. In eastern Europe the results of enlightened absolutism were modest, and absolutism remained strong.
  3. By combining state building with the culture and critical thinking of the Enlightenment, absolute monarchs succeeded in expanding the role of the state in the life of society.

Review Questions

Check your understanding of this chapter by answering the following questions.

1. Contrast the old Aristotelian-medieval world-view with that of the sixteenth and seventeenth centuries. What were the contributions of Copernicus, Brahe, Kepler, Galileo, and Newton? What is meant by Newton's "synthesis"?

2. How did the new scientific theory and discoveries alter the concept of God and religion? Did science, in fact, come to dictate humanity's concept of God?

3. What were the scientific and religious implications of Copernicus's theory?

4. Discuss the origins and the momentum of the scientific revolution in terms of (a) its own "internal logic," and (b) external and nonscientific causes.

5. How did Bacon and Descartes contribute to the development of the modern scientific method?

6. Did the Catholic and Protestant churches retard or foster scientific investigation? Explain.

7. What were the consequences of the rise of modern science?

8. What were the central concepts of the Enlightenment?

9. Who were the philosophes, and what did they believe?

10. In what ways were Frederick of Prussia and Catherine of Russia enlightened monarchs?

11. What was the effect of Catherine's reign on (a) the Russian nobility, (b) the Russian serfs, and (c) the position of Russia in the European balance of power?

12. What was the nature of the power struggle between the aristocrats and Louis XV of France?

Study-Review Exercises

Define the following key concepts and terms.

Aristotelian world-view

empirical method

Copernican hypothesis

deductive reasoning

rationalism

progress

secular

skepticism

tabula rasa

Parlement of Paris

Enlightenment

enlightened absolutism

philosophes

Gresham College

Identify and explain the significance of each of the following people.

Diderot

Bayle

Kepler

Galileo

Bacon

Descartes

D'Holbach

Newton

Montesquieu

Voltaire

Copernicus

Brahe

Catherine the Great

Frederick the Great

Maria Theresa

Louis XV

Joseph II

Explain the new ideas of each the following books. What were some of the consequences of these ideas?
On the Revolutions of the Heavenly Spheres

New Astronomy or Celestial Physics

Two New Sciences

Principia

Conversations on the Plurality of Worlds

Historical and Critical Dictionary

The Spirit of the Laws

Essay Concerning Human Understanding

Philosophical Dictionary

Encyclopedia: The Rational Dictionary of the Sciences, the Arts, and the Crafts

The Social Contract

Test your understanding of the chapter by providing the correct answers.

1. According to Aristotle, the sublunar world was made up of four elements: air, fire,

    _____ , and _____ .

2. Copernicus *did/did not* attempt to disprove the existence of God.

3. Galileo claimed that *motion/rest* is the natural state of all objects.

4. The key feature in Newton's synthesis was the law of _____ .

5. In the medieval universities, science emerged as a branch of _____ .

6. The method of finding latitude came out of study and experimentation in the country

   of _____ .

7. The idea of "progress" *was/was not* widespread in the Middle Ages.

8. In the seventeenth and eighteenth centuries, a close link between pure (theoretical) science and applied technology *did/did not* exist.

9. A _____ is one who believes that nothing can ever be known beyond all doubt.

10. Voltaire believed that _____ was history's greatest man because he used his genius to benefit humanity.

11. Overall, Joseph II of Austria *succeeded/failed* as an enlightened monarch.

Place the following ideas in correct chronological order.

Copernicus's idea that the sun is the center   1. _____
of the universe

Montesquieu's theory of the separation   2. _____
of powers

D'Holbach's theory that human beings   3. _____
are machines

Aristotle's view of a motionless earth at   4. _____
the center of the universe

Newton's law of universal gravitation   5. _____

Multiple-Choice Questions

1. Catherine the Great accomplished which of the following?
   a. Annexed part of Poland
   b. Freed the Russian serfs
   c. Denied any sort of religious toleration
   d. Persecuted the philosophes of France

2. "Enlightened" monarchs believed in all of the following *except*
   a. reform.
   b. democracy.
   c. cultural values of the Enlightenment.
   d. secularism.

3. Geoffrin and Deffand were
   a. scientific writers.
   b. religious leaders in France.
   c. leaders of Enlightenment salons.
   d. leaders of the serf uprising in France.

4. The philosophes were
   a. mainly university professors.
   b. generally hostile to monarchial government.
   c. enthusiastic supporters of the Catholic church.
   d. satirists who wished to reform society and humanity.

5. The social setting of the Enlightenment
   a. excluded women.
   b. was characterized by poverty and boredom.
   c. was dominated by government officials.
   d. was characterized by witty and intelligent conversation.

6. Catherine the Great
   a. believed the philosophes were dangerous revolutionaries.
   b. freed the serfs to satisfy Diderot.
   c. increased the size of the Russian Empire.
   d. established a strong constitutional monarchy.

7. According to medieval thought, the center of the universe was the
   a. sun.
   b. earth.
   c. moon.
   d. heaven.

8. The Aristotelian world-view placed emphasis on the idea of
   a. the sun as the center of the universe.
   b. the rejection of Christian theology.
   c. an earth that moves in space.
   d. crystal spheres moving around the earth.

9. Copernicus's theory of a sun-centered universe
   a. suggested the universe was small and closed.
   b. questioned the idea that crystal spheres moved the stars around the earth.
   c. suggested that the worlds of heaven and earth were radically different from each other.
   d. suggested an enormous and possibly infinite universe.

10. The first astronomer to prove his theories through the use of mathematical equations was
    a. Galileo.
    b. Kepler.
    c. Brahe.
    d. Newton.

11. D'Holbach, Hume, and Rousseau are examples of the later Enlightenment trend toward
    a. rigid systems.
    b. social satire.
    c. religion.
    d. the idea of absolutism.

12. The French philosopher who rejected his contemporaries and whose writings influenced the romantic movement was
    a. Rousseau.
    b. Voltaire.
    c. Diderot.
    d. Condorcet.

13. The gathering ground for many who wished to discuss the ideas of the French Enlightenment was the
    a. salon.
    b. lecture hall.
    c. palace at Versailles.
    d. University of Paris.

14. Frederick II is considered an enlightened monarch because he
    a. regained Silesia from Prussia.
    b. wrote poetry and improved the legal and bureaucratic systems.
    c. kept the aristocrats in a dominant position socially and politically.
    d. avoided war.

15. Catherine the Great of Russia hardened her position on serfdom after the
    a. Pugachev rebellion.
    b. Moscow rebellion.
    c. Polish rebellion.
    d. "Five Year" rebellion.

16. After Louis XIV's death
    a. the nobility lost considerable power.
    b. the lower classes secured judicial positions in the Parlement.
    c. the French government struggled with severe economic difficulties.
    d. absolutism remained firmly entrenched during the succeeding reign.

17. Which of the following used the War of the Austrian Succession to expand Prussia into a great power?
    a. Joseph II
    b. Frederick II
    c. Frederick William I
    d. Louis XIV

18. The aggressiveness of Prussia, Austria, and Russia led to the disappearance of which eastern European kingdom from the map after 1795?
    a. Hungary
    b. Sweden
    c. Brandenburg
    d. Poland

19. Francis Bacon's great contribution to scientific methodology was
    a. the geocentric theory.
    b. the notion of logical speculation.
    c. the philosophy of empiricism.
    d. analytic geometry.

20. Which of the following men set the stage for the modern study of astronomy by building an observatory and collecting data?
    a. Darwin
    b. Hume
    c. Newton
    d. Brahe

21. The Parlement of Paris was
    a. a high court dominated by nobles who were formerly middle class.
    b. a center of royal absolutism.
    c. used by Maupéou to strengthen the king's position.
    d. not interested in tax reform or finance.

22. Maria Theresa was a devout Catholic who
    a. sought to limit the church's influence in Austria.
    b. was not interested in the Enlightenment.
    c. did nothing to improve the lot of the agricultural population.
    d. was a weak monarch unable to hold the Austrian Empire together.

23. After 1715 in France, the direction of political change was
    a. toward greater absolutism.
    b. away from Enlightenment political thought.
    c. in favor of opposition forces—largely the nobility and the Parlement of Paris.
    d. toward "enlightened absolutism."

24. In his famous book *Emile*, Rousseau argued that
    a. children are born with corrupting ideas and must be tamed.
    b. women should be taught the same subjects as men.
    c. boys and girls should be taught to operate in separate spheres.
    d. children should be exposed to corruption at an early age so that they know how to reject it.

25. Descartes's idea was that the world consists of two fundamental entities or substances, which we can call
    a. the physical and the spiritual.
    b. water and air.
    c. reason and passion.
    d. deduction and induction.

Major Political Ideas

1. Describe the concept of enlightened absolutism in terms of its political and legal goals. Did it work? What was the response of the aristocracy to this political concept?

2. This chapter emphasizes the difference between a secular and religious view of the world. What is meant by *secular* and what effect did a secular world-view have on political loyalties?

Issues for Essays and Discussion

In the course of the eighteenth century the basic outlook on life and society held by many men and women changed dramatically. In what ways did this transformation affect scientific, political, religious, social, and economic thought? In working out your argument, explain how specific new scientific ideas and methods of reasoning led directly to new political and social ideas.

Interpretation of Visual Sources

Study the print of Louis XIV's visit to the Royal Academy in 1671 on page 666 of the textbook. Write a paragraph on how this print illustrates the relationship between science and politics. Did the scientific revolution have a great effect on how kings ran their states? Why were some monarchs interested in science? Does this print give any clues?

Geography

Compare Map 20.1 to Map 19.3 in the text. Describe what the "partition of Poland" was, when it took place, why, and who benefited.

Understanding History Through the Arts

How did the Enlightenment affect the arts? This period is often referred to as the age of the baroque style, and the achievements of its great artists are discussed in M. Kitson, *The Age of the Baroque* (1966). See also Chap. 6 in N. Pevsner, *An Outline of European Architecture* (7th ed., 1963), and E. Kaufmann, *Architecture in the Age of Reason—Baroque and Post-Baroque in England, Italy, and France* (1955, *1968). On the subject of the Scottish Enlightenment, see T. A. Markus, ed., *Order and Space: Architectural Form and Its Context in the Scottish Enlightenment* (1982). Few artists captured English life as well as the painter Hogarth, whose *Rake's Progress* and *Harlot's Progress* point to the consequences of moral decay. Hogarth's paintings can be seen and studied in W. Gaunt, *The World of William Hogarth* (1978), and D. Bindman, *Hogarth** (1981). For a description of French life by painters of the time, see T. E. Crow, *Painters and Public Life in Eighteenth-Century Paris* (1985).

*Available in paperback.

Problems for Further Investigation

1. Write an essay in which you describe and analyze an important work of the Enlightenment. What were the ideas set forth by the author, and how do these ideas reflect or illustrate Enlightenment thought and change? The two greatest philosophes of the age of Enlightenment were Rousseau and Voltaire. Rousseau's ideas on education and natural law are set forth in *Emile,* and Voltaire's most-praised work is *Candide,* a funny and sometimes bawdy parody of eighteenth-century life and thought. Selections from the great *Encyclopedia* are found in S. Gendzier, ed., *Denis Diderot: The Encyclopedia: Selections* (1967). Much of the fiction of the eighteenth century reflects, often in satire, the spirit of the new world-view—Jonathan Swift's *Gulliver's Travels,* Daniel Defoe's *Moll Flanders,* and Henry Fielding's *Tom Jones* are just a few of the many novels of this period. In Germany, the Sturm und Drang (storm and stress) movement embraced the ideas of the Enlightenment and romanticism and produced works such as Lessing's *Nathan the Wise,* which stressed a universal religion.

2. How have historians interpreted the meaning and impact of the Enlightenment? Students interested in this topic will want to begin with two books that set forth some of the major issues and schools of interpretation on the subject: B. Tierney, et al., eds., *Enlightenment—The Age of Reason** (1967), and R. Wines, ed., *Enlightened Despotism** (1967).

3. Why was it not until the seventeenth century that rational science emerged? What has been the relationship between science and religion in Western society? What ideas did Darwin and modern biologists draw from the scientific revolution of 1500–1800? These are just a few of the questions asked by scholars of the subject. Begin your investigation with H. Butterfield, *The Origins of Modern Science* (1951); A. R. Hall, *From Galileo to Newton, 1630–1720* (1963); G. Sarton, *Introduction to the History of Science* (1927–1948, 5 vols.); or L. Thorndike, *History of Magic and Experimental Science* (1923–1958). On particular figures in science see F. S. Taylor, *Galileo and the Freedom of Thought* (1938); A. Armitage, *Copernicus, the Founder of Modern Astronomy* (1938); M. Casoar, *Johannes Kepler,* C. Heffman, trans. (1959); L. T. More, *Isaac Newton* (1934); and I. Cohen, *Franklin and Newton* (1956).

*Available in paperback.

Studying Effectively—Exercise 4

Learning to Classify Information According to Sequence

As you know, a great deal of historical information is classified by sequence, in which things follow each other in time. This kind of *sequential order* is also known as *time order* or *chronological order*.

Attention to time sequence is important in the study of history for at least two reasons.

1. It helps you organize historical information effectively.

2. It promotes historical understanding. If you know the order in which events happen, you can think intelligently about questions of cause and effect. You can begin to evaluate conflicting interpretations.

Since time sequences are essential in historical study, the authors have placed a number of timelines in the text to help you organize the historical information.

Two Fallacies Regarding Time Sequences

One common fallacy is often known by the famous Latin phrase *post hoc, ergo propter hoc:* "after this, therefore because of this." This fallacy assumes that one happening that follows another *must* be caused by the first happening. Obviously, some great development (such as the Protestant Reformation) could come after another (the Italian Renaissance) without being caused by it. *Causal relationships must be demonstrated, not simply assumed on the basis of the "after this, therefore because of this" fallacy.*

A second common, if old-fashioned, fallacy assumes that time sequences are composed only of political facts with precise data. But in considering social, intellectual, and economic developments, historians must often speak with less chronological exactitude—in terms of decades or even centuries, for example. Yet they still use time sequences, and students of history must recognize them. For example, did you realize that the sections on "The Scientific Revolution" and "The Enlightenment" in Chapter 20 are very conscientious about time sequence, even though they do not deal with political facts?

Exercise

Reread the large section in Chapter 20 on "The Scientific Revolution" with an eye for dates and sequential order. Then take a sheet of notebook paper and with the book open make a "Timeline for the Scientific Revolution." Pick out at least a dozen important events and put them in the time sequence, with a word or two to explain the significance when possible.

Suggestion: Do not confine yourself solely to specific events with specific dates. Also, integrate some items from the subsection on the causes of the scientific revolution into the sequence. You may find that constructing timelines helps you organize your study.

After you have completed your timeline, compare it with the one on the following page, which shows how one of the authors of the text did this assignment.

Timeline on the Scientific Revolution

(1300–1500)	Renaissance stimulates development of mathematics
early 1500s	Aristotle's ideas on movement and universe still dominant
1543	Copernicus publishes *On the Revolution of the Heavenly Spheres*
1572, 1577	New star and comet create more doubts about traditional astronomy
1546–1601	Tycho Brache—famous astronomer, creates mass of observations
1571–1630	Johannes Kepler—his three laws prove Copernican theory and demolish Aristotle's beliefs
1589	Galileo Galilei (1564–1642) named professor of mathematics
1610	Galileo studies moon with telescope and writes of experience
1561–1626	Francis Bacon—English scientific enthusiast, advocates experimental (inductive) method
1596–1650	René Descartes—French philosopher, discovers analytical geometry in 1619 and advocates theoretical (deductive) method
to about 1630	All religious authorities oppose Copernican theory
about 1632	Galileo tried by papal inquisition
1622	Royal Society of London founded—brings scientists and practical men together
1687	Isaac Newton publishes his *Principia*, synthesizing existing knowledge around idea of universal gravitation
to late 1700s	Consequences of scientific revolution primarily intellectual, not economic

CHAPTER 21

The Life of the People in Europe

Chapter Questions

After reading and studying this chapter, you should be able to answer the following questions:

How did the common people wring a living out of the land, and how was cottage industry growing to complement these efforts? What changes in marriage and family were occurring in the eighteenth century? What was it like to be a child in preindustrial society? What did people eat, and how did diet and medical care affect people's health? What were the patterns of popular religion in the era of Enlightenment?

Chapter Summary

Until recently scholars have not been very interested in how men and women lived in preindustrial society. The aspects of everyday life, such as family relations, sex, marriage, health, and religion, took a secondary place in history. As a result, much of our understanding of these subjects is often based on myth rather than on solid historical research and interpretations. This chapter corrects some of the long-standing myths and provides a close look at the life of the people.

Contrary to early belief, for example, it appears that in western Europe the nuclear rather than the extended family was very common among preindustrial people. Furthermore, preindustrial people did not marry in their early teens, and illegitimacy was not as common as usually thought, and certainly less so than today. The concept of childhood as we know it hardly existed. The text also points out that when the poor got enough to eat their diet was probably almost as nutritionally sound as that of rich people. As for medical science, it probably did more harm than good in the eighteenth century. Also explained in this chapter are the reasons for a kind of "sexual revolution," particularly for women, beginning in the mid-eighteenth century, when young people began engaging in sex at an earlier age and illegitimacy began to rise. These changes accompanied new patterns of marriage and work—

much of which were connected to the growth of new economic opportunities for men and women.

Education and literacy improved significantly, particularly in countries like Prussia and Scotland. In the area of religion the eighteenth century witnessed a tug of war between the Enlightenment's attempt to demystify Christianity and place it on a more rational basis and a popular movement to retain traditional ritual, superstition, and religious mysteries. In Protestant and Catholic countries alike, rulers and religious leaders sought to purify religion by eliminating many ritualistic practices. The response to this reform by the common people in Catholic countries was a resurgence of religious ritual and mysticism, while in Protestant Germany and England there occurred a popular religious revival based on piety and emotional conversion. Meanwhile, most of Europe—Catholic and Protestant—saw the state increase its control over the church.

Study Outline

Use this outline to preview the chapter before you read a particular section in your textbook and then as a self-check to test your reading comprehension after you have read the chapter section.

    I. Agriculture and population in eighteenth-century Europe
        A. Frequent poor harvests and bad weather led to famine and disease and a search for new sources of food and income.
        B. Working the land
            1. The medieval open-field system divided the land into a few large fields, which were then cut up into long, narrow strips.
            2. The fields were farmed jointly, a portion of the arable land was always left fallow, and output was low.
            3. Common lands were set aside for community use.
            4. The labor and tax system throughout Europe was unjust, but eastern European peasants suffered the most.
            5. By the eighteenth century most peasants in western Europe were free from serfdom and many owned some land.
            6. Crop rotation eliminated the need for fallowing and broke the old cycle of scarcity; more fodder meant more animals, which meant more food.
            7. Enclosure of the open fields to permit crop rotation also meant the disappearance of common land.
        C. The balance of numbers
            1. The traditional checks on growth were famine, disease, and war.
            2. The use of "famine foods" made people weak and susceptible to illness and epidemics.
            3. These checks kept Europe's population rate fairly low.
            4. Quarantine of ports and the elimination of the black rat by the brown rat helped reduce the bubonic plague.

5. An increase in the food supply—aided by improved transportation—meant fewer famines and epidemics.

6. But population growth in the eighteenth century led to new pressures on resources and labor.

D. The growth of cottage industry

1. Population increase caused the rural poor to take in manufacturing work to supplement their income.

2. This cottage industry challenged the monopoly of the urban craft guilds.

3. It was based on rural workers' producing cloth, or other goods, in their homes for merchant-capitalists, who supplied the raw materials and paid for the finished goods.

4. This system reduced the problem of rural unemployment and provided cheap goods.

5. The textile industry in England was an example of the putting-out system; it was often a family enterprise.

II. Marriage and the family

A. Extended and nuclear families

1. The nuclear family, not the extended family, was prevalent in preindustrial western and central Europe.

2. Early marriage was not common prior to 1750, and many women (perhaps as much as half) never married at all.

3. Marriage was often delayed because of poverty and/or local law and tradition.

B. Work away from home

1. Many boys left home to work as craftsmen or laborers.

2. Girls left to work as servants—and they often were physically and sexually mistreated.

C. Premarital sex and birth-control practices

1. Illegitimate children were not common in preindustrial society.

2. Premarital sex was common, but marriage usually followed.

3. Coitus interruptus was the most common form of birth control.

D. New patterns of marriage and illegitimacy

1. The growth of cottage industry (and later, the factory) resulted in people marrying earlier and for love.

2. The explosion of births and the growth of prostitution from about 1750 to 1850 had several causes.

   a. Increasing illegitimacy signified rebellion against laws that limited the right of the poor to marry.

   b. Pregnant servant girls often turned to prostitution, which also increased illegitimacy.

E. The question of sexual emancipation for women

1. Women in cities and factories had limited economic independence.

2. Poverty caused many people to remain single—leading to premarital sex and illegitimate births.

III. Women and children in preindustrial society
    A. Child care and nursing
        1. Infant mortality was very high.
        2. Breast-feeding of children was common among poor women.
        3. Middle- and upper-class women hired wet nurses.
        4. The occupation of wet-nursing was often exploitative of lower-class women.
    B. Foundlings and infanticide
        1. "Killing nurses" and infanticide were forms of population control.
        2. Foundling hospitals were established but could not care for all the abandoned babies.
            a. Some had as many as 25,000 children.
            b. A high proportion of children were abandoned as foundlings.
    C. Attitudes toward children
        1. Attitudes toward children were different from those of today, partly because of the frequency of death.
            a. Parents and doctors were generally indifferent to children.
            b. Children were often neglected or treated brutally.
        2. The Enlightenment brought about more humane treatment of children.
            a. Critics like Rousseau called for more love and understanding of children.
            b. The practice of swaddling was discouraged.
    D. Schools and education
        1. Education for common people began in the seventeenth and eighteenth centuries.
        2. Protestantism encouraged popular education.
        3. Literacy increased, especially in France and Scotland, between 1700 and 1800.

IV. Food and medicine
    A. The life span of Europeans increased from twenty-five years to thirty-five years between 1700 and 1800, largely because diet improved and plagues disappeared.
    B. Diet and nutrition
        1. The major improvements were in the area of prevention, or "preventive medicine"—particularly because of more food.
        2. The diet of ordinary people improved.
            a. Poor people ate mainly grains and vegetables.
            b. Milk and meat were rarely eaten.
        3. Rich people ate quite differently from the poor.
            a. Their diet was rich in meat and wine.
            b. They spurned fruits and vegetables.
    C. The impact of diet on health
        1. There were nutritional advantages and disadvantages to the diet of the poor.
            a. Their breads were very nutritious.
            b. Their main problem was getting enough green vegetables and milk.
        2. The rich often ate too much rich food.

D. New foods and new knowledge about diet
   1. The potato substantially improved the diet of the poor.
      a. For some poor people, particularly in Ireland, the potato replaced grain as the primary food in the eighteenth century.
      b. Elsewhere in Europe, the potato took hold more slowly, but became a staple by the end of the century.
   2. There was a growth in market gardening and an improvement in food variety in the eighteenth century.
   3. There was some improvement in knowledge about diet, and Galen's influence declined.
   4. Greater affluence caused many to turn to less nutritious food such as white bread and sugar.
E. The medical professionals
   1. The demonic view of disease was common, and faith healers were used to exorcise the demons.
   2. Pharmacists sold drugs that were often harmful to their patients.
   3. Surgeons often operated without anesthetics and in the midst of dirt.
   4. Physicians frequently bled or purged people to death.
F. Hospitals and mental illness
   1. Patients were crowded together, often several to a bed.
   2. There was no fresh air or hygiene.
   3. Hospital reform began in the late eighteenth century.
   4. Mental illness was misunderstood and treated inhumanely.
   5. Some attempts at reform occurred in the late eighteenth century.
   6. Nevertheless, many wildly erroneous ideas about mental illness persisted.
G. Medical experiments and research
   1. Much medical experimentation was creative quackery.
   2. The conquest of smallpox was the greatest medical triumph of the eighteenth century.
      a. Montague and Jenner's work on inoculation was the beginning of a significant decline in smallpox.
      b. Jenner's work laid the foundation for the science of immunology in the nineteenth century.

V. Religion and Christian churches
A. The institutional church
   1. Despite the critical spirit of the Enlightenment, the local parish church remained important in daily life, and the priest or pastor was the link between the people and the church hierarchy.
   2. The Protestant belief in individualism in religion was tempered by increased state control over the church and religious life.
   3. Catholic monarchs also increased state control over the church, making it less subject to papal influence.
      a. Spain took control of ecclesiastical appointments and the Inquisition and, with France, pressured Rome to dissolve the Jesuits.

       b. In Austria, Maria Theresa and Joseph II greatly reduced the size and influence of the monasteries and convents.

   B. Catholic piety

      1. In Catholic countries the old religious culture of ritual and superstition remained popular.

      2. Catholic clergy reluctantly allowed traditional religion to survive.

   C. Protestant revival

      1. Pietism stressed religious enthusiasm, popular education, and individual religious development.

      2. In England, Wesley was troubled by religious corruption, decline, and uncertainty.

         a. His Methodist movement rejected the Calvinist idea of predestination and stressed salvation through faith.

         b. Wesley's ministry brought on a religious awakening, particularly among the lower classes.

Review Questions

Check your understanding of this chapter by answering the following questions.

1. Was the typical preindustrial family extended or nuclear? What evidence can you cite to support your answer?

2. In *Romeo and Juliet*, Juliet was just fourteen and Romeo was not too many years older. Is this early marriage typical of preindustrial society? Why did so many people not marry at all?

3. When did the custom of late marriage begin to change? Why?

4. Did preindustrial men and women practice birth control? What methods existed?

5. How do you explain that prior to 1750 there were few illegitimate children, but illegitimacy increased thereafter?

6. It is often claimed that factory women, as opposed to their rural counterparts, were sexually liberated. Is this claim correct? Explain.

7. How and why did life expectancy improve in the eighteenth century?

8. What were the differences in the diets of the rich and the poor in the eighteenth century? What nutritional deficiencies existed?

9. How important was the potato in the eighteenth century? Is it important enough to merit more attention from historians?

10. How important were the eighteenth-century advances in medical science in extending the life span?

11. What was the demonic view of disease?

12. It is said that when it came to medical care, the poor were better off than the rich because they could not afford doctors or hospitals. Why might this have been true?

13. Why was there so much controversy over the smallpox inoculation? Was it safe? What contribution did Edward Jenner make to the elimination of this disease?

14. How was mental illness regarded and treated in the eighteenth century?

15. What effect did changes in church-state relations have on the institutions of the church?

16. In what forms did popular religious culture survive in Catholic Europe?

17. Define pietism. How is it reflected in the work and life of John Wesley?

Study-Review Exercises

Define the following key concepts and terms.

extended family

nuclear family

preindustrial childhood

demonic view of disease

illegitimacy explosion

Methodists

coitus interruptus

purging

"killing nurses"

Jesuits

Identify and explain the significance of the following people.
Lady Mary Montague

Edward Jenner

James Graham

Joseph II

John Wesley

Test your understanding of the chapter by providing the correct answers.

1. It is apparent that the practice of breast-feeding *increased/limited* the fertility of lower-class women.

2. The teenage bride *was/was not* the general rule in preindustrial Europe.

3. Prior to about 1750, premarital sex usually *did/did not* lead to marriage.

4. In the eighteenth century, the _____ was the primary new food in Europe.

5. People lived *longer/shorter* lives as the eighteenth century progressed.

6. The key to Jenner's discovery was the connection between immunity from smallpox

   and _____ , a mild and noncontagious disease.

7. In Catholic countries it was largely *the clergy/the common people* who wished to keep traditional religious rituals and superstitions.

8. The Englishman who brought religious "enthusiasm" to the common folk of England.

_____

Multiple-Choice Questions

1. One of the chief deficiencies of the diet of both rich and poor Europeans was the absence of sufficient
   a. meat.
   b. fruit and vegetables.
   c. white bread.
   d. wine.

2. A family in which three or four generations live under the same roof under the direction of a patriarch is known as a(n)
   a. nuclear family.
   b. conjugal family.
   c. industrial household.
   d. extended family.

3. Prior to about 1750, marriage between two persons was more often than not
   a. undertaken freely by the couple.
   b. controlled by law and parents.
   c. based on romantic love.
   d. undertaken without economic considerations.

4. The establishment of foundling hospitals in the eighteenth century was an attempt to
   a. prevent the spread of the bubonic plague.
   b. isolate children from smallpox.
   c. prevent willful destruction and abandonment of newborn children.
   d. provide adequate childbirth facilities for rich women.

5. Which of the following statements about preindustrial society's attitudes toward children is *false*?
   a. Parents often treated their children with indifference and brutality.
   b. Poor children were often forced to work in the early factories.
   c. Doctors were the only people interested in the children's welfare.
   d. Killing of children by parents or nurses was common.

6. It appears that the role of doctors and hospitals in bringing about improvement in health in the eighteenth century was
    a. very significant.
    b. minor.
    c. helpful only in the area of surgery.
    d. helpful only in the area of preventive medicine.

7. In the seventeenth and early eighteenth centuries people usually married
    a. surprisingly late.
    b. surprisingly early.
    c. almost never.
    d. and divorced frequently.

8. Which of the following was *not* a general characteristic of the European family of the eighteenth century?
    a. The nuclear family
    b. Late marriages
    c. Many unmarried relatives
    d. The extended family

9. The overwhelming reason for postponement of marriage was
    a. that people didn't like the institution of marriage.
    b. lack of economic independence.
    c. the stipulation of a legal age.
    d. that young men and women valued the independence of a working life.

10. In the second half of the eighteenth century, the earlier pattern of marriage and family life began to break down. Which of the following was *not* a result of this change?
    a. A greater number of illegitimate births
    b. Earlier marriages
    c. Marriages exclusively for economic reasons
    d. Marriages for love

11. The "illegitimacy explosion" of the late eighteenth century was encouraged by all but which one of the following?
    a. The laws, especially in Germany, concerning the right of the poor to marry
    b. The mobility of young people needing to work off the farm
    c. The influence of the French Revolution, which repressed freedom in sexual and marital behavior
    d. The decreasing influence of parental pressure and village tradition

12. Which of the following statements best describes the attitude toward children in the first part of the eighteenth century?
    a. They were protected and cherished.
    b. They were never disciplined.
    c. They were treated as they were—children living in a child's world.
    d. They were ignored, often brutalized, and often unloved.

13. Most of the popular education in Europe of the eighteenth century was sponsored by
    a. the church.
    b. the state.
    c. private individuals.
    d. parents, in the home.

14. Which of the following would most likely be found in an eighteenth-century hospital?
    a. Isolation of patients
    b. Sanitary conditions
    c. Uncrowded conditions
    d. Uneducated nurses and poor nursing practices

15. The greatest medical triumph of the eighteenth century was the conquest of
    a. starvation.
    b. smallpox.
    c. scurvy.
    d. cholera.

16. The practice of sending one's newborn baby to be suckled by a poor woman in the countryside was known as
    a. the cottage system.
    b. infanticide.
    c. wet-nursing.
    d. overlaying.

17. Which of the following was *not* a common food for the European poor?
    a. Vegetables
    b. Beer
    c. Dark bread
    d. Milk

18. It appears that the chief dietary problem of European society was the lack of an adequate supply of
    a. vitamins A and C.
    b. vitamin B complex.
    c. meat.
    d. sugar.

19. Most probably the best thing an eighteenth-century sick person could do with regard to hospitals would be to
    a. enter only if an operation was suggested by a doctor.
    b. enter only if in need of drugs.
    c. enter only a hospital operating under Galenic theory.
    d. stay away.

20. The country that led the way in the development of universal education was
    a. Britain.
    b. Prussia.
    c. France.
    d. Austria.

21. In which of the following countries did a religious conviction that the path to salvation lay in careful study of the Scriptures lead to an effective network of schools and a very high literacy rate by 1800?
    a. Austria
    b. England
    c. France
    d. Scotland

22. The desire for "bread as white as snow" led to
    a. a decline in bacterial diseases.
    b. a significant nutritional advance.
    c. an increase in the supply of bread.
    d. a nutritional decline.

23. The general eighteenth-century attitude toward masturbation was that it
    a. was harmless and perhaps healthy.
    b. was unacceptable for women but okay for men.
    c. caused insanity and therefore must be prevented.
    d. did not exist.

24. The general trend in Catholic countries was for monarchs to follow the Protestant lead in
    a. limiting the power and influence of the church.
    b. adopting the idea of predestination.
    c. casting off all allegiance to the papacy.
    d. protecting the poor.

25. During the eighteenth century the Society of Jesus
    a. found its power and position in Europe rise.
    b. gained considerable land in Portugal and France.
    c. was ordered out of France and Spain.
    d. avoided politics and property accumulation altogether.

Major Political Ideas

1. Did the standard of living have a "class" bias? In other words, did one class benefit more than another when economic conditions improved? Did material advances reduce or widen the gap between the rich and the poor?

2. Was society more or less divided in terms of gender roles? In terms of class?

Issues for Essays and Discussion

1. Did the common people of preindustrial Europe enjoy a life of simple comfort and natural experiences? Or was theirs a life of brutal and cruel exploitation? Discuss this in terms of the nature of family life, childhood, diet and health, and education and religion.

2. In general, was life, by the late eighteenth century, getting better or worse?

Interpretation of Visual Sources

Study the reproduction of the print entitled *The Five Senses* on page 708 of your textbook. What is the theme of this print? What does it tell us about the treatment of children? Is this typical of how society treated children? How does the illustration mirror some of the ideas of the Enlightenment? (Refer to Chapter 20.)

Understanding History Through the Arts

1. What can art tell us about childhood in the preindustrial era? Preindustrial childhood is the subject of *Children's Games* by Pieter Brueghel the Elder, a lively, action-packed painting of over two hundred children engaged in more than seventy different games. The painting is the subject of an interesting article by A. Eliot, "Games Children Play," *Sports Illustrated* (January 11, 1971): 48–56.

2. How is preindustrial life portrayed in literature and film? Samuel Richardson wrote a novel about the life of a household servant who became the prey of the lecherous son of her master, *Pamela, or Virtue Rewarded** (1740). Tom Jones, eighteenth-century England's most famous foundling, was the fictional hero of Henry Fielding's *Tom Jones* and the

*Available in paperback.

subject and title of director Tony Richardson's highly acclaimed, award-winning film version of Fielding's novel. Starring Albert Finney, Susannah York, and Dame Edith Evans, the film re-creates, in amusing and satirical fashion, eighteenth-century English life. A more recent film adaptation is Richardson's *Joseph Andrews*, based on another Fielding novel.

3. Was urban life more comfortable than rural life? What was the great attraction of the city? London was the fastest growing city in the eighteenth century. How people lived in London is the subject of two highly readable and interesting books: M. D. George, *London Life in the Eighteenth Century** (3rd ed., 1951), and R. J. Mitchell and M. D. R. Leys, *A History of London Life** (1963).

Problems for Further Investigation

1. What was daily life like for poor women in this period? Few men in preindustrial society earned enough to support a family. This, in part, explains why and when women married, and why most women worked. The preindustrial woman, therefore, was not in any modern sense a homemaker. The subject of women and the family economy in eighteenth-century France is discussed by O. Hufton in *The Poor of Eighteenth-Century France* (1974).

2. What was the cause of the so-called population explosion? Did medical science contribute to an improvement in eighteenth-century life? Until about twenty years ago, it was fashionable to believe that the population explosion was due to improvements made by medical science. Although this theory is generally disclaimed today, it appears to be enjoying a slight revival. For both sides of the argument, begin your study with M. Anderson, *Population Change in North-Western Europe, 1750–1850** (1988), and then read the following journal articles (which also have bibliographies): T. McKeown and R. G. Brown, "Medical Evidence Related to English Population Change," *Population Studies* 9 (1955); T. McKeown and R. G. Record, "Reasons for the Decline in Mortality in England and Wales During the Nineteenth Century," *Population Studies* 16 (1962); and P. Razzell, "Population Change in Eighteenth-Century England: A Reinterpretation," *Economic History Review*, 2nd series, 18-2 (1965). For the history of disease, see D. Hopkins, *Princes and Peasants: Smallpox in History* (1977).

*Available in paperback.

CHAPTER 22

African Kingdoms and Societies, ca 1450–1800

Chapter Questions

After reading and studying this chapter, you should be able to answer the following questions:

What kinds of economic and social structures characterized African societies? What impact did Islam have on African societies? What kinds of literary sources survive? What role did slavery play in African societies before European intrusion? What were the geographical and societal origins of the African slaves shipped to America and to Asia?

Chapter Summary

African states and societies of the fifteenth through eighteenth centuries were made up of a wide variety of languages, cultures, and kinds of economic and political development. By 1450, Africa consisted of a number of kingdoms and societies that were held together by class structure, kingship, and family or kinship ties: the Senegambian states on the West African coast, the kingdom of Songhay that dominated much of the Sudan, Kanem-Bornu and Hausa city-states, and the Swahili city-states on the east coast of Africa. This chapter describes the varied social and political developments across Africa and discusses how Africa was influenced by Christian European and Islamic societies.

The transatlantic slave trade was one of the great forced migrations of world history. It resulted in terrible misery and degradation. It led to neither economic nor technological growth in Africa, and its political and demographic consequences were varied. West Africa lost an enormous labor supply, but the coast of Angola suffered the greatest loss in population. In the long term, the overall impact of the slave trade on Africa was marginal. Although French culture influenced the coastal fringes of Senegal, the English maintained factories along the Gold Coast, and the Portuguese held Angola and Mozambique. By 1800, European influence had hardly penetrated the African interior.

Study Outline

Use this outline to preview the chapter before you read a particular section in your textbook and then as a self-check to test your reading comprehension after you have read the chapter section.

I. Senegambia and Benin
  A. The Senegambian states of the West African coast possessed a homogeneous culture.
    1. They served as a center in the trade from North Africa and the Middle East.
    2. They became an important center for the transatlantic slave trade.
  B. Ghana and Mali controlled much of Senegambia, but other states remained independent.
  C. Senegambian social and political structure
    1. The three Senegambian language groups were Wolof, Serer, and Pulaar.
    2. Wolof and Serer culture had clearly defined classes: royalty, nobility, warriors, peasants, artisans, and slaves.
      a. Senegambian slavery was harsh but also different from Western slavery; most slaves were not considered property.
      b. Some slaves served as royal advisers and had great power.
    3. The Wolof nobility elected the king, who appointed village chiefs.
    4. In stateless societies, age-grade cultures evolved.
      a. Age-grades were groups of men and women initiated into adulthood at the same time.
      b. Age-grades cut across family ties and created communitywide loyalties.
    5. The typical Senegambian community was a self-supporting agricultural village made up of family farms.
      a. Work was understood more in terms of social relationships.
      b. Millet and sorghum were supplemented by plantains, beans, bananas, fish, and small game.
  D. The forest kingdom of Benin (now southern Nigeria) emerged in the fifteenth and sixteenth centuries.
    1. A balance of power between the king (*oba*) and the nobility evolved under Ewuare.
    2. Ewuare expanded the state east to the Niger River, west to Yoruba country, and south to the Gulf of Guinea.
      a. The capital, Benin City, was large and wealthy.
      b. From 1485 on, the Portuguese and other Europeans tried unsuccessfully to play a role in Benin.
      c. Reasons for its decline in the eighteenth and nineteenth centuries remain a mystery.

II. The Sudan: Songhay, Kanem-Bornu, and Hausaland
  A. Songhay dominated the Niger region of western and central Sudan.
    1. Muhammad Toure tried to introduce political centralization and Muslim reforms into the Songhay Empire.

2. Leo Africanus visited Timbuktu in 1513; he reported it to be a sophisticated and prosperous urban society.
3. In Songhay slaves produced the main crops, and Muhammad Toure increased the number of royal slaves greatly.
4. Muhammad Toure's reforms failed because of diverse groups and resistance to Islamic institutions.
5. His death left the country politically unstable, and it fell to Moroccan armies.

B. Kanem-Bornu thrived under Idris Alooma's leadership.
1. A strong military-feudal state was established.
2. Agriculture and trade with North Africa flourished.
3. Idris Alooma's great feats were described by the historian Ibn Fartua in *The Kanem Wars*.
4. He introduced Muslim religion and law into Kanem-Bornu.
5. The empire declined after his death.

C. The Hausa were agricultural people who lived in small villages.
1. Trade with North Africa resulted in the evolution of important city-states such as Katsina and Kano.
2. Kano and Katsina became Muslim intellectual centers.
3. King Muhammad Rimfa of Kano introduced the practice of purdah, or seclusion of women, and the use of eunuchs in high political offices.

III. Ethiopia
A. The East African Christian kingdom of Ethiopia faced numerous invaders.
1. The Muslim state of Adal defeated Emperor Lebna Dengel and then devastated the land and forced many to convert to Islam.
2. The Adal Muslims were defeated by the Portuguese in 1541.
3. The Galla peoples occupied parts of Ethiopia, and the Ottoman Turks seized Massawa and other coastal cities.

B. Portuguese Jesuits tried to replace the Coptic Christian tradition with Roman Catholicism.
1. In spite of these overzealous attempts, the Coptic Christian church remained the cornerstone of Ethiopian national identity.
2. The Jesuits were expelled in 1633.

C. For the next two centuries, hostility to foreigners, weak political leadership, and regionalism characterized Ethiopia.

IV. The Swahili city-states
A. The Swahili city-states on the east coast of Africa prospered greatly in the late fifteenth century.
1. Mogadishu, Mombasa, Kilwa, and Sofala traded ivory, gold, and slaves with Arabian and Persian Gulf ports and the Far East.
2. Kilwa dominated the cities, which were cosmopolitan and wealthy.

B. In 1498, the Portuguese, under da Gama, conquered many of the city-states.
1. Some well-fortified northern cities, such as Mogadishu, survived as important ports.

      2. Some towns were deserted and their peoples migrated north, as passive resistance worked to block Portuguese control of trade.

      3. The Portuguese base at Fort Jesus eventually collapsed.

V. The transatlantic slave trade

  A. By the sixteenth century, slavery had a long history in Africa.

      1. Islam had heavily influenced African slavery.

      2. African rulers justified slavery with the Muslim argument that prisoners of war could be sold.

  B. Portugal dominated the slave trade from 1493 to 1600, sending many slaves to Brazil.

  C. From 1690 to 1807, England was the leading carrier of African slaves.

  D. Population density and supply conditions along the African coast and the sailing time to New York determined the sources of slaves.

  E. Most slaves were intended for sugar and coffee plantations.

      1. Most were obtained through trade with African dealers.

      2. Whites did not participate in the inland markets.

  F. The four centuries of slave trade involved the brutalization and exploitation of millions of people.

      1. At the ports the slaves were treated harshly and given poor food.

      2. They were branded a number of times.

      3. In ships they were packed below deck and received little food and water.

  G. The Portuguese colony of Brazil provided the ships, capital, and goods for the slave trade.

      1. Credit played a major role in the trade.

      2. The African operators frequently ended up in debt to the merchants.

      3. Despite high demand, Portuguese merchants tried to maintain only a trickle of slaves to Rio de Janeiro.

  H. The British slave trade was dominated by London, Bristol, and Liverpool; the British traded textiles, gunpowder and flint, and liquor for slaves.

  I. European traders and African dealers all looked for profits.

      1. The "sorting" was the system of trading goods for slaves.

      2. The Europeans established factory-forts, or fortified trading posts, as centers for slave trade.

      3. The shore method of trading allowed the slave ship to move easily from market to market.

  J. A northbound trade in slaves went across the Sahara to Algiers, Tripoli, and Cairo—and survived into the twentieth century.

  K. The economic, social, and political impact of the European slave trade on African societies was varied.

      1. The trade did not lead to the economic development of Africa because slave-trade income was usually spent on luxury and consumer goods or firearms.

      2. The trade encouraged slavery within Africa, encouraged population growth, and resulted in a métis, or mulatto, class.

         a. The métis came to exercise considerable economic and social power.

    b.   However, European culture did not penetrate West African society beyond the coast.

  3. Demographic and political consequences varied greatly from state to state.

    a.   West Africa lost an enormous labor supply.

    b.   The coast of Angola suffered the greatest loss.

    c.   Many African societies, however, suffered no significant population loss.

Review Questions

Check your understanding of this chapter by answering the following questions.

1. What was the political and social structure of Senegambia?

2. What was the extent of Benin territory, what was its political structure, and why was it attractive to the Portuguese invaders?

3. What were Muhammad Toure's goals in Songhay, and what success did he have?

4. What were Idris Alooma's accomplishments in the state of Kanem-Bornu?

5. Who were the Hausa people, and what was their culture like?

6. What external threats faced the Ethiopians in the sixteenth century, and what was the outcome?

7. What was the economic basis of Swahili prosperity? Why did the Swahili city-states crumble?

8. What were the origins of the African slave trade, which European countries were involved, and what were the African areas of supply?

9. What was the relationship between Portugal, its colony Brazil, and the African slave trade?

10. What was the economic and demographic impact of the slave trade on African societies?

11. What were the two systems of exchange of slaves adopted by European traders?

12. What were the political consequences of the slave trade on African society?

Study-Review Exercises

Identify and explain the significance of the following people and terms.

métis

factory-forts

shore trading

purdah

Solomonid dynasty

Timbuktu

oba

Galla peoples

Swahili city-states

Benin City

Coptic Christianity

transatlantic slave trade

Ewaure

Muhammad Toure

Idris Alooma

Leo Africanus

Vasco da Gama

Test your understanding of the chapter by providing the correct answer.

1. On the east coast of Africa are the *Hausa/Swahili* city-states.

2. The Senegambian states of the West African coast possessed a *homogeneous/heterogeneous* culture.

3. *Kanem-Bornu/Songhay* dominated the Niger region of the western and central Sudan.

4. The Adal Muslims were defeated by the *Spanish/Portuguese* in 1541.

5. From 1690 to 1807, *Portugal/England* was the leading carrier of African slaves.

6. In the Portuguese colony of Brazil, credit *did/did not* play a major role in the slave trade.

7. The economic, social, and political impact of the European slave trade on African societies *was generally the same/varied* throughout the continent.

Multiple-Choice Questions

1. In the kingdom of Benin, the oba was the
    a. clan system.
    b. king.
    c. supreme god.
    d. priesthood.

2. Benin's political history was marked by struggles between the king and
    a. European slave traders.
    b. the nobility.
    c. Muslim traders.
    d. the peasants.

3. In the Sudanese kingdoms, the religion of Islam
   a. was embraced by the masses.
   b. was popular primarily with the rulers.
   c. made deep changes in the legal system.
   d. was forbidden by royal decree.

4. The Coptic church is an ancient branch of
   a. Hinduism.
   b. Islam.
   c. Christianity.
   d. animism.

5. The country that monopolized the slave trade until 1600 was
   a. Portugal.
   b. England.
   c. the United States.
   d. Holland.

6. Most Portuguese slave ships were bound for
   a. the United States.
   b. the West Indies.
   c. Brazil.
   d. Argentina.

7. African trade with Europe
   a. led to technological progress for the Africans.
   b. soaked up the Africans' surplus wealth.
   c. increased the African standard of living.
   d. brought badly needed gold to Europe.

8. The métis were
   a. French slave traders.
   b. blacks who spoke French.
   c. mulattos.
   d. ex-slaves.

9. Which of the following statements about the slave trade is most accurate?
   a. African kingdoms broke down.
   b. Populations were depleted and economies destroyed.
   c. The trade enriched and strengthened economies.
   d. Consequences varied from place to place.

10. Most New World slaves came from the region of
    a. Ghana.
    b. Mali.
    c. Sudan.
    d. Senegambia.

11. In the fifteenth and sixteenth centuries, a great forest kingdom emerged in what is now southern Nigeria called the kingdom of
    a. Senegambia.
    b. Oba.
    c. Benin.
    d. Songhay.

12. The militaristic king of Kanem-Bornu who replaced tribal customs with Islamic rule was
    a. Muhammad Toure.
    b. Idris Alooma.
    c. Legna Dengel.
    d. Ahman ibn-Ghazi.

13. The Swahili city-states were on the
    a. east coast of Africa.
    b. north coast of Africa.
    c. south coast of Africa.
    d. west coast of Africa.

14. Portuguese merchants in Angola and Brazil sought to keep the flow of slaves from Africa to Brazil down to a trickle because they did not
    a. want to depopulate Angola too quickly.
    b. approve of the slave trade and wanted eventually to stop it for good.
    c. want to depress the American market.
    d. want to pay exorbitant transportation costs.

15. The slave trade that lasted late into the nineteenth century and even into the twentieth century was the
    a. North Atlantic trade.
    b. Angola-Brazil trade.
    c. northbound trade across the Sahara.
    d. eastbound trade via the Indian Ocean.

16. The slave trade produced the greatest demographic losses to the slaving coast of
    a. Angola.
    b. South Africa.
    c. the Gold Coast.
    d. Mali.

17. The typical Senegambian community was a
    a. highly urban community that avoided agriculture.
    b. city with a strong and dominating central government.
    c. community that rejected age-grade systems.
    d. small, self-supporting agricultural village.

18. Leo Africanus was
    a. the governor of Songhay.
    b. a Moroccan scholar who worked for Pope Leo X.
    c. the military leader of Kanem-Bornu and Hausaland.
    d. the general who inflicted military defeat on the Ethiopians.

19. The European country that did not have a strong mercantile class involved in "slaving" was
    a. Britain.
    b. France.
    c. the Netherlands.
    d. Portugal.

Major Political Ideas

What is meant by the age-grade system of social organization? How does it differ from African societies organized according to class and kingship?

Issues for Essays and Discussion

1. Define and describe the similarities and differences between the African societies of Senegambia, the Sudan, Ethiopia, and the Swahili city-states.

2. What impact did Islam have on African societies?

3. Discuss the role of slavery and its impact on African societies before and after European intrusion.

Interpretation of Visual Sources

Study the photograph of "The Oba of Benin" on page 728 of the textbook. What was the oba, and how does this illustration indicate his role and significance in African society?

Geography

On Outline Map 22.3 provided, and using Maps 22.1 and 22.2 in the text as references, locate the following:

1. The kingdoms of Kanem-Bornu and Hausaland; the Hausa city-states of Katsina and Kano; the kingdom of Ethiopia; and the Swahili city-states of Mogadishu, Mombasa, Kilwa, and Sofala.

2. In the space below, describe briefly the kinds of products each of these areas traded and the directions in which its trade flowed.

_____

_____

_____

_____

_____

_____

Remember that duplicate maps for class use are at the back of this book.

Outline Map 22.3

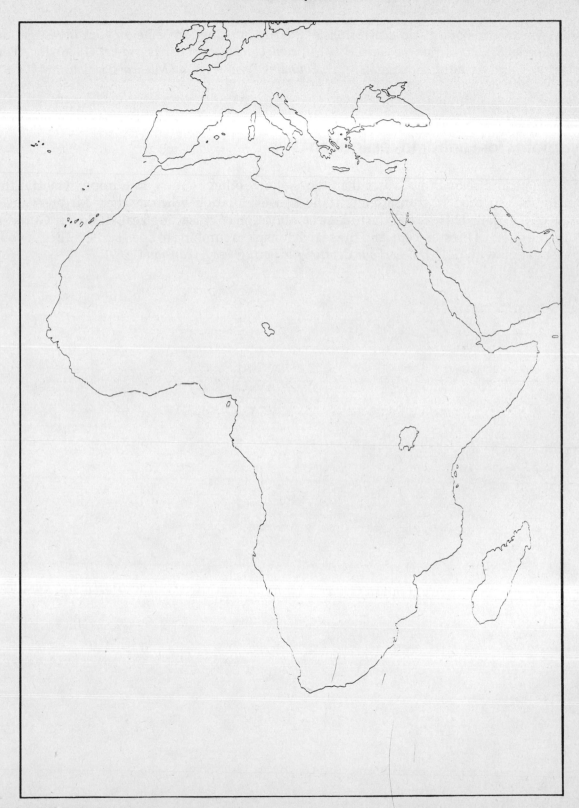

Understanding History Through the Arts

What were the major artistic expressions of the African kingdoms? Begin your investigation with *African Sculpture from the University Museum, University of Pennsylvania** (1986), by Allen Wardwell, and Arthur P. Bourgeois, et al., *Sounding Forms: African Musical Instruments** (1989).

Problems for Further Investigation

With ships and seamen no better than those of any other country in Europe, why did the Portuguese succeed in transatlantic trade and exploration whereas their Mediterranean predecessors failed? How did the unique combination of crusading zeal, desire for Guinean gold, the quest of Prester John, and the search for spices combine to spell success? Begin your investigation with C. R. Boxer, *Four Centuries of Portuguese Expansion* (1969).

*Available in paperback.

PRIMARY SOURCES
The Transatlantic Slave Trade

The transatlantic slave trade was one of the great forced migrations of world history—in which an estimated nine to twelve million people were exported from Africa (see textbook Tables 22.1 and 22.2). Here is an account of that experience from one person, Olaudah Equiano (1745?–1797) who was born in Benin and captured and sold into slavery when he was about eleven. He grew up in Philadelphia and lived part of his adult life in Britain. He was given his freedom by his Quaker master in the late 1760s. The following is from his autobiography.

How was Equiano captured? What were his experiences as a slave in Africa? What were the conditions of his transport across the Atlantic? Why do you suppose he received special treatment? Overall what is your assessment of the slaving process?

Equiano's Introduction to Slavery*

Generally when the grown people in the neighborhood were gone far in the fields to labor, the children assembled together in some of the neighbors' premises to play, and commonly some of us used to get up a tree to look out for any assailant or kidnapper that might come upon us, for they sometimes took those opportunities of our parents' absence to attack and carry off as many as they could seize. . . . One day, when all our people were gone out to their works as usual and only I and my dear sister were left to mind the house, two men and a woman got over our walls, and in a moment seized us both, and without giving us time to cry out or make resistance they stopped our mouths and ran off with us into the nearest wood. . . .

For a long time we had kept to the woods, but at last we came into a road which I believed I knew. I had now some hopes of being delivered, for we had advanced but a little way before I discovered some people at a distance, on which I began to cry out for their assistance: but my cries had no other effect than to make them tie me faster and stop my mouth, and then they put me into a large sack. They also stopped my sister's mouth and tied her hands, and

*Source: Paul Edwards, ed. and tr., Equiano's Travels, pp. 25–42. Heinemann Educational Books (Oxford). Used by permission.

in this manner we proceeded till we were out of sight of these people. When we went to rest the following night they offered us some victuals, but we reused it, and the only comfort we had was in being in one another's arms all that night and bathing each other with our tears. But alas! we were soon deprived of even the small comfort of weeping together. The next day proved a day of greater sorrow than I had yet experienced, for my sister and I were then separated while we lay clasped in each other's arms. It was in vain that we besought them not to part us; she was torn from me and immediately carried away, while I was left in a state of distraction not to be described. I cried and grieved continually, and for several days I did not eat anything but what they forced into my mouth. At length, after many days' traveling, during which I had often changed masters, I got into the hands of a chieftain in a very pleasant country. This man had two wives and some children, and they all used me extremely well and did all they could to comfort me, particularly the first wife, who was something like my mother. . . . This first master of mine, as I may call him, was a smith, and my principal employment was working his bellows, which were the same kind as I had seen in my vicinity. . . . I believed it was gold he worked, for it was of a lovely bright yellow color and was worn by the women on their wrists and ankles. I was there I suppose about a month, and they at last used to trust me some little distance from the house. . . .

In a small time afterwards he recovered and I was again sold. I was now carried to the left of the sun's rising, through many different countries and a number of large woods. The people I was sold to used to carry me very often when I was tired either on their shoulders or on their backs. I saw many convenient well-build sheds along the roads at proper distances, to accommodate the merchants and travelers who lay in those buildings along with their wives, who often accompany them; and they always go well armed. . . .

I was again sold and carried through a number of places till, after traveling a considerable time, I came to a town called Tinmah in the most beautiful country I had yet seen in Africa. . . . I was sold here . . . by a merchant who lived and brought me there. I had been about two or three days at his house when a wealthy widow, a neighbor of his, came there one evening and brought with her an only son, a young gentleman about my own age and size. Here they saw me; and, having taken a fancy to me, I was bought of the merchant and went home with them. . . . The next day I was washed and perfumed, and when meal-time came I was led into the presence of my mistress, and ate and drank before her with her son. This filled me with astonishment, and I could scarce help expressing my surprise that the young gentleman should suffer me, who was bound, to eat with him who was free; and not only so, but that he would not at any time either eat or drink till I had taken first, because I was the eldest, which was agreeable to our custom. Indeed everything here, and all their treatment of me, made me forget that I was a slave. . . . There were likewise slaves daily to attend us, while my young master and I with other boys sported with our darts and bows and arrows, as I had been used to do at home. In this resemblance to my former happy state I passed about two months; and I now began to think I was to be adopted into the family, and was beginning to be reconciled to my situation, and to forget by degrees my misfortunes, when all at once the delusion vanished; for without the least previous knowledge, one morning early, while my dear master and companion was still asleep, I was wakened out of my reverie to fresh sorrow, and hurried away. . . .

At last I came to the banks of a large river, which was covered with canoes in which the people appeared to live with their household utensils and provisions of all kinds. I was beyond measure astonished at this, as I had never before seen any water larger than a pond or a rivulet:

and my surprise was mingled with no small fear when I was put into one of these canoes and we began to paddle and move along the river. We continued going on thus till night, and when we came to land and made fires on the banks, each family by themselves, some dragged their canoes on shore, others stayed and cooked in theirs and laid in them all night. . . . Thus I continued to travel, sometimes by land, sometimes by water, through different countries and various nations, till at the end of six or seven months after I had been kidnapped I arrived at the sea coast.

The Slave Ship

The first object which saluted my eyes when I arrived on the coast was the sea, and a slave ship which was then riding at anchor and waiting for its cargo. These filled me with astonishment, which was soon converted into terror when I was carried on board. I was immediately handled and tossed up to see if I were sound by some of the crew, and I was now persuaded that I had gotten into a world of bad spirits and that they were going to kill me. Their complexions too differing so much from ours, their long hair and the language they spoke (which was very different from any I had ever heard) united to confirm me in this belief. Indeed such were the horrors of my views and fears at the moment that, if ten thousand worlds had been my own, I would have freely parted with them all to have exchanged my condition with that of the meanest slave in my own country. When I looked round the ship too and saw a large furnace or copper boiling and a multitude of black people of every description chained together, every one of their countenances expressing dejection and sorrow, I no longer doubted of my fate; and quite overpowered with horror and anguish, I fell motionless on the deck and fainted. When I recovered a little I found some black people about me, who I believed were some of those who had brought me on board and had been receiving their pay; they talked to me in order to cheer me, but all in vain. . . .

I was soon put down under the decks, and there I received such a salutation in my nostrils as I had never experienced in my life: so that with the loathsomeness of the stench and crying together, I became so sick and low that I was not able to eat, nor had I the least desire to taste anything. I now wished for the last friend, death, to relieve me; but soon, to my grief, two of the white men offered me eatables, and on my refusing to eat, one of them held me fast by the hands and laid me across I think the windlass, and tied my feet while the other flogged me severely. I had never experienced anything of this kind before, and although, not being used to the water, I naturally feared that element the first time I saw it, yet nevertheless could I have got over the nettings I would have jumped over the side, but I could not; and besides, the crew used to watch us very closely who were not chained down to the decks, lest we should leap into the water: and I have seen some of these poor African prisoners most severely cut for attempting to do so, and hourly whipped for not eating. This indeed was often the case with myself. In a little time after, amongst the poor chained men I found some of my own nation, which in a small degree gave ease to my mind. I inquired of these what was to be done with us; they gave me to understand we were to be carried to these white people's country to work for them. I then was a little revived, and thought if it were no worse than working, my situation was not so desperate: but still I feared I should be put to death, the white people looked and acted, as I thought, in so savage a manner; for I had never seen among my people such instances of brutal cruelty, and this not only shown towards us blacks but also to some of the whites themselves. One white man in particular I saw, when we were permitted to be on deck, flogged so unmercifully with a large rope near the foremast that he died in consequence of it; and they tossed him over the side as they would have done a brute. This made me fear these people the more, and I expected nothing less than to be treated in the same manner. . . .

At last, when the ship we were in had got in all her cargo, they made ready with many fearful noises, and we were all put under deck so that we could not see how they managed the vessel. But this disappointment was the last of my sorrow. The stench of the hold while we were on the coast was so intolerably loathsome that it was dangerous to remain there for any time, and some of us had been permitted to stay on the deck for the fresh air; but now that the whole ship's cargo were confined together it became absolutely pestilential. The closeness of the place and the heat of the climate, added to the number in the ship, which was so crowded that each had scarcely room to turn himself, almost suffocated us. This produced copious perspirations, so that the air soon became unfit for respiration from a variety of loathsome smells, and brought on a sickness among the slaves, of which many died, thus falling victims to the improvident avarice, as I may call it, of their purchasers. This wretched situation was again aggravated by the galling of the chains, now become insupportable, and the filth of the necessary tubs, into which the children often fell and were almost suffocated. The shrieks of the women and the groans of the dying rendered the whole a scene of horror almost inconceivable. Happily perhaps for myself I was soon reduced so low here that it was thought necessary to keep me almost always on deck, and from my extreme youth I was not put in fetters. . . .

One day, when we had a smooth sea and moderate wind, two of my wearied countrymen who were chained together (I was near them at the time), preferring death to such a life of misery, somehow made through the nettings and jumped into the sea: immediately another quite dejected fellow, who on account of his illness was suffered to be out of irons, also followed their example; and I believe many more would very soon have done the same if they had not been prevented by the ship's crew, who were instantly alarmed. Those of us that were the most active were in a moment put down under the deck, and there was such a noise and confusion amongst the people of the ship as I never heard before, to stop her and get the boat out to go after the slaves. However two of the wretches were drowned, but they got the other and afterwards flogged him unmercifully for thus attempting to prefer death to slavery. In this manner we continued to undergo more hardships than I can now relate, hardships which are inseparable from this accursed trade. Many a time we were near suffocation from the want of fresh air, which we were often without for whole days together. This and the stench of the necessary tubs carried off many. . . .

At last we came in sight of the island of Barbados, at which the whites on board gave a great shout and made many signs of joy to us. We did not know what to think of this, but as the vessel drew nearer we plainly saw the harbor and other ships of different kinds and sizes, and we soon anchored amongst them off Bridgetown. Many merchants and planters now came on board, though it was in the evening. They put us in separate parcels and examined us attentively. They also made us jump, and pointed to the land, signifying we were to go there. . . .

We were not many days in the merchant's custody before we were sold after their usual manner, which is this: On a signal given, (as the beat of a drum) the buyers rush at once into the yard where the slaves are confined, and made choice of that parcel they like best. The noise and clamor with which this is attended and the eagerness visible in the countenances of the buyers serve not a little to increase the apprehensions of the terrified Africans, who may well be supposed to consider them as the ministers of that destruction to which they think themselves devoted. In this manner, without scruple, are relations and friends separated, most of them never to see each other again. I remember in the vessel in which I was brought over, in the men's apartment there were several brothers who, in the sale, were sold in different lots; and it was very moving on this occasion to see and hear their cries at parting. O, ye nominal Christians! might not an African ask you, Learned you this from your God who says unto you, Do unto all men as you would men shall do unto you?

CHAPTER 23

The Middle East and India, ca 1450–1800

Chapter Questions

After reading and studying this chapter, you should be able to answer the following questions:

Who were the Ottomans and the Safavids? What political and religious factors gave rise to the Ottoman and Safavid empires? What were the sources of Ottoman and Safavid power, and how were the two empires governed? What intellectual developments characterized the Ottoman and Safavid cultures? What external and domestic difficulties caused the decline of the Ottoman Empire and Safavid Persia? How did Muslim government reform and artistic inspiration affect the dominant Hindu population in India?

Chapter Summary

The Ottoman Turkish empire had its origins in the fourteenth century as a border state between Islam and Byzantine Christianity. The political cornerstone of the empire was the jihad, or holy war, and from about 1389, when the south European Serbs and Bosnians were defeated, to 1570, when Cyprus was taken, the Ottomans built an enormous empire that stretched into Europe and across the North African coast. The imperial phase of Ottoman history began with the conquest of Constantinople in 1453, and the Ottoman threat continued to raise fears in Christian Europe for centuries to follow.

The great Turkish militarist, political administrator, and law giver was Suleiman I—"the Magnificent." His reign, from 1520 to 1566, represents the peak of Ottoman influence and culture. This chapter stresses how European prejudice against Islam has resulted in a neglect of the great literary and artistic achievements of Suleiman's state—a cultural explosion that rivaled the achievement of the European Renaissance.

The chapter also shows why the Ottoman Empire did not develop a feudal structure such as that in Europe. One important reason was that all property belonged to the sultan, and hence the Turkish nobility could not put down roots. Also, the system of slave recruitment called devshirme meant social advancement for many slaves but blocked the development of a feudal military/bureaucratic class. Finally, royal corruption and factionalism led to real power being held by the janissaries, the elite slave class that came to control the military.

A turning point in Ottoman history came with the Treaty of Karlowitz in 1699, by which the Ottomans gave up claims to Hungary and Transylvania. This was followed by a long period of decline. Changes in the Western economy furthered the decline: new trade routes by-passed the old Middle Eastern routes, and raw materials were exported to Europe rather than fed to Turkish industry. Foolishly, the Ottomans gave European states trade privileges called capitulations that in effect drained the Ottoman economy. By 1800 the Ottoman Empire was known as "the sick man of Europe."

Persia, known as Iran since 1935, emerged as a powerful Muslim state under the Safavid dynasty in the early sixteenth century. Three features contributed to the strength of the state. First, it had the loyalty and military support of the Qizilbash nomadic tribesmen. Second, the Safavid state utilized the skills of urban bureaucrats and made them an essential part of the government machinery. The third source of strength was the Shi'ite faith. The strength of the Safavid power reached its peak under Shah Abbas (r. 1587–1629), labeled "the Great" for his military achievements, support for trade, commerce, and the arts. Shah Abbas was succeeded by inept rulers.

The Mughal period in India began in 1525 with Babur's conquests of northern India. Akbar, Babur's grandson, gave the Mughal state its form. Assisted by the military leader, Bairam Khan, Akbar added Malwa, Gondwana, Gujarat, and Bengal to the empire. He developed an efficient bureaucracy, sought universal religious tolerance, abolished taxes on non-Muslims, and supported the arts. Akbar created the Din-i-Ilahi which was a mix of a number of religions. Akbar built a new city, Fatehpur-Sikri, which combined Muslim and Hindu traditions.

Akbar was followed by his son, Jahangir and his grandson, Shah Jahan. Jahangir consolidated rule in Bengal; Shah Jahan moved the court to Delhi and built the Peacock Throne and the Taj Mahal. The absence of a formal procedure for imperial succession led to Aurangzeb's puritanical rule. After his death the provincial governors began to rule independently.

Shortly before Babur's invasion of India, the Portuguese opened the subcontinent to Portuguese trade and established the port of Goa on the Arabian Sea as their headquarters. The Portuguese controlled the spice trade over the Indian Ocean for nearly a century after sweeping the Muslims, through a policy of piracy and terrorism, off the Indian and Arabian Oceans.

In 1602, the Dutch formed the Dutch East India Company with the stated goal of wresting the enormously lucrative spice trade from the Portuguese. Shortly thereafter appeared the British East India Company with similar designs. The French were the last to arrive in India. From 1740 to 1763, Britain and France were almost continually engaged in a tremendous global struggle. The Treaty of Paris of 1763 recognized British control of much of India, and scholars acknowledge the treaty as the beginning of the British Empire in India. By the beginning of the nineteenth century, British rule of India rested on three foundations: the support of puppet Indian princes; a large army of sepoys of dubious loyalty; and an increasingly effective civil service, staffed almost entirely of Englishmen, with Hindus and Muslims in minor positions.

Study Outline

Use this outline to preview the chapter before you read a particular section in your textbook and then as a self-check to test your reading comprehension after you have read the chapter section.

I. The splendor of the Ottoman state
   A. The Ottoman state grew out of the expansionist activities of Osman, a Turkish ruler (1299–1326).
      1. The first Ottoman state expanded out of western Anatolia.
      2. Its rulers were the leaders of the Ghazis, fighters in the holy war.
      3. The principle of jihad, or holy war, was central to the Ottoman state.
      4. The Ottomans pushed into the Balkans, and under Mehmed II conquered Constantinople (1453).
         a. The conquest of Constantinople inaugurated the imperial phase of the Ottomans.
         b. They threatened Italy and conquered much of the territory surrounding the Mediterranean, including the Italian port of Otranto.
         c. Selim the Grim added Syria, Palestine, and Egypt to the empire, and extended the empire across North Africa as far as Algeria.
         d. Suleiman extended the empire farther, adding Greece and the Balkans, and attacking Vienna.
         e. Ottoman success was due to the weakness and disunity of their enemies as well as to Turkish military organization and skill.
      5. The Ottomans did not completely dominate the sea; they struggled with the Habsburgs for control of the Mediterranean.
         a. A Turkish victory at Preveze in 1538 assured Turkish control of the Ionian and Aegean seas.
         b. Cyprus was conquered in 1570 and settled by Turks.
      6. Pope Pius V organized the Holy League against the Turks, smashing the Turkish fleet at the battle of Lepanto in 1571, although the naval competition continued.
      7. Military organization and goals dominated Ottoman life.
   B. The class organization of society
      1. The ruling class was Muslim and loyal to the sultan; all property belonged to the sultan; thus, a European-type feudal structure did not emerge.
      2. Slaves were acquired through purchase, through capture in battle, or through devshirme, a system that placed boys in the sultan's service.
         a. For some, devshirme meant social advancement; the top 10 percent went to the palace school.
         b. Other boys went into military training, to become janissaries (army elite).
         c. Pashas were the sultan's highest servants: generals, governors, police officers, and others.
   C. Suleiman I's reign was one of extraordinary artistic flowering.
      1. Suleiman, through the slave-poet Lütfi Pasa, is known as a lawgiver (Kanuni).
         a. His legal code prescribed penalties for most crimes.

      b. It sought to end corruption and imprisonment without trial, and it introduced the idea of a balanced budget.

      c. These decrees, or Kanuns, became imperial law.

2. Suleiman was known as "the Magnificent" because of the grandeur of his court and the cultural advances achieved during his reign.

      a. His expenditures surpassed any European monarch; he used his wealth to adorn Constantinople with palaces and mosques and built new public water systems.

      b. Pasha Sinan designed hundreds of public buildings, the best being the Shehzade and Suleimaniye mosques.

      c. Great achievements were made in poetry, painting, history, mathematics, geographical literature, astronomy, and medicine.

      d. Poetry was the main literary expression; Diwan poetry consisted of collections of poems.

      e. The troubadours conveyed traditional folk wisdom with short stories and anecdotes; Dede Korkut's collection is a major source for historians.

      f. Ottoman rulers used historical writing to justify their power and position; Kemalpaşazêde was perhaps the greatest historian, while Piri Reis wrote an extremely detailed book on geography.

      g. A large number of hospitals were founded under Suleiman, and important books were written on medicine and drugs.

D. Grave political, social, and economic difficulties afflicted the Ottoman state in the seventeenth and eighteenth centuries.

1. The tradition of giving the imperial heir training in administration and fighting was abandoned following Suleiman's reign.

      a. Hence the sultans tended to be corrupt and ignorant, which invited factionalism.

      b. This enabled the janissaries to destroy the influence of the old families and make their positions hereditary; thus, the janissaries became the powerful class.

2. Muhammad Kuprili, the vizier, abolished the widespread corruption and strengthened the state, but defeat at Vienna in 1683 led to decline once again.

3. The Treaty of Karlowitz in 1699, by which the Ottomans lost Hungary and Transylvania to Austria, represents the decline of Ottoman power in Europe.

4. Population increase and economic decline led to further weakness, as well as to famine, inflation, and revolt.

      a. The population doubled as a result of the end of the plague.

      b. New trade routes and modernization in Europe left Turkey in economic decline.

      c. The capitulations gave Europeans great power over the Turkish economy.

      d. By 1800 the Ottoman state was known as the "sick man of Europe."

II. The Persian theocratic state
   A. All of Persia (now Iran) was united by Shah Ismail, the founder of the Safavid dynasty, between 1502 and 1510.
      1. The strength of the Safavid dynasty rested on three features.
         a. First was the loyalty of the Qizilbash tribesmen, who provided the shah with troops in return for vast grazing lands.
         b. Second, the state utilized the skills of urban bureaucrats; the wakēl was the highest official next to the shah.
         c. Third, the Shi'ite faith became the official religion of Persia—and shaped the cultural and political nature of the state, making it a theocracy.
      2. Safavid power reached its height under Shah Abbas the Great.
         a. He built a national army and adopted English military skills.
         b. He captured Baghdad, Mosul, and Diarbakr.
         c. He built the carpet trade into a major export business and imported Chinese potters to establish a new tile industry.
      3. The most important city was Isfahan—the center of Persian arts trade and a city of great architecture and gardens.
      4. Shah Abbas was succeeded by inept rulers, and in the eighteenth century Persia was divided among the Turks, Afghans, and Russians.

III. India: From Mughal domination to British dominion (ca 1498–1805)
   A. The Mughal (or Muslim) period of Indian history began in 1525.
   B. The rule of the Mughals
      1. Mughal rule in India began with Babur's conquests of northern India.
      2. Babur's grandson, Akbar, gave the Mughal state its form, although his father, Humayun, gave it a strong artistic base.
         a. As badshah the young Akbar was assisted by the military leader Bairam Khan.
         b. Akbar continued Bairam Khan's expansionist policy—adding Mala, Gondwana, Gujarat, and Bengal to the empire.
         c. Akbar developed an efficient bureaucracy, including a bureau of finance and a royal mint.
         d. He appointed mansabdars to administer imperial policy at the local level.
      3. Akbar sought universal religious tolerance, or sulahkul.
         a. He worked for the mutual assimilation of Hindus and Muslims.
         b. Under the principle of sulahkul, he assumed responsibility for all his subjects.
         c. He abolished taxes (jizya) on non-Muslims, married Hindu women, and employed Hindus in his government.
         d. From his mediation of religious disputes he created the Din-i-Ilahi, which was a mix of a number of religions.
         e. Din-i-Ilahi led to serious Muslim rebellions.
         f. Akbar built a great new city, Fatehpur-Sikri, which combined Muslim and Hindu traditions.
         g. He supported artists and writers.

    4. Akbar was followed by his son, Jahangir, and his grandson, Shah Jahan.
        a. Jahangir consolidated rule in Bengal and supported the arts.
        b. Shah Jahan moved the court to Delhi and built the Peacock Throne and the Taj Mahal.
    5. The absence of a formal procedure for imperial succession led to Aurangzeb's puritanical rule.
        a. He reimposed laws and taxes against the non-Muslim majority.
        b. His religious policies proved unpopular with the Hindus.
        c. His attempt to conquer the south was only partly successful.
        d. After Aurangzeb's death the provincial governors began to rule independently.
        e. The Marathas revolted and fought the Afghans, who were led by the Persian Nadir Shah.

C. European rivalry for the Indian trade
    1. From their port of Goa, the Portuguese used piracy and terrorism to push the Muslims from the Indian and Arabian oceans; they claimed that international law did not apply to non-Westerners.
    2. The Dutch and British formed trading companies.
        a. The Dutch East India Company sought profits in the spice trade.
        b. Madras and Bombay became British trade centers.
        c. The British pushed the Portuguese out of the India trade, while Indonesia came under Dutch control.

D. Factory-fort societies
    1. A "factory" was a European trade settlement.
        a. At first the British company discouraged involvement in local politics.
        b. To deal with local disorder, however, the company came to exert political control over its factory-forts and surrounding territory.
        c. The one-way nature of the trade led to demands in England to prohibit the import of certain goods, particularly Indian cloth.

E. The rise of the British East India Company
    1. Colbert's French East India Company established factories in India in the 1670s.
    2. Joseph Dupleix advocated use of sepoys and alliances with princes to accomplish French hegemony.
        a. India was a battleground in the French-British struggle.
        b. British seapower, along with Clive's victory at Plassey (1757), led to British control of India.
    3. Hastings implemented the parliamentary legislation that transferred some power from the East India Company to a governor.
        a. He laid the foundations for the civil service, instituted reforms, and blocked Indian coalition.
        b. After his resignation, the British imposed a new landholding system on India and tightened control over the local princes.
    4. At the beginning of the nineteenth century, Britain controlled India through the support of the Indian princes, a large army of sepoys, and the civil service.

Review Questions

Check your understanding of this chapter by answering the following questions.

1. What role did religion and militarism play in the Ottoman state?

2. What were the chief accomplishments of Suleiman the Magnificent?

3. What role did the janissaries play in Turkish history?

4. What was the relationship between Shah Abbas and the Shi'ite religion? What were Abbas's accomplishments?

5. What was the significance of the Battle of Lepanto in 1571?

6. Describe the Ottoman system of devshirme. What impact did this system have on the distribution of political power within the Turkish state?

7. What were the basic features of Suleiman's law codes?

8. What were the reasons for the economic decay of the Ottoman Empire? Were the capitulations a wise idea?

9. Trace the religious and political policies and accomplishments of the Mughal state under Akbar.

10. What were the contributions of Jahangir and Shah Jahan?

11. Why is Aurangzeb's rule described as "puritanical"? What was his attitude toward his grandfather's policies of religious toleration?

12. What were the goals, interests, and trade practices of the Dutch and British East India companies?

13. What were Dupleix's ideas of colonial policy in India? Describe how the British adopted these policies under Hastings.

Study-Review Exercises

Define the following key concepts and terms.

jihad

pashas

Diwan poetry

Kanuni

devshirme

janissaries

Shi'ism

sulahkul

mansabdars

sati

factory-fort societies

capitulations

Mughal

Identify and explain the significance of each of the following people and terms.

sepoys

Taj Mahal

Robert Clive

British East India Company

Treaty of Karlowitz (1699)

Battle of Lepanto (1571)

Suleiman's law codes

Pope Pius's Holy League

Din-i-Ilahi

Fatehpur-Sikri

Safavid dynasty

Explain why each of the following people was important.

Suleiman the Magnificent

Akbar

Shah Ismail

Muhammad Kuprili

Piri Reis

Şeyhi of Kütahya

Pasha Sinan

Selim the Grim

Osman the Turk

Aurangzeb

Multiple-Choice Questions

1. The janissaries were originally
   a. provincial governors.
   b. a slave army.
   c. Ottoman officials.
   d. Muslim monks.

2. An important point of Akbar's policy was
   a. religious toleration.
   b. territorial expansion.
   c. strong central government.
   d. suppression of Hinduism.

3. Sepoys were
   a. native soldiers.
   b. Muslim wise men.
   c. concubines.
   d. Indian-born Europeans.

4. Which of the following was *not* a basis for British rule in India?
   a. Support of the Indian princes
   b. The British navy
   c. The sepoys
   d. The civil service

5. The Ottomans captured Constantinople during the reign of
   a. Mehmet II.
   b. Suleiman the Magnificent.
   c. Mustafa Naima.
   d. Muhammad Kuprili.

6. The military leader of the Ottoman Empire who tried unsuccessfully to capture Vienna in 1683 was
   a. Suleiman the Magnificent.
   b. Muhammad Kuprili.
   c. Mehmet II.
   d. Kara Mustafa.

7. The founder of the Safavid dynasty was
   a. Shah Abbas.
   b. Shah Ismail.
   c. Babur.
   d. Suleiman II.

8. Babur was a
   a. Mongol.
   b. Safavid.
   c. Turk.
   d. Mughal.

9. Which of the following statements best describes Akbar's rule in India?
   a. He developed an efficient bureaucracy.
   b. He employed only Muslim officials.
   c. He demanded religious conformity.
   d. He instituted the jizya, a tax on non-Muslim adult males.

10. The decline of the Mughal state began under Aurangzeb, whose unsuccessful reforms were basically
    a. economic in nature.
    b. bureaucratic in nature.
    c. religious in nature.
    d. political in nature.

11. Britain fought for control of India with
    a. France.
    b. Portugal.
    c. Spain.
    d. Holland.

12. The British governor general of India who defeated the Mysore was
    a. Charles Cornwallis.
    b. Richard Wellesley.
    c. Warren Hastings.
    d. Robert Clive.

13. The class of slave recruits in Ottoman Turkey who rose to secure permanent military and administrative positions was the
    a. janissaries.
    b. Kanuni.
    c. jihad.
    d. Diwan.

14. The Battle of Lepanto ended with
    a. a great Ottoman victory.
    b. a victory for Uluç Ali Pasha.
    c. an Ottoman defeat but no decisive change in sea power.
    d. mastery of the Mediterranean shifting decisively to the West.

15. The cultural developments under Suleiman I
    a. were of minor consequence.
    b. were possibly equal to those of the European Renaissance.
    c. applied only to military affairs.
    d. centered exclusively in the field of poetry.

16. By the Treaty of Karlowitz in 1699, the Ottomans
    a. gained Vienna.
    b. gained the North African coast.
    c. lost Vienna.
    d. lost Hungary and Transylvania.

17. The Ottoman capitulations were
    a. concessions given to Christian crusaders after a battle.
    b. military districts.
    c. law codes.
    d. trade and economic concessions given to European powers.

18. The ruling dynasty that united all of Persia was the
    a. Ottoman dynasty.
    b. East India Company dynasty.
    c. Qizilbash dynasty.
    d. Safavid dynasty.

19. Serious economic and commercial decline in Turkey from the sixteenth century on was due, in part, to
    a. depopulation.
    b. imperial expansion.
    c. rapid modernization.
    d. European capitalistic imperialism.

20. The Mughal rulers of India
    a. brought Islamic law and religion to India.
    b. ended Islamic influence in India.
    c. closed India to the "factory-fort" system.
    d. failed to develop an efficient bureaucracy.

Major Political Ideas

The Persian state under the Safavids was a theocratic state. What does this mean? Where did power reside, and what was its source?

Issues for Essays and Discussion

1. The Ottoman Empire was one of the world's great empires. Why did it emerge, and what was the source and extent of its power? Were its accomplishments purely military, as many westerners have claimed? Why did it become the so-called "sick man of Europe"?

2. What impact did the Mughals have on Indian society? It is said that under Akbar the Mughal state of India took definite form. What was this form? What happened to Indian society following Akbar's death?

3. Discuss the Portuguese, Dutch, British, and French entry into India. What was their purpose, and how were their goals carried out? Was this entry strictly an economic venture, or was it political as well? Did European intervention contribute to India becoming a "wounded" civilization, or was it beneficial to Indian society?

Interpretation of Visual Sources

Study the photograph "Taj Mahal at Agra" on page 759 of the textbook. What is the purpose of this building? In what ways does it signify the influence of the Mughal dynasty?

Geography

On Outline Map 23.1 provided, and using Map 23.1 in the textbook as your guide, indicate the farthest extent of the Ottoman Empire. Was it a Middle Eastern, European, or African empire? Mark the location of Turkish Hungary, Buda and Pest, Istanbul (Constantinople), Mecca, Cyprus, Mesopotamia, Baghdad, Syria, Egypt, Tripoli, Tunis. (Remember that duplicate maps for class use are at the back of this book.)

Outline Map 23.1

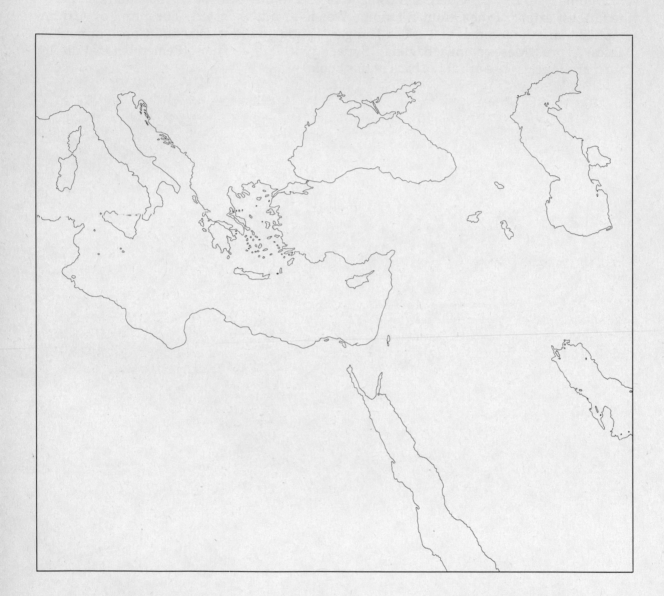

Understanding History Through the Arts

1. What were the architectual and artistic achievements of the reign of Suleiman the Magnificent? Did the cultural explosion of his reign affect the lives of common men and women? Begin your study with G. Goodwin, *A History of Ottoman Architecture* (1971), and A. Stratton, *Sinan* (1972).

2. Persian art, with its detailed ornamentation, use of color, floral decoration, balanced patterns, landscape imagery, and intricate craftsmanship, is extremely beautiful. What are some of the best examples of this art? Does it mirror Persian society? Begin your study with R. W. Ferrier, ed., *The Arts of Persia* (1989).

3. Travel guides often provide helpful information for the historian. Two guides of interest are G. Tillotson, *Mughal India** (1990), and J. Freely, *Classical Turkey** (1990).

Problems for Further Investigation

Do individuals change the course of history, or are their actions the result of uncontrolled economic or political events? Consider this great historical problem by looking into the lives of three interesting and important people discussed in this chapter, Clive, Akbar, and Suleiman I. Begin your investigation with M. Edward, *Clive, The Heaven-Born General* (1977); L. Binyon, *Akbar* (1932); and H. Lamb, *Suleiman the Magnificent—Sultan of the East* (1951).

*Available in paperback.

CHAPTER 24
China and Japan, ca 1400–1800

Chapter Questions

After reading and studying this chapter, you should be able to answer the following questions:

What features characterized the governments of the Ming and Ch'ing dynasties in China and the Tokugawa Shogunate in Japan? How were the Chinese and Japanese societies affected by agricultural and commercial developments? How did Chinese thinkers interpret the shift from the Ming to the Ch'ing dynasties? What were the Chinese and Japanese attitudes toward Western missionary efforts?

Chapter Summary

In China the Ming Dynasty replaced Mongol rule. Under the Ming, China experienced a remarkable upsurge in agricultural and commercial development. An important agricultural revolution took place between 1370 and 1398, which included not only agricultural innovations and new crops but land reclamation, reforestation, and repopulation of devastated regions. This revolution encouraged advancements in culture and economics as well. The state became highly centralized and rested on rule by bureaucracy (often to the dismay of the emperors), which, in the end, fell to corruption and greed. In the seventeenth century, the extravagances of Yung Lo and his court, his neglect of the merchant classes, high taxes, and a weakened military provoked riots and foreign intervention. The invading Manchus became the new Ch'ing Dynasty. The Ch'ing Dynasty brought a long period of peace, prosperity, and population expansion. The Ch'ing Empire supported a population of 380 million in 1812, compared to only 193 million in all of Europe in 1800. China also enjoyed a favorable balance of trade, which brought to it a large portion of the bullion from Latin American mines. However, by the early nineteenth century China was stagnating under an excessive bureaucracy, graft, an extravagant court, and the opium trade.

At about the same time, Japan was reaping the rewards of two centuries of peace and social order. Steady economic growth and improved agricultural technology had swelled the population. This chapter outlines the important aspects of Japanese feudalism and shows how the great samurai Nobunaga won control of most of Japan and went on to unite the country by means of a central government and a policy of conciliation. Nobunaga was followed by the Tokugawa regime, which inaugurated a long era of peace while it sealed Japan's borders from the outside world. Prosperity led to urbanization and population increase, while the samurai were transformed into urban consumers and bureaucrats.

Much of this chapter is devoted to Chinese and Japanese life. More than anywhere else, the family in China exercised great social control. Marriages were arranged, and education and employment were determined by the family. Life was very much influenced by agriculture, although important new jobs were created in the textile and porcelain industries. Women held an inferior position within China, but Chinese society did not develop the rigid social strata that characterized European society. Christianity's influence was limited, although the Jesuits were important agents in a scientific-mathematical exchange between Europe and China. Ordinary life in Japan is best exemplified by the oppressed peasant, although by 1800 a class of rich peasants existed, and many peasants had turned to manufacture and urban life. The nobility were stripped of much of their power and the samurai lifestyle emerged, as did an important urban-merchant class.

Study Outline

Use this outline to preview the chapter before you read a particular section in your textbook and then as a self-check to test your reading comprehension after you have read the chapter section.

I.   China: From the Ming Dynasty to the mid-Manchu Dynasty (ca 1368–1795)
   A.   Hung Wu, founder of the Ming Dynasty, pushed the Mongols out of China.
   B.   The Ming agricultural and commercial revolutions
      1.   The Ming agricultural revolution was in part a recovery from the economic chaos of Mongol rule.
         a.   Rice supplied almost the total nourishment of the people of central and south China; the main staple in north China was wheat.
         b.   Improvements in rice production, such as Champa rice, led to two yearly harvests.
         c.   Irrigation, fish farming, and new crops also resulted in an increased food supply.
         d.   Land reclamation, repopulation, and reforestation led to agricultural growth as well.
      2.   Agricultural development had social consequences.
         a.   A population boom began in about 1550, although per capita income actually decreased.

b. Towns and small cities multiplied, but urbanization meant the growth of small towns and market centers rather than the development of large cities.

C. The government of Hung Wu
1. Hung Wu instituted a number of reforms.
   a. He centralized his rule by confiscating land and giving it to the peasants.
   b. He relied on land taxes and carried out a land survey and population census.
   c. All members of the three hereditary classes—peasants, artisans, and soldiers—had to provide service to the state.
   d. The emperor was absolute, and all power was dispersed from his court.
   e. Later, Hung Wu divided China into principalities run by his sons.
   f. The civil service was reformed by the creation of an arduous examination system.
   g. After 1426 the emperor's eunuchs came to hold much state power.
2. In foreign affairs Hung Wu sought to strengthen China.
   a. He strengthened and extended the Great Wall.
   b. He demanded that foreign traders pay him tribute, but later emperors proved unable to restrict foreign trade.

D. Maritime expansion
1. The Ming era is also marked by important naval accomplishments under Yung Lo between 1405 and 1433.
2. They resulted in new trade, new tribute, navigational publications, and Chinese emigration into Asia and India.

E. Decline of the Ming Dynasty
1. After Hung Wu died, his son, Yung Lo, won a struggle for the throne, but the extravagances of his court hurt China's economy.
   a. Yung Lo moved the capital north to Peking and continued his father's policies.
   b. This, along with Yung Lo's extravagance, displeased the new gentry and mercantile groups.
   c. The emperor and his court lived in splendor in the Forbidden City, surrounded by the Imperial City.
2. Yung Lo's successors had difficulties in foreign affairs.
   a. They could not hold back the Mongol invaders, and in 1449 the emperor was captured.
   b. The Chinese invasion of Vietnam led to a Vietnamese liberation movement.
   c. Japan accelerated its raids on the China coast.
   d. The army was weak because taxes were not paid by the people.
3. Nevertheless, Chinese trade with the West resulted in prosperity, as China exchanged her goods for the Europeans' silver.
   a. Silver became the medium of exchange.
   b. Foreign trade flourished.
   c. Large silk- and cotton-weaving and papermaking industries grew up.

d. By the mid-sixteenth century, China was developing into an urban mercantile society as investment switched from land to crafts and industry.

e. Nonetheless, China did not undergo an industrial revolution like the West, probably because of its financial and political problems, external threats, and its value system.

4. By 1600 China faced grave political and economic problems.

a. The treasury was drained by war, royal extravagance, and enormous allowances for the extended imperial family.

b. The military was weak and corrupt.

c. New taxes provoked riots, and the eunuchs fomented terrorism and factionalism.

d. The civil bureaucracy was faction-ridden and greedy, and it blocked imperial reform.

5. According to Confucian theory, the Mings forfeited the Mandate of Heaven because their own greed and self-interest were passed on to their officials, which invited unrest and eventual downfall.

6. Under Nurhachi, the Manchus conquered Ming China.

F. Manchu rule

1. The Manchus established the Ch'ing Dynasty in 1644.

a. They purged the civil service of factions and eunuchs.

b. Eighteenth-century China covered much of Asia, including Manchuria, Mongolia, Tibet, and Sinkiang, and received tribute from other states such as Burma, Laos, and Korea.

2. Manchu rule rested on traditional Chinese methods.

a. The emperor was supreme and ruled by the Mandate of Heaven.

b. The central bureaucracy (civil service) continued to manage the state, but the Manchus kept themselves separate and above the Chinese.

c. Ming and Manchu agricultural improvements continued to encourage population explosion, and by 1800 population growth outpaced agricultural output.

d. Under Emperor K'ang-hsi, the emperorship was revitalized, literary and artistic work flourished, domestic revolt was crushed, and the Mongolian threat eliminated.

e. The reign of Ch'ien-lung was marked by the cultivation of new crops and the expansion of Chinese rule into central Asia, but corruption led to revolts.

G. The life of the people

1. The family exercised great social influence.

a. The family directed education of children, marriage, religious life, and welfare services.

b. Although poor families were "nuclear," middle- and upper-class families were "extended"; power in both rested with the father.

c. Marriages were arranged between parents; the bride became a part of the husband's family and was expected to bear sons.

         d. Divorce was open only to men, and men held a higher position in society than women; female babies were unwanted.

         e. Young brides came under the control of their mothers-in-law, who were often cruel and severe.

         f. Age was respected.

         g. Wealthy women had little to do, whereas poor women worked in the fields.

    2. The educational system during the Ming and Ch'ing periods had both virtues and weaknesses.

         a. The village schools for boys stressed preparation for civil service examinations, but the curriculum was limited.

         b. Still, they produced a highly literate society.

         c. Girls received training that prepared them to be wives and mothers.

    3. Unlike Europe, China did not have rigid social strata based on hereditary rights.

         a. Upward mobility was possible for intelligent children.

         b. Scholars held the highest rank in the social order.

    4. The Chinese had a variety of forms of relaxation and recreation.

         a. Gambling at cards, frequenting teahouses, drinking alcohol, and patronizing theaters were common entertainments.

         b. Athletics and racing were looked down on.

II. Japan (ca 1400–1800)

  A. During the Ashikaga Shogunate (fourteenth to sixteenth centuries), Japan was thrust into civil war among the daimyos, or lords; historians describe this era as a period of feudalism.

  B. Feudalism in Japan

    1. Feudalism in Japan evolved from a combination of the native warrior tradition and Chinese Confucian ethics.

    2. The two main elements of Japanese feudalism appeared between the eighth and twelfth centuries.

         a. The shoen, or land, which tended to be widely scattered, and its shiki, or rights to the income or rice produced by the land

         b. The military warrior clique

         c. By 1500 the samurai warriors had no land; they lived according to Bushido, a code that stressed honor, loyalty, and hardship.

    3. The number of shoen decreased in the sixteenth century, while the daimyos consolidated their territories and primogeniture became common.

    4. The nature of warfare changed as the cannon and musket made the mounted samurai obsolete.

  C. Nobunaga and national unification

    1. The samurai Nobunaga slowly extended his power and emerged as ruler of central Japan by 1568.

         a. 1568–1600 is the period of "national unification," during which Nobunaga subdued most of Japan by force.

         b. To do so, he had to destroy Japan's most powerful Buddhist monastery.

   c. He augmented his conquests with able rule and a policy of reconciliation.

   d. Trusted daimyos were favored, castles were built, and his reforms encouraged economic growth.

  2. Nobunaga was succeeded by his general, Hideyoshi.

   a. Hideyoshi brought the province of Mori and the island of Kyushu under his domination.

   b. He reduced the threat of the daimyos.

   c. He extended his control over agriculture and peasants through a great land survey and through taxes.

 D. The Tokugawa regime

  1. Ieyasu completed the work begun by Nobunaga and Hideyoshi.

   a. He left the emperor rich and sovereign in theory, but the real power resided in his Tokugawa Shogunate.

   b. The daimyos became his hostages at his capital at Edo.

   c. He employed strategies similar to those used by Louis XIV and William the Conqueror in limiting the power of the nobility.

   d. Taxes were imposed on villages, not individuals.

   e. Class mobility ended, and class stratification was encouraged.

  2. Sakoku, or the closed country policy, was instituted by Ieyasu's descendants.

   a. To maintain stability and peace, the Japanese were not allowed to leave.

   b. Foreigners were excluded.

 E. The life of the people

  1. Japanese life changed profoundly in the seventeenth and eighteenth centuries.

   a. Stripped of power, the nobility passed their lives in the pursuit of pleasure.

   b. The warrior class was gradually ruined by overindulgence in drink, sex, and costly living.

   c. Women were subordinate to men, marriage was arranged, and women of the samurai class were limited to home management.

   d. Middle-class women began to work in the silk industry, in entertainment, and elsewhere; poor parents sold their daughters—to become geishas.

   e. For men, life became divided into leisure and amusement, and family and business.

   f. The kabuki theater, with its crude and bawdy skits, was a favorite pastime of the nobility.

   g. Homosexuality, long accepted in Japan, was practiced by the samurai warrior class.

  2. Peasants were sometimes severely oppressed and led miserable lives.

   a. Peasant village life was highly regulated by the state.

   b. In the eighteenth century, 50 percent of the peasant rice crop was paid in taxes.

   c. Low rice prices and overpopulation led to frequent peasant revolts, such as in Iwaki in 1739.

   d. Famines in the 1780s and 1830s made the peasants' lot worse.

  3. The peasant society was not homogeneous.

   a. By the early 1800s, a large class of wealthy and educated peasants existed.

b. A shortage of farm labor reflected the fact that many peasants worked in manufacturing.
4. In theory the urban merchant class occupied the bottom rung of the social ladder.
   a. Merchants had no political power, but they accumulated great wealth.
   b. The growing cities offered social mobility to the poor peasants.
   c. Population growth, the samurai lifestyle, and urbanization encouraged the production of consumer goods and the formation of guilds and banks.

Review Questions

Check your understanding of this chapter by answering the following questions.

1. Describe the various factors that gave rise to the Ming agricultural revolution. What were the social consequences of this revolution?

2. How did Hung Wu strengthen and reform China? Compare and contrast the new and old Chinese methods of governing.

3. Why did the Ming Dynasty decline after Hung Wu's death? In what ways did the nation's economy reflect both decay and prosperity?

4. Describe the Forbidden City. In what ways does it symbolize China after Hung Wu's death?

5. What changes did the Manchus bring to China, and how successful were they in making China powerful?

6. What were marriage customs and family life, education, social status, and entertainment like during the Ming and Ch'ing periods?

7. What caused the civil war in Japan during the Ashikaga Shogunate, and by what term is this period known?

8. How did feudalism evolve in Japan? What two distinctive elements appeared between the eighth and twelfth centuries?

9. Who unified Japan, and how did he encourage economic growth? Why did he have to destroy Japan's most powerful Buddhist monastery?

10. Compare the regime of Ieyasu and his Tokugawa Shogunate with those of his European counterparts Louis XIV and William the Conqueror. What was the fate of Christianity during this period and why?

11. Why did Japanese life change profoundly during the seventeenth and eighteenth centuries? Describe the somewhat contradictory position of the urban merchant class.

Study-Review Exercises

Define the following key concepts and terms.

Ming agricultural revolution

Mandate of Heaven

china manufacture

Chinese civil service examinations

Chinese family

samurai

harakiri

kabuki

sakoku policy

Japan's period of "national unification"

Identify and explain the significance of the following people and terms.

Forbidden City

Ming Dynasty

Ch'ing Dynasty

Emperor Hung Wu

Emperor K'ang-hsi

Nobunaga

daimyos

shoen

Hideyoshi

Tokugawa Shogunate

Test your understanding of the chapter by providing the correct answers.

1. The peasant founder of China's Ming Dynasty. _____

2. Under the later Ming rulers, such as Yung Lo, the costs of the imperial court *increased/decreased*, while the balance of trade between China and Europe grew *more/less* favorable.

3. Compared to Europe at the time, China during the Ming and Ch'ing periods *was/was not* a society of rigid social strata.

4. Homosexuality *was/was not* accepted in Japan.

5. The eighteenth century was a period of economic and demographic *growth/decay* in both Japan and China.

Multiple-Choice Questions

1. During the Ming era in China, there was a proliferation of
   a. towns.
   b. small cities.
   c. large cities.
   d. both a and b.

2. In Ming times the entire Chinese population was divided into three categories according to
   a. place of residence.
   b. occupation.
   c. religion.
   d. wealth.

3. Ming China regarded foreigners as
   a. pirates.
   b. curiosities.
   c. barbarians.
   d. enemies.

4. The flow of silver into China caused a(n)
   a. abandonment of the gold standard.
   b. prospering of the wealthy merchant class.
   c. decline in the value of paper money.
   d. sharp drop in the price of silver.

5. Emperor Wan-Li was unable to accomplish his ends because
   a. bureaucracy and precedent stood in his way.
   b. war interrupted his reforms.
   c. he died very young.
   d. the nobility opposed him.

6. Under the Tokugawa government, Japan was ruled by the
   a. emperor.
   b. shogun.
   c. Tokugawa regent.
   d. council of samurai.

7. Kabuki theater usually depicted
   a. crude love and romance.
   b. historical events.
   c. scenes from court life.
   d. folk tales.

8. In more recent times, female roles in the kabuki theater were played by
   a. boys.
   b. prostitutes.
   c. eunuchs.
   d. divorcees.

9. It may be generally said that during the Tokugawa era in Japan
   a. the country enjoyed peace and development.
   b. the country suffered continuous civil strife.
   c. people lost their faith in the monarchy.
   d. the standard of living declined.

10. The shogun Ieyasu kept effective control over the feudal lords by
    a. executing their prominent leaders.
    b. forcing them to spend alternate years in the capital.
    c. imposing heavy taxes.
    d. requiring their personal oath of loyalty.

11. Japan expelled Christian missionaries because they
    a. were spies for European nations.
    b. encouraged Japanese Christians to participate in feudal revolts.
    c. preached the overthrow of the shogun.
    d. interfered with Japan's traditional culture.

12. The founder of the Ming Dynasty and leader of the Red Turbans was
    a. Hung Wu.
    b. Wan-Li.
    c. Wu Ti.
    d. Wang Chih.

13. The Ming agricultural and commercial revolutions were closely linked with
    a. an expansion of foreign trade.
    b. dramatic improvements in rice production.
    c. deurbanization.
    d. new methods of government spending.

14. "Fish farming" refers to
    a. big net fishing off the Chinese coast.
    b. fish hatching in government aquariums.
    c. farming for half the year and fishing the other half.
    d. stocking fish in the rice paddies.

15. Hung Wu moved the Chinese capital to
    a. Peking.
    b. Nanking.
    c. Chungking.
    d. Shanghai.

16. Hung Wu's most enduring reform was his
    a. reorganization of the state ministry.
    b. implementation of a yearly census.
    c. reinstatement of civil service examinations.
    d. hereditary categories.

17. The naval expeditions of Yung Lo during the Ming period reached as far as
    a. the east coast of India.
    b. the east coast of Africa.
    c. the west coast of India.
    d. southeast Asia.

18. Yung Lo moved the capital to
    a. Peking.
    b. Nanking.
    c. Hong Kong.
    d. Shanghai.

19. The Forbidden City was built by
    a. Hung Wu.
    b. Yung Lo.
    c. Wan-Li.
    d. Liu Chin.

20. During the later Ming Dynasty
    a. China avoided all foreign trade.
    b. China achieved peace with its northern invaders.
    c. costs of the imperial court decreased.
    d. China became involved in the world economy.

21. The Ch'ing Dynasty was established by the
    a. Manchus.
    b. Mongols.
    c. Japanese.
    d. Vietnamese.

22. Early on, the Ch'ing gained the support of
    a. peasants.
    b. intellectuals.
    c. eunuchs.
    d. landowners.

23. The zenith of the Ch'ing Dynasty was achieved during the reign of
    a. K'ang-hsi.
    b. Wan-Li.
    c. Wang Chih.
    d. Liu Chin.

24. The code by which the samurai lived was called
    a. harakiri.
    b. seppuku.
    c. Bushido.
    d. shoen.

25. The leader who began the Japanese period of national unification was
    a. Ieyasu.
    b. Tokugawa.
    c. Nobunaga.
    d. Ashikaga.

26. In Tokugawa Japan the commercial class
    a. was outlawed.
    b. was considered lowly.
    c. was highly esteemed.
    d. rose to great power.

27. To maintain dynastic stability and internal peace, the Japanese imposed measures called sakoku, which
    a. introduced the concept of primogeniture.
    b. limited the power of the samurai.
    c. was a closed-country policy.
    d. outlawed Buddhism.

Major Political Ideas

What role has the civil service played in Chinese history? Was it an arm of despotism? How much power did it exercise? What did the Manchus do to reform the system?

Issues for Essays and Discussion

1. How were Chinese and Japanese societies affected by agricultural developments? What were the main features of the Chinese economic recovery of the late fourteenth century?

2. Describe the life of the people in both China and Japan. What are the major differences and the major similarities? Which of the two countries had the most advanced standard of living?

3. Why did China's political and economic systems begin to deteriorate in the late eighteenth and early nineteenth centuries? How does this compare to events and developments in Japan?

Interpretation of Visual Sources

Study the illustration "Chinese Scholars" on page 781 of the textbook. What are these people doing? How do these examinations appear to have been administered? Do women appear to have participated? Why was this such an important activity?

Geography

Using Outline Map 24.1 provided, mark the boundaries of the Ch'ing Empire. What additional areas came under annexation in the eighteenth century? Indicate the location of the following: Sinkiang, Tibet, Shensi, Manchuria, Mongolia, Korea, Vietnam, Laos, Annam, Nepal, the Yellow and Yangtze rivers, and the Great Wall. (Remember that duplicate maps for class use are at the back of this book.)

Outline Map 24.1

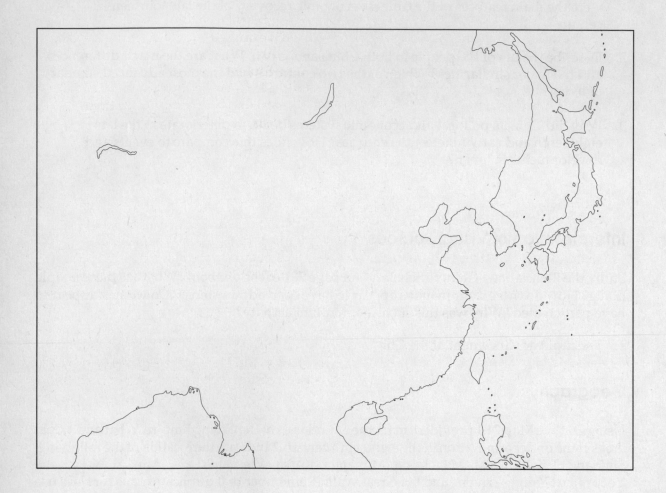

Understanding History Through the Arts

Trade between China and the West is currently attracting much interest. But the movement of Chinese goods—including paintings, china, and the decorative arts—goes back many centuries. C. L. Crossman's *The China Trade** (1972) looks at the export of furniture and other objects from China, and M. Tregear's *Chinese Art** (1985) examines Chinese art since 5000 B.C. Japan's art history is told in J. Stanley-Baker, *Japanese Art** (1984). The student interested in architecture and engineering will want to study Liang Ssu'eng, *A Pictorial History of Chinese Architecture,* ed. W. Fairbank (1984). Japan experienced a long tradition of women as artists—as painters, printmakers, and in other arts. For a discussion of this subject and examples of individual work, see Patricia Fister, *Japanese Women Artists, 1600–1900* (1988).

Problems for Further Investigation

1. How did Japanese feudalism compare with feudalism in the West? Japanese feudalism shared some similarities with its Western counterpart, and Japan's feudal values, such as loyalty and discipline, played a crucial role in the nation's modernization in the nineteenth century. For further information, see G. B. Sansom, *Japan: A Short Cultural History* (1962), and E. Reischauer, *Japan: The Story of a Nation* (1981).

2. The rapid advancement of the Chinese economy around the tenth century led to important developments in Chinese art. What, if any, influence did those developments have on Chinese art of later periods? For further investigation see M. Sullivan, *The Arts of China* (1979).

*Available in paperback.

PRIMARY SOURCES

Japan and China in the Early Seventeenth Century: Reaction to the West

The following two readings relate to Chinese and Japanese reactions to the West in the early seventeenth century. The first reading is from the journal of the Jesuit Christian scholar-missionary Matteo Ricci (refer to your textbook page 578). Here he records the reaction of the Confucian Magistrates to the presence of the Western visitors, the Jesuits. The second reading is an edict of the Shogun (in 1635) which limited contact between Japanese and foreigners.

In the first reading, what do the Jesuits appear to be doing in China at this time? What were the complaints of the Confucian leaders (the Magistrates) against the Jesuits and why did these critics attach the issue of Jesuit activity to the issue of public order?

In the Shogun's Edict of 1635, what do you detect to be the reasons the Japanese have decided to limit foreign contacts? Is the issue one of economics or culture? or otherwise? What is the punishment for Japanese who go abroad? What appears to be the major trade dealings in Japanese ports and what limits have been placed on such dealings?

Ricci's Account of the Conflict Between Confucian and Christian Leaders*

During 1606 and the year following, the progress of Christianity in Nancian was in no wise retarded. . . . The number of [converts increased] by more than two hundred, all of whom manifested an extraordinary piety in their religious devotions. As a result, the reputation of the Christian religion became known throughout the length and breath of this metropolitan city. . . .

Through the efforts of Father Emanuele Dias another and a larger house was purchased, in August of 1607, at a price of a thousand gold pieces. This change was necessary, because the house he had was too small for his needs and was situated in a flood area. Just as the community was about to change from one house to the other, a sudden uprising broke out against them. . . .

*Source: From *China in the Sixteenth Century: The Journals of Matthew Ricci: 1583–1610*, translated by Louis J. Gallagher, S. J. Copyright 1953 by Louis J. Gallagher, S. J. Reprinted by permission of Random House, Inc.

At the beginning of each month, the Magistrates hold a public assembly . . . in the temple of their great Philosopher [Confucius]. When the rites of the new-moon were completed in the temple, and these are civil rather than religious rites, one of those present took advantage of the occasion to speak on behalf of the others, and to address the highest Magistrate present. . . . "We wish to warn you," he said, "that there are certain foreign priests in this royal city, who are preaching a law, hitherto unheard of in this kingdom, and who are holding large gatherings of people in their house." Having said this, he referred them to their local Magistrate, . . . and he in turn ordered the plaintiffs to present their case in writing, assuring them that he would support it with all his authority, in an effort to have the foreign priests expelled. The complaint was written out that same say and signed with twenty-seven signatures. . . . The content of the document was somewhat as follows.

"Matthew Ricci, Giovanni Soerio, Emanuele Dias, and certain other foreigners from western kingdoms, men who are guilty of high treason against the throne, are scattered amongst us, in five different provinces. They are continually communicating with each other and are here and there practicing brigandage on the rivers, collecting money, and then distributing it to the people, in order to curry favor with the multitudes. They are frequently visited by the Magistrates, by the high nobility and by the Military Prefects, with whom they have entered into a secret pact, binding unto death.

"These men teach that we should pay no respect to the images of our ancestors, a doctrine which is destined to extinguish the love of future generations for their forebears. Some of them break up the idols, leaving the temples empty and the gods to be pitied, without any patronage. In the beginning they lived in small houses, but by this time they have bought up large and magnificent residences. The doctrine they teach is something infernal. It attracts the ignorant into its fraudulent meshes, and great crowds of this class are continually assembled at their houses. Their doctrine gets beyond the city walls and spreads itself through the neighboring towns and villages and into the open country, and the people become so wrapt up in its falsity, that students are not following their courses, laborers are neglecting their work, farmers are not cultivating their acres, and even the women have no interest in their housework. The whole city has become disturbed, and, whereas in the beginning there were only a hundred or so professing their faith, now there are more than twenty thousand. These priests distribute pictures of some Tartar or Saracen [the reference is to Jesus Christ], who they say is God, who came down from heaven to redeem and to instruct all of humanity, and who alone, according to their doctrine, can give wealth and happiness; a doctrine by which the simple people are very easily deceived. These men are an abomination on the face of the earth, and there is just ground for fear that once they have erected their own temples, they will start a rebellion. . . . Wherefore, moved by their interest in the maintenance of the public good, in the conservation of the realm, and in the preservation, whole and entire, of their ancient laws, the petitioners are presenting this complaint and demanding, in the name of the entire province, that a rescript of it be forwarded to the King, asking that these foreigners be sentenced to death, or banished from the realm, to some deserted island in the sea." . . .

Each of the Magistrates to whom the indictment was presented asserted that the spread of Christianity should be prohibited, and that the foreign priests should be expelled from the city, if the Mayor saw fit, after hearing the case, and notifying the foreigners. . . . But the Fathers [the Jesuits], themselves, were not too greatly disturbed, placing their confidence in Divine Providence, which had always been present to assist them on other such dangerous occasions. . . .

A few days later, the court decision was pronounced and written out . . . [and] was then posted at the city gates as a public edict. The following is a summary of their declaration. Having examined the cause of Father Emanuele and his companions, it was found that these men had come here from the West because they had heard so much about the fame of the great Chinese Empire, and that they had already been living in the realm for some years, without any display of ill-will. Father Emanuele should be permitted to practice his own religion, but it was not considered to be the right thing for the common people, who are attracted by novelties, to adore the God of Heaven. For them to go over to the religion of foreigners would indeed be most unbecoming. . . . It would therefore seem to be . . . [in] . . . the best interests of the Kingdom, to . . . [warn] . . . everyone in a public edict not to abandon the sacrifices of their ancient religion by accepting the cult of foreigners. Such a movement might, indeed, result in calling together certain gatherings, detrimental to the public welfare, and harmful also to the foreigner, himself. Wherefore, the Governor of this district, by order of the high Magistrates, admonishes the said Father Emanuele to refrain from perverting the people, by inducing them to accept a foreign religion. The man who sold him the larger house is to restore his money and Emanuele is to buy a smaller place, sufficient for his needs, and to live there peaceably, as he has done, up to the present. Emanuele, himself, has agreed to these terms and the Military Prefects of the district have been ordered to make a search of the houses there and to confiscate the pictures of the God they speak of, wherever they find them. It is not permitted for any of the native people to go over to the religion of the foreigners, nor is it permitted to gather together for prayer meetings. Whoever does contrary to these prescriptions will be severely punished, and if the Military Prefects are remiss in enforcing them, they will be held to be guilty of the same crimes. To his part of the edict, the Director of the Schools added, that the common people were forbidden to accept the law of foreigners, and that a sign should be posted above the door of the Father's residence, notifying the public that these men were forbidden to have frequent contact with the people.

The Shogun's Edict of 1635*

1. Japanese ships are strictly forbidden to leave for foreign countries.

2. No Japanese is permitted to go abroad. If there is anyone who attempts to do so secretly, he must be executed. The ship so involved must be impounded and its owner arrested, and the matter must be reported to the higher authority.

3. If any Japanese returns from overseas after residing there, he must be put to death.

4. If there is any place where the teachings of padres [Catholic missionaries] is practiced, the two of you must order a thorough investigation.

5. Any informer revealing the whereabouts of the followers of padres must be rewarded accordingly. If anyone reveals the whereabouts of a high ranking padre, he must be

*Source: Ryusaku Tsunoda, William Theodore de Bary, Donald Keene, and others, eds. and trs., Sources of Japanese Tradition. Copyright © 1927 and 1958 Columbia University Press. Used by permission.

given one hundred pieces of silver. For those of lower ranks, depending on the deed, the reward must be set accordingly.

6. If a foreign ship has an objection (to the measures adopted) and it becomes necessary to report the matter to Edo, you may ask the Ōmura domain to provide ships to guard the foreign ship. . . .

7. If there are any Southern Barbarians [Westerners] who propagate the teachings of padres, or otherwise commit crimes, they may be incarcerated in the prison. . . .

8. All incoming ships must be carefully searched for the followers of padres.

9. No single trading city shall be permitted to purchase all the merchandise brought by foreign ships.

10. Samurai are not permitted to purchase any goods originating from foreign ships directly from Chinese merchants in Nagasaki.

11. After a list of merchandise brought by foreign ships is sent to Edo, as before you may order that commercial dealings may take place without waiting for a reply from Edo.

12. After settling the price, all white yarns [silk] brought by foreign ships shall be allocated to the five trading cities [Kyoto, Edo, Osaka, Sakai, and Nagasaki] and other quarters as stipulated.

13. After settling the price of white yarns, other merchandise (brought by foreign ships) may be traded freely between the (licensed) dealers. However, in view of the fact that Chinese ships are small and cannot bring large consignments, you may issue orders of sale at your discretion. Additionally, payment for goods purchased must be made within twenty days after the price is set.

14. The date of departure homeward of foreign ships shall not be later than the twentieth day of the ninth month. Any ships arriving in Japan later than usual shall depart within fifty days of their arrival. As to the departure of Chinese ships, you may use your discretion to order their departure after the departure of the Portuguese *galeota* [ship].

15. The goods brought by foreign ships which remained unsold may not be deposited or accepted for deposit.

16. The arrival in Nagasaki of representatives of the five trading cities shall not be later than the fifth day of the seventh month. Anyone arriving later than that date shall lose the quota assigned to his city.

17. Ships arriving in [the island of] Hirado must sell their raw silk at the price set in Nagasaki, and are not permitted to engage in business transactions until after the price is established in Nagasaki.

You are hereby required to act in accordance with the provisions set above. It is so ordered.

CHAPTER 25
The Revolution in Western Politics, 1775–1815

Chapter Questions

After reading and studying this chapter, you should be able to answer the following questions:

What were the causes of the political revolutions between 1775 and 1815 in America and France? What were the ideas and objectives of the revolutionaries in America and France? Who won and who lost in these revolutions?

Chapter Summary

The French and American revolutions were the most important political events of the eighteenth century. They were also a dramatic conclusion to the Enlightenment, and both revolutions, taken together, form a major turning point in human history. This chapter explains what these great revolutions were all about.

The chapter begins by describing classical liberalism, the fundamental ideology of the revolution in politics. Liberalism, which had deep roots, called for freedom and equality at a time when monarchs and aristocrats took their great privileges for granted. The immediate cause of the American Revolution, the British effort to solve the problem of war debts, was turned into a political struggle by the American colonists, who already had achieved considerable economic and personal freedom. The American Revolution stimulated reform efforts throughout Europe.

It was in France that the ideas of the Enlightenment and liberalism were put to their fullest test. The bankruptcy of the state gave the French aristocracy the chance to grab power from a weak king. This move backfired, however, because the middle class grabbed even harder. It is significant that the revolutionary desires of the middle class depended on the firm support and violent action of aroused peasants and poor urban workers. It was this action of the common people that gave the revolution its driving force.

In the first two years of the French Revolution, the middle class, with its allies from the peasantry and urban poor, achieved unprecedented reforms. The outbreak of an all-European war against France in 1792 then resulted in a reign of terror and a dictatorship by radical moralists, of whom Robespierre was the greatest. By 1795, this radical patriotism wore itself out. The revolutionary momentum slowed, and the Revolution deteriorated into a military dictatorship under the opportunist Napoleon. Yet, until 1815 the history of France was that of war, and that war spread liberalism to the rest of Europe. French conquests also stimulated nationalism. The world of politics was turned upside down.

Study Outline

Use this outline to preview the chapter before you read a particular section in your textbook and then as a self-check to test your reading comprehension after you have read the chapter section.

I. Liberty and equality
  A. In the eighteenth century, liberty meant human rights and freedoms and the sovereignty of the people.
  B. Equality meant equal rights and equality of opportunity.
  C. The roots of liberalism
    1. The Judeo-Christian tradition of individualism, reinforced by the Reformation, supported liberalism.
    2. Liberalism's modern roots are found in the Enlightenment concern for freedom and legal equality, as best expressed by Locke and Montesquieu.
    3. Liberalism was attractive to both the aristocracy and the middle class, but it lacked the support of the masses.

II. The American Revolution (1775–1789)
  A. Some argue that the American Revolution was not a revolution at all but merely a war for independence.
  B. The origins of the Revolution
    1. The British wanted the Americans to pay their share of imperial expenses.
      a. Americans paid very low taxes.
      b. Parliament passed the Stamp Act (1765) to raise revenue.
      c. Vigorous protest from the colonies forced its repeal (1766).
    2. Although no less represented than Englishmen themselves, many Americans believed they had the right to make their own laws.
      a. Americans had long exercised a great deal of independence.
      b. Their greater political equality was matched by greater social and economic equality—there was no hereditary noble or serf class.
    3. The issue of taxation and representation ultimately led to the outbreak of fighting.

C. The independence movement was encouraged by several factors.
1. The British refused to compromise, thus losing the support of many colonists.
2. The radical ideas of Thomas Paine, expressed in the best-selling *Common Sense*, greatly influenced public opinion in favor of independence.
3. The Declaration of Independence, written by Thomas Jefferson and passed by the Second Continental Congress (1776), further increased the desire of the colonists for independence.
4. Although many Americans remained loyal to Britain, the independence movement had wide-based support from all sections of society.
5. European aid, especially from the French government and from French volunteers, contributed greatly to the American victory in 1783.
D. Framing the Constitution and the Bill of Rights
1. The federal, or central, government was given important powers—the right to tax, the means to enforce its laws, and the regulation of trade—but the states had important powers too.
2. The executive, legislative, and judicial branches of the government were designed to balance one another.
3. The Anti-Federalists feared that the central government had too much power; to placate them, the Federalists wrote the Bill of Rights, which spells out the rights of the individual.
   a. Liberty did not, however, necessarily mean democracy.
   b. Equality meant equality before the law, not equality of political participation or economic well-being.
E. The American Revolution reinforced the Enlightenment idea that a better world was possible, and Europeans watched the new country with fascination.

III. The French Revolution (1789–1791)
A. The influence of the American Revolution
1. Many French soldiers, such as Lafayette, served in America and were impressed by the ideals of the Revolution.
2. The American Revolution influenced the French Revolution, but the latter was more violent and more influential; it opened the era of modern politics.
B. The breakdown of the old order
1. By the 1780s, the government was nearly bankrupt.
2. The French banking system could not cope with the fiscal problems, leaving the monarchy with no choice but to increase taxes.
C. Legal orders and social realities: the three estates
1. The first estate, the clergy, had many privileges and much wealth, and it levied an oppressive tax (the tithe) on landowners.
2. The second estate, the nobility, also had great privileges, wealth, and power, and it taxed the peasantry for its own profit.
3. The third estate, the commoners, was a mixture of a few rich members of the middle class, urban workers, and the mass of peasants.

4. Revisionist historians challenge the traditional interpretation of the origins of the French Revolution.
    a. They argue that the bourgeoisie was not locked in conflict with the nobility, that both groups were highly fragmented.
    b. The nobility remained fluid and relatively open.
    c. Key sections of the nobility were liberal.
    d. The nobility and the bourgeoisie were not economic rivals.
5. Nevertheless, the old interpretation, that a new social order was challenging the old, is still convincing and valid.

D. The formation of the National Assembly of 1789
1. Louis XVI's plan to tax landed property was opposed by the Assembly of Notables and the Parlement of Paris.
2. Louis then gave in and called for a meeting of the Estates General, the representative body of the three estates.
    a. Two-thirds of the delegates from the clergy were parish priests.
    b. A majority of the noble representatives were conservative, but fully a third were liberals committed to major change.
    c. The third estate representatives were largely lawyers and government officials.
    d. The third estate wanted the three estates to meet together to ensure the passage of fundamental reforms.
    e. According to Sieyès in *What Is the Third Estate?*, the third estate constituted the true strength of the French nation.
3. The dispute over voting in the Estates General led the third estate to break away and form the National Assembly, which pledged, in the Oath of the Tennis Court, not to disband until it had written a new constitution.
4. Louis tried to reassert his monarchial authority and assembled an army.

E. The revolt of the poor and the oppressed
1. Rising bread prices in 1788–89 stirred the people to action.
2. Fearing attack by the king's army, angry Parisians stormed the Bastille on July 14, 1789.
    a. The people took the Bastille, and the king was forced to recall his troops.
    b. This uprising of the masses saved the National Assembly.
    c. All across France peasants began to rise up against their lords.
    d. The Great Fear seized the countryside.
3. The peasant revolt forced the National Assembly to abolish feudal obligations.

F. A limited monarchy established by the bourgeoisie
1. The National Assembly's Declaration of the Rights of Man (1789) proclaimed the rights of all citizens and guaranteed equality before the law and a representative government.
2. Meanwhile, the poor women of Paris marched on Versailles and forced the royal family and the government to move to Paris.
3. The National Assembly established a constitutional monarchy and passed major reforms.
    a. The nobility was abolished as a separate legal order.

       b.   All lawmaking power was placed in the hands of the National Assembly.
       c.   The jumble of provinces was replaced by 83 departments.
       d.   The metric system was introduced.
       e.   Economic freedom was promoted.
   4.   The National Assembly nationalized the property of the church and abolished the monasteries.
   5.   This attack on the church turned many people against the Revolution.

IV. World war and republican France (1791–1799)
   A. Foreign reactions and the beginning of war
      1.   Outside France, liberals and radicals hoped that the revolution would lead to a reordering of society everywhere, but conservatives such as Burke (in *Reflections on the Revolution in France*) predicted it would lead to chaos and tyranny.
      2.   Wollstonecraft challenged Burke (in *A Vindication of the Rights of Woman*), arguing that it was time for women to demand equal rights.
      3.   Fear among European kings and nobility that the revolution would spread resulted in the Declaration of Pillnitz (1791), which threatened the invasion of France by Austria and Prussia.
      4.   In retaliation, the patriotic French deputies, most of them Jacobins, declared war on Austria in 1792.
         a.   France was soon retreating before the armies of the First Coalition.
         b.   A wave of patriotic fervor swept France.
      5.   In 1792 a new National Convention proclaimed France a republic and imprisoned the king.
   B. The "second revolution" and rapid radicalization in France
      1.   The National Convention proclaimed France a republic in 1792.
      2.   However, the convention was split between the Girondists and the Mountain, led by Robespierre and Danton.
      3.   Louis XVI was tried and convicted of treason by the National Convention and guillotined in early 1793.
      4.   French armies continued the "war against tyranny" by declaring war on nearly all of Europe.
      5.   In Paris, the struggle between the Girondists and the Mountain for political power led to the political rise of the laboring poor.
      6.   The sans-culottes—the laboring poor—allied with the Mountain and helped Robespierre and the Committee of Public Safety gain power.
   C. Total war and the Terror (1793–1794)
      1.   Robespierre established a planned economy to wage total war and aid the poor.
         a.   The government fixed prices on key products and instituted rationing.
         b.   Workshops were nationalized to produce goods for the war effort, and raw materials were requisitioned.
      2.   The Reign of Terror was instituted to eliminate opposition to the Revolution, and many people were jailed or executed.

      3. The war became a national mission against evil within and outside of France, and not a class war.
        a. The danger of foreign and internal foes encouraged nationalism.
        b. A huge army of patriots was led by young generals who relied on mass attack.
    D. The Thermidorian reaction and the Directory (1794–1799)
      1. Fear of the Reign of Terror led to the execution of its leader, Robespierre.
      2. The period of the Thermidorian reaction following Robespierre's death was marked by a return to bourgeois liberalism.
        a. Economic controls were abolished.
        b. Riots by the poor were put down.
        c. The Directory, a five-man executive body, was established.
      3. The poor lost their fervor for revolution.
      4. A military dictatorship was established in order to prevent a return to peace and monarchy.

V. The Napoleonic era (1799–1815)
    A. Napoleon's rule of France
      1. Napoleon appealed to many, like Abbé Sieyès, who looked for a strong military leader to end the country's upheaval.
      2. Napoleon was named first consul of the republic in 1799.
      3. He maintained order and worked out important compromises.
        a. His Civil Code of 1804 granted the middle class equality under the law and safeguarded its right to own property.
        b. He confirmed the gains of the peasants.
        c. He centralized the government, strengthened the bureaucracy, and granted amnesty to nobles.
        d. He signed the Concordat of 1801, which guaranteed freedom of worship for Catholics.
      4. Napoleon brought order and stability to France but betrayed the ideals of the Revolution by violating the rights of free speech and press and free elections.
        a. Women had no political rights.
        b. There were harsh penalties for political offenses.
    B. Napoleon's wars and foreign policy
      1. He defeated Austria (1801) and made peace with Britain (1802), the two remaining members of the Second Coalition.
      2. Another war (against the Third Coalition—Austria, Russia, Sweden, and Britain) resulted in British naval dominance at the Battle of Trafalgar (1805).
      3. Napoleon used the fear of a conspiracy to return the Bourbons to power to get himself proclaimed emperor in 1804.
      4. The Third Coalition collapsed at Austerlitz (1805), and Napoleon reorganized the German states into the Confederation of the Rhine.
      5. In 1806, Napoleon defeated the Prussians at Jena and Auerstädt.
        a. In the Treaty of Tilsit (1807), Prussia lost half its population, while Russia accepted Napoleon's reorganization of western and central Europe.
        b. Russia also joined with France in a blockade against British goods.

      6.   Napoleon's Grand Empire in Europe meant French control of continental Europe.
         a.   Napoleon introduced many French laws, abolishing feudal dues and serfdom in the process.
         b.   However, he also levied heavy taxes.
      7.   The beginning of the end for Napoleon came with the Spanish revolt (1808) and the British blockade.
      8.   The French invasion of Russia in 1812 was a disaster for Napoleon.
      9.   Napoleon was defeated by the Fourth Coalition (Austria, Prussia, Russia, and Britain) and abdicated his throne in 1814, only to be defeated again at Waterloo in 1815.
     10.   The Bourbon dynasty was restored in France under Louis XVIII.
  C. The revolutions of France and America were liberal revolutions; the French Revolution was not a failure, for it resulted in a society based on wealth and achievement rather than legal orders and absolutism.

Review Questions

Check your understanding of this chapter by answering the following questions.

1.   The ideas of liberty and equality were the central ideas of classical liberalism. Define these ideas. Are they the same as democracy?

2.   According to Locke, what is the function of government?

3.   Did the Americans or the British have the better argument with regard to the taxation problem?

4.   Why is the Declaration of Independence sometimes called the world's greatest political editorial?

5.   What role did the European powers play in the American victory? Did they gain anything?

6.   What was the major issue in the debate between the Federalists and the Anti-Federalists?

7.   Did the American Revolution have any effect on France?

8.   Describe the three estates of France. Who paid the taxes? Who held the wealth and power in France?

9. With the calling of the Estates General, "the nobility of France expected that history would repeat itself." Did it? What actually did happen?

10. What were the reforms of the National Assembly? Do they display the application of liberalism to society?

11. What were the cause and the outcome of the peasants' uprising of 1789?

12. What role did the poor women of Paris play in the Revolution?

13. Why were France and Europe overcome with feelings of fear and mistrust?

14. Why did the Revolution turn into war in 1792?

15. Who were the sans-culottes? Why were they important to radical leaders such as Robespierre? What role did the common people play in the Revolution?

16. Why did the Committee of Public Safety need to institute a Reign of Terror?

17. Describe the Grand Empire of Napoleon in terms of its three parts. Was Napoleon a liberator or a tyrant?

18. What caused Napoleon's downfall? Was it inevitable?

Study-Review Exercises

Define the following key concepts and terms.

liberalism

checks and balances

natural or universal rights

republican

popular sovereignty

tithe

Identify and explain the significance of each of the following people and terms.

Stamp Act

Battle of Trafalgar

American Bill of Rights

Loyalists

Constitutional Convention of 1787

Jacobins

Girondists

Mountain

Reign of Terror

National Assembly

Declaration of the Rights of Woman

Bastille

sans-culottes

"the baker, the baker's wife, and the baker's boy"

Lord Nelson

Mary Wollstonecraft

Edmund Burke

Marie Antoinette

Marquis de Lafayette

Thomas Jefferson

Robespierre

John Locke

Abbé Sieyès

Test your understanding of the chapter by providing the correct answers.

1. Napoleon's plan to invade England was made impossible by the defeat of the French and Spanish navies in the Battle of _____ in 1805.

2. Overall, the common people of Paris played a *minor/an important* role in the French Revolution.

3. The author of the best-selling radical book *Common Sense.* _____

4. Prior to the crisis of the 1760s, American colonists had exercised *little/a great deal of* political and economic independence from Britain.

5. The peasant uprising of 1789 in France ended in *victory/defeat* for the peasant class.

6. By the 1790s, people like Sieyès were increasingly looking to *the people/a military ruler* to bring order to France.

Multiple-Choice Questions

1. Eighteenth-century liberals stressed
   a. economic equality.
   b. equality in property holding.
   c. equality of opportunity
   d. racial and sexual equality.

2. Which came first?
   a. Formation of the French National Assembly
   b. Execution of King Louis XVI
   c. American Bill of Rights
   d. Seven Years' War

3. The French Jacobins were
   a. aristocrats who fled France.
   b. monarchists.
   c. priests who supported the Revolution.
   d. revolutionary radicals.

4. The French National Assembly was established by
   a. the middle class of the Third Estate.
   b. King Louis XVI.
   c. the aristocracy.
   d. the sans-culottes.

5. The National Assembly did all but which of the following?
   a. Nationalized church land
   b. Issued the Declaration of the Rights of Man
   c. Established the metric system of weights and measures
   d. Brought about the Reign of Terror

6. In 1789 the influential Abbé Sieyès wrote a pamphlet in which he argued that France should be ruled by the
   a. nobility.
   b. clergy.
   c. people.
   d. king.

7. In 1799, Sieyès argued that authority in society should come from
   a. the people.
   b. the leaders of the third estate.
   c. a strong military leader.
   d. the Directory.

8. In the first stage of the Revolution the French established
   a. a constitutional monarchy.
   b. an absolutist monarchy.
   c. a republic.
   d. a military dictatorship.

9. Edmund Burke's *Reflections on the Revolution in France* is a defense of
   a. the Catholic church.
   b. Robespierre and the Terror.
   c. the working classes of France.
   d. the English monarchy and aristocracy.

10. Generally, the people who did not support eighteenth-century liberalism were the
    a. elite.
    b. members of the middle class.
    c. masses.
    d. intellectuals.

11. Most eighteenth-century demands for liberty centered on
    a. the equalization of wealth.
    b. a classless society.
    c. better welfare systems.
    d. equality of opportunity.

12. Americans objected to the Stamp Act because the tax it proposed
    a. was exorbitant.
    b. was not required of people in Britain.
    c. would have required great expense to collect.
    d. was imposed without their consent.

13. The American Revolution
    a. had very little impact on Europe.
    b. was supported by the French monarchy.
    c. was not influenced by Locke or Montesquieu.
    d. was supported by almost everyone living in the United States.

14. Which of the following was a cause of the outbreak of revolution in France in 1789?
    a. Peasant revolt in the countryside
    b. The death of Louis XVI
    c. The demand of the nobility for greater power and influence
    d. The invasion of France by foreign armies

15. The first successful revolt against Napoleon began in 1808 in
    a. Spain.
    b. Russia.
    c. Germany.
    d. Italy.

16. Prior to about 1765, the American people were
    a. fairly independent of the British government.
    b. subject to heavy and punitive British controls.
    c. paying a majority share of British military costs.
    d. under the direct control of the East India Company.

17. The major share of the tax burden in France was carried by the
    a. peasants.
    b. bourgeoisie.
    c. clergy.
    d. nobility.

18. The participation of the common people of Paris in the revolution was initially attributable to
    a. their desire to be represented in the Estates General.
    b. the soaring price of food.
    c. the murder of Marat.
    d. the large number of people imprisoned by the king.

19. For the French peasants, the Revolution of 1789 meant
    a. a general movement from the countryside to urban areas.
    b. greater landownership.
    c. significant political power.
    d. few, if any, gains.

20. The group that announced that it was going to cut off Marie Antoinette's head, "tear out her heart, and fry her liver" was the
    a. National Guard.
    b. Robespierre radicals.
    c. revolutionary committee.
    d. women of Paris.

21. The group that had the task of ridding France of any internal opposition to the revolutionary cause was the
    a. Revolutionary Army.
    b. secret police.
    c. republican mob of Paris.
    d. Committee of Public Safety.

22. In her writings, Mary Wollstonecraft argues that
    a. the liberating promise of the French Revolution must be extended to women.
    b. British life is threatened by the revolutionary chaos in France.
    c. Burke is correct in his defense of inherited privilege.
    d. women should devote themselves to education, not politics.

23. Some historians have questioned the traditional interpretation of the French Revolution by arguing that
    a. the Revolution was solely the result of a clash of economic classes.
    b. the key to the Revolution was the social and economic isolation of the nobility.
    c. fundamental to the Revolution was the clash between the bourgeois and noble classes.
    d. the nobility and the bourgeoisie had common political and economic interests.

24. The abolition of many tiny German states and the old Holy Roman Empire and the reorganization of fifteen German states into a Confederation of the Rhine was the work of
    a. the Congress of Vienna.
    b. Frederick William III of Prussia.
    c. the Continental system.
    d. Napoleon.

25. Napoleon's plan to invade Britain was scrapped as a result of
    a. the Treaty of Amiens.
    b. the Battle of Trafalgar.
    c. the fall of the Third Coalition.
    d. economic restraints in France.

Major Political Ideas

1. Define liberalism. What did it mean to be a liberal in the eighteenth- and nineteenth-century sense? How does this liberalism compare to twentieth-century liberalism? To democracy? What is the relationship between liberalism and the Enlightenment idea of natural law?

2. How did Americans interpret the term *equality* in 1789? Has it changed since then? Are the definitions of liberalism and equality unchangeable, or do they undergo periodic redefinition?

Issues for Essays and Discussion

1. What were the causes, both immediate and long term, of the French Revolution? Was it basically an economic event? A social or political struggle? Support your argument by making reference to specific events and ideas.

2. Why did the French Revolution become violent? Is it inevitable that all revolutions turn into violence and dictatorship?

3. Was the American Revolution a true revolution or a war of independence? Support your argument with reference to specific events and ideas.

Interpretation of Visual Sources

Study the reproduction of the print "Storming the Bastille" on page 807 of your textbook. Who are the participants, and what are their motives? Is a recognizable social class represented here? Did demonstrations such as this have any impact on the course of the Revolution?

Geography

On Outline Map 25.1 provided, and using Map 25.1 in the textbook as a reference, mark the following:

1. The boundaries of France before the outbreak of war in 1792, and the areas acquired by France by 1810.

2. Look closely at Map 25.1 in the text. Can you find the four small British outposts scattered throughout Europe? How were these outposts necessary to and a reflection of Britain's military power? What did these outposts mean for smugglers and Napoleon's efforts to stop British trade with continental countries?

Remember that duplicate maps for class use are at the back of this book.

Outline Map 25.1

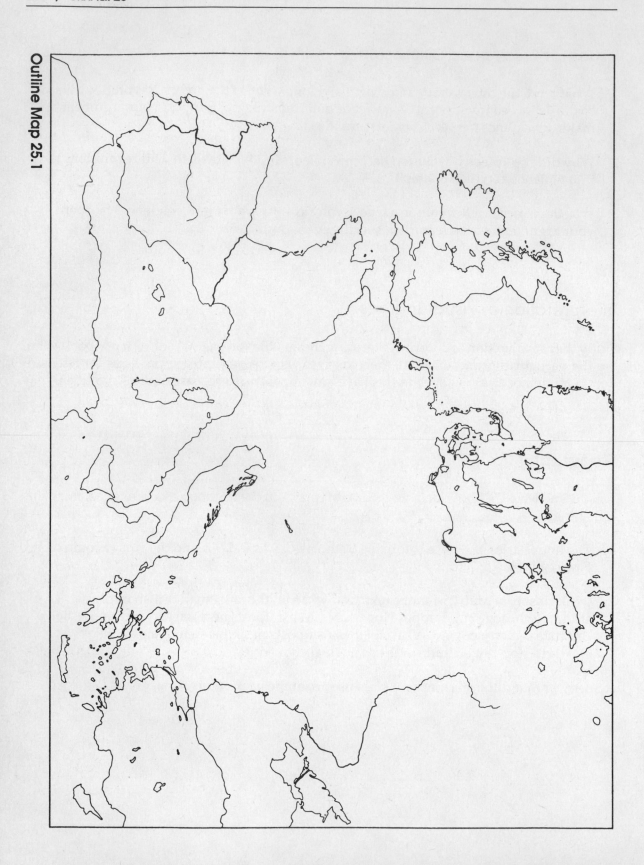

Understanding History Through the Arts

1. How did the era of revolution affect architecture? Out of the Enlightenment and the upheaval of the Revolution, and in response to the desire to create a new social order based on principles of natural law, French architects took traditional classical and baroque features and merged them with an interest in natural geometrical shapes. The result was an original architecture of bold and gigantic buildings. The leading architects in this movement were Etienne Louis Boullée and Claude-Nicolas Ledoux. Their work can be found in most general histories of architecture, but the student may wish to begin with E. Kaufmann, *Architecture in the Age of Reason** (1954), and A. Vidler, *Claude-Nicolas Ledoux, Architecture and Social Reform at the End of the Ancien Régime* (1990).

2. What was the impact of the French Revolution on art? The Revolution in France forced art to become a statement of politics and political ideals. The style was a "new classicism" based on simplicity and rationality, with references to Roman civic virtue. This new style, whose goal was to inspire patriotism, was made popular by Jacques Louis David. David, a member of the National Convention, painted a number of emotional masterpieces that glorified first the Revolution—such as *Oath in the Tennis Court* and *The Death of Marat*—and later the patriotic aims of Napoleon. For a view of David and other revolutionary artists of the late eighteenth century, see E. Kennedy, *A Cultural History of the French Revolution* (1989), and R. Paulson, *Representations of Revolution, 1789–1820** (1987).

Problems for Further Investigation

1. Do individuals determine history, or is history the product of the environment? The various arguments of scholars over the motives and contributions of Napoleon are brought together in D. H. Pinkney, ed., *Napoleon: Historical Enigma** (1969). The story of Admiral Lord Nelson, Britain's hero and victor of great sea battles, is interestingly told in R. Hough, *Nelson, A Biography* (1980).

2. King George III of Britain has often been viewed, in American history, as the archenemy of liberty and constitutionalism. Is this a fair assessment? The debate over his role has gone on for a number of years and is the subject of a book of collected opinions, *George III: Tyrant or Constitutional Monarch?** (1964), edited by E. A. Reitan.

3. How important were women in the French Revolution? Did the people of Paris play a role in determining the Revolution's political ideas? Group action in a revolution makes for an interesting study. The role of women in the Revolution in France (and in other times) is well handled in E. Boulding, *The Underside of History: A View of Women Through Time* (1976). The people (which includes the Paris mob) who participated in the

*Available in paperback.

Revolution in France are the subject of the interesting study by George Rudé, *The Crowd in the French Revolution** (1959).

4. How did the French Revolution start? Students interested in the origins of the French Revolution will want to check R. W. Greenlaw, ed., *The Economic Origins of the French Revolution** (1958), and those interested in political theory may want to consider a study of liberalism, beginning with H. Schultz, ed., *English Liberalism and the State: Individualism or Collectivism** (1972).

*Available in paperback.

PRIMARY SOURCES

The Rights of Man and of Woman

Drawing upon the ideas of the Enlightenment, particularly those of John Locke and Jean-Jacques Rousseau, the bourgeois-dominated French National Assembly issued on August 26, 1789, *The Declaration of the Rights of Man and of the Citizen*. Thousands of copies of this document circulated in France, and it became the ideological manifesto of the Revolution. Its influence on the rest of Europe and the world was equally noteworthy. In 1792 an Englishwoman, Mary Wollstonecraft, wrote *A Vindication of the Rights of Woman*, which was a reply to Edmund Burke's attack on the French Revolution and the starting point for the debate over whether the natural rights of man should apply, in full, to women.

What, according to these documents, are the principle rights of man and woman? In what principles are these rights grounded? What Enlightenment views do these documents illustrate?

Declaration of the Rights of Man and of the Citizen, 1789

The representatives of the French people, organized as a National Assembly, believing that the ignorance, neglect, or contempt of the rights of man are the sole cause of public calamities and of the corruption of governments, have determined to set forth in a solemn declaration the natural, unalienable, and sacred rights of man, in order that this declaration, being constantly before all the members of the Social body, shall remind them continually of their rights and duties; in order that the acts of the legislative power, as well as those of the executive power, may be compared at any moment with the objects and purposes of all political institutions and may thus be more respected, and, lastly, in order that the grievances of the citizens, based here-after upon simple and incontestable principles, shall tend to the maintenance of the constitution and redound to the happiness of all. Therefore the National Assembly recognizes and proclaims, in the presence and under the auspices of the Supreme Being, the following rights of man and of the citizen:

Article

1. Men are born and remain free and equal in rights. Social distinctions may be founded only upon the general good.

2. The aim of all political association is the preservation of the natural and imprescriptible rights of man. These rights are liberty, property, security, and resistance to oppression.

3. The principle of all sovereignty resides essentially in the nation. No body nor individual may exercise any authority which does not proceed directly from the nation.

4. Liberty consists in the freedom to do everything which injures no one else; hence the exercise of the natural rights of each man has no limits except those which assure to the other members of the society the enjoyment of the same rights. These limits can only be determined by law.

5. Law can only prohibit such actions as are hurtful to society. Nothing may be prevented which is not forbidden by law, and no one may be forced to do anything not provided for by law.

6. Law is the expression of the general will. Every citizen has a right to participate personally, or through his representative, in its foundation. It must be the same for all, whether it protects or punishes. All citizens, being equal in the eyes of the law, are equally eligible to all dignities and to all public positions and occupations, according to their abilities, and without distinction except that of their virtues and talents.

7. No person shall be accused, arrested, or imprisoned except in the cases and according to the forms prescribed by law. Any one soliciting, transmitting, executing, or causing to be executed, any arbitrary order, shall be punished. But any citizen summoned or arrested in virtue of the law shall submit without delay, as resistance constitutes an offense.

8. The law shall provide for such punishments only as are strictly and obviously necessary, and no one shall suffer punishment except it be legally inflicted in virtue of a law passed and promulgated before the commission of the offense.

9. As all persons are held innocent until they shall have been declared guilty, if arrest shall be deemed indispensable, all harshness not essential to the securing of the prisoner's person shall be severely repressed by law.

10. No one shall be disquieted on account of his opinions, including his religious views, provided their manifestation does not disturb the public order established by law.

11. The free communication of ideas and opinions is one of the most precious of the rights of man. Every citizen may, accordingly, speak, write, and print with freedom, but shall be responsible for such abuses of this freedom as shall be defined by law.

12. The security of the rights of man and of the citizen requires public military forces. These forces are, therefore, established for the good of all and not the personal advantage of those to whom they shall be intrusted.

13. A common contribution is essential for the maintenance of the public forces and for the cost of administration. This should be equitably distributed among all the citizens in proportion to their means.

14. All the citizens have a right to decide, either personally or by their representatives, as to the necessity of the public contribution; to grant this freely; to know to what uses it is put; and to fix the proportion, the mode of assessment and of collection and the duration of the taxes.

15. Society has the right to require of every public agent an account of his administration.

16. A society in which the observance of the law is not assured, nor the separation of powers defined, has no constitution at all.

17. Since property is an inviolable and sacred right, no one shall be deprived thereof except where public necessity, legally determined, shall clearly demand it, and then only on condition that the owner shall have been previously and equitably indemnified.

Mary Wollstonecraft, *The Vindication of the Rights of Woman*, 1792*

Contending for the rights of woman, my main argument is built on this simple principle, that if she be not prepared by education to become the companion of man, she will stop the progress of knowledge and virtue; for truth must be common to all, or it will be inefficacious with respect to its influence on general practice. And how can woman be expected to co-operate unless she know why she ought to be virtuous? Unless freedom strengthen her reason till she comprehend her duty, and see in what manner it is connected with her real good? If children are to be educated to understand the true principle of patriotism, their mother must be a patriot; and the love of mankind, from which an orderly train of virtues spring, can only be produced by considering the moral and civil interest of mankind; but the education and situation of woman, at present, shuts her out from such investigations.

In this work I have produced many arguments, which to me were conclusive, to prove that the prevailing notion respecting a sexual character was subversive of morality, and I have

*Source: Mary Wollstonecraft, from the Dedication of the first edition, *The Vindication of the Rights of Woman* (1792).

contended, that to render the human body and mind more perfect, chastity must more universally prevail, and that chastity will never be respected in the male world till the person of woman is not, as it were, idolized, when little virtue sense embellish it with the grand traces of mental beauty, or the interesting simplicity of affection.

Consider, sir, dispassionately, these observations—for a glimpse of this truth seemed to open before you when you observed, "that to see one half of the human race excluded by the other from all participation of government, was a political phenomenon that, according to abstract principles, it was impossible to explain." If so, on what does your constitution rest? If the abstract rights of man will bear discussion and explanation, those of woman, by a parity of reasoning, will not shrink from the same test: though a different opinion prevails in this country, built on the very arguments which you use to justify the oppression of woman—prescription.

Consider—I address you as a legislator—whether, when men contend for their freedom, and to be allowed to judge for themselves respecting their own happiness, it be not inconsistent and unjust to subjugate women, even though you firmly believe that you are acting in the manner best calculated to promote their happiness? Who made man the exclusive judge, if woman partake with him the gift of reason?

But, if women are to be excluded, without having a voice, from a participation of the natural rights of mankind, prove first, to ward off the charge of injustice and inconsistency, that they want reason—else this flaw in your NEW CONSTITUTION will ever show that man must, in some shape, act like a tyrant; and tyranny, in whatever part of society it rears its brazen front, will ever undermine morality.

I have repeatedly asserted, and produced what appeared to me irrefragable arguments drawn from matters of fact, to prove my assertion, that women cannot, by force, be confined to domestic concerns; for they will, however ignorant, intermeddle with more weighty affairs, neglecting private duties only to disturb, by cunning tricks, the orderly plans of reason which rise above their comprehension.

Besides, whilst they are only made to acquire personal accomplishments, men will seek for pleasure in variety, and faithless husbands will make faithless wives: such ignorant beings, indeed, will be very excusable when, not taught to respect public good, nor allowed any civil rights, they attempt to do themselves justice by retaliation.

The box of mischief thus opened in society, what is to preserve private virtue, the only security of public freedom and universal happiness?

Let there be then no coercion established in society, and the common law of gravity prevailing, the sexes will fall into their proper places. And, now that more equitable laws are forming your citizens, marriage may become more sacred: your young men may choose wives from motives of affection, and your maidens allow love to root out vanity.

The father of a family will not then weaken his constitution and debase his sentiments by visiting the harlot, nor forget, in obeying the call of appetite, the purpose for which it was implanted. And, the mother will not neglect her children to practise the arts of coquetry, when sense and modesty secure her the friendship of her husband.

But, till men become attentive to the duty of a father, it is vain to expect women to spend that time in their nursery which they, "wise in their generation," choose to spend at their glass; for this exertion of cunning is only an instinct of nature to enable them to obtain indirectly a little of that power of which they are unjustly denied a share: for, if women are not permitted to enjoy legitimate rights, they will render both men and themselves vicious, to obtain illicit privileges.

I wish, sir, to set some investigations of this kind afloat in France; and should they lead to a confirmation of my principles, when your constitution is revised the Rights of Woman may be respected, if it be fully proved that reason calls for this respect, and loudly demands JUSTICE for one half of the human race.—I am, sir, your respectfully,

M. W.

CHAPTER 26

The Industrial Revolution in Europe

Chapter Questions

After reading and studying this chapter, you should be able to answer the following questions:

What was the Industrial Revolution, what caused it, and how did it evolve? How did the Industrial Revolution affect people and society in an era of continued population growth? Was it a blessing or a disaster?

Chapter Summary

The world we live in today is largely a product of a revolution in industry and energy that began in England in the 1780s and lasted until about 1850. This revolution is still a highly controversial subject among scholars—and so a number of important problems of interpretation relating to it are discussed in this chapter.

The chapter first considers why the Industrial Revolution occurred when it did, and why it began in England. Important causes of English industrialization, some of which were discussed in detail in Chapter 21, were foreign and home demand for manufactured goods, agricultural improvements, a large free-trade area, good transportation, and a fairly advanced banking system. The pressure of a growing demand for textiles led to better spinning and weaving machinery, which, in turn, led to the creation of the world's first modern factories. In addition, a severe energy crisis resulted in new production methods: abundant coal replaced scarce wood in the all-important iron industry and fueled Watt's magnificent new steam engine. For the first time, the English people had almost unlimited energy for useful work.

The chapter next considers the gradual spread of the new industrial methods from England to continental Europe. It was not easy for continental countries to copy the English achievement, but with the coming of the railroad, rapid progress was made by the 1840s. The difficult problem of assessing the impact of the Industrial Revolution on the lives of the men and

254

women of the working class is then examined. Was industrialization mainly a blessing or a disaster for the workers? After evaluating consumption patterns, the text concludes, with qualifications, that the lot of ordinary men and women improved only after about 1820, and more particularly between 1840 and 1850. Equally important, the Industrial Revolution affected women differently than it did men, as a sexual division of labor created "separate spheres," wherein women were assigned to low-paying and dead-end jobs or became home-makers. Several theories about why this happened are examined.

Study Outline

Use this outline to preview the chapter before you read a particular section in your textbook and then as a self-check to test your reading comprehension after you have read the chapter section.

I. The initial breakthrough: the Industrial Revolution in England
   A. The eighteenth-century origins of the Industrial Revolution
      1. A colonial empire, the expanding Atlantic trade, and a strong and tariff-free home market created new demands for English manufactured goods.
      2. Cheap food also increased this demand.
      3. Available capital, stable government, economic freedom, and mobile labor in England encouraged growth.
      4. The Industrial Revolution began in England in the 1780s and on the Continent after 1815.
   B. The agricultural revolution, first in Britain and then in the Low Countries, promoted economic growth.
      1. Dutch leadership was due to population pressure, urban growth, and the initiative of the people.
      2. Dutch land drainage techniques were skillfully adopted in England.
      3. Tull, Townsend, and others in England advocated new crops and new agricultural methods.
   C. The cost of enclosure
      1. Many historians and social observers have argued that enclosure left the small farmer without "common rights" and, generally, worse off.
      2. The fencing of open fields probably did not harm the poor people who lived off the land, as some historians have claimed.
      3. Enclosure resulted in more, not less, agricultural employment for wage workers.
   D. The growth of foreign trade
      1. Mercantilism is an economic system whereby the state uses a variety of means to regulate the economy.
      2. The mercantilists claimed that a favorable balance of trade was necessary for the nation's survival.

3. The Navigation Acts were a form of economic warfare against the Dutch and gave Britain a virtual trade monopoly with its colonies.
4. The French quest for power in Europe and North America led to international wars.
5. The loss of the War of the Spanish Succession and the Seven Years' War forced France to cede all its North American possessions to Britain.
6. Colonies helped relieve European poverty and surplus population as settlers eagerly took up farming.
   a. The English colonists made up for a decline in English trade on the Continent.
   b. Colonial and home demand encouraged industrial growth in England.

E. Land and wealth in North America
1. Free land combined with population growth led to economic equality and a very high standard of living in colonial America.
2. The availability of land made labor expensive and encouraged the growth of black slavery.

F. The first factories in the cotton textile industry
1. Growing demand for textiles led to the creation of the world's first large factories.
   a. The putting-out system could not keep up with demand.
   b. Hargreaves's spinning jenny and Arkwright's water frame speeded up the spinning process.
   c. Cotton spinning was gradually concentrated in factories.
2. Cotton goods became cheaper and more widely available.
3. The wages of weavers rose rapidly, and many agricultural workers became handloom weavers.
4. Abandoned children became a prime source of labor in the early factories.

II. Energy and transportation
A. The problem of energy
1. The search for a solution to the energy problem was a major cause of industrialization.
2. From prehistoric to medieval times the major energy sources were plants and animals, and human beings and animals did most of the work.
3. Energy from the land was limited.
   a. By the eighteenth century, England's major source of fuel, wood, was nearly gone.
   b. A new source of power and energy was needed, so people turned to coal.

B. The steam engine breakthrough
1. Before about 1700, coal was used for heat but not to produce mechanical energy or to run machinery.
2. Early steam engines, such as those of Savery (1698) and Newcomen (1705), were inefficient but revolutionary converters of coal into energy.
3. In the 1760s, in Scotland, James Watt increased the efficiency of steam engines and began to produce them.

4. Steam power was used in many industries, and it encouraged other breakthroughs.
   a. It enabled the textile industry to expand.
   b. The iron industry was transformed as steam power made coke available.
   c. Cort's puddling furnace led to increased production of pig iron.
C. The coming of the railroads
   1. Stephenson's steam-powered *Rocket* (1825) was Europe's first locomotive, and the Liverpool and Manchester Railway was the first important railroad.
   2. The railroad boom (1830–1850) meant lower transportation costs, larger markets, and cheaper goods.
   3. Railroad building took workers from their rural life and made them more inclined to become urban dwellers.
   4. The railroad changed the outlook and values of the entire society.
D. Industry and population
   1. The 1851 Great Exposition, held in the Crystal Palace, reflected the growth of industry and population in Britain and confirmed that Britain was the "workshop of the world."
   2. GNP grew by 400 percent and population boomed, but average consumption grew only by 75 percent.
      a. Malthus argued that the population would always exceed the food supply.
      b. Ricardo said that wages would always be low.

III. Industrialization in continental Europe
   A. National variations
      1. Statistics show that between 1750 and 1830, Britain industrialized more rapidly than other countries.
      2. Belgium followed Britain's lead, with France showing gradual growth.
      3. By 1913, Germany and the United States were closing in on Britain; the rest of Europe (along with Japan) grew, while some Asian states (India, China) lost ground.
   B. The challenge of industrialization
      1. Revolutions and wars on the Continent slowed economic growth after 1789.
      2. Continental countries found it difficult to compete with Britain after 1815 because it was so economically and technologically advanced.
      3. However, continental countries had three advantages.
         a. Most continental countries had a rich tradition of putting-out enterprise, merchant-capitalists, and urban artisans.
         b. Britain had done the developmental pathbreaking, so other countries could simply copy the British way of doing things.
         c. The power of strong central governments could be used to promote industry.
   C. Agents of industrialization in continental Europe
      1. Cockerill, in Belgium, was one of many Englishmen who brought British industrial secrets to other parts of Europe.

2. Harkort's failed attempt to industrialize Germany illustrates the difficulty of duplicating the British achievements.
3. Governments aided industrialists by erecting tariffs, building roads and canals, and financing railroads.
4. Many thinkers and writers, such as List in Germany, believed that industrialization would advance the welfare of the nation.
   a. List supported the idea of a tariff-free zone in Germany, the Zollverein (1834).
   b. Henceforth, goods could move among the German member states without tariffs, but goods from other nations were subject to a tariff.
5. Banks played a more important role in industrialization on the Continent than in Britain.
   a. Industrial banks, such as the Crédit Mobilier, became important in France and Germany in the 1850s.
   b. These industrial banks mobilized the savings of thousands of small investors and invested them in transportation and industry.

IV. Capital and labor in the age of the Industrial Revolution
   A. The new class of factory owners
      1. Capitalist owners were locked into a highly competitive system.
      2. The early industrialists came from a variety of backgrounds.
      3. As factories grew larger, opportunities declined.
   B. The new factory workers and their working conditions
      1. Many observers claimed that the Industrial Revolution brought misery to the workers.
         a. The romantic poets Blake and Wordsworth protested the life of the workers and the pollution of the land and water.
         b. The Luddites smashed the new machines they believed were putting them out of work.
         c. Engels wrote a blistering attack on the middle classes, *The Condition of the Working Class in England* (1844).
      2. Others, such as Ure and Chadwick, claimed that life was improving for the working class.
      3. The statistics with regard to purchasing power of the worker (real wages) shows that there was little or no improvement between 1780 and 1820.
         a. Between 1792 and 1815, living conditions actually declined as food prices rose faster than wages.
         b. Only after 1840 did a substantial improvement in real wages occur.
         c. Even in this era of improving purchasing power, hours of labor increased and unemployment was present.
      4. Diet probably improved, as did the supply of clothing, but housing did not.
   C. Conditions of work
      1. Working in the factory meant more discipline and less personal freedom.
      2. The refusal of cottage workers to work in factories led to child labor.
         a. The use of pauper children was forbidden in 1802.

b. Urban factories attracted whole families, as did coal mining, and tended to preserve kinship ties.

c. Children and parents worked long hours.

3. Parliament acted to limit child labor.

a. Robert Owen, a successful manufacturer in Scotland, proposed limiting the hours of labor and child labor.

b. The Factory Act of 1833 limited child labor and the number of hours children could work in textile factories.

c. Factory owners were required to establish elementary schools for the children of their employees.

4. Subcontracting led to a close relationship between the subcontractor and his work crew, many of whom were friends and relations.

a. Subcontracting helped maintain kinship ties.

b. Many workers (such as in Liverpool and Glasgow) were Irish and were thus held together by ethnic and religious ties.

5. Some firms were large, but the survival of small workshops and artisan crafts gave many workers an alternative to factory employment.

6. Many traditional jobs, such as farming and domestic service, lived on.

7. Workers created a labor movement to improve working conditions.

a. The Combination Acts, which outlawed unions and strikes, were repealed in 1824.

b. Robert Owen experimented with cooperative and socialist communities and then formed a national union in 1834 in Britain.

c. The British labor movement turned once again, after 1851, in the direction of craft unions.

8. Chartism was a workers' political movement that sought universal male suffrage, shorter work hours, and cheap bread.

D. The sexual division of labor

1. A new pattern of "separate spheres" emerged.

a. The man emerged as the family's primary wage earner, while the woman found only limited job opportunities.

b. Married women were much less likely to work outside the house after the first child arrived.

c. Women were confined to low-paying, dead-end jobs.

2. The reasons for this reorganization of paid work along gender lines are debated.

a. One argument centers on the idea of a deeply ingrained patriarchal tradition, which predates the economic transformation.

b. Others claim that the factory conflicted with strong incentives on the part of mothers to concentrate on child care; this theory centers on the claim that women saw division of labor as the best strategy for family survival in the industrializing society.

c. Others argue that sexual division of labor was part of an effort to control the sexuality of working-class youth.

Review Questions

Check your understanding of this chapter by answering the following questions.

1. Why did the Industrial Revolution begin in England?

2. Describe the energy crisis in England. How was it solved?

3. What was the relationship between the steam engine and the coal mine? The railroad and the coal mine?

4. What impact did the railroad have on (a) the factory system, (b) the rural workers, and (c) the outlook and values of society?

5. What did James Watt do to increase the efficiency of the steam engine?

6. How did the change in textile production affect employment in spinning and weaving for adults and children?

7. What effect did the French Revolution and the wars of 1792–1815 have on the economies of the continental states? What were the variations in the timing and extent of industrialization in the United States, Belgium, Germany, and France?

8. What disadvantages and advantages were felt by countries that industrialized after Great Britain?

9. What do the careers of Cockerill, Harkort, and List tell us about the problems and methods of industrialization on the Continent?

10. What was the purpose of the Zollverein? Of the Crédit Mobilier?

11. Did Britain's new industrial middle class ruthlessly exploit the workers?

12. Did the standard of living improve or decline between 1790 and 1850? What about other factors, such as diet and working conditions?

13. What was the effect of the factory system in Britain on the family?

14. What was the subcontract system, and how did it work? Did it have a negative or a positive impact on working-class life?

15. What were the goals and accomplishments of the Chartists?

16. What is meant by the term *sexual division of labor*? What are the various theories about its emergence?

17. Was the enclosure movement a disaster for the common farm worker?

18. What was the agricultural revolution? Where did it begin and why?

Study-Review Exercises

Define the following key concepts and terms.

agricultural revolution

mercantilism

War of the Spanish Succession

War of the Austrian Succession

Seven Years' War

cottage workers

enclosure system

domestic system

Industrial Revolution

protective tariff

Chartist movement

energy crisis of the eighteenth century

real wages

sexual division of labor

Identify and explain the significance of the following people and terms.
Jethro Tull

Charles Townsend

Thomas Malthus

David Ricardo

Andrew Ure

Crystal Palace

Cartwright's power loom

spinning jenny

Zollverein

Factory Act of 1833

Crédit Mobilier

Combination Acts

parish "apprentices" in cotton mills

Henry Cort

James Hargreaves

Robert Owen

James Watt

Friedrich List

George Stephenson

Grand National Consolidated Trades Union

Emile and Isaac Pereire

Friedrich Engels

craft union

Test your understanding of the chapter by providing the correct answers.

1. The Industrial Revolution began in England in about _____ in the

    _____ industry.

2. A decrease in food prices led to an *increased/decreased* demand for manufactured goods.

3. The Scotsman who improved the steam engine. _____

4. Henry Cort developed a new process of using coke to improve the output of

    _____ .

5. The first railroad line was the _____ line, and the first effective

    locomotive was Stephenson's _____ .

6. The railroads tended to *increase/decrease* the number of cottage workers.

7. The architectural wonder of the 1851 industrial fair in London. _____

8. Between 1780 and 1820, purchasing power in Britain *increased/decreased*.

9. The role of the government in bringing about industrialization was *greater/less* in continental countries than in Britain.

10. The economic and trade agreement formed in 1834 that allowed goods to move

    among German member states without tariffs. _____

11. The possibility of a worker becoming a successful industrialist *increased/decreased* as the nineteenth century wore on.

12. With the _____ Act of 1833, the employment of children in British factories tended to *increase/decrease*.

Multiple-Choice Questions

1. In the 1830s, the most technologically advanced country in the world was
   a. Belgium.
   b. the United States.
   c. France.
   d. Britain.

2. Which of the following was a period of falling real wages for English workers?
   a. 1792–1815
   b. 1815–1850
   c. 1840–1850
   d. 1850–1890

3. Which of the following was used by continental countries to meet British competition?
   a. The adoption of free trade
   b. Closing the doors to skilled British workers
   c. Exchanging the secrets of technology with one another
   d. Government grants and loans

4. Which of the following was most likely to characterize a cottage worker?
   a. Worked at his or her own pace
   b. Never worked alongside other members of his or her family
   c. Worked at a steady and constant rate
   d. Would probably prefer factory work to domestic industry work

5. Which of the following contributed to England's early industrialization?
   a. Colonial trade
   b. Very weak central banking system
   c. High food prices due to inadequate crops
   d. A domestic market with many local protective barriers

6. The energy crisis of the eighteenth and nineteenth centuries was solved by reliance on
   a. wood.
   b. coal and steam.
   c. electricity.
   d. water power.

7. According to Friedrich List, the promotion of industry
   a. was dangerous for the well-being of the peasants.
   b. was vital for the defense of the nation.
   c. increased the poverty of the population.
   d. required free trade between nations.

8. The most significant technological advance made during the Industrial Revolution was the
   a. first large factory.
   b. cotton-spinning jenny.
   c. steam engine.
   d. water frame.

9. Which of the following was passed by the British Parliament to outlaw unions and strikes?
   a. The Factory Act of 1833
   b. The Combination Acts
   c. The Mines Act of 1842
   d. The Grand National Consolidated Trades Union Act

10. The Industrial Revolution in France
    a. developed at a faster pace than it did in Germany.
    b. developed more rapidly than in Britain.
    c. occurred largely prior to 1780.
    d. lagged behind that of Britain.

11. The growth of the railroad caused all of the following *except*
    a. a reduction in the cost of overland freight.
    b. an increase in the demand for cottage industry goods.
    c. the growth of a class of urban workers.
    d. the widening of markets.

12. The first continental country to industrialize was
    a. Belgium.
    b. France.
    c. Italy.
    d. Germany.

13. The industrial development of continental Europe was delayed by
    a. a lack of resources.
    b. the French Revolution and Napoleonic wars.
    c. the plague.
    d. a labor shortage.

14. To understand more fully the impact of the Industrial Revolution, historians concentrate their studies on
    a. England.
    b. France.
    c. Ireland.
    d. Belgium.

15. Before the 1830s, the
    a. family continued to work as a unit in the factories.
    b. factory employed only females.
    c. mother and father worked together while their children went to factory schools.
    d. factory employed only the males.

16. The British workers' campaign to gain the franchise between 1838 and 1848 was called the
    a. Ten Hours' movement.
    b. Luddite movement.
    c. Chartist movement.
    d. democratic movement.

17. Which of the following was *not* characteristic of Robert Owen?
    a. He was a scholar who wanted to implement his socialist ideas.
    b. He experimented with cooperative and socialist communities.
    c. He organized one of Britain's first national unions.
    d. He tried to improve the working conditions of his workers.

18. The first factories were
    a. steel mills.
    b. chemical firms.
    c. clothing companies.
    d. textile mills.

19. The early industrialists in Britain very often were
    a. aristocrats taking advantage of new economic opportunities.
    b. members of the established church.
    c. Irish immigrants.
    d. Quakers and Scots.

20. Workers who smashed the machines that put them out of work were known as
    a. Luddites.
    b. anti-Modernists.
    c. Chartists.
    d. apprentices.

21. William Cockerill, a Lancashire carpenter, built an industrial empire in
    a. the English Midlands.
    b. London.
    c. Belgium.
    d. North America.

22. By the end of the nineteenth century, large decreases in per capita industrial levels
    had occurred in
    a. India and China.
    b. France.
    c. Britain.
    d. Germany.

23. For women, the Industrial Revolution
    a. provided a greater chance of economic equality with men.
    b. discouraged marriage and children.
    c. provided new career opportunities in high-level jobs.
    d. caused them to be confined to low-paying, dead-end jobs.

24. It appears that during the Industrial Revolution in Britain the gross national product
    a. rose at about the same rate as the per capita consumption of goods.
    b. rose more rapidly than the per capita consumption of goods.
    c. rose less rapidly than the per capita consumption of goods.
    d. fell below the per capita consumption of goods.

25. The daily requirement of calories that adult men and women need to fuel their bodies, work, and survive is
    a. 1,000.
    b. 5,000 to 6,000.
    c. 200 to 400.
    d. 2,000 to 4,000.

26. The nation that benefited most from the Anglo-Dutch War, the War of the Austrian Succession, and the Seven Years' War was
    a. France.
    b. the Netherlands.
    c. Spain.
    d. Britain.

Major Political Ideas

1. What role did the government play in the process of industrialization? Did this role vary from country to country?

2. Why, with the Factory Act of 1833, did the British government turn toward some state intervention?

Issues for Essays and Discussion

1. What were the causes of the Industrial Revolution in Britain? Which of the causes, in your opinion, were the most important?

2. Historians have long argued whether the Industrial Revolution was a blessing or a disaster for the workers who lived through it. What is your opinion? What information exists that allows us to measure the impact of industrialization? Did the Industrial Revolution affect women and men alike?

Interpretation of Visual Sources

Study the reproduction of the engraving titled "Girl Dragging Coal Tubs" on page 857 of your textbook. What seems to be the motive of those who produced and published this print? Could this illustration have supported the argument for "separate spheres" for men and women?

Geography

1. Compare Maps 26.1 and 26.4 in the textbook in terms of the major industrial areas and transportation networks shown on each. How do these maps explain why an ever-greater portion of the English population lived in the north as time passed? What different stages in the development of English transportation are illustrated by these maps? Write your answers in the space provided below.

_____

_____

_____

2. Study Maps 26.4 and 26.5 in the textbook. Using the space below, compare British and continental industrialization by 1850 in terms of (a) railroads, (b) coal deposits, and (c) industrial centers. What role did geography play in Britain's early industrial lead?

_____

_____

_____

3. Four of Europe's most important centers of modern industry are (a) the Manchester-Sheffield area, (b) the Ruhr valley, (c) the Liège region, and (d) the Roubaix region. Locate these regions on Maps 26.4 and 26.5. What countries are they in? What do they have in common?

_____

_____

_____

Understanding History Through the Arts

1. What was the impact of photography on society? Few nineteenth-century inventions had as great an impact on society as the invention of the camera in 1839. Photography allowed society to examine itself with a closeness never before experienced. In the late 1860s, for example, Thomas Annan took a series of photographs of the slums of Glasgow, and thus encouraged interest in sanitary reform and urban improvement. Annan's photographs have been reproduced by Dover Press as T. Annan, *Photographs*

of the Old Closes and Streets of Glasgow, 1868–1877* (1977). M. Hiley, *Victorian Working Women* (1980), is a view of the habits and life of Victorian women through photography.

2. How did artists depict the changes brought by the Industrial Revolution? Begin your study with the path-breaking study by F. D. Klingender, *Art and the Industrial Revolution,** edited and revised by A. Elton (1970). An unrivaled source of visual material associated with Britain's early industrial history is A. Briggs, *Iron Bridge to Crystal Palace: Impact and Images of the Industrial Revolution* (1979), and more recently his book *Victorian Things* (1988).

Problems for Further Investigation

1. When did the Industrial Revolution begin? Some historians do not agree with the traditional interpretation that the Industrial Revolution began in the late eighteenth century. One such historian is John Nef, who argues that it actually began in the sixteenth century. He places considerable emphasis on the importance of the coal industry and the early energy crisis. Some of his ideas are found in J. Nef, "The Early Energy Crisis and Its Consequences," *Scientific American* (Nov. 1977), and "The Progress of Technology and the Growth of Large-Scale Industry in Great Britain, 1540–1640," *Economic History Review* 5 (Oct. 1984). Students interested in the causes of the Industrial Revolution will also want to read the series of debates by six historians in R. M. Hartwell, ed., *The Causes of the Industrial Revolution in England** (1967).

2. What was the impact of the Industrial Revolution on the working class? The issue of whether the Industrial Revolution was a blessing or a curse for the working class has fueled a long-lasting debate. Many of the arguments of the optimists and the pessimists are collected in two small books: P. A. M. Taylor, ed., *The Industrial Revolution in Britain** (rev. ed., 1970), and C. S. Doty, ed., *The Industrial Revolution** (1969). The impact of industrialization on women is one of the themes of Louise Tilly and Joan Scott in *Women, Work and Family** (1978). The most important (and controversial) book on the impact of industrialization on the working class is E. P. Thompson, *The Making of the English Working Class** (1966). Emile Zola's *Germinal** is a powerful novel about life and conditions in Belgian and French coal mines. Popular novels by Charles Dickens and Elizabeth Gaskill are among the suggested readings in the text. The machine breakers in England (1811–1817) are the subject of M. I. Thomis's *The Luddites** (1970–1972). Those interested in reading about the new industrial working class may want to begin with J. Kuczynski, *The Rise of the Working Class* (1967), or two collections of essays on the subject—M. L. McDougal, ed., *The Working Class in Modern Europe* (1975), and E. J. Hobsbawm, ed., *Labouring Men: Studies in the History of Labour** (1964).

*Available in paperback.

PRIMARY SOURCES

Industrialization and Urban Life for the Working Classes

Most historians agree that, given the poverty and uncertainty of preindustrial life, the process of urbanization and industrialization brought more benefits than hardships. Nevertheless, a large number of people continued to live in filthy environments and work under exploitative conditions. The following readings do two things. First, they show how the state, in this case the British state, became increasingly absorbed in defining and solving the problems faced by the less advantaged classes. Second, they show what life and labor was like for many people at the bottom—particularly women, children, and elderly people, who gained the least from the economic advances of the time. All of these excerpts are from parliamentary hearings, and all led to specific legislative reform.

Eldin Hargrave was a boy from the great city of Leeds, which was the center of Britain's wool cloth manufacture. He was brought to London on April 13, 1832, to testify before the parliamentary committee of Mr. Sadler, M.P., a committee that was set up to uncover the evils of child labor in order to gain public support for a factory protection act. It appears they provided him with a new suit—and it also appears that he may have lost his job for testifying. The act, passed in 1833, was the first effective factory legislation in Britain.

If Hargrave is typical of children who worked in the early textile factories, what are the ages at which children began their work? Their hours of labor? Wages? What effect did factory work have on their health and morals?

Child Labor in the Textile Factories, 1832*

Eldin Hargrave, called in; and Examined (13 April, 1832):

755.　What age are you?—I shall be 15 next month.
756.　Have you a father?—No.
757.　Your father is dead?—Yes.
758.　Have you a mother?—Yes, I have a mother.
759.　What age were you when you were sent to the mill?—I was about eight years old.
760.　You come from Leeds?—Yes.
761.　To whose mill did you go?—I went to Messrs. Shaun & Driver's.
762.　Did you work there as a premer?—Yes.
763.　What were your hours of labour there?—I worked from 6 to 7.
764.　You worked 13 hours, with two hours for meals?—Yes.
765.　How long did you stop at that work?—A year.
766.　What wages did you have for that?—Three shillings a week.
767.　Where did you go then?—I went to Lord & Robinson's.
768.　What did you do there?—I was a carper there.
769.　What is a carper?—There are some prickles on the top of the tassels, and they had a pair of scissors to clear them off.
770.　Did you find that work easier?—Yes.
771.　Had you less wages for that?—I had half-a-crown.
772.　How many hours did you work at Lord & Robinson's?—From 5 to 9.
773.　Why did you leave Shaun & Driver's?—Because they went to a fresh mill, and one of the master's cousins went in my place.
774.　How long did you stop at Lord & Robinson's?—About half a year.
775.　Why did you leave that?—Because I could not clip tassels fast enough.
776.　Did they discharge you?—Yes.
777.　Where did you seek for employment then?—At Mr. Brown's mill.
778.　What age were you then?—About 10 years old.
779.　In what situation were you there?—I was a sweeper and errand-boy.
780.　What were your wages there?—Three shillings.
781.　What hours did you work there?—I went from 6 to 7.
782.　How long were you a sweeper?—About a year.
783.　What situation did you get after that?—I was a brusher.
784.　What wages did you get as a brusher?—I had 3s. 6d.[1] a week; and I had sometimes 1s. for over-hours, and sometimes 1s. 3d.; I had three-farthings an hour.
785.　How long did you work when you worked over-hours?—I went from 5 to 10.

*Source: "Report from the Select Committee on the Bill to Regulate the Labour of Children in Mills and Factories of the United Kingdom, with Minutes of Evidence, August, 1832," *Parliamentary Papers, 1831–32, Vol. XV.*
[1]There were 12 pence ("d") in a shilling and 20 shillings ("s") in a pound (£).

786. Supposing you had refused to work over-hours, what would have happened?—I was forced to work over-hours, otherwise I must seek a fresh shop.

787. For what length of time did you so work?—I worked for that time for a year round.

788. What did you do after that?—I went to mind Lewises.

789. At the same mill?—Yes.

790. Did you work at the broad or the narrow Lewis?—I worked at the broad.

791. What had you for working at the Lewis?—I had 5s. a week and over-hours.

792. How much had you for over-hours?—I had a penny an hour.

793. Will you describe the labour you had to do in attending to the Lewis.—I had a stool to stand on, and then I had to reach over as far as I could reach to put the list on.

794. Did you find that harder work than brushing?—Yes, that was harder work than any that I had.

795. In attending to this machine, are you not always upon the stretch, and upon the move?—Yes, always.

796. Do not you use your hand a good deal in stretching it out?—Yes.

797. What effect had this long labour upon you?—I had a pain across my knee, and I got crooked.

798. Was it the back of your knee, or the side of your knee?—All round.

799. Will you show your limbs?—[Here the Witness exposed his legs and knees.]

800. Were your knees ever straight at any time?—They were straight before I went to Mr. Brown's mill.

801. Are there any other boys at work at that mill that have crooked knees beside yourself?—Yes, there is one.

802. Did you ever hear any boys in the mill complain that by working there they got crooked knees or bad legs?—Yes, one.

803. Have you had bad health generally, besides the pain in your knee?—Yes; I have been very weak and poorly sometimes.

804. What sort of clothes had you before you put these on?—They were middling good trousers.

805. Have you only one suit?—No, I have only one suit.

806. You have no better suit for Sunday?—Not before I got this.

807. You say that you worked for 17 hours a day all the year round; did you do that without interruption?—Yes.

808. Could you attend any day or night-school?—No.

809. Can you write?—No.

810. Can you read?—I can read a little in a spelling book.

811. Where did you learn that; did you go to a Sunday-school?—No, I had not clothes to go in.

812. Did you ever go to church?—Yes, sometimes.

813. When you were a sweeper and errand-boy, had you any thing to do with the manufacturing?—Yes; I took one of the boys' places at the Lewises when they went out.[2]

814. What situation did you like best?—I liked sweeping best.

815. What is the most you have earned in a week, since you have worked at the broad Lewises?—I have earned 6s. 3d. and 6s. 6d. sometimes; very seldom 6s. 6d.

816. Have you any brothers?—I have four.

817. Are they working in manufactories?—No; I have only a sister working.

818. Where are your brothers working?—I have not a brother working at present.

819. You say that your regular hours of working at the broad Lewises were from 6 in the morning to 6 at night, and that you had four extra hours, and that you get a penny an hour; how much did you ever get extra?—Sometimes 1s. 3d. and sometimes 1s. 6d.; but very seldom 1s. 6d.

820. Were you paid for every extra hour you worked?—Yes.

821. What time did you leave off on Saturday?—Sometimes at half-past 4, sometimes 5.

822. Did you get paid for all the over-hours that you worked?—Yes.

823. They never cheated you out of any time?—No.

824. When did you begin on Saturday?—Sometimes at 5, and sometimes at 6; but I went a great deal oftener at 5 than at 6.

825. Are you still working at Mr. Brown's?—I have got turned off for going to London.

826. Till you came, did you work at Mr. Brown's, at the Lewis?—Yes.

827. How came you to be turned off; what did they tell you?—They told me I was to go no more.

828. Did you ask to leave to go away?—Yes, I told the overlooker a day or two before.

829. When they turned you away, did they tell you that you could not come back because they must put another boy in your place, or did they seem angry with you for going?—They looked very cross with me for going.

830. Did they say any thing?—They say that I was not to come any more again, if I went.

831. Have you been working at this last place from 5 to 10?—No; we have been going from 8 to half-past 5.

832. Did they ever beat you at Mr. Brown's mill?—Yes; the overlooker used to beat us for not going to school.

833. Did they ever beat you for not working?—No.

834. Did Mr. Brown desire you to go to school?—I do not know; but the overlooker used to beat us for not going.

835. Did Mr. Brown keep a school upon the premises?—No.

836. Had you any other school to go to but the Sunday-school?—No.

[2]On strike.

837. Was it then for not going to the Sunday-school that you were beat?—Yes, it was.
838. What were you flogged with?—With a strap.
839. Did it hurt you very much?—Yes.
840. When was it he beat you for not going to the Sunday-school, was it upon a Sunday?—No, Monday morning.
841. Did the schoolmaster tell that you had not been there?—He used to ask us all every Monday morning, and I used to always tell him the truth.
842. What Sunday-school did you go to?—I did not go to any, because I had no clothes.
843. What Sunday-school should you have gone to if you had gone to any?—I might have gone to any that I liked.
844. When did you work last from 5 till 10?—About a year and a half since.
845. Were you working at the broad Lewis when you came away?—Yes.
846. Are you pretty well in health?—No, I am very weak.
847. Have you no appetite?—No, I do not eat much.
848. When you were an errand-boy and sweeper, was that hard work?—It was middling hard work.
849. When you came to be a brusher, did that tire you very much?—Yes, I was rather tired, but brushing is a good deal easier than minding Lewises.
850. Did you feel fatigued with 12 hours of daily labour?—Yes.
851. Has it affected your health?—Yes.
852. And you believe that it has deformed your limbs?—Yes, it has.
853. Were you obliged either to work those long hours, or to leave your employment?—Yes.
854. Would you have liked it better to have worked a smaller length of time, even though your wages would have been less?—Yes, I would have liked to have worked less, but then the wages would have been lower.
855. When you were a brusher, how came you to go the Lewises; did you wish to go there?—Yes, it was not work that I looked at, but wages.
856. How far did you live from the mill?—About half a mile.
857. Did you go home when you left work?—Yes.
858. What time was that?—Sometimes 10, and sometimes 9.
859. When you went home, what did you do?—I got my supper, and went to bed.
860. What time did you get up?—About half-past 4, and sometimes a quarter to 5, and then I went to work at 5.
861. Who waked you in the morning?—My mother.
862. At this place you have been working short hours?—Yes.
863. What wages have your got?—I have got 4s. from 8 till half-past 5.
864. If you had left these manufactories could you have got any other work?—No, I do not think I could.
865. Do you know what boys got that worked with farmers?—I do not know.
866. Had you rather work now as you are doing, from 8 to half-past 5, and get 4s., or work the 11 hours and get 5s.?—I had gather go 11 hours and get 5s., because it is more wages; we have very little coming in at our house;

there is only another sister besides me working, and she has 7s. 6d. a week.

867. What is the most wages you ever got when you were working the 17 hours?—I sometimes got 6s. 3d. and sometimes 6s. 6d.

868. Would you rather work the long hours and get the 6s. 3d. or work the short hours and get the 4s?—I would as lief work the short hours.

869. Would your health enable you to endure the 17 hours of labour?—No, it would not.

870. Has your mother any parochial relief[3]?—Yes, she has 5s. a fortnight.

871. Does your mother work at the mill?—No, she goes out washing.

872. How old is your sister?—Going on 24.

873. Does she work the same length of time that you do?—She goes at 7 in the morning and works till half-past 6 at night.

874. You said that the working 17 hours fatigued you, does working from 8 till half-past 5 fatigue you?—No.

875. When you go back, shall you go to Mr. Brown's mill and ask for the work again?—Yes, I shall go and ask.

876. Do you hope they will take you in again?—Yes, I do.

877. Are you capable of doing any other work but working in a manufactory?—No, nothing but working in a manufactory of cloths.

In the early 1840s a British civil servant by the name of Edwin Chadwick undertook, for the government, an investigation into the "sanitary condition of the labouring population" in various cities of Britain. Following is an excerpt from a report on the city of Glasgow, in Scotland, by one of Chadwick's fellow researchers, Charles Baird, in March 1841. Glasgow was the second largest city in Britain—a city of great wealth but also of great poverty. What impression does Baird convey with regard to the standard of living of the average working-class family in Glasgow? What were the "many causes" by which the workers could be reduced to poverty? What proportion of Glasgow's population was working class? How did people survive in times of distress?

Working-Class Life in Glasgow, 1842*

That many of the operatives in Glasgow live in comfort and are able to clothe themselves and families, and to educate their children, is well known to all who know anything of them, and must be evident even to the passing stranger who sees the thousands pouring along the streets on the sabbath-day, apparently well fed and well clad, to their respective places of worship. I rejoice to be able to add, that numbers of them can do more—they give their quota of charity

---

[3]Welfare subsidy provided by the local poor law guardians.

*Source: Charles Baird, "On the General and Sanitary Condition of the Working Classes and the Poor in the City of Glasgow," included in *Reports of the Sanitary Conditions of the Labouring Populations of Scotland, 1842*, 165–168.

(far more in proportion than the higher classes do)—they assist in supporting their clergymen, as witness the payments for church-seats, and the donations, especially at the dissenting churches, and not a few of them save money. In proof of this last fact I call attention to our savings banks, and to the class of depositors therein. By the last Report (dated 2nd January, 1841) of the National Security Savings Bank of Glasgow, I find that, out of 20,076 individual depositors, there were—

Mechanics, artificers, and their wives	6,736
Factory operatives	1,574
Labourers, carters, and their wives	867
In all, of these descriptions	9,177

And it is proper to mention, that there are nearly 2,000 other depositors, whose "descriptions are not stated."

While, however, many of the working classes in Glasgow are able to live in comfort, and a number of them, by proper economy and prudence, to save money, it must be kept in view that they are subject to many causes by which even the most prudent and economical may be reduced to penury, such, for instance, as the want of employment: it may be from the inclemency of the weather, which almost every winter (and peculiarly during the last winter) interrupts the masons, slaters, and out-door labourers; the sudden convulsions and fluctuations of trade, by which the means of subsistence are frequently withdrawn from large masses; the high price of provisions; and, above all, their liability to diseases, especially those of an epidemic nature.

Like the population of every other manufacturing city or town, the working classes of Glasgow have frequently suffered very severely from sudden depressions and fluctuations of trade, and the consequent want of employment. In 1816–17 the distress was such that it was found necessary to raise a large sum of voluntary subscription. At that time 9,653£. 6s. 2d. was distributed among 23,130 persons. In 1819–20 large distributions of clothing, meal, and fuel were made to persons who could find no employment. Upwards of 600 men were employed in breaking stones for the roads, and 340 weavers at spade-work in the public green. From April, 1826, till October, 1827, was another period of great mercantile distress, and about 9,000£. was laid out for the amelioration of the working classes. In 1829, 2,950£. for the like purpose. In 1832, the memorable cholera year, the condition of these classes was most lamentable. About 10,000£. was then raised by voluntary subscription, and 8,000£. under the Cholera Assessment Act, and (with the exception of 1,854£.) was expended in feeding and clothing the destitute, washing the houses, attending to the sick, and providing coffins, &c. &c. Down till 1837 there was no other period of great distress; but in the spring of that year, owing to the depressed state of trade, the want of employment, and the high price of provisions, a large number of the working classes in Glasgow were reduced to very necessitous circumstances: 5,200£. was raised by voluntary subscription, with which, and 3,000£. handed over by a former relief committee, 3,072 adults were employed at out door work, as preparing road-metal, or at weaving, and 3,800 adults, besides children, in all about 18,500 persons, were daily supplied with food at the soup-kitchens then established; besides which considerable sums were expended in providing fuel, and in redeeming bedding and clothes from pawn. Even during last winter, although it was generally admitted that there was no great scarcity of employment, and that the operatives were in a much better condition than they had been at previous times, owing to the great severity of the weather the relief committee thought it was necessary to give extraordinary aid; and accordingly, in the city and suburbs, upwards of 3,000 persons were assisted in various ways, particularly with food, during the months of January and February last.

Much, however, as the working classes in Glasgow have suffered from the depressions or fluctuations of trade, the want of employment, and the high prices of provisions, I conceive that their sufferings from these causes have been trifling indeed when compared to what they have annually suffered from disease, especially of an epidemic nature.

From deductions made on an extensive scale by our most eminent statists, it may be said to be established that "when 1 person in 100 dies annually, 2 are constantly sick." Let this axiom be applied to Glasgow, in which, last year, the deaths were as 1 to 31,969 (and the mean annual mortality for the last 5 years 1 in 31,738). Let it be taken into account that the deaths from fever alone, in 1840, were 1,229, being 1 to 7,177, or 13,921 per cent of the whole deaths. Let it be also considered the fever here, as elsewhere, chooses its victims in the prime of life, and consequently most frequently the parents of large young families; and let it be recollected that, as above stated, at least four-fifths of the population of Glasgow and suburbs consist of the working classes, or their families: so that if, as is too often the case, the father is laid on a bed of sickness or cut off by death, there is no provision for the other members of the family, I say let these considerations be duly weighed, and even a passing thought given to the sufferings, the watching, want and wretchedness which accompanies sickness and death, especially in the poor man's house, and any right-constituted mind will contemplate with horror the amount of misery which must have been the lot of countless thousands of our working classes.

Instead of dwelling longer here upon the vast amount of suffering incident to these classes from the fearful extent of disease and mortality which has afflicted our city for many years past, I shall now proceed to the next head of my report, viz., on the sanitary state of Glasgow, and there give tables, or data, from which any person interested in the condition of the working and poorer classes may draw deductions; and I may here mention that I make a separate chapter, and place it in position I do, as the tables and statements in it illustrate the condition of both the working classes and the poor, and also show the great extent of destitution which must exist in the city of Glasgow. With these characteristics, the chapter on the sanitary condition of our city will form an intermediate and proper connecting link in my report.

Mary Hayes was a widow who lived in London and worked as a tailoress (a "trouser finisher") in what was called a "sweated industry." "Sweated" work was very common in most large cities of Europe and America, and for the most part undertaken in their homes by women, children, and immigrant Jews. What were the circumstances under which Mrs. Hayes worked? Can you tell from this testimony what her work consisted of? What her hours of labor were? Wages? Diet? How did she get her work from the business for whom she worked? What were the advantages of this sort of work to the manufacturer who hired her?

Women in "Sweated Labor" in London, 1888*

Mrs. MARY HAYES, is called in; and, having been sworn, is Examined, as follows (24th, April 1888):

1563. [Chairman.] Where do you live?
14, Maplin-street.

1564. What is your trade?
Trouser finishing.

1565. Your husband was a soldier, was he not?
Yes.

1566. How long have you been in this trade?
I was in the trade before I was married, but when I got married to my husband of course I had to do the army work, such as washing; and since the death of my husband of course I have done the work, because I knew it from a girl; I was always in the line.

1567. How long is it since your husband died?
Nineteen years on the 5th of next June.

1568. You have been 19 years at trouser finishing?
Yes.

1569. Have you any children?
Yes.

1570. What ages, and how many?
I have got three children; I say "children." I have two daughters at home. I have got one that has been in the infirmary since she has left a situation. Off and on she has been laid up with rheumatism, and likewise with rheumatic fever.

1571. And the other?
The other has been a delicate girl from the birth; she has never been fit for any situation, but she assists me with the work as far as she can.

1572. Perhaps you will tell the Committee the prices you get for these trousers?
I get from 2 3/4d. to 3d.[1] I have had more years ago; I have had 4 1/2d. for twist holes, and I have had 4d. for all cotton holes; but then that is some years ago.

---

*Source: "First Report from the Select Committee of the House of Lords on the Sweating System, together with Proceedings of the Committee, Minutes of Evidence, and Appendix," *Parliamentary Papers, 1888, Vol. XX.*
[1]There were 12 pence ("d") in a shilling and 20 shillings ("s") in a pound (£).

1573. You have had 4d. and 4 1/2d. for what you now get 2 3/4d. and 3d. for?
Yes, for what I now get 2 3/4d. for I used five years ago to get 4d.; they are all cotton holes.

1574. How many can you make a week?
With me and my assistant, my daughter, I do about eight pair a day. I call it a day, but it is not a day; I do not feel able to sit the hours I used to do. Sometimes I sit from eight in the morning until 10, or sometimes 11 at night.

1575. Did you hear what the witness before you said as to the price of materials, and so on; I suppose you would have to pay the same price?
The same price; because I suppose, to take the trimmings of the work, that there is hardly a farthing difference in all the work so far as that goes.

1576. How much can you make a day?
With me and my daughter, the hours that we sit, we do about eight pairs a day; that is when I can get them.

1577. What will that come to?
If they are 2 3/4d.; if I have a day's work, that is 1s. 10d. for the day.

1578. And out of that you find materials?
Yes, I have to find threads and cottons.

1579. And what do you consider you can clear?
Of course, when I take my trimmings and all that out, it leaves me but a very little clear; to take the average I do not suppose it leaves above 5s. 6d. a week when trimmings are taken; I do not think I am much out of the way in saying that.

1580. During the winter have you good work?
No, I lose a deal by slack time in the winter.

1581. How long is the slack time?
About two months before Christmas; this year it has been very bad indeed.

1582. Do you find any other kind of work to do then?
I do not feel able to do much other sort of work; I have not very good health myself since I have been left a widow. I have got now, at this present time, an abscess at the back of the left eye that I have been suffering from for years.

1583. You work now from about eight in the morning till 10 or 11 at night?
Yes.

1584. Used you ever to work longer hours than that?
I used to work longer when I was younger.

1585. You used to work harder?
Yes; of course I cannot do that now.

1586. What could you earn when prices were better, five or six years ago?
When the children were little I could earn, I dare say, from 10s. to 11s. a week at that time; but then that is some years ago.

1587. When did prices begin to get so bad?
That is a good many years ago now; but then I daresay for this last five years they have come down a great deal more than that.

1588. Do you think there are more people engaged in the same business now than there were then?
I think so.

1589. What is your ordinary food?
I am almost ashamed to tell the gentlemen. Of course you must know that it cannot be very good food; I know that very little meat comes to the house out of it.

1590. What do you pay for meat?
When I do get any it is 8d. a pound, and if I get a pound of it, it has to be for Sunday; that is as much as I can get when I can afford to be out of that little money.

1591. Do you have meat once a week?
Sometimes I do, and sometimes I do not. I generally try to struggle to have a bit on a Sunday, if I can possibly at all.

1592. And what is your ordinary diet, bread?
Bread and a cup of tea, and such as a bit of fish, or anything of that sort.

1593. What rent do you pay?
Two shillings a week.

1594. How do you manage to pay that during the slack times in the winter?
I have to pay it as well as I possibly can; I owe nothing of it.

1595. Do you have to fetch your work?
My daughter, she goes after the work.

1596. How far has she to go?
It is not a great distance from where I am living.

1597. [Earl of Aberdeen.] About the rent, if you get into arrears, how much time are you allowed?
She is a very good landlady that I am now living with; she will not compel me to any particular time; I could pay it the best way I could get it.

1598. [Lord Monkswell.] What were your former hours when you were strong; how many used you to work?
Perhaps it might be 12 o'clock at night and much earlier, beginning in the morning.

1599. How early beginning?
I might begin, perhaps, at six, sometimes at seven.

1600. And work generally till 12, or only sometimes?
Only sometimes.

1601. When did you leave off, usually, if you began at six or seven, when you were strong?
Sometimes about 10 o'clock.

1602. Then your hours would be usually from 6 or 7 to 10 at night?
Yes.

1603. How many days a week did you work like that?
I might have a little time just to do a bit of cleaning, either me or my daughter.

1604. Otherwise you would work the whole seven days; could you afford not to work on Sunday?
I never do any work on a Sunday, not such as that work.

1605. You say you earn 5s. 6d. a week; does that include your daughter's earnings?
That is with me; she does not do much, because she has to run about.

1606. When you get 1s. 10d. a day, that must make more than 5s. 6d. a week?
Sometimes I have trousers that I get 3d. for.

1607. Then how much would you deduct for materials?
There is firing, and the thread and the twist, and the oil; I know it comes to 1s. 6d.; that is with the firing and the trimming.

1608. One shilling and sixpence a week?
Yes, because I have all colours of thread and cotton to find.

1609. [Chairman] Do you work by gas light?
With a lamp.

1610. I forgot to ask you whether you use a sewing machine in your work?
No.

1611. Why not?
I do not use any sewing machine; I am a finisher.

1612. Do you mean that a sewing machine could not be used in finishing?
Of course it can be, but I am too old to do it now; I could not use the machine.

1613. Why not?
My nerves would never let me; I have hard work sometimes to see to thread the needle, much more a machine.

1614. Other finishers do use a machine?
Oh, yes; there are some that can finish and machine together.

1615. Could you earn better wages if you were able to use a machine?
I dare say I could, if I was able to do such a thing; but I cannot properly sit in a room when I hear the noise of a machine.

The Witness is directed to withdraw.

Studying Effectively—Exercise 5

Learning to Identify Main Points That Are Causes or Reasons

In Exercise 3 we considered cause and effect and underlined a passage dealing with effects or results. This exercise continues in this direction by focusing on causes or reasons.

Exercise

Read the following passage in its entirety. Then reread it and underline or highlight each cause (or factor) contributing to the Industrial Revolution in England.

Note that there are several causes and that they are rather compressed. (This is because the author is summarizing material presented in previous chapters before going on to discuss other causes or factors—notably technology and the energy problem—in greater detail.) Since several causal points are presented in a short space, this is a very good place to number the points (and key subpoints) in the margin. After you have finished, compare your underlining or highlighting with that in the suggested model that follows.

Eighteenth-Century Origins

Although many aspects of the English Industrial Revolution are still matters for scholarly debate, it is generally agreed that the industrial changes that did occur grew out of a long process of development. First of all, the expanding Atlantic economy of the eighteenth century served mercantilist England remarkably well. The colonial empire that England aggressively built, augmented by a strong position in Latin America and in the African slave trade, provided a growing market for English manufactured goods. So did England itself. In an age when it was much cheaper to ship goods by water than by land, no part of England was more than 20 miles from navigable water. Beginning in the 1770s, a canal-building boom greatly enhanced this natural advantage. Nor were there any tariffs within the country to hinder trade, as there were in France before 1789 and in politically fragmented Germany.

Agriculture played a central role in bringing about the Industrial Revolution in England. English farmers were second only to the Dutch in productivity in 1700, and they were continuously adopting new methods of farming as the century went on. The result, especially before 1760, was a period of bountiful crops and low food prices. The ordinary English family did not have to spend almost everything it earned just to buy bread. It could spend more on other items, on manufactured goods—leather shoes or a razor for the man, a bonnet or a shawl for the woman, toy soldiers for the son, and a doll for the daughter. Thus demand for goods within the country complemented the demand from the colonies.

England had other assets that helped give rise to industrial leadership. Unlike eighteenth-century France, England had an effective central bank and well-developed credit markets. The monarchy and the aristocratic oligarchy, which had jointly ruled the country since 1688, provided stable and predictable government. At the same time the government let the domestic economy operate fairly freely and with few controls, encouraging personal initiative, technical change, and a free market. Finally, England had long had a large class of hired agricultural laborers, rural proletarians whose numbers were further increased by the enclosure movement of the late eighteenth century. These rural wage earners were relatively mobile—compared to village-bound peasants in France and western Germany, for example—and along with cottage workers they formed a potential industrial labor force for capitalist entrepreneurs.

All these factors combined to initiate the Industrial Revolution, a term first coined by awed contemporaries in the 1830s to describe the burst of major inventions and technical changes they had witnessed in certain industries. This technical revolution went hand in hand with an impressive quickening in the annual rate of industrial growth in England. Thus industry grew at only 0.7 percent between 1700 and 1760—before the Industrial Revolution—but it grew at the much higher rate of 3 percent between 1801 and 1831, when industrial transformation was in full swing. The decisive quickening of growth probably came in the 1780s, after the American war for independence and before the French Revolution.

Eighteenth-Century Origins

causes
1
a
b
c

2
a
b

c

3

4
5

6

The Industrial Revolution grew out of the expanding Atlantic economy of the eighteenth century, which served mercantilist England remarkably well. The colonial empire, augmented by a strong position in Latin America and in the African slave trade, provided a growing market for English manufactured goods. So did England itself. In an age when it was much cheaper to ship goods by water than by land, no part of England was more than 20 miles from navigable water. Beginning in the 1770s, a canal building boom greatly enhanced this natural advantage. Nor were there any tariffs within the country to hinder trade, as there were in France before 1789 and in politically fragmented Germany.

Agriculture played a central role in bringing about the Industrial Revolution in England. English farmers were second only to the Dutch in productivity in 1700, and they were continuously adopting new methods of farming as the century went on. The result, especially before 1760, was a period of bountiful crops and low food prices. The ordinary English family did not have to spend almost everything it earned just to buy bread. It could spend more on other items, on manufactured goods—leather shoes or a razor for the man, a bonnet or a shawl for the woman, toy soldiers for the son, and a doll for the daughter. Thus, demand for goods within the country complemented the demand from the colonies. England had other assets that helped give rise to industrial leadership. Unlike eighteenth-century France, England had an effective central bank and well-developed credit markets. The monarchy and the aristocratic oligarchy, which had jointly ruled the country since 1688, provided stable and predictable government. At the same time the government let the domestic economy operate fairly freely and with few controls, encouraging personal initiative, technical change, and a free market. Finally, England had long had a large class of hired agricultural laborers, rural proletarians, whose numbers were further increased by the enclosure movement of the late eighteenth century. These rural wage earners were relatively mobile—compared to village-bound peasants in France and western Germany, for example—and along with cottage workers they formed a potential industrial labor force for capitalist entrepreneurs. All these factors combined to initiate the Industrial Revolution, a term first coined by awed contemporaries in the 1830s to describe the burst of major inventions and technical changes they had witnessed in certain industries. This technical revolution went hand in hand with an impressive quickening in the annual rate of industrial growth in England. Thus industry grew at only 0.7 percent between 1700 and 1760—before the Industrial Revolution—but it grew at the much higher rate of 3 percent between 1801 and 1831, when industrial transformation was in full swing. The decisive quickening of growth probably came in the 1780s, after the American war for independence and just before the French Revolution.

CHAPTER 27

Ideologies and Upheavals in Europe, 1815–1850

Chapter Questions

After reading and studying this chapter, you should be able to answer the following questions:

What ideas did thinkers develop to describe and shape the great political and economic transformation that was taking place? How and why did conservatives and radicals view liberalism and nationalism differently? How did the artists and writers of the romantic movement reflect and influence the era? How and why did political revolution break out once again? Why did the revolutionary surge triumph in 1848, then fail almost completely?

Chapter Summary

This chapter examines a number of extremely important ideas: liberalism, nationalism, socialism, and romanticism. Studying these ideas helps us understand the historical process in the nineteenth and twentieth centuries—including the contemporary world. A key aspect of that process was the bitter and intense struggle between the conservative aristocrats, who wanted to maintain the status quo, and the middle- and working-class liberals and nationalists, who wanted to carry on the destruction of the old regime of Europe that had begun in France in 1789. The symbol of conservatism was Prince Metternich of Austria, Europe's leading diplomat. Metternich was convinced that liberalism and nationalism had to be repressed, or else Europe would break up into warring states. In opposition to Metternich, liberals and nationalists saw their creeds as the way to free humanity from the burden of supporting the aristocracy and from foreign oppression. Metternich's convictions were shared by the other peacemakers at Vienna in 1814, while those of the liberals fanned the fires of revolution, first in 1830 and, more spectacularly, in 1848. Political liberalism, combined with the principles of economic liberalism, with its stress on unrestricted economic self-interest as the avenue to human happiness, was extremely attractive to the middle class. Of the major powers, only Britain was transformed by reform and untouched by revolution.

The chapter shows that although many believed nationalism led to human happiness, it contained in reality the dangerous ideas of national and racial superiority. To make the turbulent intellectual world even more complex, socialism emerged as another, equally powerful set of ideas regarding the creation of a just and happy society. Early socialists were idealistic and utopian, but the socialism of Karl Marx, which later became dominant, claimed to be realistic and scientific. Socialism contributed to the split between the middle and lower classes. This split explains the failure of these classes in the face of the common enemies in the revolutions of 1848. The chapter also discusses romanticism, which was a reaction to the rationalism of the previous century. Romanticism was the central mood of the nineteenth century and the emotional background of its painting, music, and literature.

Study Outline

Use this outline to preview the chapter before you read a particular section in your textbook and then as a self-check to test your reading comprehension after you have read the chapter section.

I. The peace settlement
    A. The Congress of Vienna
        1. By 1814 the conservative monarchs of Europe had defeated the French armies and checked the spread of the French Revolution.
        2. The victors restored the French boundaries of 1792 and the Bourbon dynasty.
        3. They made other changes in the boundaries of Europe, establishing Prussia as a "sentinel" against France and creating a new kingdom out of Belgium and Holland.
        4. It was believed that the concept of the balance of power—an international equilibrium of political and military forces—would preserve peace in Europe.
        5. But the demands of the victors, especially the Prussians and the Russians, for compensation threatened the balance.
            a. The Russian demands for Poland and the Prussian wish for Saxony led to conflict among the powers.
            b. Castlereagh, Metternich, and Talleyrand forced Russia and Prussia into a compromise whereby Russia got part of Poland and Prussia received two-fifths of Saxony.
    B. Intervention and repression
        1. Under Metternich, Austria, Prussia, and Russia led a crusade against liberalism.
            a. They formed a Holy Alliance to check future liberal and revolutionary activity.
            b. When liberals succeeded in Spain and in the Two Sicilies, these powers intervened to restore conservatism.
            c. However, Britain blocked intervention in Latin America and encouraged the Monroe Doctrine (1823).

2. Metternich's policies also dominated the German Confederation.
    a. Metternich had the Carlsbad Decrees issued in 1819.
    b. These decrees repressed subversive ideas and organizations.
C. Metternich and conservatism
    1. Metternich represented the view that the best state blended monarchy, bureaucracy, and aristocracy.
    2. He hated liberalism, which he claimed stirred up the lower classes and caused war and bloodshed.
        a. Liberalism also stirred up national aspirations in central Europe, which many feared could lead to war and the breakup of the Austrian Empire.
        b. The empire, which was dominated by the minority Germans, contained many ethnic groups, including Hungarians and Czechs, which was a potential source of weakness and dissatisfaction.

II. Radical ideas and early socialism
A. Liberalism
    1. Liberalism demanded representative government, equality before the law, and individual freedoms such as freedom of speech and assembly.
    2. Early nineteenth-century liberalism opposed government intervention in social and economic affairs.
    3. Economic liberalism was known as laissez faire—the principle that the economy should be left unregulated.
        a. Adam Smith was critical of mercantilism and argued that a free economy would bring wealth for all, including workers.
        b. British businessmen often used the principle of laissez faire in self-serving ways, backed up by the theories of Malthus, who believed that the population would always grow faster than the supply of food, and of Ricardo, who claimed that because of the pressure of population, wages would always be low.
    4. After 1815, political liberalism became increasingly a middle-class doctrine, used to exclude the lower classes from government and business.
        a. Some foes of conservatism called for universal voting rights for men.
        b. Many people who believed in democracy also believed in the republican form of government and were more radical than the liberals.
B. Nationalism
    1. Nationalism was a second radical idea in the years after 1815.
        a. It evolved from cultural unity.
        b. Nationalists sought to turn cultural unity into political reality, so the territory of each people coincides with its state boundaries.
        c. Modern nationalism had its roots in the French Revolution and the Napoleonic wars.
    2. Nationalists believed that common language and traditions would bring about unity and common loyalties and, therefore, self-government.
    3. On the negative side, nationalism generated ideas of racial and cultural superiority.
        a. The German pastor Herder claimed that nationalities are different.

      b.   Palacký, Mazzini, and Michelet all spoke of national mission and the superiority of one nation over others.

C. French utopian socialism.
1. Early French socialists proposed a system of greater economic equality planned by the government.
    a. They believed the rich and poor should be more nearly equal economically.
    b. They believed that private property should be abolished.
2. Saint-Simon and Fourier proposed a planned economy and socialist communities.
    a. Saint-Simon was a moralist who believed that a planned society would bring about improved conditions for the poor.
    b. Fourier proposed new planned towns; he also criticized middle-class family life and sexual and marriage customs—and advocated the total emancipation of women.
3. Blanc believed that the state should set up government-backed workshops and factories to guarantee employment.
4. Proudhon, often considered an anarchist, claimed that the worker was the source of all wealth.

D. The birth of Marxian socialism
1. The *Communist Manifesto* (1848), by Marx and Engels, is the key work of socialism.
    a. Marx saw all of previous history in terms of an economic class struggle.
    b. The industrial society was characterized, according to Marx, by the exploitation of the proletariat (workers) by the bourgeoisie (middle class).
2. He predicted that the future would bring a violent revolution by workers to overthrow the capitalists.
3. Marx argued that profits were really wages stolen from the workers.
4. His theory of historical evolution came from Hegel.
    a. Hegel believed that each age is characterized by a dominant set of ideas, which produces opposing ideas and eventually a synthesis.
    b. Marx retained Hegel's view of history as a dialectic process of change but made economic relationships between classes the driving force.

III. The romantic movement
A. Romanticism was partly a revolt against classicism and the Enlightenment.
1. Romantics rejected the classical emphasis on order and rationality.
    a. Romanticism was characterized by a belief in emotional exuberance, imagination, and spontaneity.
    b. Romantics stressed individualism and the rejection of materialism.
2. Romantics used nature as a source of inspiration, and they emphasized the study of history.
    a. History was seen as the key to an organic, dynamic universe.
    b. Reading and writing history was viewed as the way to understand national destiny.

B. Romanticism in literature
1. Romantic literature first developed fully in Britain, as exemplified by the poets Wordsworth, Coleridge, Scott, Byron, Shelley, and Keats.
   a. Wordsworth and Coleridge rejected classical rules of poetry; Wordsworth's work points to the power of nature to elevate and instruct.
   b. The Scottish novelist and poet Walter Scott romanticized history.
2. In France, Victor Hugo emphasized strange settings and human emotions.
3. Romantics such as the Frenchwoman George Sand rebelled against social conventions.
4. In central Europe romanticism reinforced nationalism.
C. Romanticism in art and music
1. Delacroix, Turner, and Constable were three of the greatest romantic painters.
2. Romantic composers rejected well-defined structure in their efforts to find maximum range and emotional intensity.
   a. Liszt was the greatest pianist of his age.
   b. Beethoven was the first master of romantic music.

IV. Reforms and revolutions
A. National liberation in Greece
1. Greek nationalists led by Ypsilanti in 1821 fought for freedom from Turkey.
2. The Great Powers supported the Ottoman Empire, but Britain, France, and Russia supported Greek nationalism, and Greece became independent in 1830.
B. Liberal reform in Great Britain
1. The British aristocracy, which controlled the Tory party, feared liberalism and worked to repress it.
2. The Corn Laws, which protected the English landowners by prohibiting the importation of foreign grain unless the domestic price rose above a certain level, is an example of aristocratic class power and selfishness.
   a. The change in the Corn Laws in 1815 led to protests by urban laborers, supported by radical intellectuals.
   b. Parliament responded by passing the Six Acts (1819), which eliminated all mass meetings.
3. The growth of the middle class and its desire for reform led to the Reform Bill of 1832, which significantly increased the number of voters.
   a. The House of Commons emerged as the major legislative body.
   b. The new industrial areas of the country gained representation in Commons.
   c. Many "rotten boroughs" were eliminated.
4. The Chartist demand for universal male suffrage failed, but the Anti-Corn Law League succeeded in getting the Corn Laws repealed in 1846 and free trade established.
5. By 1846, both the Tory and Whig parties were interested in reform.
   a. The Ten Hours Act (1847) limited the workday for women and young people in factories to ten hours.

      b. The reform efforts did not extend to Ireland, where potato crops failed in 1846, 1848, and 1851, causing the Great Famine.

      c. Fully 1 million Irish fled and at least 1.5 million died; the British efforts at relief were too little, and Ireland remained a conquered province.

C. The revolution of 1830 in France

  1. Louis XVIII's Constitutional Charter of 1814, although undemocratic, protected the people against a return to royal absolutism and aristocratic privilege.

  2. Charles X, Louis's successor, tried to re-establish the old order and repudiated the Constitutional Charter in 1830.

  3. The reaction was an immediate insurrection that brought the expulsion of Charles X.

  4. The new king, Louis Philippe, accepted the Constitutional Charter but did little more than protect the rich upper middle class.

V. The revolutions of 1848

A. A democratic republic in France

  1. The refusal of King Louis Philippe and his chief minister, Guizot, to bring about electoral reform sparked a revolt in Paris in 1848.

  2. The revolt led to the establishment of a provisional republic that granted universal male suffrage and other reforms.

  3. The revolutionary coalition couldn't agree on a common program, as the moderate, liberal republicans split with the socialist republicans.

  4. National workshops were a compromise between the socialists' demands for work for all and the moderates' determination to provide only temporary relief for the massive unemployment.

  5. The fear of socialism led to a clash of classes.

      a. The workers invaded the Constituent Assembly and tried to proclaim a new revolutionary government.

      b. The Assembly dissolved the workshops in Paris.

  6. The closing down of the workshops led to a violent uprising (the June Days).

  7. Class war led to the election of a strongman, Louis Napoleon, as president in 1848.

B. The Austrian Empire

  1. The revolution in France resulted in popular upheaval throughout central Europe, but in the end conservative reaction won.

  2. Hungarian nationalism resulted in revolution against the Austrian overlords.

      a. Under Kossuth, the Hungarians demanded national autonomy, civil liberties, and universal suffrage.

      b. Emperor Ferdinand I promised reforms and a liberal constitution.

      c. Serfdom was abolished.

  3. Conflict among the different nationalities (Hungarians against Croats, Serbs, and Romanians; Czechs against Germans), encouraged by the monarchy, weakened the revolution.

  4. The alliance of the working and middle classes soon collapsed.

  5. The conservative aristocrats crushed the revolution.

   6. Francis Joseph was crowned emperor in 1848.
   7. The Russian army helped defeat the Hungarians.
C. Prussia and the Frankfurt Assembly
   1. Middle-class Prussians wanted to create a unified, liberal Germany.
   2. Inspired by events in France, the working-class people of Prussia demanded and received a liberal constitution.
   3. Further worker demands for suffrage and socialist reforms caused fear among the aristocracy.
   4. The Frankfurt National Assembly of 1848 was a middle-class liberal body that began writing a constitution for a unified Germany.
   5. War with Denmark over the provinces of Schleswig and Holstein ended with a rejection of the Frankfurt Assembly by the newly elected Frederick William and the failure of German liberalism.

Review Questions

Check your understanding of this chapter by answering the following questions.

1. What is the "dual revolution"?

2. Describe the treatment of defeated France by the victors in 1814. Why wasn't the treatment harsher?

3. What is meant by the term *balance of power*? What methods were used by the Great Powers to preserve the balance of power?

4. What were the Hundred Days?

5. Who were the participants and what was the purpose of the Holy Alliance and the congress system?

6. Describe the make-up of the Austrian Empire. How and why were nationalism and liberalism regarded as dangerous to those in power?

7. Describe laissez-faire economic philosophy. Why did laissez-faire liberals see mercantilism as undesirable?

8. What are the links between nationalism and liberalism?

9. What are the goals of socialism? How do the ideas of Saint-Simon, Fourier, Blanc, and Proudhon illustrate socialist thought?

10. What was Marx's view of history? What was the role of the proletariat?

11. What is romanticism? What were the romantics rebelling against?

12. In what ways was romantic music a radical departure from the past? What was the purpose of romantic music?

13. Compare and contrast the political developments in Britain and France between 1814–15 and 1832. Who were the winners and the losers?

14. What were the causes and the outcome of the Greek revolution of 1821–32?

15. What were the goals of the Chartists? The Anti-Corn Law League?

16. What was the Reform Bill of 1832?

17. Why did Charles X lose his throne?

18. Describe what happened in France in 1848. Why did the French voters turn their backs on the Revolution and elect a strongman as president?

19. Was the national workshop plan a wise compromise for the French socialists?

20. Why did the revolutionary coalition in Hungary in 1848 break down?

21. Why couldn't the middle-class liberals and the urban poor in Austria cooperate in destroying their common enemies?

22. What was the role of the Archduchess Sophia in the preservation of the Austrian Empire?

23. What were the goals of the Frankfurt Assembly? Why did it fail?

Study-Review Exercises

Define the following key concepts and terms.

romanticism

conservatism

dual revolution

liberalism

nationalism

radicalism

laissez faire

iron law of wages

socialism

Marx's theory of historical evolution

classicism

republicanism

Identify and explain the significance of the following people and terms.
Quadruple Alliance

Constitutional Charter of 1814 (France)

Napoleon's Hundred Days

Congress of Troppau

congress system

Corn Laws

Ten Hours Act of 1847 (Britain)

national workshops

Wealth of Nations

Frankfurt Assembly

Schleswig-Holstein question

Louis Kossuth

Jules Michelet

Johann Herder

Frederick William IV

Alexander Ypsilanti

Chartists

Thomas Malthus

Karl Marx

Louis Philippe

Communist Manifesto

Robert Peel

Explain what ideas the following romantic figures attempted to convey to their audiences.

William Wordsworth

Walter Scott

George Sand

Victor Hugo

Eugène Delacroix

Ludwig van Beethoven

Explain the objectives of the participants at the peace conferences of 1814–15 by completing the following table.

Name of Diplomat	Country	Objective
Metternich		
Castlereagh		
Alexander I		
Talleyrand		
Hardenburg	Prussia	

Explain the objectives of the revolutionaries in the following countries and evaluate how successful they were. In each case explain why the revolution failed or succeeded.

Country	Year	Revolutionary Goals and Outcome
Spain	1820–1823	
Two Sicilies	1820–1821	
Greece	1821–1832	
France	1830	
France	1848	
Hungary	1848	
Prussia	1848	

Test your understanding of the chapter by providing the correct answers.

1. In the long run, the revolution in Germany in 1848 resulted in the *victory/defeat* of German liberalism.

2. The new president of France in 1848. _____

3. The romantic painter whose masterpiece was *Liberty Leading the People.*

    _____

4. Laissez-faire economists believed that the state *should/should not* regulate the economy.

5. Hungary was part of the _____ Empire.

6. This German pastor and philosopher argued that every national group has its own particular spirit and genius. _____

7. This mid-nineteenth-century Frenchman, author of *Organization of Work,* believed that the right to work was sacred and should be guaranteed by the state.

   _____

8. The revolution of 1848 in Austria saw *cooperation/competition* between national groups and the eventual *victory/defeat* of the old aristocracy and conservatism.

Multiple-Choice Questions

1. Which one of the following people was part of the romantic movement of the nineteenth century?
   a. George Sand
   b. Count Metternich
   c. Louis Blanc
   d. Alexis de Tocqueville

2. The British Corn Laws were passed to give economic advantage to the
   a. landed aristocracy.
   b. middle class.
   c. urban working class.
   d. agricultural workers.

3. The term *dual revolution* refers to
   a. political revolution in France and Russia.
   b. an economic and political revolution.
   c. improved health care and population increase.
   d. a revolution in both literature and music.

4. Which of the following statements about the peace settlement worked out at the Congress of Vienna is true?
   a. It was harsh toward the defeated French and rejected the restoration of the Bourbon monarchy.
   b. France gained a few colonies in addition to territories it had conquered in Italy, Germany, and the Low Countries.
   c. Belgium and Holland were united, and Prussia received territory on France's eastern border.
   d. Russia lost some western territory to Poland.

5. The problem that almost led to war among the major powers in 1815 was
   a. the refusal of France to participate in the Vienna conference.
   b. the British takeover of the South American trade routes.
   c. Russian and Prussian territorial demands.
   d. the traditional idea about balance of power.

6. The major demand of the English Chartists was for
   a. universal male suffrage.
   b. improved prison conditions.
   c. tariff protection for poor farmers.
   d. government-sponsored cooperative workshops.

7. The Holy Alliance consisted of
   a. Russia, Britain, and Austria.
   b. Britain, France, and Prussia.
   c. Prussia, Austria, and Russia.
   d. France, Austria, and Prussia.

8. Metternich's conservative policies prevailed in
   a. South America.
   b. western Europe.
   c. central Europe.
   d. Great Britain and its colonies.

9. Adam Smith would have been likely to agree that
   a. monopolies are good for a state.
   b. increased competition benefits all classes of society.
   c. increasing workers' wages is harmful in the long run.
   d. population will always grow too fast.

10. The Vienna peace settlement was largely the product of
    a. liberals.
    b. nationalists.
    c. socialists.
    d. conservatives.

11. One of the most influential French utopian socialists was
    a. the count de Saint-Simon.
    b. Talleyrand.
    c. Louis Philippe.
    d. Eugène Delacroix.

12. In 1848, great revolutions occurred in all of the following countries *except*
    a. Prussia.
    b. Hungary.
    c. Italy.
    d. Great Britain.

13. After the peace settlement of Vienna there were
    a. still over three hundred independent German political entities.
    b. thirty-eight independent German states, including Austria and Prussia.
    c. only two German states: Austria and Prussia.
    d. approximately one hundred independent German states dominated by Austria.

14. Those conservatives who opposed liberal thought would have supported
    a. representative government.
    b. equality before the law.
    c. individual freedoms, e.g., freedom of the press, freedom of speech.
    d. legally separated classes.

15. In his writings, Karl Marx drew heavily on the ideas of
    a. French writers on absolutism.
    b. English mercantilist economists.
    c. Hegel, especially the dialectic process of history.
    d. Christianity and middle-class views of the family.

16. The first great nationalist rebellion of the 1820s involved the
    a. Germans against the Austrians.
    b. Greeks against the Turks.
    c. Irish against the English.
    d. Greeks against the Russians.

17. The English Corn Laws prohibited
    a. the exporting of British grain.
    b. raising the price of British grain above that of continental prices.
    c. the importing of foreign grain unless the price of British grain reached harvest-disaster prices.
    d. the domination of the British grain market by the aristocracy.

18. The English Reform Bill of 1832 provided for
    a. representation in Parliament for the new industrial areas.
    b. the working-class vote.
    c. the supremacy of the House of Lords over the House of Commons.
    d. universal womanhood suffrage.

19. Generally, the revolutions of 1848 resulted in
    a. success for the liberal forces in France.
    b. slow gains at first for the liberals, followed by complete realization of their goals.
    c. a consolidation of moderate, nationalistic middle classes.
    d. the end of the age of romantic revolution.

20. The nineteenth-century romantic writer famous for his fascination with fantastic characters (including his "human gargoyle"), strange settings, and human emotion was
    a. William Wordsworth.
    b. Walter Scott.
    c. Victor Hugo.
    d. J. M. W. Turner.

21. The writer and poet influenced by German romanticism who wrote novels and poems based on romantic history, particularly that of Scotland, was
    a. William Wordsworth.
    b. Walter Scott.
    c. Adam Smith.
    d. Samuel Coleridge.

22. The greatest master of romantic music was
    a. Liszt.
    b. Paganini.
    c. Hugo.
    d. Beethoven.

23. Romanticism originated in
    a. Britain and Germany.
    b. France.
    c. Italy.
    d. Russia.

24. Marx believed that the key to understanding history is
    a. religion.
    b. feudalism.
    c. the power of the aristocracy.
    d. class struggle.

25. The Austrian Empire and Austrian society were dominated by which one of the following ethnic groups?
    a. German
    b. Hungarian
    c. Czech
    d. Bohemian

Major Political Ideas

1. Compare and contrast conservatism and liberalism. What are the principal beliefs of each, who were their major supporters, and how successful was each?

2. Define nationalism. Why did it become a major political force in the nineteenth century? Why did many conservatives oppose it? Did nationalism exist in the eighteenth century or earlier?

3. How were the ideas of economic liberals like Smith, Malthus, and Ricardo used by the industrialist middle class to further its own interests?

Issues for Essays and Discussion

The early nineteenth century saw the rise of a number of profoundly influential ideologies—conservatism, liberalism, nationalism, and socialism. What are the contents of these ideologies, and what are their origins? Are there any connections between them? Which were the most influential?

Interpretation of Visual Sources

Study the reproduction of the painting *Liberty Leading the People* by Delacroix on page 887 of the textbook. What is the "message" of this painting? Could it be described as an ideological painting? What are some of the characteristics of the painting in terms of composition and subject portrayal that have caused it to be described as romantic?

Geography

Study carefully Map 27.1, "Europe in 1815," to better understand the Vienna peace settlement and the balance of power in the nineteenth century. Identify the five Great Powers and fix their boundaries in your mind. Also study the boundaries of the reorganized German Confederation. What are the two main states in the confederation, and what are some of the smaller ones? Now, refer to Map 25.1 and see how France had lost and Prussia had gained in the Rhineland area. Note how Poland virtually disappeared as an independent state. How do you explain this? Finally, were Italy, Germany, and Austria clearly defined national states?

Now close the text and test your understanding with Outline Map 27.1 provided. Shade in the five Great Powers and their boundaries, trace the boundary of the German confederation, and name and locate (approximately) the capital cities of the five Great Powers. (Remember that duplicate maps for class use are at the back of this book.)

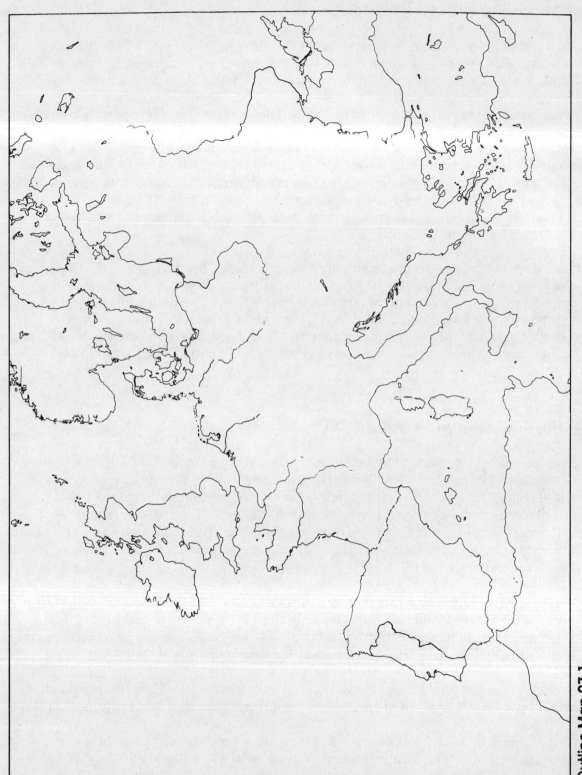

Outline Map 27.1

Understanding History Through the Arts

1. How did politics affect art in France? Begin your investigation with M. Marrian, *Painting Politics for Louis-Philippe* (1988); N. Athanassoglou, *French Images from the Greek War of Independence* (1989); and P. Mainardi, *Art and Politics of the Second Empire** (1987).

2. What do novels reveal about the period? Great novels that accurately portray aspects of the times are Victor Hugo's *Les Miserables,** an exciting story of crime and passion among France's poor; Honoré de Balzac's *Cousin Bette** and *Pere Goriot**; Thomas Mann's *Buddenbrooks** (1902), a wonderful historical novel that traces the rise and fall of a prosperous German family over three generations during the nineteenth century; and Charles Dickens's *A Tale of Two Cities*, a portrait of London and Paris during the dual revolution. A more recent historical novel about nineteenth-century life is J. Fowles's *The French Lieutenant's Woman** (1969).

3. How does Beethoven's music exemplify romantic ideals? Beethoven was the first great master of romantic music, even though in his early period he was influenced by the classical works of Haydn and Mozart. Beethoven's Ninth Symphony, the Choral Symphony, was greatly influenced by the ideas of the French Revolution—liberty, equality, and fraternity—and the symphony's "Ode to Joy" is based on Schiller's "Ode to Freedom. " The score was dedicated to Frederick William III, the king of Prussia.

Problems for Further Investigation

1. Was the 1848 revolution in France a modern class struggle in the Marxist sense? Much of the answer depends on whether or not one can show that the working class was of the new proletarian type—that is, modern factory workers rather than traditional artisan craftsmen. Begin your investigation with G. Rudé, *The Crowd in History: A Study of Popular Disturbances in France and England, 1730–1848** (1964), Chaps. 9 and 11. For the other side of the argument, see C. Tilly, "The People of June, 1848," in R. Price, ed., *Revolution and Reaction* (1977).

2. Did the British aristocrats give power to the middle class (in the Reform Bill of 1832) because they were afraid that it was the only alternative to violent revolution? This and other questions of interpretation of the famous bill are considered by seventeen different historians in W. H. Maehl, Jr., ed., *The Reform Bill of 1832** (1967).

3. What were the origins of romanticism? Those interested in the subject of romanticism should see J. B. Halsted, ed., *Romanticism: Definition, Explanation, and Evaluation** (1965).

4. Has nationalism been a force for good or for evil? A good starting point for an investigation of nationalism is H. Kohn, *Nationalism: Its Meaning and History** (1955).

*Available in paperback.

CHAPTER 28

Life in European Urban Society

Chapter Questions

After reading and studying this chapter, you should be able to answer the following questions:

What was life like in the cities? What did the emerging urban-industrial society mean for its rich, poor, and in-between members? Did the quality of life improve? What impact did the city have on family life, sexuality, marriage, and child rearing? What changes in science, thought, and culture grew out of the new urban civilization?

Chapter Summary

Life in the new urban society was exciting and complex—as well as full of problems. Although some historians argue that conditions were improving by 1850, others conclude that a deterioration in the quality of life canceled out higher wages and greater opportunity. This chapter shows that although the urban environment had long been crowded and unhealthy, the rapid growth of urban population made such problems worse. However, by the 1840s, urban problems were attacked and partly solved in Great Britain and the continental countries. For example, throughout Europe a movement for better public health brought about sewer and water systems and gradually cleaned up the worst filth. Likewise, there were revolutionary breakthroughs in preventive medicine in the 1860s and after as Pasteur and his followers discovered how germs spread disease and how disease could be controlled. Urban planning and public transportation helped people move to better, less crowded housing. Thus, by the late nineteenth century the quality of life in cities had improved dramatically for ordinary people and the working classes.

However, enormous social and economic differences between upper and lower classes continued to exist as urban and industrial growth created new classes, class conflict, and a more complex social hierarchy. The chapter illustrates these differences by describing the different classes and some of the details of their distinctive lifestyles. During this period, family life, sexual practices, and the role of women changed dramatically. In general, family life became more stable and affectionate in the later nineteenth century, but economic activities became rigidly separated according to sex—with most women relegated to the position of mother and homemaker. Only in poor families did women work. Women were subordinated to their husbands in law as well, although it appears that their power in the home increased. The result of this discrimination was the emergence of a feminist movement among middle- and working-class women. At the same time family size declined and children were treated in a more affectionate (and more calculated) manner—so much so that family life in the nineteenth century became extremely intense.

Major intellectual developments in the urban society included an expansion of scientific knowledge and the rise of realism as the dominant literary mode. Scientific thought scored theoretical triumphs, which resulted in practical improvements, a growing faith in progress, and great prestige for scientists and their methods. Influential social thinkers such as Comte and Marx sought to determine society's unalterable scientific laws, while Social Darwinists applied Darwin's theory of natural selection to human affairs. The trend toward secular thinking strengthened. Literary realism, characterized by its fascination with scientific laws, ordinary people, and urban problems, fully reflected the spirit of the age.

Study Outline

Use this outline to preview the chapter before you read a particular section in your textbook and then as a self-check to test your reading comprehension after you have read the chapter section.

I. Taming the city
   A. Industry and the growth of cities
      1. Deplorable urban conditions of congestion, filth, and disease existed long before the Industrial Revolution.
      2. The Industrial Revolution and population growth made urban reform necessary.
         a. In Britain, the percent of population living in cities of 20,000 or more jumped from 17 percent in 1801 to 54 percent in 1891.
         b. Housing was crowded and poor, and living conditions unhealthy.
         c. Many people lived surrounded by sewage and excrement.
      3. Several reasons for these conditions can be pinpointed.
         a. A lack of transportation, which necessitated the crowding, and the slowness of government enforcement of sanitary codes contributed to the problem.
         b. The legacy of rural housing also contributed to the problem.
   B. The public health movement
      1. The reformer Chadwick was influenced by Bentham's ideas of the greatest good for the greatest number.
         a. He believed that cleaning the city would curtail disease.

        b. He proposed the installation of running water and sewers.
    2. New sanitation methods and public health laws were adopted all over Europe from the 1840s on.
  C. The bacterial revolution
    1. The prevailing theory of disease (the miasmatic theory) was that it was caused by bad odors.
    2. Pasteur's theory that germs caused disease was a major breakthrough, and its application meant disease could be controlled through vaccines.
    3. Through the work of Koch and others, the organisms responsible for many diseases were identified and effective vaccines developed.
    4. Lister developed the concept of sterilization of wounds.
    5. Mortality rates began to decline rapidly in European countries.
  D. Urban planning and public transportation
    1. Better urban planning contributed to improved living conditions.
    2. After 1850, Paris was transformed by Haussmann and became a model city.
        a. Broad, straight, tree-lined boulevards cut through the center of the city.
        b. Parks were created throughout the city.
        c. Sewers were improved and aqueducts built.
    3. Zoning expropriation laws were a major tool of the new urbanism.
    4. Electric streetcars revolutionized urban life and enabled the cities to expand.

II. Rich and poor and in between
  A. Social structure
    1. Between about 1850 and 1906, the standard of living for the average person improved substantially.
    2. But differences in wealth continued to be enormous; society remained stratified in a number of classes.
  B. The middle classes
    1. The upper middle class was composed of successful business families who were attracted to the aristocratic lifestyle.
    2. The middle middle-class group contained merchants, lawyers, and doctors—people who were well off but not wealthy.
    3. Next came the lower middle class: shopkeepers, small businessmen, white-collar workers.
    4. Experts, such as engineers, chemists, accountants, and managers, were also considered members of the middle class.
    5. The middle-class lifestyle included large meals, dinner parties, servants, an interest in fashionable dressing, and good education.
    6. The middle-class code of expected behavior stressed hard work, self-discipline, religion, and restraint from vices.
  C. The working classes
    1. The vast majority of people belonged to the working class, yet the class had varying lifestyles and little unity.
    2. The most highly skilled workers constituted a fluid "labor aristocracy."
        a. They developed a lifestyle of stern morality.
        b. They considered themselves the leaders of the working class.

      c. They had strong political and philosophical beliefs.

    3. Next came the semiskilled and unskilled urban workers.

      a. Workers in the crafts and factory workers constituted the semiskilled workers.

      b. Domestic servants, mostly female, were one of the largest subgroups of the unskilled workers.

      c. Women employed in the "sweated industries" were another large group.

      d. Drinking was a favorite leisure activity of the working class; other pastimes included sports and music halls.

    4. In Europe, church attendance by the working class declined, while in the United States churches thrived and were a way to assert ethnic identity.

III. The family

    A. Premarital sex and marriage

      1. "Romantic love" had triumphed over economic considerations in the working class by 1850.

      2. Economic considerations remained important to the middle class.

      3. Both premarital sex and illegitimacy increased.

      4. After 1850, illegitimacy decreased, indicating the growing morality and stability of the working class.

    B. Prostitution

      1. Men commonly turned to prostitutes because marriages were so often made later in life, especially in the middle and upper classes.

      2. Brutal, sexist behavior was a part of life.

    C. Kinship ties

      1. Marriage and family ties were often strong.

      2. Kinship networks were an important source of mutual support and welfare.

    D. Women and family life

      1. The preindustrial pattern of women working outside the home disappeared except for working-class women.

      2. Women became full-time mothers and homemakers, not wage earners.

      3. Women were excluded from good jobs; the law placed women in an inferior position.

      a. A wife in England had no legal identity and no right to own property.

      b. The Napoleonic Code gave women few legal rights in France.

      4. Women's struggle for rights occurred on two fronts.

      a. Middle-class feminists campaigned for equal legal rights, equal opportunities in education and the professions, and the right to vote.

      b. Socialist women, especially in Germany, called for the liberation of working-class women through revolution.

      5. Meanwhile, women's control and influence in the home increased.

      a. The wife usually determined how the family's money was spent and made all the major domestic decisions.

      b. Running the household was complicated and demanding, and many women sacrificed for the welfare and comfort of their husband.

6. The home increased in emotional importance in all social classes; it symbolized shelter from the harsh working world.
7. Strong emotional bonds between mothers and children and between wives and husbands developed.

E. Child rearing
1. There was more breast-feeding and less swaddling and abandonment of babies.
2. The birthrate declined, so each child became more important and could receive more advantages.
   a. The main reason for the reduction in family size was the parents' desire to improve their economic and social position and that of their children.
   b. Children were no longer seen as an economic asset.
3. Many children were too controlled by parents, however, and suffered the effects of excessive parental concern.
   a. Parents were obsessed with the child's sexual behavior—particularly the possibility of masturbation.
   b. Relations between fathers and children were often tense; fathers tended to be very demanding.
4. In studying family dynamics, Freud developed his theory of the Oedipal complex: that the son competes with his father for the mother's love.
5. Working-class youths probably had more avenues of escape from family tensions than middle class youths.

IV. Science and thought
A. The triumph of science
1. Theoretical discoveries resulted increasingly in practical benefits, as in thermodynamics, chemistry, and electricity.
2. Scientific achievements strengthened faith in progress and gave science unrivaled prestige.
B. Social science and evolution
1. Many thinkers, such as Comte, tried to study society scientifically—using data collected by the government—and find general social laws.
   a. Comte argued that the third and final stage of knowledge is that of science, or what he called the "positivist method."
   b. Positivism would allow social scientists to develop a disciplined and harmonious society ruled by science and experts.
2. Theories of dynamic development and evolution fascinated the nineteenth century.
   a. Lyell set forth the principle of uniformitarianism, and Lamarck asserted that all forms of life had arisen through adjustment to the environment.
   b. Building on the ideas of Lyell and Lamarck, Darwin theorized that all life had evolved gradually from a common origin through an unending "struggle for survival" that led to the survival of the fittest by natural selection.
   c. Social Darwinists, such as Spencer, applied Darwin's ideas to human affairs.

C. Realism in literature
1. Realism, which stressed that heredity and environment determined human behavior, replaced romanticism as the dominant literary trend from the 1840s through the 1890s.
2. Realist writers, led by Zola, gloried in everyday life, taboo subjects, and the urban working class.
3. The realists were strict determinists and believed that human actions were caused by unalterable natural laws.
4. Balzac and Flaubert, along with Zola, were the leading French realists.
5. Mary Ann Evans (George Eliot) and Hardy in Britain, and Tolstoy in Russia were also great realists.

Review Questions

Check your understanding of this chapter by answering the following questions.

1. To what extent was industrialization responsible for the deplorable conditions of the cities in the early nineteenth century?

2. Who was Edwin Chadwick? What role did he play in the health movement?

3. What was the miasmatic theory of disease? How did it retard progress?

4. What contributions did Pasteur, Koch, and Lister make to life in urban Europe? Give examples.

5. What were the reasons for the rebuilding of Paris? Who was responsible for this change?

6. Why was the electric streetcar so important in improving urban life?

7. Marx claimed that as a result of industrialization there was an increasing polarization of society into rich and poor. Do the facts warrant such a conclusion?

8. Describe the differences and similarities between groups within the middle class. What separated and what united them?

9. What were the goals of the middle class?

10. Describe the "labor aristocracy." What were the interests of its members? How did they differ from the rest of the working class?

11. What were the interests, motives, and lifestyle of the working class? How were they changing by the late nineteenth century?

12. Why was there a decline in illegitimacy after 1850?

13. Why did middle-class men marry late? What effect did this have on their sexual behavior?

14. How common was prostitution in the nineteenth century? What sort of evidence on the subject exists?

15. Did kinship ties disappear in the new urban environment? Explain.

16. What was the social and economic position of women in the nineteenth century? Were they better off than in preindustrial society?

17. What changes occurred in child care and the attitudes toward children in the nineteenth century?

18. What was the nineteenth-century view of masturbation?

19. Overall, did family life improve in the nineteenth century? Explain.

20. In what practical ways did breakthroughs in scientific inquiry transform life for the general population of the nineteenth century?

21. What impact did science have on the study of society?

22. What were the new evolutionary views of biological development, and how did these views influence religious and social thought?

23. What was the realist movement in literature? Who were the major writers of this movement, and how did they differ from previous writers?

Study-Review Exercises

Define the following key concepts and terms.

antiseptic principle

Darwin's theory of biological evolution

sweated industries

labor aristocracy

realist movement

miasmatic theory

middle-class morality

Comte's positivism

Study Figures 28.2 and 28.4 in the textbook. What important characteristics of nineteenth-century society do they reveal?

_____

_____

_____

_____

Explain how each of the following people contributed to the improvement of nineteenth-century life.
Edwin Chadwick

Louis Pasteur

Robert Koch

Jean Baptiste Lamarck

Charles Darwin

Sigmund Freud

Gustave Flaubert

Emile Zola

Auguste Comte

Joseph Lister

Baron Georges Haussmann

Gustave Droz

Test your understanding of the chapter by providing the correct answers.

1. The birthrate *increased/decreased* in the last half of the nineteenth century.

2. He advocated the principle of "the greatest good for the greatest number."

    _____

3. Lister believed that infection could be controlled by the application of the

    "_____ principle."

4. Electric streetcars first came to the city in about the year _____ .

5. Overall, treatment of children and infants *improved/deteriorated* in the nineteenth century.

6. Generally speaking, the European aristocracy experienced *no change/a decrease* in relative income in the nineteenth century.

7. The highly skilled upper 15 percent of the working class was known as the

    _____ .

8. The status and income of schoolteachers and nurses *rose/fell* during the nineteenth century.

9. "It is to the _____ that the vast body of the working people look for recreation and entertainment."

10. By 1850, working-class young people tended to marry for *love/economic reasons*.

11. Kinship ties tended to grow *stronger/weaker* as a result of urban society.

12. Sex roles for men and women in the nineteenth century tended to become *more/less* rigid.

13. Women's economic power in the nineteenth century *increased/decreased* compared to the eighteenth century.

Multiple-Choice Questions

1. Compared to preindustrial society, the relative distribution of wealth among the three classes in industrial society
   a. probably did not change.
   b. shifted in favor of the working class.
   c. shifted significantly in favor of the middle class.
   d. shifted toward the aristocracy.

2. Which group was most opposed to drinking?
   a. Aristocracy
   b. Middle class
   c. Working class
   d. Slum dwellers

3. Comte's "stages of knowledge" theory held that the third and final stage of all intellectual activity was
   a. scientific.
   b. theological, or fictitious.
   c. metaphysical, or abstract.
   d. ideological.

4. The new movement in writing, found in the works of Zola, Flaubert, and Hardy, which pursued the typical and commonplace and claimed that human action was a result of heredity and environment, was called
   a. romanticism.
   b. secularism.
   c. realism.
   d. the positivist method.

5. Which of the following factors was a reason for the deplorable conditions of English cities up to the 1850s?
   a. Peoples' acceptance of dirt
   b. The abundance of urban land
   c. The presence of too many urban transportation facilities
   d. The slow growth of urban population

6. The development of urban society between 1850 and 1900 brought
   a. a decrease in wages.
   b. a drop in the average standard of living.
   c. less of a gap between the income of rich and poor.
   d. more diversity of occupation in the middle and lower classes.

7. By 1900, people of the working class
   a. were divided into well-defined subclasses.
   b. had generally similar lifestyles.
   c. were united against the rich.
   d. were largely agricultural workers.

8. One change the nineteenth century brought to women was
   a. less distinction between the duties of husband and wife.
   b. a rise in factory employment after marriage.
   c. more equal employment opportunities.
   d. legal subordination to men.

9. The birthrate declined in the later nineteenth century for all of the following reasons *except* the
   a. desire to give more individual care and attention to children.
   b. desire to give more educational opportunities to children.
   c. acceptance of birth-control practices by the Catholic church.
   d. declining value of children as an economic asset.

10. After 1850, ordinary women
    a. were more likely to marry for money.
    b. were more likely to breast-feed their babies.
    c. hardly ever got pregnant before marriage.
    d. generally cut themselves off from parents and relatives after they got married.

11. White-collar workers generally
    a. grew in importance in the nineteenth century.
    b. were uninterested in moving up in society.
    c. kept many servants.
    d. felt a common tie with manual workers.

12. The country in which the problems of urban congestion and deplorable conditions occurred first and most acutely was
    a. France.
    b. Germany.
    c. Great Britain.
    d. Ireland.

13. Freud's most revolutionary idea was that
    a. unconscious psychological energy was sexual energy.
    b. masturbation was a source of psychological disturbance.
    c. spontaneous affection was damaging.
    d. family life had little to do with mental illness.

14. Comte's social philosophy of positivism was based on the idea that the laws of human relations were discoverable through
    a. God.
    b. political action.
    c. social science.
    d. Marxism.

15. The realist writers held to which of the following principles in their writing?
    a. The romantic search for the sublime
    b. An emphasis on rural life
    c. A general approval of middle-class values and life
    d. A focus on everyday life, particularly that of the working classes

16. The transformation of Paris in the 1850s encompassed all of the following *except*
    a. new streets and boulevards.
    b. improved sewer and water systems.
    c. a decrease in the number of parks and amount of open space.
    d. comprehensive urban planning.

17. After the Industrial Revolution, the general standard of living
    a. decreased for everyone except the very rich.
    b. increased for everyone except for the middle class.
    c. stayed about the same for most people.
    d. improved, but did not close the gap between rich and poor.

18. The typical nineteenth-century middle-class social occasion was
    a. a trip to the music hall.
    b. gambling.
    c. a dinner party.
    d. a relaxing evening at the local pub.

19. By the late nineteenth century, indulging in heavy drinking and practicing cruel sports like cockfighting
    a. were on the increase because of more leisure time.
    b. were both in decline.
    c. fluctuated from year to year.
    d. resulted in the prohibition of such activities.

20. After 1850, the illegitimacy rate in Europe
    a. increased.
    b. decreased.
    c. remained about the same.
    d. fluctuated depending on economic conditions.

21. During the nineteenth century, the working class viewed which of the following as the most important consideration for marriage?
    a. Mercenary concerns
    b. Pregnancy
    c. Romantic love
    d. Social improvement

22. It is most likely that kinship ties within the typical nineteenth-century working-class family
    a. hardly existed.
    b. were greater than often believed.
    c. did not exist after marriage.
    d. existed only in crisis situations.

23. The division of labor by sex in the last half of the nineteenth century tended to
    a. increase.
    b. decrease.
    c. not change from the earlier period.
    d. decrease only for middle-class women.

24. Late-nineteenth-century roles of father and mother tended to become
    a. more alike.
    b. more rigid and defined.
    c. more democratic, with the father showing more affection.
    d. more equal as economic power shifted to women.

25. In nineteenth-century Europe, the working classes consisted of about
    a. four out of every five people.
    b. half the population.
    c. one out of every three people.
    d. one-quarter of the population.

Major Political Ideas

1. Define working class and working classes. Which term best describes nineteenth-century society? Many historians and political thinkers have argued that industrialization produced a single, unified working class. Do you agree? Was there such a thing as a working-class culture with values and beliefs different from other classes in society?

2. Was there a gender division of power within nineteenth-century society? Compared to previous societies, were women better or worse off in terms of their power within society? What changes had taken place?

Issues for Essays and Discussion

What was life like in the new urban society, and in what ways had it changed from previous centuries? Discuss this by describing developments in the area of (1) public health and transportation, (2) class structure, (3) family life, and (4) science and thought. Who were the winners and who were the losers in this process—or did all members of society gain?

Interpretation of Visual Sources

Study the drawing entitled "Apartment Living in Paris" on page 904 of your textbook. Name the various classes shown. Besides showing the social hierarchy, how does this illustration show the social and gender division of labor?

Geography

Study Map 28.1 in your textbook. Approximately how many more cities of 100,000 or more population existed in 1900 as compared to 1800? Where did the new concentration of urban growth take place? Why?

Understanding History Through the Arts

1. How does the art of the era reflect the times? Victorian social and moral codes were expressed in narrative, or "modern-life," paintings. These highly popular works of the

time (which have since fallen out of fashion) are interestingly described (and shown) in C. Wood, *Victorian Panorama: Paintings of Victorian Life* (1977), and J. Hadfield, *Every Picture Tells a Story: Images of Victorian Life* (1985). Impressionist painting is very popular today, but a new light on how it related to the social change of the time is sketched out in T. Clark, *The Painting of Modern Life: Paris in the Art of Manet and His Followers* (1985). Socialism and art was a subject taken up by the influential Englishman William Morris, who is himself the subject of A. Briggs, *William Morris, Selected Writings and Designs* (1957).

2. How does nineteenth-century architecture mirror nineteenth-century urban life? The student interested in architecture and the city should begin with M. Girouard, *Cities and People* (1985); D. Olsen, *The City as a Work of Art* (1986); A. Sutcliffe, ed., *Metropolis, 1890–1940* (1984); and F. Loyer, *Paris: Nineteenth-Century Architecture and Urbanism* (1988), C. L. Clark, trans. For an important development in nineteenth-century German architecture, see D. Watkin and T. Mellinghoff, *German Architecture and the Classical Ideal* (1987); and for a discussion of how architects viewed the society within which they worked, see J. Schmiechen, "The Victorians, the Historians, and the Idea of Modernism," in the *American Historical Review* 93, No. 2, April 1988.

3. How does music reflect the social changes of the nineteenth century? The tragedy of industrial-urban life for the lower classes is woven into Puccini's highly popular and romantic opera *La Bohème*, which takes place in Paris. Many recordings of this opera are available.

4. What can fiction reveal about the nineteenth century? The best way to learn about life for the common people is to read historical novels. The life of a family in early twentieth-century Scotland (Ayrshire) is told in W. McIlvanney's *Docherty* (1975); the London underworld of crime is mixed with upper-class life in M. Crichton's exciting *The Great Train Robbery** (1975); and life in a slum is the subject of Robert Robert's autobiography, *The Classic Slum** (1973). Charles Dickens's *Hard Times** has become a classic statement about life in the new industrial society, as has E. Gaskill's *Mary Barton**. A. Trollope's six novels of the Chronicles of Barsetshire, of which *Barchester Towers** (1857) is the most popular, tell of middle-class intrigues of ambition and love. An interesting fictional account of hardship and survival among the nineteenth-century working class is C. Kingsley, *Alton Locke**.

Problems for Further Investigation

1. What was life like for members of the nineteenth-century working class? Historians are just now beginning to understand how they lived. One of the problems, however, is that the working people wrote little about themselves. Some autobiographical and biographical material that exists for the British working classes is H. Mayhew, *London*

*Labour and London Poor** (reprint, 3 vols., 1969); E. Yeo, *The Unknown Mayhew** (1972); J. Burnett, ed., *Annals of Labour* (1974); P. Thompson, *The Edwardians* (1975); and J. Saville and J. Bellamy, eds., *Dictionary of Labour Biography* (6 vols., 1973–1988). For accounts of the lives of two German women, see P. Knight (with R. Knight), *A Very Ordinary Life* (1974), and A. Pott, *The Autobiography of a Working Woman*, trans. E. C. Harvey (1913).

2. In what ways did male and female roles change in Germany during this age of urbanization? Begin your study with R. Evans and W. R. Lee, *The German Family* (1981). What were some of the problems faced by women in German society in the nineteenth century? Begin your inquiry with J. Fout, ed., *German Women in the Nineteenth Century: A Social History* (1984); R. Evans, *The Feminist Movement in Germany, 1884–1933* (1976); and J. Quataert, *Reluctant Feminists in German Social Democracy, 1885–1917* (1979).

*Available in paperback.

CHAPTER 29
The Age of Nationalism in Europe, 1850–1914

Chapter Questions

After reading and studying this chapter, you should be able to answer the following questions:

How did nation building transform the major states of nineteenth-century Europe? Why did nationalism become a universal faith in Europe between 1850 and 1914? How did it evolve so that it gained the support of the broad masses of society?

Chapter Summary

The theme of this chapter is the triumph of nationalism and modernism after the unsuccessful nationalist revolutions of 1848. Between 1850 and 1914, strong nation-states developed, which won the enthusiastic support of all the social classes, caused a shift in the balance of international political power, and pulled the masses away from the socialist doctrine of class war.

Napoleon III of France played a pioneering role in this triumph of nationalism. His mild dictatorship, which came into being illegally and which lasted from 1852 to 1870, showed how the national state and its programs could appeal to rich and poor, conservative and radical. In this way, the national state became a way of coping with the challenge of rapid political and economic change. In 1860, Count Cavour, the moderate nationalist leader of the kingdom of Sardinia, managed to unify most of Italy into a single political state that was far from radical in social and economic matters. Shortly thereafter, in 1862, Otto von Bismarck became chief minister of Prussia. A master of power politics, Bismarck skillfully fought three wars to unify the states of Germany into a single nation under Prussian leadership. In doing so, Bismarck strengthened German nationalism and gave it a conservative and antiliberal thrust. Nationalism was also important in Russia. There it led to major reforms after the Crimean War: in 1861 the serfs were freed, and the government encouraged the development of railroads and modern industry. In effect, "modernization" was under way. It is with Russia that the chapter introduces the concept of "modernism"—a set of changes that enable a country to compete effectively with other countries. Frustrated nationalism was an important factor in the Russian revolution of 1905, after defeat in a war with Japan.

Nationalism continued to grow in strength in the emerging urban society of the late nineteenth century. This was because national governments and politicians responded effectively to many of the political demands and social needs of the people. Throughout most of Europe socialists and socialist political parties looked increasingly toward unions and parliaments for continued gradual improvement. They paid only lip service to the idea of radical, violent revolution and class war. The growing moderation of European socialists reflected the great appeal of nationalism for the masses. Only in multinational states, most notably the Austro-Hungarian Empire, did the growth of competing nationalisms promote fragmentation instead of unity.

Study Outline

Use this outline to preview the chapter before you read a particular section in your textbook and then as a self-check to test your reading comprehension after you have read the chapter section.

I. Napoleon III in France
   A. The Second Republic and Louis Napoleon
      1. The reasons for Napoleon's election include middle-class and peasant fears of socialism and a disgust with class politics.
      2. Many people wanted a strong national leader who would serve all the people and help them economically.
      3. Louis Napoleon believed the state had an obligation to provide jobs and stimulate the economy.
      4. Napoleon cooperated with the conservative National Assembly, but it refused to change the constitution so he could run for another term.
      5. Therefore, he seized power in a coup d'état in 1851 and dismissed the Assembly; these actions were approved by the voters.
   B. Napoleon III's Second Empire
      1. Napoleon III's greatest success was improving the economy of France.
         a. His government encouraged new investment banks and massive railroad construction.
         b. The government also sponsored an ambitious program of public works, including the rebuilding of Paris.
         c. He granted workers the right to form unions and to strike.
      2. His political system allowed only limited opposition.
         a. He restricted the Assembly and tied reform to support of his candidates.
         b. In the 1860s he allowed the Assembly greater power, gave the opposition more freedom, and granted a new constitution.

II. Nation building in Italy and Germany
   A. Italy to 1850: a battleground for great powers
      1. Italy prior to 1860 was divided; much of it was under the control of Austria and the pope.
      2. Between 1815 and 1848, the goal of national unity began to appeal to Italians.
      3. Sardinia was the logical leader in the nationalist movement.
      4. Pope Pius IX opposed nationalism and other modern ideas.
   B. Cavour and Garibaldi
      1. Cavour, the liberal minister of Sardinia, built Sardinia into a liberal and economically sound state.
         a. He was a moderate nationalist who sought unity only for the northern and perhaps central areas of Italy.
         b. He worked in the 1850s to consolidate Sardinia as a liberal state capable of leading northern Italy.
      2. Cavour used France to engineer a war with Austria to further his plans for unification.
      3. Central Italy was united with Sardinia in 1860.
      4. Garibaldi "liberated" southern Italy and Sicily, and Italy was further unified.
      5. Except for Rome and Venice, Italy was politically united by 1860.
         a. However, there were strong class divisions.
         b. There were also strong cultural divisions between the northern and southern areas.
   C. Germany before Bismarck
      1. In the aftermath of 1848, the German states were locked in a political stalemate.
      2. The Zollverein became a crucial factor in the Austro-Prussian rivalry.
      3. William I of Prussia wanted to double the size of the army, but he was opposed by the parliament, which rejected the military budget in 1862.
   D. Bismarck takes command.
      1. Bismarck was an ultraconservative Junker politician whose main goal was to strengthen Prussia's power and status.
      2. He concluded that the path to this goal was to weaken Austria.
         a. He supported German nationalism.
         b. His view was that middle-class parliamentary liberalism was not the way to unify Germany—"blood and iron" was.
   E. The Austro-Prussian War of 1866—the first step toward unification
      1. Denmark's attempted annexation of Schleswig-Holstein led first to an alliance with Austria in a war against Denmark (1864) and then to a war with Austria in 1866.
         a. The German Confederation was dissolved and a new North German Confederation, led by Prussia, formed.
         b. Austria withdrew from German affairs.
      2. Bismarck's goal of Prussian expansion was being realized.
   F. The taming of Parliament
      1. Bismarck believed the middle class could be led to prefer national unity to liberal institutions.

2. Bismarck outmaneuvered the liberals in the parliament, and the middle class ended up supporting monarchial authority.

G. The Franco-Prussian War (1870–71)
   1. Bismarck used war with France to bring southern Germany into the union.
   2. As a result of military success, semi-authoritarian nationalism in Germany won out over liberalism.

III. The modernization of Russia
   A. *Modernization* is defined as those changes that enable a country to compete effectively with leading countries of the time.
   B. The "Great Reforms"
      1. Serfdom was still the basic social institution of agrarian nineteenth-century Russia.
      2. The Crimean War (1853–1856) speeded up the modernization of Russia.
         a. Russia's defeat showed how badly the country had fallen behind the industrializing West.
         b. The war also created the need for reforms because its hardships led to the threat of peasant uprisings.
      3. Serfdom was abolished in 1861, collective ownership of the land was established, and other reforms were undertaken.
         a. Local assemblies (zemstvos) were established.
         b. The legal system was reformed.
   C. The industrialization of Russia
      1. Railroad construction stimulated the economy and inspired nationalism and imperialism.
      2. The assassination of Alexander II (1881) brought political reform to an end.
      3. Economic reform was carried out by Sergei Witte, the minister of finance from 1892 to 1903.
         a. More railroads were built, notably the trans-Siberian line.
         b. Protective tariffs were raised.
         c. Foreign ideas and money were used to build factories and create modern coal, steel, and petroleum industries.
   D. The revolution of 1905
      1. Imperialist ambitions brought defeat at the hands of Japan in 1905 and political upheaval at home.
         a. Separatist nationalism (e.g., among the Ukranians) emerged among the empire's minorities.
         b. The "Bloody Sunday" massacre, when the tsar's troops fired on a crowd of protesting workers, produced a wave of indignation.
         c. By the summer of 1905, strikes, uprisings, revolts, and mutinies were sweeping the country.
      2. A general strike in October forced Nicholas II to issue the October Manifesto, which granted full civil liberties and promised a popularly elected parliament (Duma).
      3. The Social Democrats rejected the manifesto and led a bloody workers' uprising in Moscow in December.

4. Middle-class moderates helped the government repress the uprising and survive as a constitutional monarchy.

IV. The responsive national state, 1871–1914
   A. Characteristics of the new national state
      1. Ordinary people felt increasing loyalty to their governments.
      2. By 1914, universal male suffrage was the rule, and women were beginning to demand the right to vote too.
   B. The German Empire
      1. In 1871, the German Empire was a union of twenty-five German states governed by a chancellor (Bismarck) and a parliament (the Reichstag).
      2. Bismarck and the liberals attacked the Catholic church (the Kulturkampf) in an effort to maintain the superiority of state over church, but abandoned the attack in 1878.
      3. Worldwide agricultural depression after 1873 resulted in the policy of economic protectionism in Germany.
      4. Bismarck outlawed socialist parties in 1878.
      5. Bismarck gave Germany an impressive system of social-welfare legislation, partly to weaken socialism's appeal to the workers.
      6. William II dismissed Bismarck in 1890 to try to win the support of the workers, but he couldn't stem the rising tide of socialism.
      7. The Social Democratic party became the largest party in the parliament, but it was strongly nationalistic, not revolutionary.
   C. Republican France (the Third Republic)
      1. The defeat of France in 1871 led to revolution in Paris (the Commune).
      2. The Paris Commune was brutally crushed by the National Assembly.
      3. A new Third Republic was established and led by skilled men such as Gambetta and Ferry.
      4. The Third Republic passed considerable reforms, including legalizing trade unions and creating state schools, and it built a colonial empire.
      5. The Dreyfus affair (1898–99) weakened France and caused an anti-Catholic reaction.
         a. Between 1901 and 1905, the government severed all ties between the state and the Catholic church.
         b. Catholic schools were put on their own financially and lost many students.
   D. Great Britain and Ireland
      1. The reform bills of 1867 and 1884 further extended the franchise in Britain, and political views and the party system became more democratic.
         a. Nevertheless, some, like John Stuart Mill, explored the problem of safeguarding individual differences and unpopular opinions.
         b. The conservative leader Disraeli supported extending the vote.
         c. The Third Reform Bill of 1884 gave the vote to almost every adult male.
      2. Led by David Lloyd George, the Liberal party ushered in social-welfare legislation between 1906 and 1914 by taxing the rich.

3. The issue of home rule (self-government) divided Ireland into the northern Protestant Ulsterites, who opposed it, and the southern Catholic nationalists, who favored it.
    a. Gladstone supported home rule for Ireland in 1886 and 1893, but the bills failed to pass.
    b. The question of home rule was postponed because of war in 1914.
E. The Austro-Hungarian Empire
    1. After 1866, the empire was divided in two, and the nationalistic Magyars ruled Hungary.
    2. Austria suffered from competing nationalisms, which pitted ethnic groups against one another and weakened the state.
        a. A particularly divisive issue was the language used in government and elementary education.
        b. From 1900 to 1914 the parliament was so divided that a majority could not be obtained.
        c. Anti-Semitism grew rapidly, especially in Vienna.
        d. In Hungary the Magyar nobility dominated the peasantry and the minorities.
        e. Unlike other states, nationalism weakened the Austro-Hungarian Empire.

V. Marxism and the socialist movement
    A. The Socialist International
        1. A rapid growth of socialist parties occurred throughout Europe after 1871.
        2. With Marx's help, socialists united in 1864 to form an international socialist organization known as the First International; it was short-lived but had a great psychological impact.
        3. The Second International—a federation of national socialist parties—lasted until 1914.
    B. Unions and revisionism
        1. There was a general rise in the standard of living and quality of life for workers in the late nineteenth century, so they became less revolutionary.
        2. Unions were gradually legalized in Europe, and they were another factor in the trend toward moderation.
        3. Revisionist socialists (such as Bernstein) believed in working within capitalism (through labor unions, for example) and no longer saw the future in terms of capitalist-worker warfare.
        4. In the late nineteenth century, the socialist movements within each nation became different from one another and thereby more and more nationalistic.

Review Questions

Check your understanding of this chapter by answering the following questions.

1. How was Germany unified? Describe Bismarck's methods. What were the long-term results?

2. Why did nationalism become a universal faith in Europe between 1850 and 1914?

3. How did nationalism gain the support of the broad masses of society?

4. Why did the voters of France elect Louis Napoleon president in 1848? Why did they elect him emperor a few years later?

5. What were some of the benefits Napoleon bestowed on his subjects?

6. Did Napoleon allow any political opposition to exist? Describe his political system and explain why it eventually broke down.

7. Why was Italy before 1860 merely a "geographical expression"?

8. What were the three basic approaches to Italian unification? Which one prevailed?

9. What was the nature and significance of Garibaldi's liberation of Sicily and Naples in 1860? Why was Cavour so nervous about Garibaldi?

10. What were the causes and results of the Austro-Prussian War?

11. What was the significance of the Zollverein in German history?

12. Why did the Prussian liberals make an about-face and support their old enemy Bismarck after 1866?

13. Why did nationalism weaken rather than strengthen the Austro-Hungarian Empire?

14. What is "modernization" and how was it introduced into Russia? Which was the most "modern" of the states of Europe at the middle of the nineteenth century?

15. What was the status of the Russian serf in the early nineteenth century? How beneficial was the reform of 1861 to the serf?

16. Why was the Crimean War a turning point in Russian history?

17. How did Russia use the West to catch up with the West?

18. Was the new Germany a democracy? Where did power reside in the Germany of 1871?

19. What was Bismarck's relationship (after 1871) with (a) the Catholic church, (b) the liberals, and (c) the socialists?

20. What were the German social-welfare laws? What were their origins?

21. What were the causes and outcome of the Dreyfus affair in France?

22. What were the major political developments and issues in Britain and Ireland in the late nineteenth century? Was the Irish problem solvable?

23. In what ways were ethnic rivalries and growing anti-Semitism related in Austro-Hungary?

24. How does one account for the rapid growth of socialist parties in Europe in the last quarter of the nineteenth century?

25. What was the purpose of the socialist internationals? To what degree did they represent working-class unity?

26. What were the general arguments of the revisionist socialists? Were they true Marxists?

Study-Review Exercises

Identify and explain the significance of the following people.

Benjamin Disraeli

Emmeline Pankhurst

Jules Ferry

Sergei Witte

Alexander II

Camillo Benso di Cavour

Edward Bernstein

Pius IX

William Gladstone

Giuseppe Garibaldi

William II

John Stuart Mill

Explain what the following events were, who participated in them, and why they were important.
The People's Budget (Britain)

Napoleon III's coup d'état

May Day

assassination of Tsar Alexander II

establishment of the Zollverein (1834)

establishment of the Austro-Hungarian monarchy

Treaty of Villafranca

Paris Commune of 1871

Ulster revolt of December 1913

Explain the outcome and significance of each of the following wars by completing the following table.

	Year	Outcome and Significance
Danish War		
Austro-Prussian War		
Franco-Prussian War		
Crimean War		
Russo-Japanese War		

Test your understanding of the chapter by providing the correct answers.

1. In 1851, the French voters *approved/disapproved* of Louis Napoleon's seizure of power.

2. Increasingly, the main opposition to Napoleon III came from the *middle/working/upper* class.

3. The Russian *victory/defeat* in the Crimean War of 1853–1856 contributed to *freedom/serfdom* for the Russian peasants after 1861.

4. After 1848, the pope *supported/opposed* Italian unification.

5. After 1873, the price of wheat on the world market *rose/fell* dramatically.

6. The minority Irish Ulsterites were *Catholic/Protestant* and *for/against* home rule.

7. Bismarck used war with *Austria/France/Russia* to bring the south Germans into a united Germany.

Multiple-Choice Questions

1. The most industrialized, socialized, and unionized continental country by 1914 was
   a. France.
   b. Germany.
   c. Italy.
   d. Belgium.

2. The Russian zemstvo was a(n)
   a. industrial workers' council.
   b. local government assembly.
   c. terrorist group.
   d. village priest.

3. The Kulturkampf in Germany was an attack on
   a. liberals.
   b. socialists.
   c. the Catholic church.
   d. Prussian culture.

4. The first modern social security laws were passed in the 1880s in
   a. Britain.
   b. France.
   c. Russia.
   d. Germany.

5. The general tendency of unions toward the end of the century was
   a. to move closer to Marxism.
   b. to move toward evolutionary socialism.
   c. to reject socialism altogether.
   d. increasingly to favor revolution.

6. After 1850, the disciples of nationalism in Italy looked for leadership from
   a. Prussia.
   b. the papacy.
   c. Sardinia-Piedmont.
   d. the kingdom of the Two Sicilies.

7. Cavour's program for the unification of northern Italy included
   a. improved transportation.
   b. increased power for the Catholic church.
   c. restriction of civil liberties.
   d. compromise and cooperation with Austria.

8. Russian social and political reforms in the 1860s could best be described as
   a. revolutionary.
   b. totally ineffective.
   c. halfway measures.
   d. extremely effective.

9. Witte's plans for the economic development of Russia included
   a. lowering protective tariffs.
   b. taking Russia off the gold standard.
   c. encouraging foreign investment.
   d. bringing Russian Marxists into the government.

10. Bismarck's fundamental goal for Prussia was
    a. democratic reform.
    b. expansion.
    c. the elimination of nationalism.
    d. the elimination of the monarchy.

11. Which of the following groups fought for the defense of Captain Dreyfus in France?
    a. The Catholics
    b. The army
    c. The radical republicans
    d. The anti-Semites

12. Among those opposing home rule in Ireland were
    a. Catholics.
    b. Ulsterites.
    c. Irish peasants.
    d. William Gladstone.

13. After 1870, Marxian socialists
    a. accepted the revisionist theories of Edward Bernstein.
    b. failed to grow in number.
    c. formed a second international organization.
    d. refused to participate in national elections.

14. Which of the following statements about German unification is true?
    a. It was completed in 1891 with a war between Prussia and Russia.
    b. The chief architect of the movement was the emperor of Austria.
    c. The unification process was directed by the German state of Austria.
    d. Unification did not include liberal and democratic ideas and methods.

15. A new institution of local government established in Russia in 1864 was the
    a. zemstvo.
    b. Reichstag.
    c. Duma.
    d. Zollverein.

16. Changes that enable a country to compete effectively with leading countries at a given time are called
    a. nationalism.
    b. modernization.
    c. revisionism.
    d. reconstruction.

17. Which of the following was *not* an action taken by the Third French Republic?
    a. Crushing the Paris Commune of 1871
    b. Passing considerable reforms
    c. Legalization of trade unions
    d. Expansion of the traditional Catholic school system

18. The Russian defeat in the Crimean War of 1853–1856
    a. signaled the end of the modernization of Russia for nearly fifty years.
    b. resulted in legal and local political reform.
    c. delayed the abolition of serfdom.
    d. was relatively insignificant militarily and politically.

19. The German Zollverein was
    a. a trade union.
    b. a customs union.
    c. an "all-German" parliament.
    d. a political party.

20. Bismarck's policy toward the Social Democrats was one of
    a. limited support.
    b. political alliance to defeat the military party.
    c. total repression.
    d. official tolerance.

21. The sometime popular emperor-dictator of France who granted France a new constitution in 1869 was
    a. Napoleon III.
    b. Baron Haussmann.
    c. Alexander H. Stephens.
    d. Sergei Witte.

22. The new popularly elected parliament in Russia after 1905 was known as the
    a. House of Commons.
    b. National Assembly.
    c. Reichstag.
    d. Duma.

23. The People's Budget of David Lloyd George in Britain was, in effect, a tax on
    a. the rich.
    b. those who wanted national health insurance.
    c. the urban masses.
    d. the middle classes.

24. After the adoption of the 1867 constitution, Hungary was dominated by
    a. the peasantry.·
    b. the middle classes.
    c. the Croatians and Romanians.
    d. the Magyar nobility.

25. Between 1906 and 1913 in Germany, the working classes
    a. increasingly rejected unions and unionism.
    b. adopted revolutionary Marxist principles.
    c. looked to collective bargaining as a substitute for revolution.
    d. rejected Bernstein's revisionist thought.

Major Political Ideas

1. What is meant by the term *responsive national state*? Why did it come to serve as a new unifying principle? Give examples of how this new concept of state worked. How did this state differ from earlier ones in terms of its objectives and its appeal? Which nation best exemplifies this development?

2. By 1914 a large number of Europeans had adopted social democracy as their political and cultural ideology. What were the goals of the Social Democratic party in Germany and elsewhere? How revolutionary was this socialist movement, and what were the ideas behind revisionism, or evolutionary socialism?

Issues for Essays and Discussion

Between about 1850 and 1914, nationalism became almost a new religion in Europe and the United States. Why? What were the characteristics of nationalism that were so appealing? Define the goals of nationalism and then compare and contrast how nationalist goals were implemented in France, Germany, Italy, and Russia. Was nationalism, in your opinion, a positive or negative force in history?

Interpretation of Visual Sources

Study the reproduction of the print entitled "Rebuilding Paris" on page 932 of your textbook. What appears to be the purpose of this demolition? What do you imagine the original site looked like compared to its successor? Note the irregular thoroughfare to the center right. Why do you think this sort of passage was regarded as undesirable? How is this project tied to the idea of the responsive national state? (This topic is also discussed in Chapter 28 under the heading "Urban Planning and Public Transportation.")

Geography

On Outline Map 29.2, and using Map 29.2 in the textbook for reference, mark the following: the boundaries of both the old German Confederation and the new Germany of 1871, Prussia before 1866, the territory added to Prussia as a result of the Austro-Prussian War in 1866, the territory joined to Prussia to form the North German Confederation of 1867, the territory joined to all of the preceding to make up the new German Empire in 1871, Berlin, Bavaria, Wurtenburg, Baden, Hanover, Mecklenburg, Oldenburg, Schleswig, Saxony, and the Oder, Rhine, Danube, and Elbe rivers. (Remember that duplicate maps for class use are at the back of this book.)

Outline Map 29.2

Understanding History Through the Arts

1. What were the achievements in the arts in the nineteenth century? British achievements in architecture, design, literature, drama, and music are surveyed in B. Ford, ed., *The Cambridge Guide to the Arts in Britain: The Later Victorian Age* (1989). The book includes a chapter on the Scottish city of Glasgow, which was the center of much artistic activity. Another city that excelled in the arts was Vienna; it is the subject of C. Schorske, *Fin-de-Siècle Urban Politics and Culture** (1980).

2. What is the music of the era like? In music the mood of the last half of the nineteenth century was romantically nationalistic. Brahms wrote *Song of Triumph* to celebrate the German victory over France in 1870, while Smetana, the first great Czech nationalist composer, glorified the folk history of the Czech people in *My Country*. In opera, Moussorgsky wrote *Boris Godunov* (1874), a historical drama about Russia during the time of Ivan the Terrible. The popularity of German heroic music-drama continued to grow, and it drew added inspiration from Wagner's *The Ring of the Nibelung* (four parts, 1869–1876), a monumental national epic of Germany based on Nordic mythology. All of these works are available on a number of recordings.

Problems for Further Investigation

1. Who was Napoleon III, and what were his motives? Begin your investigation with B. D. Gooch, ed., *Napoleon III—Man of Destiny** (1963).

2. Why was it so difficult to unify Italy? The problems of interpreting the Italian unification movement are discussed by a number of historians in C. F. Delzell, *The Unification of Italy** (1963).

3. How did the workers become politicized? Those interested in the political activities of British workers will want to start with H. Pelling, *The Origins of the Labour Party* (1954), and, for the interesting story of the politicization of the German working class from Marx to the present, begin with H. Grebing, *The History of the German Labour Movement* (1969).

4. How did the Franco-German War change the course of history? French-German relations and French history took a tragic turn in 1870 with the siege of Paris and the grim civil war that followed. This is the subject of A. Horne, *The Fall of Paris: The Siege and the Commune of 1870–1** (1965, 1981).

5. What were the goals and interests of women in the nineteenth century? Begin with T. Lloyd, *Suffragettes International: The World-Wide Campaign for Women's Rights** (1971);

*Available in paperback.

M. Thomis and J. Grimmett, *Women in Protest, 1800–1850** (1983); and O. Banks, *Faces of Feminism* (1981). Further, in an era in which most women were confined to either the kitchen or drawing room, three Victorian women, Josephine Butler, Octavia Hill, and Florence Nightingale, became important makers of social policy. They are the subjects of N. Boyd, *Three Victorian Women Who Changed Their World* (1982). Women and socialism is the subject of C. Sowerwine, "The Socialist Women's Movement from 1850 to 1940," in R. Bridenthal, C. Koonz, and S. Stuard, eds., *Becoming Visible: Women in European History** (1987). One of the horror stories of working-class history is the plight of women and children caught up in the infamous "sweating system"—a story retold in J. Schmiechen, *Sweated Industries and Sweated Labor* (1984). One of the most interesting women of the century was Queen Victoria of Britain, whose life is dealt with in the lively biography *Queen Victoria** (1964) by E. Longford.

6. Was socialism a positive or negative force in the struggle for reform? The nineteenth century saw the publication of many books based on the idea that humanity could transform itself and build a new world ruled by justice and equality. One of the most popular of these utopian works in Europe was written by an American, Edward Bellamy, whose *Looking Backward** was first published in 1888. One of the most influential socialist thinkers and writers in Britain was William Morris, whose book *News From Nowhere** (1890) is a masterpiece of the socialist utopian style of writing that inspired many to work for reform of the present system. Also important were H. H. Hyndman's *England for All** (1883) and the very popular socialist (but not Marxist) little book *Merrie England* (1894) by R. Blatchford. Blatchford's aim was to explain the meaning of socialism to the common man.

*Available in paperback.

PRIMARY SOURCES
Varieties of Socialism

One of the most important political developments of late-nineteenth-century Europe was the popularity of socialism as an alternative to the capitalist organization of society. Although Karl Marx was important in this process, he was neither the most popular nor the most influential of the socialist writers. The documents that follow illustrate the varieties of socialist thought that existed in the late nineteenth century.

Edward Bernstein (1850–1932) was a German Social Democrat who challenged the predictions of Marx that capitalism would end in catastrophe and that the bourgeois parliamentary state is an enemy of the working classes. According to Bernstein, what advances have the workers made that were not anticipated by Marx and Engels? What goals should the working class set for itself? What are the predictions of Marx and Engels that Bernstein believes to be mistaken or contradictory?

Eduard Bernstein, *Evolutionary Socialism**

I set myself against the notion that we have to expect shortly a collapse of the bourgeois economy, and that social democracy should be induced by the prospect of such an imminent, great, social catastrophe.[1] . . .

The adherents of this theory of a catastrophe base it especially on the conclusions of the *Communist Manifesto*. This is a mistake in every respect.

The theory which the *Communist Manifesto* sets forth of the evolution of modern society was correct as far as it characterised the general tendencies of that evolution. But it was mistaken

---

**Source:* Edward Bernstein, *Evolutionary Socialism, A Criticism and Affirmation*, intro. Sidney Hook, trans. E. C. Harvey (Schocken Books, first paper edition, 1961).
[1] The Marxists held that a great economic crash or revolution or some other internal disorder within capitalism, such as revolution, would cause capitalism to collapse.

in several special deductions, above all in the estimate of the time the evolution would take. The last has been unreservedly acknowledged by Friedrich Engels, the joint author with Marx of the *Manifesto,* in his preface to the *Class War in France.* But it is evident that if social evolution takes a much greater period of time than was assumed, it must also take upon itself forms and lead to forms that were not foreseen and could not be foreseen then.

Social conditions have not developed to such an acute opposition of things and classes as is depicted in the *Manifesto.* It is not only useless, it is the greatest folly to attempt to conceal this from ourselves. The number of members of the possessing classes is to-day not smaller but larger. The enormous increase of social wealth is not accompanied by a decreasing number of capitalists but by an increasing number of capitalists of all degrees. The middle classes change their character but they do not disappear from the social scale.

The concentration in productive industry is not being accomplished even to-day in all its departments with equal thoroughness and at an equal rate. In a great many branches of production it certainly justifies the forecasts of the socialist critic of society; but in other branches it lags even to-day behind them. The process of concentration in agriculture proceeds still more slowly. . . .

In all advanced countries we see the privileges of the capitalist bourgeoisie yielding step by step to democratic organisations. Under the influence of this, and driven by the movement of the working classes which is daily becoming stronger, a social reaction has set in against the exploiting tendencies of capital, a counteraction which, although it still proceeds timidly and feebly, yet does exist, and is always drawing more departments of economic life under its influence. Factory legislation, the democratising of local government, and the extension of its area of work, the freeing of trade unions and systems of co-operative trading from legal restrictions, the consideration of standard conditions of labour in the work undertaken by public authorities—all these characterise this phase of the evolution.

But the more the political organisations of modern nations are democratised the more the needs and opportunities of great political catastrophes are diminished. He who holds firmly to the catastrophic theory of evolution must, with all his power, withstand and hinder the evolution described above, which, indeed, the logical defenders of that theory formerly did. But is the conquest of political power by the proletariat simply to be by a political catastrophe? Is it to be the appropriation and utilisation of the power of the State by the proletariat exclusively against the whole non-proletarian world?

He who replies in the affirmative must be reminded of two things. In 1872 Marx and Engels announced in the preface to the new edition of the *Communist Manifesto* that the Paris Commune had exhibited a proof that "the working classes cannot simply take possession of the ready-made State machine and set it in motion of their own aims." And in 1895 Friedrich Engels stated in detail in the preface to *War of the Classes* that the time of political surprises, of the "revolutions of small conscious minorities at the head of unconscious masses" was to-day at an end, that a collision on a large scale with the military would be the means of checking the steady growth of social democracy and of even throwing it back for a time—in short, that social democracy would flourish far better by lawful than by unlawful means and by violent revolution. And he points out in conformity with this opinion that the next task of the party should be "to work for an uninterrupted increase of its votes" or to carry on a slow propaganda of parliamentary activity. . . .

[To Engels] the task of social democracy is, instead of speculating on a great economic crash, "to organise the working classes politically and develop them as a democracy and to fight for all reforms in the State which are adapted to raise the working classes and transform the State in the direction of democracy."

That is what I have said in my impugned article and what I still maintain in its full import. . . .

The conquest of political power by the working classes, the expropriation of capitalists, are not ends in themselves but only means for the accomplishment of certain aims and endeavours. . . . The conquest of political power necessitates the possession of political rights; and the most important problem of tactics which German social democracy has at the present time to solve, appears to me to be to devise the best ways for the extension of the political and economic rights of the German working class.

Robert Blatchford was a British journalist who was influenced by Carlyle, Ruskin, Mill, the Christian socialists, and Karl Marx. In his enormously popular little book, *Merrie England* (1894), he sought to explain the meaning of socialism to the average man and woman (the "John Smith" of the following excerpt). How does he define socialism? What, in effect, would practical socialism be like? How, to his mind, does this differ from the system of the time? What do you believe to be the strengths and weaknesses of this argument?

Robert Blatchford, "What Is Socialism?"*

John Smith, do you know what Socialism is? You have heard it denounced many a time, and it is said that you do not believe in it; but do you know what it is?

But before I tell you what Socialism is, I must tell you what Socialism is not. For half our time as champions of Socialism is wasted in denials of false descriptions of Socialism; and to a large extent the anger, the ridicule, and the argument of the opponents of Socialism are hurled against a Socialism which has no existence except in their own heated minds.

Socialism does not consist in violently seizing upon the property of the rich and sharing it out amongst the poor.

Socialists do not propose by a single Act of Parliament, or by a sudden revolution, to put all men on an equality, and compel them to remain so. Socialism is not a wild dream of a happy land where the apples will drop off the trees into our open mouths, the fish come out of the rivers and fry themselves for dinner, and the looms turn out ready-made suits of velvet with golden buttons without the trouble of coaling the engine. Neither is it a dream of a nation of stained-glass angels, who never say damn, who always love their neighbours better than themselves, and who never need to work unless they wish to.

No, Socialism is none of those things. It is a scientific scheme of national Government, entirely wise, just, and practical. And now let us see. . . .

Practical Socialism is so simple that a child may understand it. It is a kind of national scheme of co-operation, managed by the State. Its programme consists, essentially, of one demand,

*Source: Robert Blatchford, *Merrie England* (London, 1894), 98–102.

that the land and other instruments of production shall be the common property of the people, and shall be used and governed by the people for the people.

Make the land and all the instruments of production State property; put all farms, mines, mills, ships, railways, and shops, under State control, as you have already put the postal and telegraphic services under State control, and Practical Socialism is accomplished.

The postal and telegraphic service is the standing proof of the capacity of the State to manage the public business with economy and success.

That which has been done with the post-offices may be done with mines, trams, railways, and factories.

The differences between Socialism and the state of things now in existence will now be plain to you.

At present the land—that is, England—does not belong to the people—to the English—but to a few rich men. The mines, mills, ships, shops, canals, railways, houses, docks, harbours, and machinery do not belong to the people, but to a few rich men.

Therefore the land, the factories, the railways, ships and machinery are not used for the general good of the people, but are used to make wealth for the few rich men who own them. Socialists say that this arrangement is unjust and unwise, that it entails waste as well as misery, and that it would be better for all, even for the rich, that the land and other instruments of production should become the property of the State, just as the post-office and the telegraphs have become the property of the State.

Socialists demand that the State shall manage the railways and the mines and the mills just as it now manages the post-offices and the telegraphs.

Socialists declare that if it is wicked and foolish and impossible for the State to manage the factories, mines, and railways, then it is wicked and foolish and impossible for the State to manage the telegraphs.

Socialists declare that as the State carries the people's letters and telegrams more cheaply and more efficiently than they were carried by private enterprise, so it could grow corn and weave cloth and work the railway systems more cheaply and more efficiently than they are now worked by private enterprise.

Socialists declare that as our Government now makes food and clothing and arms and accoutrements for the army and navy and police, so it could make them for the people.

Socialists declare that as many corporations make gas, provide and manage the water-supply, look after the paving and lighting and cleansing of the streets, and often do a good deal of building and farming, so there is no reason why they should not get coal, and spin yarn, and make boots, and bread, and beer for the people.

Socialists point out that if all the industries of the nation were put under State control, all the profit, which now goes into the hands of a few idle men, would go into the coffers of the State—which means that the people would enjoy the benefits of all the wealth they create.

This, then, is the basis of Socialism, that England should be owned by the English, and managed for the benefit of the English, instead of being owned by a few rich idlers, and mismanaged by them for the benefit of themselves.

But Socialism means more than the mere transference of the wealth of the nation to the nation.

Socialism would not endure competition. Where it found two factories engaged in under-cutting each other at the price of long hours and low wages to the workers, it would step in and fuse the two concerns into one, save an immense sum in cost of working, and finally produce more goods and better goods at a lower figure than were produced before.

But Practical Socialism would do more than that. It would educate the people. It would provide cheap and pure food. It would extend and elevate the means of study and amusement. It would foster literature and science and art. It would encourage and reward genius and industry. It would abolish sweating and jerry work. It would demolish the slums and erect good and handsome dwellings. It would compel all men to do some kind of useful work. It would recreate and nourish the craftsman's pride in his craft. It would protect women and children. It would raise the standard of health and morality; and it would take the sting out of pauperism by paying pensions to honest workers no longer able to work.

Why nationalise the land and instruments of production? To save waste; to save panics; to avert trade depressions, famines, strikes, and congestion of industrial centres; and to prevent greedy and unscrupulous sharpers from enriching themselves at the cost of the national health and prosperity. In short, to replace anarchy and war by law and order. To keep the wolves out of the fold, to tend and fertilise the field of labour instead of allowing the wheat to be strangled by the tares, and to regulate wisely the distribution of the seed-corn of industry so that it might no longer be scattered broadcast—some falling on rocks, and some being eaten up by the birds of the air.

CHAPTER 30

The World and the West

Chapter Questions

After reading and studying this chapter, you should be able to answer the following questions:

What was the "new imperialism," and how and why did it occur? What were its consequences for Europe and the new colonial peoples?

Chapter Summary

We live in a world in which the consequences of nineteenth-century Western imperialism are still being felt. In the nineteenth century, Western civilization reached the high point of its long-standing global expansion. Western expansion in this period took many forms. There was, first of all, economic expansion. Europeans invested large sums of money abroad, building railroads and ports, mines and plantations, factories and public utilities. Trade between nations grew greatly, and a world economy developed. Between 1750 and 1900, the gap in income disparities between industrialized Europe and America and the rest of the world grew at an astounding rate. Part of this was due, first, to a rearrangement of land use that accompanied Western colonialism and to Western success in preventing industrialization in areas westerners saw as markets for their manufactured goods. European economic penetration was very often peaceful, but Europeans (and Americans) were also quite willing to force isolationist nations such as China and Japan to throw open their doors to westerners. Second, millions of Europeans migrated abroad. The pressure of poverty and overpopulation in rural areas encouraged this migration, but once in the United States and Australia, European settlers passed laws to prevent similar mass migration from Asia.

A third aspect of Western expansion was that European states established vast political empires, mainly in Africa but also in Asia. This "new imperialism" occurred primarily between 1880 and 1900, when European governments scrambled frantically for territory. White people came, therefore, to rule millions of black and brown people in Africa and Asia.

The causes of the new imperialism are still hotly debated. Competition for trade, superior military force, European power politics, and a racist belief in European superiority were among the most important. Some Europeans bitterly criticized imperialism as a betrayal of Western ideals of freedom and equality.

Western imperialism produced various reactions in Africa and Asia. The first response was simply to try to drive the foreigners away. The general failure of this traditionalist response then led large masses to accept European rule, which did bring some improvements. A third response was the modernist response of Western-educated natives, who were both repelled by Western racism and attracted by Western ideals of national independence and economic progress. Thus, imperialism and reactions to it spread Western civilization to non-Western lands.

Study Outline

Use this outline to preview the chapter before you read a particular section in your textbook and then as a self-check to test your reading comprehension after you have read the chapter section.

I. Industrialization and the world economy
   A. The rise of global inequality
      1. The Industrial Revolution caused a great and steadily growing gap between Europe and North America and the nonindustrializing regions of Africa, Asia, and Latin America.
         a. In 1750, the average standard of living in Europe was no higher than the rest of the world.
         b. By 1970, the average person in the rich countries had twenty-five times the wealth of the average person in the poor countries.
         c. This gap, seen first between Britain and the rest of Europe, was the result of industrialization.
         d. Only after 1945 did Third World regions begin to make gains.
      2. Some argue that these disparities are the result of the West using science and capitalism; others argue that the West used its economic and political power to steal its riches.
   B. Trade and foreign investment
      1. World trade, which by 1913 was twenty-five times what it had been in 1800, meant an interlocking economy centered in and directed by Europe.
      2. Britain played a key role in using trade to link the world.
         a. It used its empire as a market for its manufactured goods.
         b. It prohibited its colonies from raising protective tariffs.
         c. Britain sought to eliminate all tariffs on traded goods, and this free-trade policy stimulated world trade.
      3. The railroad, the steamship, refrigeration, and other technological innovations revolutionized trade patterns.

4. The Suez and Panama canals and modern port facilities fostered intercontinental trade.
5. Beginning in about 1840, Europeans invested large amounts of capital abroad and in other European countries.
   a. Most of the exported capital went to the United States, Canada, Australia, New Zealand, and Latin America, where it built ports and railroads.
   b. This investment enabled still more land to be settled by Europeans, pushing out the native peoples already living there.
C. The opening of China and Japan
   1. European trade with China increased, but not without a struggle.
      a. China was self-sufficient and had never been interested in European goods, and the Manchu Dynasty carefully regulated trade.
      b. British merchants and the Chinese clashed over the sale of opium and the opening of Chinese ports to Europeans.
      c. The opium war in 1839–1842 led to the British acquisition of Hong Kong and the opening of four cities to trade (the Treaty of Nanking).
      d. A second war in 1856–1860 resulted in more gains for Europeans.
   2. Japan also was unwilling to trade or have diplomatic relations with the West.
      a. Japan wanted to maintain its long-standing isolation.
      b. An American fleet under Perry "opened" Japan in 1853 with threats of naval bombardment.
D. Western penetration of Egypt
   1. Muhammad Ali built a modern state in Turkish-held Egypt that attracted European traders.
      a. He stepped into the power vacuum left when the French occupiers withdrew in 1801.
      b. He drafted the peasants, reformed the government, and improved communications.
      c. The peasants lost out because the land was converted from self-sufficient farms to large, private landholdings to grow cash crops for export.
   2. Ismail continued the modernization of Egypt, including the completion of the Suez Canal, but also drew the country deeply into debt.
   3. To prevent Egypt from going bankrupt, Britain and France intervened politically.
   4. Foreign financial control provoked a violent nationalistic reaction in Egypt that led to British occupation of the country until 1956.

II. The great migration from Europe and Asia
   A. The pressure of population
      1. The population of Europe more than doubled between 1800 and 1900.
      2. This population growth was the impetus behind emigration.
      3. Migration patterns varied from country to country, reflecting the differing social and economic conditions.
         a. Five times as many people migrated in 1900–1910 as in the 1850s.

      b. Between 1840 and 1920, one-third of all migrants came from Britain; German migration was greatest between 1830 and the 1880s, while Italian migration continued high until 1914.

      c. The United States absorbed about half the migrants from Europe, while in other countries an even larger proportion of their population was new arrivals.

  B. European migrants

    1. Most European migrants were peasants lacking adequate landholdings or craftsmen threatened by industrialization.

      a. Most were young and unmarried, and many returned home after some time abroad.

      b. Many were spurred on by the desire for freedom; many Jews left Russia after the pogroms of the 1880s.

      c. Italian migrants were typical in that they were small landowning peasants who left because of agricultural decline; many of them went to Brazil and Argentina but later returned to Italy.

    2. Ties of friendship and family often determined where people would settle.

    3. Many migrated because they resented the power of the privileged classes.

  C. Asian migrants

    1. Many Asians became exploited laborers—in Latin America, California, Hawaii, Australia.

    2. Asian migrants often left their initial jobs in search of greater opportunities in trade and in towns.

    3. Asian migration led to racist reactions, such as "whites only" laws in the West.

III. Western imperialism

  A. The new imperialism

    1. Between 1880 and 1914, European nations scrambled for political as well as economic control over foreign nations.

    2. This scramble led to new tensions among competing European states and wars with non-European powers.

  B. The scramble for Africa

    1. Prior to 1880, European penetration of Africa was limited.

    2. British occupation of Egypt and Belgian penetration into the Congo started the race for colonial possessions.

      a. Leopold II of Belgium sent explorers into the Congo and planted the Belgian flag.

      b. Other countries, such as France and Britain, rushed to follow.

    3. The Berlin conference (1884–85) laid ground rules for this new imperialism.

      a. European claims to African territory had to be based on military occupation.

      b. No single European power could claim the whole continent.

    4. Germany entered the race for colonies and cooperated with France against Britain; the French goal was control of Lake Chad.

     5. The British under Kitchener massacred Muslim tribesmen at Omdurman (1898) in their drive to conquer the Sudan and nearly went to war with the French at Fashoda.

C. Imperialism in Asia

     1. The Dutch extended their control in the East Indies while the French took Indochina.

     2. Russia and the United States also penetrated Asia.

D. Causes of the new imperialism

     1. Economic motives—especially trade opportunities—were important, but in the end general economic benefits were limited because the new colonies were too poor to buy much.

     2. Political and diplomatic factors also encouraged imperialism.

        a. Colonies were believed to be crucial for national security, military power, and international prestige.

        b. Many people believed that colonies were essential to great nations.

     3. Nationalism, racism, and Social Darwinism contributed to imperialism.

        a. The German historian Treitschke claimed that colonies were essential to show racial superiority and national greatness.

        b. Special-interest groups favored expansion, as did military men and adventurers.

     4. Imperialists also felt they had a duty to "civilize" more primitive, nonwhite peoples.

        a. Kipling set forth the notion of the "white man's burden."

        b. Missionaries brought Christianity and education, but also European racism.

E. Critics of imperialism

     1. The British economist J. A. Hobson set forth the argument that imperialism was the result of capitalism and that only special-interest groups benefited from colonial possessions.

     2. Others condemned imperialism on moral grounds.

        a. They rebelled against the crude Social Darwinism of the imperialists.

        b. They accused the imperialists of applying a double standard: liberty and equality at home, military dictatorship and discrimination in the colonies.

IV. Responses to Western imperialism

A. Imperialism threatened traditional society.

     1. Traditionalists wanted to drive Western culture out and preserve the old culture and society.

     2. Modernizers believed it was necessary to adopt Western practices.

     3. Anti-imperialist leaders found inspiration in Western liberalism and nationalism.

B. The British Empire in India

     1. The last traditionalist response in India was broken by crushing the Great Rebellion of 1857–58.

     2. After 1858, India was administered by a white elite that considered itself superior to the Indians.

3. An Indian elite was educated to aid the British in administration.
4. Imperialism brought many benefits, including economic development, unity, and peace.
5. But nationalistic sentiments and demands for equality and self-government grew among the Western-educated Indian elite.

C. The example of Japan
1. The Meiji Restoration (1867) was a reaction to American intrusion, unequal treaties, and the humiliation of the shogun (military governor).
2. The Meiji leaders were modernizers who brought liberal and economic reforms.
   a. They abolished the old decentralized government and formed a strong, unified state.
   b. They declared social equality and allowed freedom of movement.
   c. They created a free, competitive, government-stimulated economy.
   d. They built a powerful modern navy and reorganized the army.
3. In the 1890s, Japan looked increasingly toward the German empire and rejected democracy in favor of authoritarianism.
4. Japan became an imperial power in the Far East.
   a. Japan defeated China in a war over Korea in 1894–95.
   b. In 1904, Japan attacked Russia and took Manchuria.

D. Toward revolution in China
1. The traditionalist Manchu rulers staged a comeback after the opium wars.
   a. The traditional ruling groups produced effective leaders.
   b. Destructive foreign aggression lessened, and some Europeans helped the Manchus.
2. The Chinese defeat by Japan in 1894–95 led to imperialist penetration and unrest.
3. Modernizers hoped to take over and strengthen China.
4. Boxer traditionalists caused violence (1900–1903) and a harsh European reaction.
5. Revolutionary modernizers overthrew the Manchu Dynasty in 1912.

Review Questions

Check your understanding of this chapter by answering the following questions.

1. How large was the income gap between industrializing and nonindustrializing regions? What was the cause of this gap?

2. What factors facilitated intercontinental trade in the late nineteenth century? Where did most of the foreign investments during this period go?

3. What were the motives of both the British merchants and the Chinese government in the opium wars of 1839–1842?

4. What were some of the differences in migration patterns among the various European states?

5. Where did the European migrants go?

6. Why did the migrants leave? Why did so many return?

7. Why was migration from Italy so heavy? Who were the migrants, and where did they go?

8. Khedive Ismail once said, "My country is no longer in Africa; we now form part of Europe." What did he mean?

9. Explain the British-Egyptian conflict of 1882. What were the causes and the results?

10. What distinguished the "new imperialism" from earlier forms of European expansion in the nineteenth century?

11. Why was Leopold II of Belgium interested in Africa?

12. What was meant by "effective occupation"? Did it cause or curtail further imperialism?

13. In 1898, a British army faced a French army at Fashoda in north-central Africa. How did each power get to such a location, and how was the confrontation solved?

14. What impact did Christianity have on imperialism?

15. What was the purpose of the Great Rebellion in India in 1857–58?

16. What were the advantages and disadvantages of British rule for the Indians?

17. What was the Meiji Restoration in Japan? Why was it a turning point in Japanese history?

18. How well did the Japanese copy the Europeans? What European ideas were most attractive to them?

19. Does the Manchu Dynasty in the period 1860–1912 represent a traditionalist or a modernist response to Europe and imperialism?

Study-Review Exercises

Define the following key concepts and terms.
"new imperialism"

traditionalist response to imperialism

modernist response to imperialism

Social Darwinism

racism

"the white man's burden"

Identify and explain the significance of the following people and terms.
Manchu Dynasty

Pale of [Jewish] Settlement

International Association for the Exploration and Civilization of Central Africa

Egyptian Nationalist party

Suez Canal

Omdurman

British opium trade

Pierre de Brazza

Muhammad Ali

Leopold II

Matthew Perry

Boers

Dowager Empress Tzu Hsi

John Hobson

Heinrich von Treitschke

Explain what the following events were, who participated in them, and why they were important.
Berlin conference of 1884–85

Fashoda crisis of 1898

Great Trek of the Boers

Treaty of Nanking, 1842

Clermont experiment of 1807

Meiji Restoration of 1867

Sino-Japanese War (1894–95)

Test your understanding of the chapter by providing the correct answers.

1. He took the Sudan for the British with his victory at Omdurman. _____

2. His attempt to modernize Egypt resulted in bankruptcy and foreign intervention.

   _____

3. He was a journalist, explorer, and employee of Leopold III. _____

4. He was a paternalistic British reformer in Egypt. _____

5. He argued that the strongest nations tend to be the best. _____

6. He "opened" Japan to the West in 1853. _____

7. He was a Chinese revolutionary and republican. _____

8. Under her leadership China was able to strengthen itself and maintain its traditional

   culture. _____

Multiple-Choice Questions

1. The Treaty of Nanking (1842) ended a war between Great Britain and China that had started over
   a. Chinese expulsion of British diplomats from Canton.
   b. disagreement over shipping rights in Chinese ports.
   c. opium smuggled into China from British India.
   d. the British annexation of Manchuria.

2. The great European migration of the nineteenth century was caused by all of the following *except*
   a. population pressure.
   b. desire for political and social rights.
   c. the desire of wealthy Europeans to emigrate and settle in non-European lands.
   d. lack of employment.

3. The most persuasive Western argument against European imperialism was that
   a. it was not economically profitable.
   b. European control of nonwhites was immoral and hypocritical.
   c. not enough investment was made in colonies.
   d. it was unworthy of great nations.

4. Western influence on Japan resulted in
   a. a Westernized country that began to practice its own form of imperialism.
   b. a country subject to Britain in the same way that India was.
   c. a country subject to the United States in the same way that India was subject to Britain.
   d. no effect at all.

5. After the wars over the opium trade, China
   a. began to industrialize rapidly.
   b. recovered for a number of years under the empress dowager.
   c. defeated Japan in the Sino-Japanese war of 1894–95.
   d. established a communist dictatorship to crush the Boxer Rebellion.

6. After 1840, world trade
   a. grew slowly as prices increased.
   b. grew rapidly as prices decreased.
   c. remained about the same as during the early decades of the century.
   d. declined because of the rise of protective barriers.

7. Which of the following promoted the growth of world trade after 1840?
   a. The British policy of high tariffs and trade barriers
   b. The increase in transportation costs
   c. The opening of the Suez and Panama canals
   d. The rise in price of raw materials and food

8. Which of the following characterizes the traditional attitude of Chinese society toward Western society?
   a. Great interest in European products
   b. A desire to open trade ports to European capitalists
   c. A need for Europe as a source of capital and market for Chinese tea
   d. Considerable disinterest in Europe

9. The war between Britain and China, which ended in 1842, was caused by
   a. Chinese penetration into southeast Asia.
   b. British merchants' demand to sell opium to the Chinese.
   c. the Chinese naval blockade of the Japanese coast.
   d. British refusal to sell European goods in China.

10. Japan was "opened" by the United States as a result of
    a. a military display of force.
    b. long and arduous negotiations.
    c. a willingness on the part of Japan.
    d. the opium wars.

11. Throughout the nineteenth century, European population and emigration tended to
    a. increase.
    b. decrease slightly.
    c. remain about the same.
    d. decrease significantly.

12. The country that was most affected by the immigration of Europeans was
    a. the United States.
    b. Argentina.
    c. Russia.
    d. Peru.

13. For the most part, the people who left Europe to settle elsewhere were
    a. the poorest and least skilled of society.
    b. middle-class adventurers in search of new fortunes.
    c. small landowners and village craftsmen.
    d. urban factory workers.

14. The return of the migrant to his or her native land was
    a. rare.
    b. not uncommon.
    c. common only among the Irish.
    d. common only among those migrating to Argentina.

15. In the nineteenth century, two out of three migrants to Argentina and Brazil came from
    a. Italy.
    b. Africa.
    c. Ireland.
    d. northern Europe.

16. The groups of east European migrants least likely to return to Europe were
    a. Poles.
    b. Jews.
    c. Germans.
    d. migrants from the Balkan lands.

17. The great European scramble for possession of Africa occurred
    a. prior to 1850.
    b. after 1900.
    c. between 1880 and 1900.
    d. around 1850.

18. The victor of the Fashoda incident in Africa was
    a. Britain.
    b. France.
    c. Germany.
    d. Belgium.

19. Reasons for British colonial expansion in the late 1870s and 1880s include all of the following *except*
    a. the desire to bring Africans and Asians back to Britain and exploit them as cheap laborers.
    b. the rise of France, Germany, and America as industrial powers.
    c. the fear of "protectionism" on the part of other European powers and the United States.
    d. the increased belief that colonies were necessary to support naval supremacy.

20. The radical English economist J. A. Hobson argued in his book *Imperialism* that the motive for colonial imperialism was
    a. economic.
    b. political.
    c. military.
    d. overpopulation.

21. Between 1750 and 1913, the gap in average income between the industrializing and nonindustrializing regions
    a. stayed about the same.
    b. narrowed considerably.
    c. increased slightly.
    d. increased enormously.

22. The application of steam power to transportation affected the general economy in that it resulted in
    a. lower prices for raw materials and manufactured goods.
    b. higher prices for raw materials.
    c. decreased demand for manufactured products.
    d. higher passenger and freight rates.

23. The effect of Muhammad Ali's modernization on the average peasant was that it
    a. improved the peasant's economic independence.
    b. caused a rise in peasant income.
    c. resulted in a loss of land.
    d. allowed the peasant to become a wealthy landlord.

24. The German historian Treitschke believed that imperialism was
    a. morally wrong but historically inevitable.
    b. the result of "pure selfishness."
    c. a way for the superior races to fulfill their greatness.
    d. due to the economic needs of unregulated capitalism.

25. It appears that the nineteenth-century British policy of free trade
    a. successfully replaced mercantilism.
    b. was nothing but a hindrance and caused economic loss.
    c. caused many wars.
    d. resulted in economic growth.

Major Political Ideas

1. Define imperialism. Was it largely a political or an economic phenomenon? What was the political impact of imperialism on those who were subject to imperialist activity? How valid is the claim that imperialism caused a shift in world power in favor of the Europeans and Americans?

2. Nonwesterners responded to imperialism in a variety of ways, but it is possible to think of their responses as a spectrum, with traditionalists at one end and modernizers at the other. What do these two terms mean, and how were they implemented. Which approach was more successful?

Issues for Essays and Discussion

Was Western imperialism "pure selfishness" and the product of unregulated capitalism, as its critics claimed? Provide evidence to back up your argument.

Geography

1. On Outline Map 30.2 provided, locate and label the following and indicate to which European nation it belonged: Union of South Africa, Madagascar, Algeria, French Equatorial Africa, Belgian Congo, Orange Free State, Libya, Nigeria, German East Africa, Transvaal, Egypt, British East Africa, Gold Coast, Morocco.

2. On Outline Map 30.3 provided, locate and label the following places and indicate which Western nation exercised control or domination: French Indochina, Philippine Islands, Port Arthur, Korea, India, Canton, Macao, Manchuria, Dutch East Indies, Hong Kong, Formosa, Vladivostok.

Remember that duplicate maps for class use are at the back of this book.

Outline Map 30.2

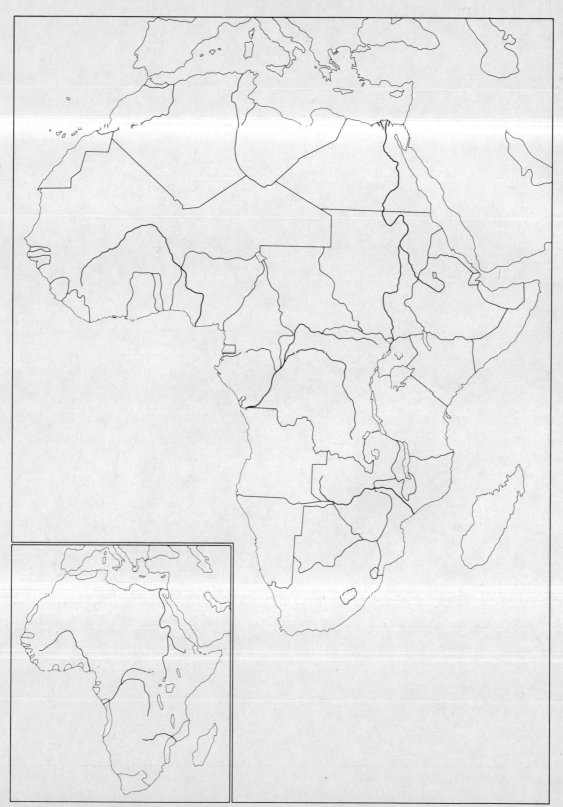

Outline Map 30.3

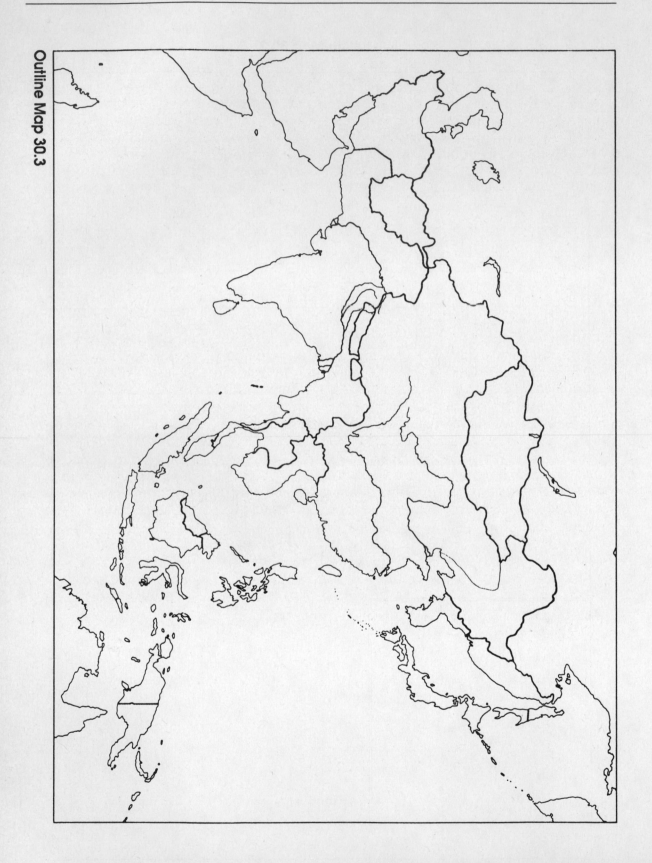

Understanding History Through the Arts

How has imperialism been depicted in opera and the movies? Few operas have enjoyed the popularity of Puccini's *Madame Butterfly* (1904). Set in Japan, the opera centers on the love between an American naval lieutenant and a Japanese woman. Imperialist adventure, and more recently imperialist exploitation, have long been subjects of filmmakers. Several recent films, available on video, are *Gandhi, The Last Emperor,* and *Empire of the Sun.*

Problems for Further Investigation

1. What impact did Western imperialism have on Chinese society? This is among the questions addressed in J. Grey, *Rebellions and Revolutions, China from the 1800s to the 1980s** (1990).

2. What were the causes of imperialism, and what made the system of "empire" work? What were the motives of its participants? The various causes for the changed nature of imperialism in the 1880s are discussed in H. M. Wright, ed., *The "New Imperialism"** (1961). Imperialism in Africa is analyzed by a number of historians in R. F. Betts, ed., *The "Scramble" for Africa** (1966), and a good general description of the greatest imperialist nation, Great Britain, can be found in B. Porter, *The Lion's Share: A Short History of British Imperialism, 1850–1970** (1975). A striking and fascinating study of one of the greatest of the imperialist-militarists is P. Magnus, *Kitchener: Portrait of an Imperialist** (1959, 1968). Imperialist adventure, as found in works such as R. Kipling, *Kim* and *In Black and White,* and J. Conrad, *Lord Jim,* has become part of the classical literature of our time. One woman's life in Africa is the subject of the award-winning film *Out of Africa* (1984), based on I. Dinesen, *Letters from Africa, 1914–1931** (1981), trans. A. Born.

3. How were immigrants treated in their new homelands? The American experience is described in L. Dinnerstein and D. Reimers, *Ethnic Americans: A History of Immigration** (1988), and Y. Ichioka, *The Issei: The World of First-Generation Japanese Immigrants, 1885–1924** (1988).

*Available in paperback.

CHAPTER 31

Nation Building in the Western Hemisphere and in Australia

Chapter Questions

After reading and studying this chapter, you should be able to answer the following questions:

How did the transformation of the United States into a great world power come about? Why and how did the Spanish colonies of Latin America shake off European domination and become nation-states? What role did "manifest destiny" play in United States history? How did the Americas absorb new peoples, and what was their social impact? How did the issue of race create serious tensions throughout the hemisphere?

Chapter Summary

It was during the nineteenth century that millions of immigrants populated and built ethnically diverse nations. This chapter examines that process.

Between 1806 and 1825, the Latin American colonies acquired independence from Spain and Portugal and established a unique racial-social structure consisting essentially of four racial groups: Creoles, peninsulares, mestizos, and mulattos. Much of the political and social history of Latin America evolves from this arrangement. Although the independence struggles grew out of a common reaction to the colonial policies of Spain—particularly the economic policies of Charles III—the struggles took different forms in different places. The Creole rulers, like the white landowners of the United States, interpreted the Enlightenment ideals in a manner that applied only to them and left the Indian and black majorities without human rights. The racism of Latin America was less rigid than that of the United States, however, because Indian and black individuals of mixed blood were more easily assimilated and enjoyed a degree of social and economic mobility. As the Comunero Revolution of 1781 illustrates, nonwhite revolt proved partially successful.

With independence in Latin America came instability, which led to military dictatorships, such as Rosas' in Argentina. The price of economic development was another kind of dictatorship—neocolonialism—as Britain and the United States came to dominate the rail-roads, mineral resources, banking, and much else. Economic development also meant a deterioration of conditions for the Latin American Indians, who were deprived of their land and fell into a cycle of debt peonage and plantation labor.

Meanwhile, massive immigration from Europe led to rapid urbanization, tenement living, and (for some) assimilation into the elite and wealthy upper class. Furthermore, because a vast majority of the immigrants were single males, immigration promoted the integration and intermixture of Europeans, Asians, and Indians. For blacks in Latin America, however, immigration proved a calamity. They were reduced to the fringes of the labor market and became the victims of racial prejudice.

The concept of manifest destiny played an important role in U.S. history. Overall, it gave the young nation justification for its relentless push across the continent and its inhuman treatment of native Americans. Another issue, that of slavery, preoccupied Americans and eventually caused a civil war. Although a powerful array of arguments—including the human rights arguments of the Enlightenment—characterized slavery as a great evil, many Americans of the liberal-democratic tradition were nonetheless committed to it. The reason for this dilemma was profits: cotton was king in the South, and slavery was necessary for the survival and expansion of the cotton economy. It was President Lincoln's Emancipation Proclamation that transformed the war from a political struggle to a moral crusade for the liberty of all Americans. The chapter discusses the impact of slavery on the black family. It describes how black women fought sexual abuse, and how the black family held itself together in spite of slavery.

After the Civil War the United States experienced a gigantic industrial boom and a surge of immigration and urbanization, both of which brought a high degree of cultural-ethnic pluralism to the new industrial cities. But industrialization and urbanization also brought serious problems: poverty and slum life, prejudice, and industrial unrest.

Canada also developed into an independent nation during the nineteenth century. Control passed to the British following the prolonged French and Indian Wars, an event central to the history of French Canadians. Widespread discontent over the lack of popular representation led to parliamentary reforms, most notably those outlined in the British North America Act of 1867, which established the Dominion of Canada and brought the Canadian constitution to its modern form. Under the Dominion's first prime minister, John A. Macdonald, Canada underwent significant expansion (incorporating all of northern North America by 1873) and development; by the century's end, Canada was enjoying an impressive industrial boom. The chapter concludes with a discussion of the establishment of a new nation in Australia—one that grew out of the British need for a penal colony and that was transformed in the nineteenth century by wool and gold.

Study Outline

Use this outline to preview the chapter before you read a particular section in your textbook and then as a self-check to test your reading comprehension after you have read the chapter section.

I. Latin America (ca 1800–1929)
   A. The Spanish Empire in the West underwent a series of upheavals that can be called revolutions, wars of independence, or civil wars.
      1. Creoles (American Spanish), peninsulares (Spanish or Portuguese natives), mestizos (mixed Spanish and Indian), and mulattos (mixed Spanish and black) fought the Spanish and one another.
      2. After 1850, millions of new immigrants flooded Latin America.
   B. The origins of the revolutions
      1. By the late seventeenth century, the Spanish colonies had achieved much economic diversity and independence.
         a. The mercantilist imperialism of Spain had faded away.
         b. Intercolonial trade had grown, and dependence on Spain had lessened.
      2. Spain's new economic policies reversed this trend after the War of the Spanish Succession.
         a. Colonial manufacture and agriculture were taxed highly, and economic development was frustrated.
         b. Under Charles III, preference was shown to Spaniards in political offices—at the expense of the Creoles.
         c. Tax reforms aggravated colonial discontent.
   C. Race relations in the colonial period
      1. Creoles did not extend the idea of "rights of man" to nonwhites.
         a. The lack of women led to mixed marriages of Indians, Spaniards, and Africans.
         b. Peninsulares and Creoles held privileged status.
         c. Dark skin was linked with servile manual labor.
         d. Indian majorities existed in Peru and Bolivia, whereas European majorities existed in Argentina and Chile.
      2. The Spanish controlled the economy.
         a. Indian land was taken by the Spanish as the Indians became slave laborers.
         b. Nevertheless, manumission was more frequent than in North America, and social mobility was not uncommon.
         c. Many black slaves fled to the jungles or mountains.
         d. Indians were subject to the mita, the repartimiento, and the new taxes of the 1770s and 1780s.
   D. The Comunero Revolution
      1. Amaru led an Indian uprising in Peru in 1779.
         a. The rebels demanded abolition of the alcabala tax and the mita and replacement of the corregidores with Indian governors.
         b. The revolt was crushed by the Spanish, but some reforms were granted.
      2. Revolution then occurred in Socorro in New Granada.
         a. Socorro had prospered as an agricultural and manufacturing center of Colombia.
         b. A large mestizo population existed.
         c. Tax increases and a new alcabala led to the Comunero Revolution.
         d. Creole captains led an Indian army on Bogotá.

       e. The government agreed to the rebels' demands but later pardoned the Creoles and turned against the rebels.

E. Independence

  1. The removal of the Spanish king by Napoleon led to revolt in Latin America.

     a. The wealthy Creoles seized power for themselves.

     b. Otherwise, there was a variety of doctrines, leaders, and organization throughout Spanish America.

     c. Each separate area went its own way.

     d. Bolívar's dream of a continental union broke down.

  2. Only Brazil won its independence without violent upheaval.

     a. The Portuguese kings had fled to Brazil.

     b. King Pedro I proclaimed Brazil's independence in 1822.

     c. Factional disputes and separatist movements were not settled until Pedro II's reign.

F. The consequences of independence

  1. The expulsion of the Spanish left a power vacuum filled by civic disorder.

     a. Creole inexperience in politics led to rule by military dictators.

     b. The dictator Rosas ruled in Argentina and Santa Anna, while other dictators ruled in Venezuela.

     c. Continual revolutions occurred in Bolivia and Venezuela.

     d. Economic prosperity was lost as warfare disrupted the economy.

  2. Slavery was abolished (except in Brazil and Cuba).

     a. Most slaves were freed and were given legal equality, but there was no redistribution of property.

     b. Blacks in Latin America enjoyed greater economic and social mobility than those in the United States.

     c. Some blacks, such as Guerrero, Flores, Santa Cruz, Guzman, and Castilla, led their countries.

     d. A three-tiered socioracial structure existed: white, colored, and black.

     e. Colored people were gradually assimilated upward—partly due to the small number of poor whites.

     f. The mass of blacks continued to experience racism.

G. Neocolonialism

  1. The advent of stable dictatorship led to economic growth.

     a. Political stability encouraged foreign investment.

     b. British and American investment in Mexico and British investment in Brazil and Chile encouraged economic development—but at a high price.

     c. By 1900 foreigners—especially the British and Americans—controlled Latin American economies.

     d. Each economy revolved around one or two export products, making them overly vulnerable to world market changes.

  2. Demand for land for the Spanish-owned haciendas led to further loss of land by the Indians.

     a. In Mexico the Díaz government encouraged appropriation of Indian land.

     b. The Indians were then exploited as laborers.

      c. Some argue that the hacienda owners, such as the Sanchez Navarro family in Mexico, ran efficient capitalist enterprises.

   H. The impact of immigration

      1. Argentina and other Latin American countries adopted Alberdi's idea that immigration was crucial, and many European countries, in turn, were overpopulated and promoted emigration.

      2. Italian, Spanish, and Portuguese people poured into Latin America.

         a. Cities like Buenos Aires grew rapidly and were cosmopolitan in nature.

         b. Immigrants worked hard and often lived in poverty in tenement dwellings known as conventillos.

         c. Many immigrants enjoyed upward mobility and imitated the lifestyle of the rich Europeans.

      3. This vast immigration changed the economy and the society.

         a. Agriculture and industry grew.

         b. Immigrant men often married Indian women, thus advancing ethnic integration.

         c. Because nonblack immigrants controlled factory jobs, urban blacks were forced into unemployment or marginal employment and experienced racism.

  II. The United States (ca 1789–1929)

   A. Manifest destiny

      1. Many agreed with O'Sullivan that God had foreordained the United States to cover the entire continent.

      2. The United States pushed its borders across the continent.

         a. During the colonial period, the Indians and the British blocked expansion westward to the Pacific.

         b. The purchase of Louisiana from France, that of Florida from Spain, and the settlement of 1814 with Britain expanded the United States south, southwest, northwest, and to the Gulf Plains.

         c. The absorption of Texas, an independent republic since 1836, led to a push further west and to war with Mexico.

         d. President Polk's war with Mexico led to U.S. acquisition of California and New Mexico.

   B. The fate of the Indians

      1. Government treatment of the Indian population was wanton and cruel.

         a. Trickery was used to obtain Indian land.

         b. Indians were moved to reservations, where many of them died.

      2. President Jackson refused to enforce the Supreme Court decision recognizing Cherokee Indian land rights.

   C. Black slavery in the South

      1. The liberal and democratic beliefs of Americans conflicted with their dependence on black slavery.

         a. Some argue that social prestige and political power were the reasons for slavery.

   b. Economic historians show that economic gain was the main motive for slavery.

  2. Slavery produced a considerable sense of guilt and psychological conflict among the planter class—particularly among women.

   a. The conflict between religious beliefs and slaveholding produced deep psychological stresses.

   b. Many white women of the South were abolitionists.

D. Westward expansion and the Civil War

  1. The growth of the cotton industry raised the question of the further expansion of slavery.

  2. Lincoln's election caused South Carolina (and then other states) to secede from the Union in 1860.

  3. Lincoln became a spokesman for the antislavery movement.

   a. However, he wanted to conduct the Civil War for the preservation of the status quo.

   b. Pressures to win the war brought Lincoln to declare the Emancipation Proclamation.

   c. The proclamation freed slaves only in the rebel states.

   d. It transformed the war into a moral crusade for all Americans.

  4. The shortage of American cotton led English textile manufacturers to secure cotton outside of the southern United States.

  5. The war had important political consequences in Europe.

   a. The English masses interpreted the North's victory as a symbol of the triumph of democracy over aristocracy.

   b. The Civil War was the first modern war.

  6. "Reconstruction" (1865–1877) of the South saw slavery disappear, but there was no practical application of social-legal equality or suffrage.

   a. Lacking cash, blacks became poor sharecroppers.

   b. Despite the Fifteenth Amendment, whites used violence and Jim Crow laws to keep blacks from exercising their rights.

E. The black family

  1. In spite of slavery, blacks established strong family units.

   a. Most slave couples had long marriages.

   b. Slaveowners encouraged slave marriage and large families.

   c. Separated couples tried to maintain the family unit.

   d. Slave women fought to retain their choice of marriage partners, and they frequently used abortion to limit family size.

   e. Sexual activity outside of marriage was rare among slave women.

   f. Until the 1920s, most black households were headed by two parents.

F. Industrialization and immigration

  1. Following the Civil War, the United States underwent an industrial boom.

   a. Government land turned over to the railroads encouraged industrial expansion.

   b. The entry of millions of new immigrants met the labor needs of growing industry.

   c. Cheap farmland in the West encouraged cultivation by pioneers.

      d. Immigration led to rapid urbanization—nearly 40 percent of the population was urban by 1900.

      e. New inventions, large factories, and manufacturing techniques (such as Ford's assembly line) led to increased production and new ways of living.

      f. Depressions led to huge trusts and monopolies.

      g. Employers constantly tried to cut labor costs, and they often neglected worker safety.

   2. Urbanization brought serious problems.

      a. Riis's investigation pointed to the sordidness of slum life for many new immigrants.

      b. Anti-immigrant prejudices—largely against non-Anglo-Saxons, Catholics, and Orientals—arose among Americans born here.

      c. Economic depression in the 1890s meant unemployment, exploitation of workers, and industrial unrest.

      d. Racist immigration laws established quotas on some groups and completely restricted others.

   3. The notion of "manifest destiny" and the process of urbanization and industrialization led to U.S. intervention in the Philippines, Cuba, and elsewhere in Latin America.

      a. The United States acquired Cuba and the Philippines as a result of the Spanish-American War of 1898.

      b. The United States practiced intervention in Latin America on numerous occasions—including Nicaragua in 1926 to bolster conservative governments.

III. Canada: from colony to nation

  A. Colonization and conflict

   1. Champlain established a trading post in 1608 on the site of present-day Quebec; the colony of New France was founded.

   2. The British challenged the French for control of the lucrative fur trade, initiating the French and Indian Wars.

   3. The British defeated the French in 1759 on the Plains of Abraham, ending the presence of the French Empire in North America; by the Treaty of Paris of 1763, France ceded Canada to Great Britain.

  B. Colonial government

   1. The British Parliament passed the Quebec Act of 1774, placing power in the hands of an appointed governor and council and denying Canadians a legislature.

   2. Civil discontent led to the Constitution Act of 1791, which divided Canada into Lower and Upper Canada; though the act provided for elective assemblies in both provinces, it gave the governor and his council the right to veto assembly decisions.

   3. The British Parliament appointed Lord Durham to recommend reforms when open rebellion broke out in Upper and Lower Canada in 1837.

C. Age of confederation (1840–1905)
1. Lord Durham's *Report on the Affairs of British North America* led to the Union Act of 1840, which united Lower and Upper Canada under one government composed of a governor, an appointed legislative council (cabinet), and an elective assembly.
2. The British North America Act of 1867 brought the Canadian constitution to its modern form; the Dominion of Canada was established.
   a. The Dominion cabinet had complete jurisdiction over internal affairs; Britain retained control over foreign policy.
   b. John A. Macdonald became the Dominion's first prime minister.
D. Expansion and development
1. Under Macdonald, Canada expanded to include all of northern North America (1868–1873).
2. The Canadian Pacific Railroad opened in 1885.
3. Between 1897 and 1912, a wave of immigrants arrived in Canada; the French Canadians resisted assimilation.
4. Supported by population growth, Canada experienced an agricultural and industrial boom between 1891 and 1914.
E. Participation in the First World War
1. Canadians powerfully supported the Allied cause.
2. The Imperial War Cabinet, composed of chief British ministers and prime ministers of the Dominion, was established.
3. In 1918 Canada received the right to participate in the Versailles Peace Conference and in the League of Nations.

IV. Australia: penal colony to nation
A. Australia was claimed for the British king by James Cook in 1770.
1. It is the world's smallest continent and has three topographical zones: a western desert and semidesert, a central eastern lowlands, and an eastern highlands.
2. Australia was inhabited by Aborigines who had emigrated from southern Asia.
   a. The Aborigines were tribal and had no domestic agriculture.
   b. Most of the Aborigines succumbed to white man's diseases and to a breakdown of tribal life.
B. Penal colony
1. After the American Revolution, the British needed new places to send convicts.
   a. Some historians argue that there were other motives in the founding of Australia, but these arguments are weak and unconvincing.
   b. Crowded English prisons led to the establishment of a penal colony at Botany Bay, although the first governor moved the colony to Port Jackson (Sydney).
   c. The convicts knew nothing of agriculture, and the colony nearly disappeared.

      d. Men outnumbered women, most women were prostitutes, and most children born in Australia were illegitimate.

      e. A gentry class called the exclusionists emerged; the former convicts were called emancipists.

C. Economic development

   1. After 1787, the policy was to have the convicts help strengthen the colonial economy.

      a. After 1815, a steady stream of people moved to Australia.

      b. Sealing was carried out until the seal herds were depleted.

      c. Wool production was introduced by John Macarthur in about 1800 and then encouraged by J. T. Bigge in 1819—who recommended that British duties on wool be removed and that convicts be used to work on wool-growing estates.

      d. After 1820, wool export became crucial to Australia's economy.

   2. Wheat farming was encouraged because of the development of a white-grained variety of wheat; by 1900 it was the country's second most important crop.

   3. Population shortage was a problem; Wakefield's plan to provide cheap land and cheap passage led to a large number of immigrants.

D. From colony to nation

   1. The gold rush of 1851–1861 greatly affected life and the economy.

      a. Great population growth occurred; transport improved; and the gold rush provided the financial basis for the promotion of education and culture.

      b. The gold rush also encouraged racism and a "white Australia policy"; anti-Chinese discrimination increased.

      c. The Commonwealth Immigration Restriction Act of 1901 closed immigration to Asians.

      d. By 1859, all of the Australia colonies were self-governing.

   2. The government of Australia combines features of the British and American systems.

      a. The Commonwealth of Australia was formed in 1901.

      b. It took its parliamentary system from Britain and its concept of decentralized government from the United States.

Review Questions

Check your understanding of this chapter by answering the following questions.

1. Describe how the economic policies of Charles III affected Spanish America.

2. What were the Spanish attitudes toward nonwhites, and how were their attitudes incorporated into colonial society?

3. The upheavals in the Spanish colonies have been described as revolutions, wars of independence, and civil wars. Why? What are the differences among the three?

4. How and why did racial mixing and freedom for slaves come about?

5. Why did the revolutions in Peru and Socorro take place? What were the outcomes?

6. How and why did the independence movement occur in Latin America? What roles did Bolívar and King Pedro I play?

7. Why did military dictatorships evolve, and what were their effects on the economy?

8. Describe how the abolition of slavery affected the blacks of Latin America.

9. Discuss how foreign immigration affected the new independent states of Latin America in terms of the economy and the racial structure of society.

10. Define and describe the notion of manifest destiny. What were its origins, and what results did it produce?

11. By citing examples, explain, in general, the U.S. government attitude and policy toward native Americans.

12. What were the motives for slavery in the United States?

13. Explain why a U.S. liberal democrat in the early nineteenth century could also be a slaveowner. What was the impact of this dilemma on society?

14. Describe how slavery affected the black family. How accurately do the facts fit previously accepted notions of slaves' family life and sexuality?

15. What was the effect of Reconstruction on blacks in the United States? Had racial discrimination disappeared?

16. In what ways did the urbanization and industrialization that followed the Civil War bring growth as well as serious problems?

17. What were the causes of U.S. intervention in Latin America? Give some examples and discuss the effects that intervention had on Latin American politics.

18. Why did the Quebec Act prove unpopular in Canada? What reforms in colonial government did the British proceed to make?

19. What were the motives and circumstances behind the settlement of Australia? Was the founding of Australia a product of economic imperialism?

Study-Review Exercises

Define the following key concepts and terms.

alcabala

mita

repartimiento

peninsulares

Creoles

mestizos

conventillos

hacienda

manifest destiny

Identify and explain the significance of the following people and terms.

Charles III of Spain

Comunero Revolution

Tupac Amaru

Simon Bolívar

Pedro I of Portugal

Juan Bautista Alberdi

Emancipation Proclamation

frontier women in the American West

Chinese Exclusion Act of 1882

Treaty of Guadalupe Hidalgo (1848)

Spanish-American War of 1898

Louisiana Purchase

Toussaint L'Ouverture

Jim Crow laws

Lord Durham

John A. Macdonald

James Cook

Edward Hargraves

Edward Gibbon Wakefield

Ripon Land Regulation Act

Commonwealth Immigration Restriction Act of 1901

Test your understanding of the chapter by providing the correct answers.

1. The people of Spanish descent born in America were known as _____ , whereas the natives of Spain and Portugal were called the _____ .

2. In his effort to make himself emperor of Europe, Napoleon indirectly *encouraged/discouraged* independence movements in Latin America.

3. During the colonial period, nonwhites in Latin America experienced *more/less* social mobility than those in North America.

4. The Comunero Revolution was led by _____ .

5. Generally, the vast immigration from Europe had a(n) *favorable/unfavorable* impact on the blacks of Latin America.

6. The countries that led the way in foreign investment in Latin America were

   _____ and _____ .

7. Most slave couples in the United States had *long/short* marriages, and sexual activity outside of marriage among slave women was *common/rare*.

8. The Emancipation Proclamation freed *all slaves/only slaves in rebel states*.

9. From slaveholding times until the 1920s, a large majority of black families were headed by *one/two* parent(s).

10. The man whose book *How the Other Half Lives* led many people to recognize the

    wretchedness of life for immigrants in New York. _____

11. French Canadians *did/did not* resist assimilation with the immigrants who arrived in Canada in the late nineteenth century.

Multiple-Choice Questions

1. The Creoles were
   a. persons of mixed Spanish-Indian blood.
   b. Americans of Spanish ancestry.
   c. Indians who absorbed European culture.
   d. the ruling class in Spanish America.

2. In the late eighteenth century, most government posts in Latin America were held by
   a. peninsulares.
   b. mestizos.
   c. mulattos.
   d. Creoles.

3. Spanish colonies resented the imposition of taxes without
   a. arbitration.
   b. consultation.
   c. representation.
   d. legislation.

4. Social status in Spanish America depended on
   a. wealth.
   b. titles of nobility.
   c. religion.
   d. racial background.

5. The majority of the population in Latin America was
   a. Indian.
   b. mestizo.
   c. European.
   d. Creole.

6. The independence movement in Latin America
   a. intended a radical redistribution of property.
   b. sought to give rights to the Indians.
   c. fought to eliminate Spanish rule.
   d. desired to place a Creole king on the throne.

7. The Latin American wars of independence ended with
   a. the election of the South American constitutional convention.
   b. a chaotic political situation.
   c. Spanish recognition of the new nations.
   d. Bolívar's election to the presidency.

8. The typical Latin American nation of the nineteenth century was a
   a. monarchy.
   b. democratic republic.
   c. republic ruled by a dictator.
   d. totalitarian state.

9. Nonwhites in Latin America
   a. had ample opportunity to rise socially.
   b. could rise economically but seldom socially.
   c. could not get ahead unless they "passed" for white.
   d. might rise socially if they were light-skinned.

10. Large-scale development of Latin American economies began when
    a. oil was discovered.
    b. foreign investment started.
    c. slavery was abolished.
    d. dictators introduced economic planning.

11. A serious economic weakness in South America was
    a. dependence on imported food.
    b. the possibility of U.S. intervention.
    c. dependence on one or two products.
    d. the use of domestic capital.

12. The term *manifest destiny* refers to the
    a. belief that the United States was destined to cover the continent.
    b. Confederacy's justification for southern independence.
    c. reason that the United States purchased Louisiana.
    d. belief that blacks were destined to be slaves.

13. According to this textbook
    a. slavery was not profitable.
    b. slaves were kept for reasons of security.
    c. slaveholders were aristocrats, not businessmen.
    d. slavery was profitable business.

14. The experience of slavery led to
    a. a weak family structure among blacks.
    b. a strong family tradition among blacks.
    c. a pattern of fatherless families among blacks.
    d. marriages of short duration among blacks.

15. Immigrants to the United States most often
    a. settled on western farms.
    b. found employment in urban industries.
    c. had difficulty finding work.
    d. worked in the mines.

16. Experiences on the U.S. frontier led to
    a. increased differentiation of sex roles.
    b. the belief that women were morally superior.
    c. a contempt for the arts as effeminate.
    d. a blurring of the sex roles.

17. The assembly line became popular because
    a. quality was more important than quantity.
    b. quantity was more important than quality.
    c. industrialists wanted interchangeable workers.
    d. industrialists like to use interchangeable parts.

18. One explanation suggested for the recurring economic depressions of the nineteenth century is
    a. strikes.
    b. overproduction.
    c. unsound monetary policy.
    d. legalization of trusts.

19. The immigrants most disliked by nativist Americans were the
    a. Roman Catholics.
    b. Slavics.
    c. Chinese.
    d. Jews.

20. The insurrections in nineteenth-century Latin America were
    a. wars of independence.
    b. civil wars.
    c. wars of revolution.
    d. all of the above.

21. Peninsulares were
    a. natives.
    b. whites born in the Americas.
    c. mulattos.
    d. native-born Spanish or Portuguese.

22. The Comunero and Tupac Amaru rebellions
    a. were total successes.
    b. were put down, yet led to some reforms.
    c. failed utterly.
    d. ended in even more severe treatment of the Indians.

23. Brazil's independence was
    a. secured peacefully by royal proclamation.
    b. obtained by treaty with Portugal.
    c. won in a bloody civil war.
    d. won by Bolívar.

24. In the late nineteenth century
    a. land reform gave farms to millions of Indians.
    b. many Indians lost their land to corrupt businessmen.
    c. foreign capitalists bought up huge tracts of land.
    d. the Mexican government nationalized vacant lands.

25. Methods of operation on the haciendas
    a. were inefficient and old-fashioned.
    b. were businesslike and efficient.
    c. were the reason for high corn prices.
    d. are disputed by scholars.

26. Juan Bautista Alberdi advocated immigration for Argentina because
    a. the nation's labor supply was totally inadequate.
    b. he believed that the Indians and blacks lacked basic skills.
    c. the constitution required it.
    d. he wished that the nation would become predominantly white.

27. The vast majority of immigrants to Argentina were
    a. family groups.
    b. unmarried males.
    c. skilled workers.
    d. northern Europeans.

28. Which of the following is *not* a reason that blacks could seldom obtain urban industrial jobs in Latin America?
    a. They lacked basic skills.
    b. Immigrants would work for lower wages.
    c. Whites were racially prejudiced.
    d. Their background was usually rural.

29. California became part of the United States as a result of the
    a. Louisiana Purchase.
    b. Treaty of Ghent.
    c. Mexican War.
    d. War of 1812.

30. It may be generally said of the American Indians that they
    a. were bloodthirsty savages.
    b. were fairly compensated for their lands.
    c. endured terrible treatment at the hands of whites.
    d. went to war out of a desire for revenge.

31. South Carolina seceded from the Union because
    a. Lincoln wanted to free the slaves.
    b. Fort Sumter had been fired on.
    c. Lincoln had been elected president.
    d. it wished to form a Southern Confederacy.

32. John A. Macdonald's crowning achievement was
    a. his *Report on the Affairs of British North America*.
    b. the opening of the Canadian Pacific Railroad.
    c. the defeat of the French on the Plains of Abraham in 1759.
    d. his championship of the Constitution Act of 1796.

Major Political Ideas

1. What did Bolívar mean by *pan-Americanism*, and why did this idea fail?

2. What was neocolonialism, and what impact did it have on Latin American nations? Give examples.

Issues for Essays and Discussion

1. Why and how did the Spanish colonies of Latin America shake off European domination? Did European domination disappear in fact as well as in name?

2. Why did slavery develop in the United States, and how did it affect the black family?

3. Compare and contrast colonization in Canada and Australia. What were the motives of immigrants in each area, and why and how did each state expand?

Interpretation of Visual Sources

Study the illustration "Domestic Scenes in Mid-Nineteenth-Century Rio" on page 1005 of the textbook. What "races" are represented here? What appears to be the ratio of servant/slave to white householder? What do specific actions in these illustrations suggest in terms of relations between servant and master/mistress?

Geography

1. Study Maps 31.1 and 31.2. Referring to the textbook when necessary, answer the following questions:
   a. Name the present-day countries that made up the Spanish viceroyalties of Peru, New Granada, and La Plata. Draw all of these areas on Outline Map 31.2 provided.
   b. In the space below, describe the products that were exported by these areas to Spain. What effect did the French revolutionary and Napoleonic wars have on Spain's administration of its colonies?

   _____

   _____

   _____

   c. Indicate the location of the Suarez River and Bogotá in New Granada. In the space below, describe the sequence of events that constituted the Comunero Revolution.

   _____

   _____

   _____

2. Using Map 31.1 in the textbook as your guide, answer the following questions as you locate the appropriate areas:
   a. What was the economic, political, and social importance of Buenos Aires in the era after independence was gained?
   b. What countries received their independence through the leadership of Simon Bolívar? Why did Bolívar say that "America is ungovernable"?

Remember that duplicate maps for class use are at the back of this book.

Outline Map 31.2

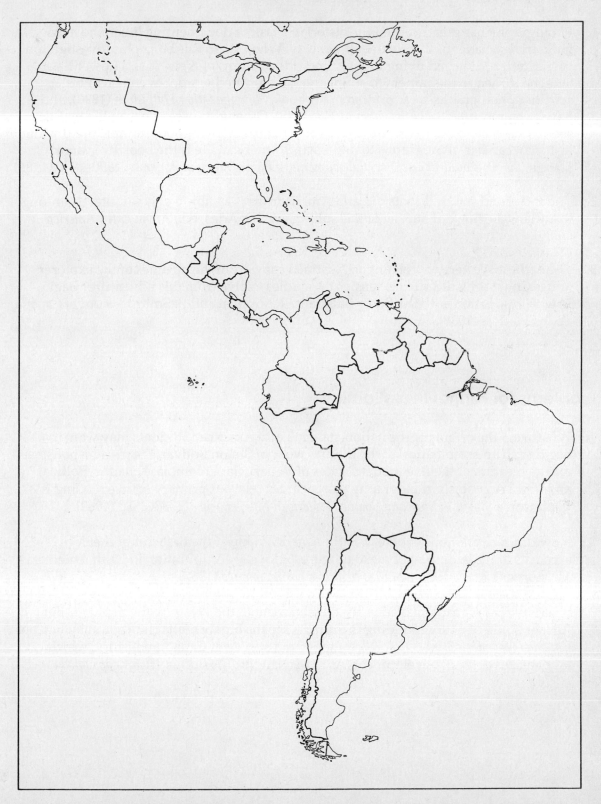

Understanding History Through the Arts

1. Photography has greatly aided the historian's task of documenting life in the new industrial societies of the nineteenth century. When Jacob Riis began his investigation of the underprivileged living in the crime-ridden slums of New York's Lower East Side, he turned to the camera to supplement the printed word. Seventeen of his startling photographs were printed in his book, *How the Other Half Lives* (1890), and have been reprinted in *U.S. Camera 1948* (1948). Other glimpses of urban life by Riis are seen in his second book, *Children of the Poor* (1895). Another good example of how the historian can use photographs to understand American life is the book by Maren Stange, *Symbols of Ideal Life: Social Documentary Photography in America, 1890–1930* (1989).

2. The social and political roots of Latin American art is a subject of great interest among historians. Begin your survey of this subject with D. Ades, ed., *Art in Latin America* (1989).

3. The earliest Western art relating to Australia came from the voyages of the explorer James Cook. Why did such extensive art studies evolve from this adventure? Begin your investigation with the finely illustrated R. Joppien and B. Smith, *The Art of Captain Cook's Voyages* (1988).

Problems for Further Investigation

1. What were the origins of the nation-state in Latin America? Students may want to begin with an examination of the life and work of Simon Bolívar, the man responsible for the creation of the five modern states of Venezuela, Colombia, Ecuador, Bolivia, and Peru. A good short biography that includes relevant primary source reading is J. Johnson's *Simon Bolivar and Spanish American Independence, 1783–1830* (1968).

2. How did race relations evolve in Latin America? One of the first comprehensive accounts of the evolution of racial mixture and racial acculturation in Latin America is M. Morner's *Race Mixture in the History of Latin America* (1967).

3. What role has Canada played in the development of the Western Hemisphere? For further study of nation-building in Canada, see the highly readable account by R. Cook, *Canada: A Modern Study* (1971). Another sound survey of Canadian history, which emphasizes cultural developments, is K. McNaught, *The Pelican History of Canada** (1976).

*Available in paperback.

CHAPTER 32

The Great Break: War and Revolution

Chapter Questions

After reading and studying this chapter, you should be able to answer the following questions:

What were the causes of the Great War? How and why did war and revolution have such enormous and destructive consequences? What impact did the war have on the ways in which people lived and thought? What were the causes of the great revolution in Russia, and what changes did this event bring to Russian society?

Chapter Summary

The First World War had enormous consequences. Western civilization changed decisively, as the war caused not only death and destruction but a variety of revolutions as well. Thus, the First World War opened a new era in European history. This chapter shows how and why this was so. Beginning with the system of alliances that had formed two hostile military blocs by 1914, the text explains how nationalism and fears of nationalism touched off a world war. Contrary to expectations, the First World War became a ghastly military stalemate. The stalemate forced each government to make a total war effort, which demanded great sacrifices and major social changes. Economic life was strictly controlled, women entered defense plants, and nationalistic propaganda strengthened genuine popular support for the war. By 1916, however, there was growing discontent and war weariness in all countries.

Russia broke first under the enormous strain of total war. In March 1917, a moderate patriotic revolution established a Russian republic. In November 1917, Lenin and the Bolsheviks took power in a socialist revolution. Lenin was a dedicated revolutionary who had reinterpreted Marxism in a radical way before 1914, and he took Russia out of the war and established a harsh dictatorship. This dictatorship allowed the Bolshevik government to survive and to defeat many different foes in a bloody civil war. Revolution also occurred in

Germany and Austria. Germany established a republic, and Austria-Hungary broke into pieces.

In 1919, the world of 1914 lay in ruins, due to the impact of total war and radical revolution. Nor did the peace settlement of Versailles bring stability, since the defeated Germans hated the peace treaty, and the victorious Americans rejected it.

Study Outline

Use this outline to preview the chapter before you read a particular section in your textbook and then as a self-check to test your reading comprehension after you have read the chapter section.

I. The First World War (1914–1918)
   A. The Bismarckian system of alliances
      1. Germany was the most powerful European country after 1871.
      2. Bismarck sought to guarantee European peace through alliances.
      3. The Three Emperors' League (Austria, Russia, and Germany) was created in 1873 to maintain the status quo; this was followed by an Austrian-German Alliance of 1879 and the Alliance of the Three Emperors in 1881.
      4. Because of tensions with France, Italy joined Germany and Austria in the Triple Alliance (1882).
      5. In 1887, the Russian-German Reinsurance Treaty promised neutrality by each state if the other were attacked.
   B. The rival blocs
      1. William II dismissed Bismarck, and his termination of the German-Russian Reinsurance Treaty led to a new Russian-French alliance.
      2. Under William II, the British-German "natural alliance" deteriorated into a bitter rivalry.
         a. The Boer War, German envy of British imperialism, and economic and military rivalry drove the British and the Germans apart.
         b. Then Britain allied with Japan and turned to France and formed the Anglo-French Entente of 1904, which further alienated Germany.
         c. Germany tested this entente in a diplomatic struggle over Morocco.
         d. The Algeciras Conference (1906) left Germany empty-handed and isolated.
      3. As a result, Germany became increasingly distrustful, and other European countries began to see Germany as a threat.
      4. German naval buildup, under Tirpitz, led to an arms race with Britain and a cycle of paranoia.
   C. The outbreak of war (August 1914)
      1. Nationalism in the Balkans threatened the Ottoman Empire and European peace.
      2. Independence was acquired by Serbia, Romania, and part of Bulgaria in 1878.

3. Austria's annexation of Bosnia and Herzegovina in 1908 greatly angered Serbia, which was forced to turn southward against the Ottomans in its nationalistic desire to expand—this was the first Balkan War (1912).
4. Serbia's dispute with Bulgaria over the spoils of victory led to the Second Balkan War in 1913.
5. The Balkan wars of 1912–13 were a victory for Balkan nationalism.
6. The assassination of the Austrian archduke Francis Ferdinand (1914) resulted in a war between Serbia and Austria as Austria tried to stem the rising tide of hostile nationalism.
7. Germany gave Austria unconditional support.
8. Military considerations dictated policy, and an all-European war resulted.
   a. Russia ordered full mobilization against Austria and Germany.
   b. Germany invaded France via Belgium.
   c. Great Britain joined France and declared war on Germany.
D. Reflections on the origins of the war
   1. Austria-Hungary deliberately started the war, goaded by Germany.
   2. German aggression in 1914 reflected the failure of all European leaders to incorporate Bismarck's empire into the international system.
   3. Nationalism contributed to war fever.
   4. All the European leaders underestimated the consequences of war.
E. The first Battle of the Marne (September 1914)
   1. The original Schlieffen plan—a German invasion of France through Belgium—had to be altered when British troops landed to help the Belgians.
   2. The Battle of the Marne turned the war into a long stalemate.
F. Stalemate and slaughter
   1. Trench warfare meant much horrible death but no end to the war.
      a. The battles of Somme and Verdun cost thousands of lives but no significant gains in territory for either side.
      b. The French army was almost destroyed at Champagne (1917), while the British lost many men at Passchendaele.
   2. The war's horrors caused a profound disillusionment with society and mankind.
      a. The war shattered an entire generation of young men.
      b. It created a gulf between veterans and civilians.
G. The widening war
   1. Despite huge Austrian losses, Austria and Germany defeated Russia and Serbia on the eastern front (1914–15).
   2. Italy and Bulgaria entered the war (1915).
   3. With Arab help, Britain defeated the Ottoman Empire (1918).
      a. The British failed to take Constantinople and the Dardanelles.
      b. The British colonel Lawrence of Arabia led the Arabs to revolt.
      c. Using imperial forces, the British smashed the old Ottoman state.
   4. The European war extended around the globe as Great Britain, France, and Japan seized Germany's colonies.
      a. The war spread to parts of East Asia and Africa; French and British colonials supported their masters.

b. Japan took German colonies in the Pacific and in China.
5. The United States entered the war in 1917 because of German submarine warfare.

II. The home front
   A. Mobilizing for total war
      1. Most people saw the war in nationalistic terms and believed their nation was defending itself against aggression.
      2. Total war meant that economic planning was necessary.
         a. Rationing, price and wage controls, and restrictions on workers' freedom of movement were imposed by government.
         b. The economy of total war blurred the distinctions between soldiers and civilians—all were involved in the war effort.
         c. The ability of governments to manage economies strengthened the cause of socialism.
      3. In Germany, food and raw materials were rationed and a universal draft was initiated.
         a. Hindenburg and Ludendorff became the real rulers of Germany.
         b. Total war led to the establishment of a totalitarian society.
      4. By 1916, the British economy was largely planned.
   B. The social impact
      1. Labor shortages brought about benefits for organized labor.
      2. The role of women changed dramatically as many women entered the labor force.
         a. Some European women gained the right to vote after the war.
         b. Women displayed a growing spirit of independence.
      3. War brought about greater social equality.
   C. Growing political tensions
      1. Wartime propaganda to maintain popular support of the war was widespread.
      2. By 1916, people were growing weary of war; morale declined.
         a. In France, Clemenceau established a virtual dictatorship to deal with strikes and those who wanted compromise to end the war.
         b. In Germany, the social conflict of the prewar years emerged.

III. The Russian Revolution (1917)
   A. The fall of imperial Russia
      1. War losses and mistakes pointed to the weak leadership of the tsar and the unresponsiveness of the Russian government.
      2. The influence of Rasputin on the royal family further weakened the government and created a national scandal.
      3. Food shortages led to revolution in March 1917.
         a. A provisional government was proclaimed by the Duma.
         b. The tsar abdicated.
   B. The provisional government (March 1917)
      1. After the March revolution, Russia became the freest country in the world.

    2. Yet the new revolutionary government, led by Kerensky, wanted to postpone land reform, fearing it would further weaken the peasant army; the continuation of the war was Kerensky's primary concern.

    3. The provisional government had to share power with the Petrograd Soviet of Workers' and Soldiers' Deputies.

        a. The Petrograd Soviet's Army Order No. 1 placed military authority in the hands of ordinary soldiers.

        b. Army discipline broke down completely, and massive desertions began.

    4. Liberty was rapidly turning into anarchy

C. Lenin and the Bolshevik Revolution

    1. Lenin believed that revolution was necessary to destroy capitalism.

    2. He also believed that a Marxist revolution could occur in Russia despite the absence of advanced capitalism if led by an intellectual elite.

    3. Russian Marxists became divided over Lenin's theories.

        a. Lenin's Bolsheviks demanded a small, disciplined, elitist party.

        b. The Mensheviks wanted a democratic party with mass membership.

    4. Lenin led an attack against the provisional government in July 1917, but it failed and he went into hiding.

    5. Kerensky's power was weakened by an attack on the provisional government by his commander in chief, Kornilov, and he lost favor with the army.

D. Trotsky and the seizure of power

    1. A radical Marxist and supporter of Lenin, Trotsky centered his power in the Petrograd Soviet.

        a. The Bolsheviks gained a majority in the Petrograd Soviet.

        b. The Bolsheviks controlled the military in the capital.

    2. Trotsky engineered a Soviet overthrow of the provisional government (November 1917).

    3. The Bolsheviks came to power because they were the answer to anarchy, they had superior leaders, and they appealed to many soldiers and urban workers exhausted by war.

E. Dictatorship and civil war

    1. Lenin gave approval to the peasants' seizure of land and the urban workers' takeover of the factories.

    2. Lenin arranged for an end of the war with Germany, but at a high price: the sacrifice of all of Russia's western territories (the Treaty of Brest-Litovsk, 1918).

    3. Free elections produced a stunning loss for the Bolsheviks, and Lenin dissolved the Constituent Assembly.

    4. Opposition to the Bolsheviks led to civil war (1918–1921).

        a. The officers of the old army (the Whites) organized the opposition to the Bolsheviks (the Reds).

        b. The Whites came from many social groups and wanted self-rule, not Bolshevik dictatorship.

    5. The Bolshevik victory in the civil war was due to a number of factors: unity, a better army, a well-defined political program, mobilization of the home front,

an effective secret police force (the Cheka), and an appeal to nationalism in the face of foreign aid to the Whites.

6. The First World War created some of the conditions that led to the Russian Revolution and a radically new government based on socialism and one-party dictatorship.

IV. The Versailles peace settlement (1918–19)
   A. The end of the war
      1. By early 1917, the German populace was weary of war, and the German army was decisively defeated in the second Battle of the Marne (1918).
      2. The Allies were strengthened by American intervention, and by September, the Allies were advancing on all fronts.
      3. The German military arranged for a new liberal German government to accept defeat.
      4. German soldiers and workers began to demonstrate for peace, and Germany surrendered in November 1918.
   B. Revolution in Germany
      1. Revolution in Austria-Hungary led to the breakup of the Austro-Hungarian Empire into new national states: Austria, Hungary, Czechoslovakia, and Yugoslavia.
      2. Revolution in Germany (November 1918) led to a victory for the moderate socialists, the Social Democrats.
         a. There was little popular support for a radical revolution.
         b. The Social Democrats wanted the gradual elimination of capitalism.
         c. They accepted defeat and used the army to crush a radical uprising led by Leibknecht and Luxemburg.
   C. The Treaty of Versailles
      1. President Wilson was obsessed with creating a League of Nations to avert future wars.
      2. Clemenceau of France and Lloyd George of England were more interested in permanently weakening Germany and making it pay for the war.
      3. The conflicting desires of the Allies led to a deadlock and finally a compromise.
         a. France gave up its demand for a protective buffer state in return for a defensive alliance with Britain and the United States.
         b. The League of Nations was created.
      4. Germany lost her colonies and territory in Europe—largely Alsace-Lorraine, Danzig, and eastern land to Poland.
      5. Germany had to limit its army, admit responsibility for the war, and pay enormous damages.
      6. Austria-Hungary and Turkey were the big losers in the separate peace treaties; the principle of self-determination still applied only to Europeans, and thus Western imperialism lived on.

D. American rejection of the Versailles treaty
1. The Versailles settlement rested on the principle of national self-determination, the League of Nations, and fear that the Bolshevik Revolution might spread.
2. Republican senators refused to ratify the treaty largely because of the issue of the League's power.
   a. Henry Cabot Lodge and others believed that requiring member states of the League of Nations to take collective action against aggression violated Congress's right to declare war.
   b. Wilson refused to compromise, and the Senate did not ratify the treaty.
3. The Senate also refused to ratify the defensive alliance with Britain and France.
   a. Britain also refused to ratify the defensive alliance.
   b. France felt betrayed and isolated.

Review Questions

Check your understanding of this chapter by answering the following questions.

1. How did Bismarck's system of alliances help maintain peace?

2. What was the purpose of the German-Russian Reinsurance Treaty? Why did it end in 1890 and with what results?

3. What were the reasons for Britain and Germany's love-hate relationship?

4. Why was the Moroccan crisis of 1905 a turning point in European diplomacy?

5. What impact did the Congress of Berlin (1878) have on the Balkan area? Who was bound to be the loser in the Balkans?

6. What were the origins and causes of the "Third Balkan War" in 1914?

7. Which of the major powers do you believe most responsible and least responsible for the First World War? Explain.

8. What impact did the war have on the economy and the people at home? How cooperative was the population?

9. Did the war have any effect on the power of organized labor? On women in society?

10. How did the war tend to have an equalizing effect on society?

11. What evidence is there that the strain of war was beginning to take its toll on the home front in Russia, Austria, France, and Germany by 1916?

12. What were the reasons for the Russian Revolution in March 1917? Was revolution inevitable?

13. What were the soviets? What role did they play in the Bolshevik Revolution?

14. What was it about Lenin's character that made him a successful revolutionary? Why were his ideas popular with peasants and urban workers?

15. Why did Kerensky and the provisional government fail?

16. What were the reasons for the Bolshevik victory in the civil war?

17. Were there one, two, or many Russian revolutions in 1917? Explain.

18. What happened to the Austro-Hungarian and Turkish empires after 1918?

19. What were the goals of Wilson, Lloyd George, and Clemenceau at the Versailles peace conference?

20. The Treaty of Versailles is often seen as a major cause of the Second World War. Do you agree? Why?

21. Compare and contrast the Versailles settlement of 1919 with the Vienna settlement of 1815. What similarities do you see? What were the most striking differences?

Study-Review Exercises

Define the following key concepts and terms.

Congress of Berlin, 1878

Schlieffen Plan

"total war"

totalitarian

western front

Bolsheviks

principle of national self-determination

war reparations

Identify and explain the significance of the following people and terms.
First Balkan War, 1912

Lawrence of Arabia

Reinsurance Treaty

Algeciras Conference of 1906

Anglo-French Entente of 1904

"Third Balkan War" (1914)

Lusitania

Admiral Tirpitz

(German) Auxiliary Service Law of 1916

David Lloyd George

Rasputin

Georges Clemenceau

Duma

Explain what role each of the following played in the Russian Revolution.
Tsar Nicholas II

Petrograd Soviet

Leon Trotsky

Petrograd bread riots (1917)

Congress of the Soviets

Kiev mutiny (1918)

Alexander Kerensky

Vladimir Lenin

Army Order No. 1

Constituent Assembly

White opposition

Treaty of Brest-Litovsk (1918)

Test your understanding of the chapter by providing the correct answers.

1. Germany violated this country's neutrality in 1914. _____

2. He was exiled to Siberia for socialist agitation. _____

3. Called "the Tiger," he wanted to punish Germany. _____

4. He was the Bolshevik war commissar. _____

5. This Russian was called "our Friend Grigori." _____

6. The name of the important German war plan designed for a two-front war.

    _____

7. The date of the assassination of Archduke Francis Ferdinand. _____

8. The president of the revolutionary provisional government in Russia.

    _____

9. Russian workers' councils. _____

10. He aroused the Arab princes to revolt in 1917. _____

11. The name of the treaty between the Germans and the Russian Bolshevik government

    in 1918. _____

12. The German chancellor fired by William II. _____

13. A Serbian revolutionary group. _____

14. The first country to mobilize for European war in 1914. _____

15. The Russian parliament that Nicholas adjourned in 1914. _____

Place the following events in correct chronological order.

Marx writes the *Communist Manifesto*   1. _____

Lenin's return from Switzerland   2. _____

Establishment of the provisional   3. _____
government

Outbreak of war between Russia   4. _____
and Germany

Kornilov plot   5. _____

Abolishment of the Constituent Assembly   6. _____

Overthrow of Kerensky and the   7. _____
provisional government

Multiple-Choice Questions

1. The Bismarckian system of alliances was meant to
   a. expand Germany's borders.
   b. help German allies expand their borders.
   c. restrain Russia and Austria-Hungary and isolate France.
   d. encourage relations with France.

2. Which group of events is in correct chronological order?
   a. The Three Emperors' League, the Alliance of the Three Emperors, the Russian-German Reinsurance Treaty
   b. The Russian-German Reinsurance Treaty, the Alliance of the Three Emperors, the Three Emperors' League
   c. The Alliance of the Three Emperors, the Russian-German Reinsurance Treaty, the Three Emperors' League
   d. The Russian-German Reinsurance Treaty, the Three Emperors' League, the Alliance of the Three Emperors

3. Which of the following strained German-British relations before the First World War?
    a. The Greek revolution
    b. A German-French entente
    c. The German naval buildup
    d. British occupation of Belgium

4. The Schlieffen Plan called for Germany to knock out
    a. England by marching through France.
    b. Russia by marching through Poland.
    c. France by marching through Belgium.
    d. Belgium by marching through France.

5. Which of the following is usually considered a cause of the First World War?
    a. British appeasement of the Germans
    b. Nationalism
    c. Germany deliberately starting the "Third Balkan War"
    d. German control over the international alliance system

6. Which of the following was a consequence of the First World War?
    a. The weakening of socialism
    b. The exclusion of labor leaders and socialists from government
    c. The right to vote for women
    d. A widening of the gap between rich and poor

7. Which of the following was a central idea of Lenin?
    a. Revolution cannot occur in a backward country.
    b. Revolution is determined by an elite leadership.
    c. A broad-based democratic workers' party is necessary.
    d. The war against Germany must continue.

8. The end of the war in 1918 brought revolution to which of the following countries?
    a. France and Britain
    b. Germany and Italy
    c. Germany and Austria-Hungary
    d. France and Italy

9. Which of the following was an accomplishment of the peace conference at Versailles after the war?
    a. The division of Germany into an East and West Germany
    b. A defensive alliance in favor of France signed by the United States and Britain
    c. The re-establishment of Russian borders
    d. The establishment of the principle of German reparations payments

10. The phrase that best describes Bismarck's attitude toward German expansion after
    1871 is
    a. German control of Europe.
    b. the annexation of Austria-Hungary to Germany.
    c. no territorial ambitions.
    d. a great German navy and German colonies.

11. The young Emperor William II of Germany made the fateful decision to reverse
    Bismarck's foreign policy by refusing to renew the treaty between Germany and
    a. Austria.
    b. Britain.
    c. France.
    d. Russia.

12. As a result of the Moroccan crisis, European powers viewed which of the following
    countries as a threat to peace and stability?
    a. France
    b. Germany
    c. Britain
    d. Japan

13. The countries with the most at stake in the Balkans and who were most fearful of
    nationalism were
    a. Germany and Austria.
    b. France and Turkey.
    c. Turkey and Austria.
    d. Russia and Germany.

14. The first country to mobilize in 1914 for general warfare was
    a. France.
    b. Germany.
    c. Russia.
    d. Britain.

15. The chief feature of the war on the western front was
    a. inconclusive battles fought in ceaseless trench warfare.
    b. the invasion of Germany by French and British troops.
    c. a series of German victories at the German-French border.
    d. a propaganda war with little actual fighting.

16. The major impact of World War I on economic thought was the
    a. promotion of government planning and involvement in the economy.
    b. strengthening of capitalism based on laissez-faire principles.
    c. reaffirmation of imperialism.
    d. proof that civilian populations were unimportant to the war economy.

17. For women in European society, the First World War brought about
    a. overall economic and political improvement.
    b. some economic gains but no political gains.
    c. a setback in the struggle for women's rights.
    d. a deterioration of their economic position.

18. The Petrograd Soviet's Army Order No. 1 resulted in
    a. a renewed and effective war effort.
    b. a complete breakdown of army discipline.
    c. increased authority of the Russian military elite.
    d. large numbers of new recruits.

19. Lenin's appeal to the people of Russia centered on
    a. ending the war and giving land to the peasants and power to the soviets.
    b. giving all power to the Duma.
    c. victory over Germany through renewed war effort.
    d. support of the Kornilov plot against Kerensky.

20. As a result of the Treaty of Brest-Litovsk, Russia
    a. acquired considerable territory.
    b. re-entered the war on the German side.
    c. agreed to spread the revolution to western Europe.
    d. lost one-third of its population.

21. Which of the following was *not* included in the Treaty of Versailles?
    a. A clause that placed blame for the war on Germany and her allies
    b. German colonies taken away
    c. German territory given to Poland
    d. Germany allowed to keep Alsace-Lorraine but forced to give up the city of Danzig

22. The most anti-German of the major powers represented at the Versailles treaty conference in 1919 was
    a. Clemenceau of France.
    b. Lloyd George of Britain.
    c. Wilson of the United States.
    d. Orlando of Italy.

23. The second Battle of the Marne resulted in
    a. a virtual stalemate.
    b. an impressive German victory that boosted morale at home.
    c. a Russian victory at the eastern front, but a French loss in the west.
    d. a decisive loss for the Germans.

24. This leader of the German left scorned moderate socialism and stressed the revolutionary character of Marxism.
    a. Theobald von Bethmann-Hollweg
    b. Tsarina Alexandra
    c. Rosa Luxemburg
    d. Alexander Kerensky

25. Which of the following battles resulted in a stalemate and the end of the German dream to use the Schlieffen Plan to capture France?
    a. The Battle of Verdun
    b. The first Battle of the Marne
    c. The Battle of the Somme
    d. The second Battle of the Marne

26. During the First World War the colonial subjects of France and Britain
    a. revolted.
    b. allied with Germany.
    c. remained neutral.
    d. provided critical supplies and armies to the French and British.

Major Political Ideas

1. What is Leninist Bolshevism? Define it by describing Lenin's principal ideas with regard to revolutionary change. How did Lenin differ from other Marxists, and why, in your view, did Lenin prevail?

2. What is a soviet and what role did soviets play in the Russian Revolution of 1917?

Issues for Essays and Discussion

The First World War has been called "the great turning point in government and society." Do you agree? Discuss this by making reference to the political, social, physical, and psychological impact of the war. Which country was most affected by the war, Russia, Austria, France, or Britain? Provide evidence to support your argument.

Interpretation of Visual Sources

Study the wartime posters on page 1052 of the textbook. What is the message of these posters? Is this propaganda? Why were posters such as these considered necessary?

Geography

1. Study Maps 32.1 and 32.2. Referring to the textbook when necessary, answer the following questions:
   a. What was the ethnic make-up of the Balkans?
   b. What was the extent of Ottoman (Turkish) control in the Balkans in 1878 and in 1914? How and why did the Turks lose territory?
   c. What were the territorial ambitions of Serbia and Austria-Hungary in the Balkans?

2. Study Map 32.3. Referring to the textbook when necessary, answer the following questions:
   a. What was the western front, and where did it exist? Compare it with the eastern front.
   b. Locate the following important battles of the First World War: Gallipoli, Passchendaele, Tannenburg, and Verdun. In each case, who fought, what was the outcome, and what was the significance?
   c. Describe the German offensive of August-September 1914 and the first Battle of the Marne. What were the strengths and the weaknesses of the German military and the Schlieffen Plan?

3. Study Map 32.4 to understand some of the changes brought about by the First World War. Use Outline Map 32.4 provided to answer the following questions and locate the following places.
   a. The boundaries of 1926 are indicated on this map. Mark the boundaries of Europe in 1914. Next, mark the location of the Polish corridor, Alsace and Lorraine, the three new Baltic states, and Galicia. What happened to each of these areas because of the First World War, and what was the significance?
   b. Mark the location of the demilitarized zone along the Rhine. How did this zone strengthen the French military position?
   c. Mark the territorial losses experienced by Germany, Austria, and Russia. How did the losses reflect the principle of self-determination?
   d. Mark the location of Paris, Berlin, Warsaw, Budapest, Vienna, Belgrade, Brussels, Amsterdam, Leningrad, Danzig, Rome, Bucharest, and Sofia.

Remember that duplicate maps for class use are at the back of this book.

Outline Map 32.4

Understanding History Through the Arts

What effect did the Russian Revolution have on art? One of the most important cultural developments to emerge from the revolution in Russia was a revolution in art. What forms did this revolution take, and who were its participants? Begin your research with C. Lodder, *Russian Constructivism** (1983); J. Milner, *Vladimir Tatlin and the Russian Avant-Garde** (1983); S. O. Dhan-Magomedov, *Rodchenko: The Complete Work* (1986); and S. White, *The Bolshevik Poster** (1988).

Problems for Further Investigation

1. Was Germany responsible for the Great War? The German people of the postwar era felt that they had been unjustly blamed. Some historians argue that the "war guilt" issue led to the rise of Hitler. Do you agree? This has been one of the most-debated subjects in political-diplomatic history in recent years. One of the chief revisionists is A. J. P. Taylor, *The Struggle for Mastery in Europe, 1848–1919* (1954), while an anti-German argument has come from E. Fischer, *The German War Aims in World War I* (1967). The debate is discussed in D. E. Lee, *The Outbreak of the First World War** (1970), and in R. Henig, *The Origins of the First World War* (1989).

2. What were the motives of the leaders of the Bolshevik Revolution? The problem of interpreting the revolution in Russia, current interpretations, and key themes are examined in a valuable anthology with a bibliography: R. Suny and A. Adams, *The Russian Revolution and Bolshevik Victory** (1990). The war, the hemophiliac child, Rasputin, and the murder of the royal family by the Bolsheviks are all brought together in an interesting book about Russia in the era of the revolution, *Nicholas and Alexandra** (1971), by R. Massie. Lenin's impact on history is best covered in L. Fischer, *The Life of Lenin** (1964, 1965), and in C. Hill, *Lenin and the Russian Revolution** (1947, 1971), while the standard work on Leon Trotsky is a three-volume work (1954–1963) by I. Deutscher. Other books on the Bolshevik leaders are R. Conquest, *V. I. Lenin* (1972), and B. Wolfe, *Three Who Made a Revolution* (1955).

3. How was the First World War portrayed in fiction? Few books have captured the tragedy of the First World War as well as Erich Remarque's novel *All Quiet on the Western Front,** while A. Home's *The Price of Glory: Verdun 1916* (1979) recounts the horror of the western-front battle that cost 700,000 lives.

*Available in paperback.

Studying Effectively—Exercise 6

Learning to Make Historical Comparisons

An important part of studying history is learning how to *compare* two (or more) related historical developments. Such comparisons not only demonstrate a basic understanding of the two objects being compared, but also permit the student historian to draw distinctions that indicate real insight.

For these reasons, "compare-and-contrast" questions have long been favorites of history professors, and they often appear on essay exams. Even when they do not, they are an excellent study device for synthesizing historical information and testing your understanding. Therefore, as the introductory essay suggests, try to *anticipate* what compare-and-contrast questions your instructor might ask. Then work up your own study outlines that summarize the points your essay answer would discuss and develop. The preparation of study outlines, of course, is also a useful preparation for essay questions that do not require you to compare and contrast.

Exercise

Read the following brief passage. Reread it and underline or highlight it for main points. Now study the passage in terms of comparison and contrast. Prepare a brief outline (solely on the basis of this material) that will allow you to compare and contrast the Russian and German revolutions of 1917–1918. After you have finished, compare your outline with the model on the following page. Remember: the model provides a *good* answer, not the *only* answer.

The German Revolution of November 1918 resembled the Russian Revolution of March 1917. In both cases, a genuine popular uprising toppled an authoritarian monarchy and established a liberal provisional republic. In both countries, liberals and moderate socialists took control of the central government, while workers' and soldiers' councils formed a counter-government. In Germany, however, the moderate socialists won and the Lenin-like radical revolutionaries in the councils lost. In communist terms, the liberal, republican revolution in Germany in 1918 was only half a revolution: a bourgeois political revolution without a communist second installment. It was Russia without Lenin's Bolshevik triumph.

There were several reasons for the German outcome. The great majority of Marxian socialist leaders in the Social Democratic party were, as before the war, really pink and not red. They wanted to establish real political democracy and civil liberties, and they favored the gradual elimination of capitalism. They were also German nationalists, appalled by the prospect of civil war and revolutionary terror. Moreover, there was much less popular support among workers and soldiers for the extreme radicals than in Russia. Nor did the German peasantry, which already had most of the land, at least in western Germany, provide the elemental force that has driven all great modern revolutions, from the French to the Chinese.

Of crucial importance also was the fact that the moderate German Social Democrats, unlike Kerensky and company, accepted defeat and ended the war the day they took power. This act ended the decline in morale among soldiers and prevented the regular army with its conservative officer corps from disintegrating. When radicals headed by Karl Liebknecht and Rosa Luxemburg and their supporters in the councils tried to seize control of the government in Berlin in January, the moderate socialists called on the army to crush the uprising. Liebknecht and Luxemburg were arrested and then brutally murdered by army leaders, an act that caused the radicals in the Social Democratic party to break away in anger and form a pro-Lenin German Communist party shortly thereafter. Finally, even if the moderate socialists had followed Liebknecht and Luxemburg on the Leninist path, it is very unlikely they would have succeeded. Civil war in Germany would certainly have followed, and the Allies, who were already occupying western Germany according to the terms of the armistice, would have marched on to Berlin and ruled Germany directly. Historians have often been unduly hard on Germany's moderate socialists.

Comparison of Russian and German Revolutions (1917–1918)

Similarities	Differences

1. Both countries had genuine liberal revolutions.
   a. Russia—March 1917
   b. Germany—November 1918
 	
 2. In both countries moderate socialists took control.
	1. Russia had a second, radical (Bolshevik) revolution; Germany did not.
	
	 2. In Germany workers and peasants gave radicals less support than in Russia.
	
	 3. In Germany the moderate socialists stopped the war immediately and therefore the German army, unlike the Russian army, remained intact to put down radical uprisings.

CHAPTER 33
Nationalism in Asia, 1914–1939

Chapter Questions

After reading and studying this chapter, you should be able to answer the following questions:

How did modern nationalism develop in Asia between the First and Second World Wars? How did national movements arise in different countries, and how did some of these parallel movements come into brutal conflict?

Chapter Summary

Many Asians viewed nationalism as the solution to all their problems. This chapter explains why nationalism was so popular in Asia and how it became a mass movement between 1914 and 1939.

The promises of independence that the imperialist Europeans made to their subject peoples during the First World War were not kept. By the end of war neither Britain nor France were prepared to give up their old holdings; in fact, they used the League of Nations mandate system (which gave them much control over the old Turkish empire and the Middle East) to increase the size of their empires. At the same time, the war enhanced the national consciousness of peoples heretofore dominated by the West by demonstrating that the Europeans were beatable. Nationalism was also encouraged by the ideas of equality and national freedom that flowed out of wartime Europe and revolutionary Russia.

During the war the British had encouraged Arab revolt against Turkey and had promised the Zionist Jews a homeland in Palestine. After the war a British and French takeover of the Middle East caused a violent reaction from the Arab, Turkish, Iranian, and Jewish nationalists and, in some instances, brought them into conflict with each other. Rejection of self-determination for the non-Western world and the smashing of the new Syrian and Iraqi states by the Allies convinced the Arabs of the European betrayal.

Meanwhile, under Mustafa Kemal, Turkey rose up against the foreigners and laid the foundations for a modern, highly nationalistic, and secularized state. Equally important, nationalism transformed Iran and Afghanistan—both of which had to first cast off the British and in both of which Islam remained a counter against secularism and modernization.

In the 1920s and 1930s the Arabs won a considerable number of victories as independence came at a gradual pace. Iraq, Egypt, and Syria freed themselves, and a new Jewish state was created in Palestine. From the beginning, however, the Arabs and the Jews were engaged in an undeclared civil war. A similar nationalist movement both unified and divided India. Here the British policy of gradualism was deemed too gradual by Indian nationalists who, under Gandhi, successfully used the tactics of militant nonviolence to reform India and gain self-rule, although the country had to be divided between Hindus and Muslims.

Also in the 1920s the revolutionary Chinese nationalist movement, which had strengthened China and redefined Chinese family life, was undermined by both a civil war and a war with Japan. Sun Yat-sen's Nationalist program to institute land reform and crush the warlords was eventually abandoned, only to become the key to Mao's Communist strategy.

In Japan, rapid industrial development created an imbalanced economy controlled by the zaibatsus, while in the political sphere the country moved from liberalism to ultranationalism. Japanese expansion into Manchuria led to war with China.

Elsewhere in Asia, nationalism transformed French Indochina, the Dutch East Indies, and the Philippines. American encouragement of independence in the Philippines laid the foundations for popular government, but Dutch and French reluctance to set their holdings free led to nationalist reaction and, in Vietnam, a complex and bloody war.

Study Outline

Use this outline to preview the chapter before you read a particular section in your textbook and then as a self-check to test your reading comprehension after you have read the chapter section.

I. The First World War and Western imperialism
   A. The First World War greatly altered relations between Asia and Europe.
      1. The Chinese and the Japanese saw the war as a family quarrel that divided Europe and made it vulnerable; in India and French Indochina the enthusiasm for war was limited but the war's impact was greater.
      2. The British and the French needed the aid and the resources of their colonial peoples.
         a. Many Asians served in the French and British armies.
         b. The war experience exposed Asians to Western democratic and republican ideas.
         c. The British and French, in turn, made promises of postwar reform and self-rule.
         d. Wilson's idea of self-determination raised hopes for the end of foreign domination.

B. However, after the war, the Western imperialists worked to retain and expand their possessions.
   1. The idea of self-determination was subordinated to the British and French plan for continued Western rule.
   2. The League of Nations mandate system increased the size of the British and French empires.
   3. This caused Asians to turn to nationalist movements.
C. Soviet communism denounced imperialism and encouraged national independence movements.
   1. Lenin and the Communists announced that the end of foreign exploitation was their immediate goal.
   2. Nationalists like Ho Chi Minh were inspired by Lenin's plea for national self-determination.
D. National self-determination also appealed to countries that were subject to indirect Western control and exploitation.
   1. The domination of the world economy by the West created hostility toward Europe and the United States.
   2. Nationalism went hand in hand with the promise of modernization.

II. The Middle East
   A. The First World War and the Arab revolt
      1. Beginning with the revolution of 1908, the Young Turks strengthened the Ottoman state at the expense of the Arabs, largely Syria and Iraq.
         a. They were determined to hold the vast and diverse empire together.
         b. After defeat in Europe (Balkan War, 1912), they concentrated on control of their Asian possessions.
         c. Instead of liberal reform, they implemented a narrow Turkish nationalism.
         d. The Turks joined forces with Germany and Austro-Hungary in 1914, hoping to regain influence in Europe.
      2. The Arabs sided with Britain and successfully revolted against the Turks in 1916.
         a. Hussein Ibn-Ali led the Arab revolt, joined by T. E. Lawrence.
         b. The Arabs expected the British to support Arab national independence.
      3. However, Britain and France secretly agreed (in the Sykes-Picot Agreement) to divide and rule the Ottoman Empire themselves.
         a. France received modern-day Lebanon, Syria, and much of southern Turkey.
         b. Britain received Palestine, Jordan, and Iraq.
      4. The British Balfour Declaration of 1917 promised the Jews a national home in Palestine—a promise that dismayed the Arabs, who thought it wrong that a small minority be permitted to establish an exclusive religious and ethnic state.
      5. Hussein's son, Faisal, who attended the Paris Peace Conference, and the Arabs felt betrayed.
         a. The idea of self-determination was not carried out by the Allies.

        b. The mandate system and the Balfour Declaration were forced on the Arabs.

    6. A Syrian revolt in 1920 led to French repression.

B. The Turkish revolution

    1. The war left Turkey dismembered and reduced to a puppet state occupied by France and Britain, while the Greeks conquered part of western Turkey.

    2. Mustafa Kemal led the Turkish national liberation movement.

        a. Kemal's forces won a great victory over the foreigners.

        b. The Treaty of Lausanne abolished hated foreign controls, but Turkey lost its Arab provinces.

    3. Kemal was a secularist and a modernizer.

        a. He deposed the sultan and established a republic with himself as president.

        b. He crushed the Armenians and the Kurds and built a one-party system in Turkey.

        c. He ended religious influence in government and education and modernized the law and the schools.

        d. Women were enfranchised and could seek divorces, Western dress codes were enforced, and a new non-Arabic script was introduced.

    4. Kemal's nationalist revolution transformed Turkey into a modern secular state.

C. Iran and Afghanistan

    1. Iran was not as successful as Turkey in building a modern state.

        a. By the late nineteenth century, Iran was weak and subject to outside demands.

        b. The Iranian revolution of 1906 ended with Russian and British occupation of Iran.

        c. By 1919, all of Iran was under British control.

        d. The new shah, Reza Pahlavi, limited foreign influence, modernized Iran, and ruled harshly.

        e. Reza Shah's secularization and tyrannical ways weakened Iran as a modern state.

    2. Afghanistan won independence but found modernization difficult.

D. The Arab states and Palestine

    1. The Arab states gradually gained independence, although the West remained a strong presence.

        a. Faisal won independence for Iraq in 1939 by agreeing to a long-term military alliance with Great Britain.

        b. The British proclaimed Egypt independent in 1932 but maintained a strong military presence.

        c. Lebanon became a republic under French protection.

        d. Syria won its independence in 1936 in return for a treaty with France.

    2. Large Arab landowners and merchants often supported the Western presence.

    3. Relations between the Arabs and the West were complicated by Palestine.

        a. The key issue was Jewish migration from Europe to Palestine.

       b. Herzl believed that only a Jewish state could guarantee security and led a Zionist movement to encourage Jews to settle in Palestine.

       c. After the First World War, Jewish migration to Palestine increased rapidly.

       d. Arab resentment over Jewish settlement, combined with cultural and economic friction, caused anti-Jewish violence and an undeclared civil war between Arabs and Jews.

    4. Jewish settlers forged a cohesive community.

       a. The kibbutz was the key unit of agricultural organization.

       b. Industry was characterized by an egalitarian socialist ideology.

III. Toward self-rule in India

    A. Promises and repression (1914–1919)

       1. India gave significant support to the British cause during the First World War.

          a. Over one million Indians volunteered for duty in Europe.

          b. Economic and health problems grew and revived the prewar nationalist movement.

          c. The Lucknow Pact brought the Muslim minority and the Hindu majority together under the banner of self-government.

       2. The British response was contradictory.

          a. The Government of India Act (1919) permitted Indians to participate in government.

          b. However, the repressive Rowlatt Acts were designed to root out opposition.

          c. The British massacre of Indian civilians at Amritsar brought India to the verge of violent civil war.

    B. Hindu society and Mahatma Gandhi

       1. Gandhi grew up in one of the "protected" states, which were least affected by British rule.

       2. He came from a wealthy Indian family of the merchant (*gandhi*) class.

       3. The extended-family structure typical of Indian society strongly influence Gandhi.

       4. Gandhi studied law in England and eventually became a lawyer in British South Africa.

    C. The roots of Gandhi's militant nonviolence

       1. Gandhi's encounters with racial discrimination caused him to examine the "new system" of slavery in British South Africa.

       2. Gandhi undertook the legal defense of Indians who had finished their terms as indentured laborers.

       3. Gandhi called his spiritual theory of social action "Satyagraha," meaning "Soul Force."

          a. Satyagraha is a means of striving for truth and social justice through love, suffering, and conversion of the oppressor.

          b. Its tactic of nonviolent resistance owed a good deal to the teachings of Christ.

4. Gandhi's movement brought tax and immigration reforms and recognition of non-Christian marriages for the nonwhites of South Africa.

D. Gandhi leads the way toward national independence.
1. On his return to India in 1915, Gandhi traveled among the common people and led agricultural and industrial strikes.
2. The Amritsar Massacre pushed him to boycott British goods and jobs and not pay taxes.
3. His call to militant nonviolence appealed to the heretofore passive masses of Hindus and pushed them and the Muslims into the Congress party.
4. Gandhi ended this campaign in 1922 when violence broke out, and he turned to helping the poor help themselves.
5. By 1929, Indian desire for a speedier path to self-rule led to Gandhi's famous march to the sea.
6. In 1931, Gandhi and the British negotiated a new constitution (that took effect in 1935) that strengthened India's parliament and paved the way to self-rule.
7. Gandhi's tactics and philosophy brought the masses into politics and nurtured national identity and self-respect—although he failed to heal the split between Hindu and Muslim.

IV. Turmoil in East Asia
A. The Chinese movement toward independence from the West and toward modernism was undermined by internal conflict and war with Japan.
B. The rise of Nationalist China
1. The fall of the Manchu Dynasty in the revolution of 1911–1912 ended the hope of preserving traditional Chinese society.
2. Yüan Shih-k'ai, the leader of the revolution against the Manchus, dissolved the parliament and ruled as a dictator.
3. Yüan's death led to a shift of power to local warlords, whose taxes, wars, and corruption caused terrible suffering.
4. Foreign imperialism made matters worse: Japan's seizure of Shantung and southern Manchuria led to the patriotic protest called the "May Fourth Movement."
5. This led to an alliance between Sun Yat-sen's Nationalists and the Chinese Communists.
   a. Sun placed nationalism above all else, including communism.
   b. To him, democracy meant order and land reform for the peasants.
   c. Sun's goal was that the Nationalist party crush the warlords and unite China under a strong government.
6. Between 1926 and 1928, the Nationalists under Chiang Kai-shek unified China under a new government at Nanking.
   a. However, China remained divided by regional differences and lack of modern communications.
   b. Japan was opposed to a strong China.
   c. Chiang's Nationalists purged the Chinese Communists, who vowed revenge.

C. China's intellectual revolution
   1. Nationalism was only one part of the New Culture Movement.
      a. It was also a Western-oriented movement that attacked traditional culture, particularly Confucian ethics.
      b. Through its widely read magazines, *New Youth* and *New Tide*, the movement advocated Western ideas such as individualism, democracy, science, and a new language.
      c. Its leading intellectual, Hu Shih, advocated a gradual adoption of Western ideas.
   2. Another aspect of the New Culture Movement was Marxian socialism.
      a. Marxism was attractive because it was a single, all-encompassing creed.
      b. It provided a means for criticizing Western dominance and explaining Chinese weakness.
      c. It was appealing as a way to free the poor peasants from their parasitic landlords.
   3. Mao Tse-tung believed that peasant revolution would free China.
      a. After the unsuccessful Autumn Harvest Uprising of 1927, he advocated equal distribution of land.
      b. He built up a self-governing Communist soviet at Juichin in southeastern China.
D. The changing Chinese family
   1. The Confucian principle of subordination placed the group over the individual and tied women to husband and family.
      a. Women were given in marriage by parents at an early age.
      b. The wife owed unquestioning obedience to her husband, could be bought and sold, and had no property rights.
   2. Lao T'ai T'ai's autobiography illustrates both old and new Chinese attitudes toward the family.
      a. Footbinding died out.
      b. Marriages for love became common, and polygamy declined.
      c. Economic and educational opportunities opened for women.
E. From liberalism to ultranationalism in Japan
   1. The First World War accelerated economic expansion and imperial growth in Japan.
   2. The early 1920s was a period of peaceful and democratic pursuit of the country's goals, although most nationalists held that Japan's mission was to protect all of Asia.
   3. Serious problems accompanied Japan's rise.
      a. Japan's population grew while natural resources and food remained scarce.
      b. Its "dualistic economy" consisted of a few giant conglomerate firms and a mass of peasants and craftsmen—and a weak middle class.
      c. Struggle between old and new political elites resulted in a lack of cohesive leadership.

4. The most serious problem was ultranationalism.
    a. The ultranationalists were violently anti-Western and rejected Western ideas and institutions.
    b. They wanted to restore traditional Japanese practices such as the samurai code.
    c. They preached foreign expansion and "Asia for Asians."
    d. The Great Depression caused many Japanese to turn to the ultranationalists.
F. Japan against China
    1. Japanese army officers in Manchuria turned to ultranationalism as a solution to Japan's problems.
    2. Manchuria was taken from China in 1931–32 by the Japanese army, and Japan's politics became increasingly chaotic.
    3. Japanese aggression caused the Chinese Nationalist government to abandon modernization and social and land reform.
        a. Half of China's land was owned by rich landlords, while the peasants owned little land and lived in poverty.
        b. Now opposed to land reform, the Nationalists strove to eliminate Mao's Communist movement.
        c. Mao's Long March in 1934 saved communism, which then undertook land reform—thus winning peasant support.
    4. Communist-Nationalist cooperation in the late 1930s could not halt further Japanese aggression.
        a. By late 1938 sizable portions of coastal China were under Japanese control.
        b. Both the Communists and the Nationalists retreated to the interior.
G. Southeast Asia
    1. Events elsewhere in Asia inspired nationalism in French Indochina and the Dutch East Indies.
    2. French imperialism in Vietnam stimulated the growth of a Communist-led nationalist opposition movement.
    3. In Indonesia, Dutch determination to keep their colonies led to the rule of a successful nationalist movement.
    4. The Philippine nationalist movement succeeded.
        a. Highly educated, the Philippine people sought independence from the United States.
        b. The United States encouraged economic growth, education, and popular government.
        c. But U.S. racism encouraged radical nationalism in the Philippines.
        d. The Great Depression encouraged the United States (in 1934) to schedule self-government for the Philippines in 1944.

Review Questions

Check your understanding of the chapter by answering the following questions.

1. What role did the colonial peoples play in the First World War? How did most Asians view that war?

2. What was the British attitude toward their colonial peoples during and after the war? The French attitude?

3. Who benefited from the League of Nations mandate system? Who lost?

4. What happened to President Wilson's idea of national self-determination? Why was it not applied to colonial peoples?

5. In what way did the Russian Revolution encourage Asian nationalism?

6. Why did the Arabs hope that the French and British would champion the cause of Arab nationalism? Why did this hope turn into a feeling of betrayal?

7. Describe Faisal's efforts to bring about Syrian independence. What was the outcome?

8. What factors were responsible for the Young Turk nationalist movement in Ottoman Turkey, and what changes did the movement bring to that society?

9. In what sense was Mustafa Kemal a true student of the Enlightenment and Western liberalism? In what sense was he not?

10. Why did the Iranian revolution of 1906 fail?

11. What were the positions of the Jews, the Arabs, and the British on the issue of a Jewish homeland in Palestine? In what way was the British position contradictory?

12. Describe the League of Nations mandate system. How did it work, whom did it affect, and why was it established?

13. What were the origins and goals of the Zionist movement? How was it implemented?

14. How did the First World War affect the Indian people, the Indian nationalist movement, and the British government in India?

15. Describe Gandhi's philosophy of Satyagraha. Why were his cultural background and his experience in South Africa important?

16. Give examples of Gandhi's militant nonviolent tactics. What impact did this movement have on the poor masses of India?

17. Describe the British government's position in India. What was the Hindu-Muslim problem, and how did it make British rule easier?

18. Describe events in China in the fifteen or so years after 1912. What problems did China face, and how successful was it in establishing unity and order?

19. Discuss and explain the three major currents in China's New Culture Movement: nationalism, modernism, and Marxian socialism. Why was each appealing to many Chinese?

20. Describe Mao Tse-tung's philosophy and his program of revolutionary reform for China. Why were the warlords opposed?

21. What were the pros and cons of traditional Confucian ethics as it related to the family and the status of women? What changes in marriage and the role of women occurred after about 1911?

22. How did the First World War affect Japan? What events can you cite to show the trend toward liberalism and democracy?

23. What were Japanese-Chinese relations in the twentieth century up to about 1938 like?

24. What problems did Japan face in the 1920s and 1930s? How did the ultranationalists propose to solve these problems?

25. How did Japanese conquest affect the Chinese Nationalist party? What were the reasons for the Nationalist-Communist struggle?

26. What were the reasons for a nationalist movement in the Philippines? What were the attitudes of the Americans toward the Filipino people?

Study-Review Exercises

Define the following key concepts and terms.

Permanent Mandates Commission

Palestine

Zionist movement

kibbutz

Majlis

protected state

maharaja

Mahatma

Satyagraha

nonviolent resistance

warlord

zaibatsu

ultranationalism

Identify and explain the significance of the following people and terms.
Turkish revolution of 1908

Sykes-Picot Agreement (1916)

Balfour Declaration (1917)

Young Turks

Hussein Ibn-Ali

Faisal

Mustafa Kemal

Iranian revolution of 1906

Reza Shah Pahlavi

Amanullah

Theodore Herzl

Lucknow Pact (1916)

Government of India Act (1919)

Amritsar Massacre

Mohandas Gandhi

Yüan Shih-k'ai

May Fourth Movement

Sun Yat-sen

Chiang Kai-shek

New Culture Movement

Hu Shih

Mao Tse-tung

Kita Ikki

Long March

Test your understanding of the chapter by providing the correct answers.

1. Territories of the defeated German and Ottoman empires that were turned over by the

   League of Nations to the victorious powers are known as _____ .

2. At the end of the First World War, Turkey faced *British and French occupation/support for its Arab subjects.*

3. In general, most Asian and Arab nationalists *accepted/rejected* the ideas of the Western Enlightenment and Western modernization.

4. The nationalist movements in Turkey under Kemal and in Iran under Reza Shah were *opposed to/in favor of* weakening traditional religion.

5. The country of Lebanon was a mandate of *Britain/France* and was dominated by its *Christian/Muslim* majority.

6. The key unit of Jewish agricultural organization in Palestine was the

   _____ .

7. After the First World War, the British government was *more/less* sympathetic to the Indian demands for independence.

8. In India, traditional Hindu family structure was *included in/excluded from* the development of Gandhi's nationalist movement, while in China, traditional Confucian ethics was *included in/excluded from* the New Culture Movement.

Multiple-Choice Questions

1. President Wilson and Lenin had a common
   a. dislike of communism.
   b. desire to continue colonial rule by Europeans.
   c. disinterest in the ideas of nationalism.
   d. belief in self-determination.

2. The position of the Paris Peace Conference (1919) and the League of Nations on the subject of Syria was
   a. acceptance of the idea of self-determination.
   b. establishment of a French mandate.
   c. acceptance of a merger of Syria with Iraq.
   d. establishment of a Zionist state in Syria.

3. The great revolutionary and nationalist leader of Turkey and "father of the Turks" was
   a. Mustafa Kemal.
   b. Hussein Ibn-Ali.
   c. T. E. Lawrence.
   d. Jamal al-Din al-Afghani.

4. The Austrian journalist who led the Zionist movement was
   a. Mustafa Kemal.
   b. Theodore Herzl.
   c. Karl Lueger.
   d. Ferdinand Lassalle.

5. In order to forge a cohesive community that could face the dangers of Arab opposition, the Jewish settlers of Palestine
   a. turned to rural development through cooperative farming.
   b. adopted a program of rapid industrialization and urbanization.
   c. adopted a philosophy of monopoly capitalism.
   d. all of the above.

6. The Arab nationalist who was deposed in Syria and then made king of Iraq by the British was
   a. Faisal.
   b. Amanullah.
   c. Mustafa Kemal.
   d. Hussein.

7. In 1907, Iran was divided into spheres of influence by
   a. Turkey and Russia.
   b. Turkey and Iraq.
   c. Russia and Britain.
   d. Britain and France.

8. As the examples of Egypt, Syria, and Lebanon indicate, by the 1930s the Arab states had
    a. freed themselves from Western political mandates.
    b. freed themselves from Western influence.
    c. acquired genuine independence.
    d. all of the above.

9. The foremost Arab leader, a direct descendant of Muhammad, who proclaimed himself king of the Arabs, was
    a. T. E. Lawrence.
    b. Hussein Ibn-Ali.
    c. Reza Shah.
    d. Mustafa Kemal.

10. During the First World War, Arab nationalists and the British found they had a common enemy in
    a. France.
    b. Soviet Russia.
    c. India.
    d. Turkey.

11. The "Great Idea" of the Greek nationalists in the years following the First World War was
    a. a return to classical learning.
    b. a modern Greek empire.
    c. the building of a Bolshevik state in Greece.
    d. liberation from Turkey.

12. After about 1921, the majority of Jewish emigrants to Palestine came from
    a. the United States.
    b. Europe (largely Poland and Germany).
    c. the Arab states.
    d. Russia.

13. The Balfour Declaration of 1917 expressed British commitment to
    a. self-rule in India.
    b. the spirit of the Versailles Treaty.
    c. unobstructed sea lanes.
    d. a Jewish homeland in Palestine.

14. In the secret Sykes-Picot Agreement, France and Britain agreed on
    a. how to defeat Germany.
    b. unconditional German surrender.
    c. how to divide the Ottoman Empire after the war.
    d. spheres of influence in Southeast Asia.

15. Shortly after World War I, Greece invaded
    a. Italy.
    b. Albania.
    c. Egypt.
    d. Turkey.

16. Mustafa Kemal in Turkey
    a. granted autonomy to ethnic minorities.
    b. created a two-party system on the British model.
    c. moved the capital to Ankara.
    d. revived the sultanate.

17. Mustafa Kemal strove to
    a. revive the Islamic religion.
    b. recover the lost Arab lands.
    c. reacquaint his people with their historic tradition.
    d. modernize on the Western model.

18. The Muslim League demanded the creation of a Muslim nation in British India called the "land of the pure," or
    a. Pakistan.
    b. Afghanistan.
    c. Ceylon.
    d. Punjab.

19. Compared to Kemal, Reza Shah's drive to modernize Iran was
    a. less successful.
    b. equally successful.
    c. slightly more successful.
    d. much more successful.

20. The main reason Amanullah failed to reform and modernize Afghanistan was
    a. British overlordship.
    b. Islam.
    c. Indian invasions.
    d. a lack of natural resources.

21. Zionism is
    a. the Jewish political system.
    b. a highly advanced system of agriculture.
    c. Jewish nationalism.
    d. a sect of Judaism.

22. Which of the following statements about the Jewish settlement of Palestine is true?
    a. Much of the land was purchased by the U.S. government.
    b. Most of the early immigrants preferred to live in urban areas.
    c. The British gave no support to the idea of a Jewish homeland.
    d. The Zionists encouraged only wealthy Jews to settle in Palestine.

23. Gandhi was
    a. Hindu.
    b. Buddhist.
    c. Moslem.
    d. Christian.

24. Hindu women
    a. were considered equal to men.
    b. were subordinate to men.
    c. could remarry if widowed.
    d. were targets of disrespect.

25. Gandhi was
    a. from the Indian peasant class.
    b. a grocer.
    c. a trained lawyer.
    d. a bachelor.

26. Gandhi advocated
    a. war between Hindus and Muslims.
    b. British rule.
    c. violent overthrow of British rule.
    d. nonviolent action protesting British rule.

27. The founder of the Kuomintang, or Nationalist party, in China was
    a. Mao Tse-tung.
    b. Chiang Kai-shek.
    c. Yüan Shih-k'ai
    d. Sun Yat-sen.

28. According to the textbook, the most serious challenge to peaceful progress in Japan was
    a. the zaibatsu.
    b. the ultranationalists.
    c. corrupt government officials.
    d. financial oligarchy.

Major Political Ideas

Define Asian nationalism. How did it differ from nationalism elsewhere? What are the bright and dark sides of Asian nationalism? Give examples.

Issues for Essays and Discussion

Was Asian nationalism successful in helping Asian peoples address and solve the problems of modern times? Make specific reference to the Arab world, India, and China.

Interpretation of Visual Sources

Study the portrait of Mao Tse-tung on page 1093 of the textbook. What does it tell us about the make-up of the Communist army in China? About the army's military tactics? Why was Marxism so appealing to these people?

Geography

Using Map 33.1 in the text, show on Outline Map 33.1, provided, the following:

1. The changes in the size of the Turkish state following the First World War. How does the size of postwar Turkey compare to that of prewar Turkey? Show which areas were British protectorates and which were League of Nations mandates.

2. Describe the causes of the changes in the size of the Ottoman Empire. What role did Greece and Britain play in this process?

   _____

   _____

   _____

3. Mark the location of Kuwait, Ankara, Istanbul, Baghdad, Riyadh, and the Smyrna coast.

Remember that duplicate maps for class use appear at the end of this book.

Outline Map 33.1

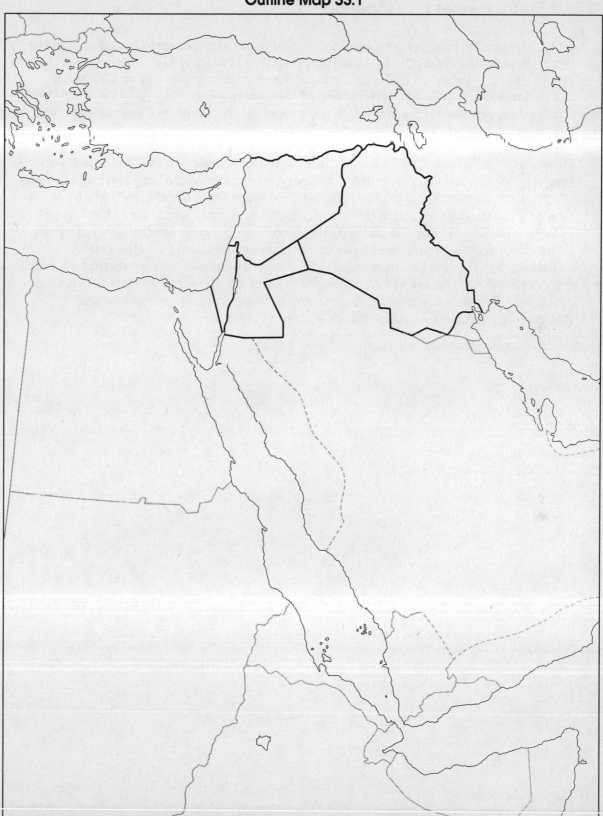

Problems for Further Investigation

1. How did Gandhi, Sun Yat-sen, and Mao Tse-tung change the world? A good place to begin to understand Gandhi is his autobiography, *The Story of My Experiments with Truth** (first published in 1927). Other helpful and interesting works on Gandhi are L. Fischer, *The Life of Gandhi** (1950), and M. Bondurant, *The Conquest of Violence** (1959). For Sun Yat-sen, see H. Shriffrin, *Sun Yat-sen and the Origins of the Chinese Revolution* (1970); and for Mao, see S. Schram, *Mao Tse-tung* (1967).

2. How was a small country like Britain able to control a vast country like India for so long a time? A good starting point in an analysis of the impact of imperial rule in India is a book of debates: *The British in India: Imperialism or Trusteeship** (1962), ed. by M. D. Lewis. The massacre of Indian civilians at Amritsar is considered one of the low points of British imperial history. If you are interested in trying your hand at working with primary source documents and have access (as most libraries do) to the British Parliamentary Papers, you may want to look at two government reports that tell of the massacre: the *Rowlatt Report* (1918, Cmd. 9190) and the *Hunter Committee Report* (1920, Cmd. 681). For an account of the last viceroy of India, Lord Mountbatten, see A. Campbell-Johnson, *Mission with Mountbatten* (1951).

*Available in paperback.

CHAPTER 34

The Age of Anxiety in the West

Chapter Questions

After reading and studying this chapter, you should be able to answer the following questions:

Why did so many people in the postwar era feel adrift in an uncertain world? How were the postwar feelings of crisis and anxiety reflected in Western thought, art, and culture? How did political leaders try to maintain peace and prosperity between 1919 and 1939? Why did they fail?

Chapter Summary

Because war and revolution had shattered so many traditional ideas, beliefs, and institutions, many people of the postwar era found themselves living in an age of anxiety and continuous crisis. Many developments in thought, science, and the arts after the war encouraged this crisis even further.

The first half of this chapter deals with major changes in ideas and culture that were connected to this age of anxiety. Some of these changes began before 1900, but they became widespread only after the great upheaval of the First World War affected millions of ordinary people and opened an era of uncertainty and searching. People generally became less optimistic and had less faith in rational thinking. Radically new theories in physics associated with Albert Einstein and Werner Heisenberg took form, while Sigmund Freud's psychology gave a new and disturbing interpretation of human behavior. Philosophy and literature developed in new ways, and Christianity took on renewed meaning for thinking people. There was also great searching and experimentation in architecture, painting, and music, all of which went in new directions. Much painting became abstract, as did some music. Movies and radio programs, which offered entertainment and escape, gained enormous popularity among the general public. In short, there were revolutionary changes in thought, art, and popular culture.

The second half of this chapter discusses efforts to re-establish real peace and political stability in the troubled era after 1918. In 1923, hostility between France and Germany led to an undeclared war when French armies occupied Germany's industrial heartland, the Ruhr. This crisis was resolved, though, and followed by a period of cautious hope in international politics between 1924 and 1929. The stock market crash in the United States in 1929, however, brought renewed economic and political crisis to the Western world. Attempts to meet this crisis in the United States, Sweden, Britain, and France were only partly successful. Thus, economic and political difficulties accompanied and reinforced the revolution in thought and culture. It was a hard time in Western society.

Study Outline

Use this outline to preview the chapter before you read a particular section in your textbook and then as a self-check to test your reading comprehension after you have read the chapter section.

I. Uncertainty in modern thought
   A. The effects of the First World War
      1. Western society began to question values and beliefs that had guided it since the Enlightenment.
      2. Many people rejected the long-accepted beliefs in progress and the power of the rational mind to understand a logical universe and an orderly society.
         a. Valéry wrote about the crisis of the cruelly injured mind; to him the war ("storm") had left a "terrible uncertainty."
         b. New ideas and discoveries in philosophy, physics, psychology, and literature encouraged this general intellectual crisis.
   B. Modern philosophy
      1. The traditional belief in progress and the rational human was attacked by Nietzsche, Bergson, and Sorel before 1914.
         a. Nietzsche believed that Western civilization was in decline because of Christian humility and the overstress on rational thinking at the expense of emotion and passion; he believed that a few superior individuals—supermen—had to become the leaders of the herd of inferior men and women.
         b. Bergson added to this the idea that immediate experience and intuition are as important as rational and scientific thinking.
         c. Sorel argued that socialism, led by an elite, would succeed through a great violent strike of all working people.
      2. The two main developments in philosophy were logical empiricism (logical positivism) in English-speaking countries and existentialism on the Continent.
         a. Logical empiricism, as defined by Wittgenstein, claimed that philosophy was nothing more than the logical clarification of thoughts—in other

words, the study of language; it could not answer the great issues of the ages such as the meaning of life.

    b. Existentialism, first developed in Germany by Heidegger and Jaspers, and then by Sartre and Camus in France, stressed that humans can overcome the meaninglessness of life by individual action.

    c. Existentialism was popular in France after the Second World War because it advocated positive human action at a time of hopelessness.

C. The revival of Christianity

    1. Before 1914, Protestant theologians, such as Schweitzer, stressed the human nature of Jesus and turned away from the supernatural aspects of his divinity; they sought to harmonize religious belief with scientific findings.

    2. A revitalization of fundamental Christianity took place after the First World War.

        a. Kierkegaard was rediscovered; he had criticized the worldliness of the church and stressed commitment to a remote and majestic God.

        b. Barth stressed the imperfect and sinful nature of man and the need to accept God's truth through trust, not reason.

        c. Catholic existential theologians, such as Marcel, found new hope in religion by emphasizing the need for its hope and piety in a broken world.

D. The new physics

    1. Prior to the 1920s, science was one of the main supports of Western society's optimistic and rational world-view.

    2. The challenge to Newtonian physics by scientists such as Planck and Einstein undermined belief in constant natural laws.

        a. Plank's work with subatomic energy showed that atoms were not the basic building blocks of nature.

        b. Einstein postulated that time and space are relative, the universe is infinite, and matter and energy are interchangeable.

    3. The 1920s was the "heroic age of physics."

        a. Rutherford split the atom.

        b. Subatomic particles were identified, notably the neutron.

        c. The new physics described a universe that lacked absolute objective reality; Heisenberg claimed that instead of Newton's rational laws, there are only tendencies and probabilities.

        d. In short, science seemed to have little to do with human experience and human problems.

E. Freudian psychology

    1. Prior to Freud, it was assumed that the conscious mind processed experiences in a rational and logical way.

    2. According to Freud, human behavior is basically irrational.

        a. The key to understanding the mind is the irrational unconscious (the id), which is driven by sexual, aggressive, and pleasure-seeking desires.

        b. Behavior is a compromise between the needs of the id and the rationalizing conscious (the ego), which mediates what a person can do, and ingrained moral values (the superego), which tell what a person should do.

   3. Instinctual drives can easily overwhelm the control mechanisms; yet rational thinking and traditional moral values can cripple people with guilt and neuroses.
   4. Many interpreted Freudian thought as an encouragement of an uninhibited sex life.
F. Twentieth-century literature
   1. The postwar moods of pessimism, relativism, and alienation influenced novelists.
   2. Literature focused on the complexity and irrationality of the human mind.
   3. Novelists like Woolf, Faulkner, and Joyce adopted the stream-of-consciousness technique, in which ideas and emotions from different time periods bubble up randomly.
   4. Some literature, such as that of Spengler, Kafka, and Orwell, was anti-utopian—it predicted a future of doom.

II. Modern art and music
   A. Architecture and design
      1. The new idea of functionalism revolutionized architecture by emphasizing efficiency and clean lines instead of ornamentation.
      2. The Chicago school of architects, led by Sullivan, pioneered in the building of skyscrapers.
      3. Frank Lloyd Wright designed truly modern houses featuring low lines, open interiors, and mass-produced building materials.
      4. In Germany, the Bauhaus school under Gropius became the major proponent of functional and industrial forms.
         a. It combined the study of fine art with the study of applied art.
         b. The Bauhaus stressed good design for everyday life.
      5. Van der Rohe brought European functionalism to Chicago—and hence steel frame and glass wall architecture.
   B. Modern painting
      1. French impressionism yielded to nonrepresentational expressionism, which sought to portray the worlds of emotion and imagination, as in the works of van Gogh, Gauguin, Cézanne, and Matisse.
      2. Cubism, founded by Picasso, concentrated on zigzagging lines and overlapping planes.
      3. Nonrepresentational art turned away from nature completely; it focused on mood, not objects.
      4. Dadaism and surrealism became prominent in the 1920s and 1930s.
         a. Dadaism delighted in outrageous conduct.
         b. Surrealists, inspired by Freud, painted wild dreams and complex symbols.
         c. Picasso's great mural *Guernica* unites cubism, surrealism, and expressionism.
   C. Modern music
      1. The concept of expressionism also affected music, as in the work of Stravinsky and Berg.

      2. Some composers, led by Schönberg, abandoned traditional harmony and tonality.

  D. Movies and radio

      1. The general public embraced movies and radio enthusiastically.

      2. The movie factories and stars like Mary Pickford, Lillian Gish, Douglas Fairbanks, Rudolph Valentino, and Charlie Chaplin created a new medium and a new culture.

      3. At first Germany led the way but by the late 1920s Hollywood dominated the film business.

      4. Moviegoing became a form of escapism and the main entertainment of the masses.

      5. Radio, which became possible with Marconi's "wireless" communication and the development of the vacuum tube, permitted transmission of speech and music, but major broadcasting did not begin until 1920.

         a. Then every country established national broadcasting networks; by the late 1930s three of four households in Britain and Germany had a radio.

         b. Dictators and presidents used the radio for political propaganda.

      6. Movies also became tools of indoctrination.

         a. Eisenstein used film to dramatize the communist view of Russian history.

         b. In Germany, Riefenstahl created a propaganda film for Hitler.

III. The search for peace and political stability

  A. Germany and the Western powers

      1. Germany was the key to lasting peace, and the Germans hated the Treaty of Versailles.

      2. France believed that an economically weak Germany was necessary for its security and wanted massive reparations to repair its devastated northern region.

      3. Britain needed a prosperous Germany in order to maintain the British economy.

         a. J. M. Keynes, an economist, argued that the Versailles treaty crippled the European economy and needed revision.

         b. His attack on the treaty contributed to guilt feelings about Germany in Britain.

         c. As a result, France and Britain drifted apart.

      4. When Germany refused to continue its heavy reparations payments, French and Belgian armies occupied the Ruhr (1923).

  B. The occupation of the Ruhr

      1. Since Germany would not pay gold, France wanted to collect reparations in coal, steel, and machinery.

      2. The Germans stopped work in the factories and France could not collect reparations, but the French occupation affected the German economy drastically.

         a. Inflation skyrocketed.

         b. Resentment and political unrest among the Germans grew.

3. Under Stresemann, Germany agreed to revised reparations payments and France withdrew its troops, but many Germans were left financially ruined and humiliated.

C. Hope in foreign affairs (1924–1929)
1. The Dawes Plan (1924) provided a solution to the reparations problem: the United States loaned money to Germany so it could pay France and Britain so they could pay the United States.
2. In 1929 the Young Plan further reduced German reparations.
3. The treaties of Locarno (1925) eased European disputes.
   a. Germany and France accepted their common border.
   b. Britain and Italy agreed to fight if either country invaded the other.
4. The Kellogg-Briand Pact (1928) condemned war, and the signing states agreed to settle international disputes peacefully.

D. Hope in democratic government
1. After 1923, democracy seemed to take root in Germany as the economy boomed.
2. However, there were sharp political divisions in the country.
   a. The right consisted of nationalists and monarchists.
   b. The communists remained active on the left.
   c. Most working-class people supported the socialist Social Democrats.
3. In France, the democratically elected government rested in the hands of the middle-class-oriented moderates, while Communists and Socialists battled for the support of the workers.
4. Northern France was rebuilt, the franc was stabilized, and Paris became the world's cultural center.
5. Britain's major problem was unemployment, and the government's efforts to ease it led the country gradually toward state-sponsored welfare plans.
   a. Britain's Labour party, committed to revisionist socialism, replaced the Liberals as the main opposition party to the Conservatives.
   b. Labour, under MacDonald, won in 1924 and 1929, yet moved toward socialism gradually.

IV. The Great Depression (1929–1939)
   A. The economic crisis
   1. The depression began with the American stock market crash (October 1929).
      a. Many investors and speculators had bought stocks on margin (paying only a small part of the purchase price and borrowing the rest from their stockbrokers).
      b. When prices started to fall, thousands of people had to sell their shares at once to pay their brokers, and a financial panic started.
   2. Financial crisis led to a decline in production, first in the United States and then in Europe, and to an unwise turn to protective tariffs.
   3. The absence of international leadership and poor national economic policies added to the depression.

B. Mass unemployment
1. As production decreased, workers lost their jobs and had no money to buy goods, which cut production even more.
2. Mass unemployment also caused great social and psychological problems.
C. The New Deal in the United States
1. Roosevelt's goal was to preserve capitalism through reform.
2. Government intervention in and regulation of the economy first took place through the National Recovery Administration (NRA), whose goal was to reduce competition and fix prices and wages for everyone's benefit.
3. The NRA was declared unconstitutional (1935), and Roosevelt decided to attack the problem of mass unemployment directly by using the federal government to employ as many people as possible.
    a. The Work Projects Administration (1935) employed millions of people.
    b. It was very popular and helped check the threat of social revolution.
4. Other social measures, such as social security and government support for labor unions, also eased the hardships of the depression.
5. Although the New Deal helped, it failed to pull the United States out of the depression.
    a. Some believe Roosevelt should have nationalized industry so national economic planning could have worked.
    b. Many economists argued that the New Deal did not put enough money into the economy through deficit financing.
D. The Scandinavian response to depression
1. Backed by a strong tradition of community cooperation, socialist parties were firmly established in Sweden and Norway by the 1920s.
2. Deficit spending to finance public works and create jobs was used to check unemployment and revive the economy after 1929.
3. Scandinavia's welfare socialism, though it depended on a large bureaucracy and high taxes, offered an appealing middle way between capitalism and communism or fascism in the 1930s.
E. Recovery and reform in Britain and France
1. Britain's concentration on its national market aided its economic recovery.
2. Government instability in France prevented recovery and needed reform.
    a. The Socialists, led by Blum, became the strongest party in France, and his Popular Front government attempted New Deal–type reforms.
    b. France was drawn to the brink of civil war, and Blum was forced to resign (1937), leaving the country to drift aimlessly.

Review Questions

Check your understanding of this chapter by answering the following questions.

1. Describe how Nietzsche, Bergson, and Sorel began the revolt against the idea of progress and the general faith in the rational human mind. How did Wittgenstein add to this belief?

2. What does Sartre's statement that "man is condemned to be free" mean? How is this thought connected to the existential belief that man must seek to define himself?

3. What impact did the loss of faith in reason and progress have on twentieth-century Christian thought?

4. Define *quanta*. What are its implications for the definition of matter and energy?

5. What is the relationship among the id, ego, and superego?

6. What are the parallels between Freud's view that human beings are basically irrational and the picture of the universe drawn by modern physics?

7. What was the stream-of-consciousness technique, and how was it used in twentieth-century literature?

8. What were the basic principles and characteristics of "modern" architecture? Where did it originate, and who were its first practitioners?

9. How do impressionism and expressionism reflect the rationality and irrationality of the nineteenth and twentieth centuries, respectively?

10. What influence did Freud have on twentieth-century painting?

11. What was the political impact of radio and film?

12. What were the attitudes of Britain, France, and Germany toward the Treaty of Versailles?

13. The most serious international crisis of the 1920s occurred in the Ruhr in January 1923. What was the crisis and what were its consequences?

14. What part was played by the United States in the economic and political settlements of the mid-1920s in Europe?

15. What problems faced the British governments of the 1920s and with what ideas did the Labour party approach these problems?

16. What were the origins, interests, and goals of the Labour and Liberal parties in Britain?

17. What were the causes of the Great Depression?

18. What was the effect of the recall of public and private loans to European countries?

19. What was the NRA, and why did it not work well?

20. The New Deal ultimately failed to halt mass unemployment. Why? Why is it said that the WPA helped prevent social revolution in the United States?

21. Why was the Scandinavian response to the economic crisis the most successful one in the Western democracies?

Study-Review Exercises

Identify and explain the significance of the following people and terms.

Gustav Stresemann

Ramsay MacDonald

"Little Entente" of 1921

Ruhr crisis of 1923

Locarno meetings of 1925

Munich beer hall "revolution" of 1923

principle of uncertainty

French Popular Front

National Recovery Administration

BBC

Raymond Poincaré

John Maynard Keynes

Guglielmo Marconi

Leni Riefenstahl

Sergei Eisenstein

Kellogg-Briand Pact, 1928

Adolf Hitler

Explain who the following people were and note how their work contributed to and reflected the uncertainty and anxiety in modern thought.

Paul Valéry

Friedrich Nietzsche

Georges Sorel

Henri Bergson

Ludwig Wittgenstein

Jean-Paul Sartre

Max Planck

Albert Einstein

Ernest Rutherford

Werner Heisenberg

Sigmund Freud

James Joyce

Marcel Proust

George Orwell

Oswald Spengler

Define the following philosophic and artistic schools and movements by describing their basic aims and characteristics and naming some participants and works.

logical empiricism

modern existentialism

functionalism in architecture

Chicago school of architecture

expressionism in painting

cubism

dadaism

surrealism

expressionism in music

atonality in music

Test your understanding of the chapter by providing the correct answers.

1. Most modern (postimpressionist) artistic movements *were/were not* concerned with the visible world of fact.

2. The Dawes Plan provided that _____ would get loans from the United States to pay reparations to _____ and _____ so that they could repay their loans to _____ .

3. The French poet and critic who wrote that "almost all the affairs of men remain in terrible uncertainty. We think of what has disappeared, and we are almost destroyed by what has been destroyed." _____

4. After 1914, people tended to *strengthen/discard* their belief in progress.

5. The works of modern physics tended to *confirm/challenge* the dependable laws of Newton.

6. The British economist who denounced the Versailles treaty and advocated a "counter-cyclical policy" to deal with depressed economies. _____

Multiple-Choice Questions

1. The country most interested in strict implementation of the Treaty of Versailles was
   a. France.
   b. Britain.
   c. the United States.
   d. Italy.

2. Which one of the following occurred during the early years of the Great Depression?
   a. Most countries went on the gold standard.
   b. Most countries raised tariffs.
   c. Americans issued massive loans to European states.
   d. Most governments increased their budgets and spending.

3. Which of the following countries was the most effective in dealing with the depression?
   a. France
   b. Britain
   c. Sweden
   d. the United States

4. Existentialists believed that
   a. the world was perfectible.
   b. only God was certain in this lost world.
   c. human beings can conquer life's absurdity.
   d. no human action can bring meaning to life.

5. The trend in literature in the postwar period was
   a. toward a new faith in God and mankind.
   b. the glorification of the state.
   c. the new belief in a world of growing desolation.
   d. utopian dreams of the future.

6. The German philosopher Friedrich Nietzsche believed that Western civilization
   a. had lost its creativity by neglecting emotion.
   b. should be rebuilt around Christian morality.
   c. needed to increase political democracy.
   d. should place more stress on social equality.

7. The modern, or international, style in architecture emphasized
   a. practical and functional construction.
   b. freedom from town planning.
   c. massive exterior ornamentation.
   d. separation of fine from applied arts.

8. The British economist J. M. Keynes argued that to ensure lasting peace and prosperity in Europe after the First World War, emphasis should be placed on
   a. a powerful France and Russia.
   b. the growth of the British Empire.
   c. the enforcement of the Treaty of Versailles.
   d. a prosperous and strong Germany.

9. Which of the following was *not* a cause of the Great Depression?
   a. Financial panic in the United States
   b. The absence of world financial leadership
   c. Unemployment
   d. The reduction of national spending

10. The British Labour party leader and prime minister in 1924 and 1929 was
    a. MacDonald.
    b. Blum.
    c. Sartre.
    d. Keynes.

11. The "spirit of Locarno" after 1924 was a general feeling in Europe that
    a. the communist overthrow of European governments was inevitable.
    b. Germany must be forced to pay its original reparation debts.
    c. European peace and security were possible.
    d. Hitler would bring about the recovery of Germany.

12. The decade following the First World War was generally a period of
    a. uncertainty and dissatisfaction with established ideas.
    b. increasing belief in the goodness and perfectibility of humanity.
    c. emphasis on the idea that a new science and technology would build a more democratic and liberal world.
    d. religious revival based on the human nature of Christ and the basic goodness of human beings.

13. The philosophy of logical empiricism held that
    a. great philosophical issues can never be decided.
    b. humanity must accept all truths as being absolute.
    c. humanity is basically sinful.
    d. there is no God.

14. The writings of Virginia Woolf, Marcel Proust, James Joyce, and William Faulkner all reflect the postwar concern with
    a. the reconstruction of society.
    b. an attempt to discover the reasons for the loss of faith in God.
    c. the conflict between materialism and spiritualism.
    d. the complexity and irrationality of the human mind.

15. Modern painting grew out of a revolt against
    a. classicism.
    b. capitalism.
    c. French impressionism.
    d. German romanticism.

16. The movement in painting that attacked all accepted standards of art and behavior and delighted in outrageous conduct was
    a. the Bauhaus movement.
    b. brutalism.
    c. dadaism.
    d. cubism.

17. The great maker of Nazi propaganda films in Germany was
    a. Sergei Eisenstein.
    b. Mack Sennett.
    c. Alban Berg.
    d. Leni Riefenstahl.

18. For the people of Britain, the greatest problem of the 1920s was
    a. increased class tension.
    b. the Irish problem.
    c. the rise of socialist dictatorship.
    d. unemployment.

19. The antifascist movement in France in 1936–37, led by Léon Blum, was known as the
    a. Radical Alliance.
    b. Communist Coalition.
    c. Popular Front.
    d. New Deal Republic.

20. In January 1923 the Ruhr was occupied by
    a. Russia.
    b. France.
    c. Britain.
    d. Austria.

21. The main entertainment of the masses until the Second World War was
    a. football.
    b. motion pictures.
    c. the music hall.
    d. the pub.

22. After 1914, religion became
    a. less popular and was largely abandoned.
    b. more interested in a reconciliation with science.
    c. more relevant and meaningful to thinking people than before the war.
    d. less occupied with spiritual matters and more worldly.

23. Surrealism in painting was inspired to a great extent by
    a. ordinary visual reality.
    b. traditional landscape painting and attention to historical accuracy.
    c. the movement to deny the concepts of anxiety and alienation.
    d. Freudian psychology.

24. The British Labour party was strongly tied to the idea of
    a. competitive capitalism.
    b. limited government control.
    c. democracy and a gradual move toward socialism.
    d. revolution and the rejection of revisionist socialism.

25. With Russia no longer a possible ally, France turned to which of the following for diplomatic support in the 1920s?
    a. Italy
    b. The new eastern European states
    c. Germany
    d. Turkey

Major Political Ideas

1. What was the purpose of a "peace treaty"? One of the most controversial political ideas in the 1920s was John Maynard Keynes's argument that the Treaty of Versailles was harsh and foolish in its treatment of Germany. Do you agree? What positions did the French, Germans, and British take on this issue?

2. The 1920s saw democracy in both Germany and France undergo considerable strain, but there was relative harmony in Britain. Describe the various political parties in each of these nations. Who supported them, and what were their objectives?

Issues for Essays and Discussion

1. The period from 1919 to 1939 was one of both hope and anxiety. Discuss this period by describing the events and ideas that pointed to a better world. What forces and events pointed in the other direction? What, in your view, were the factors that pushed Europe in the direction of another war?

2. After about 1919, European (and American) society witnessed an unprecedented upheaval in thought and the arts. What were some of these developments, and how did they reflect postwar society? Make sure you mention developments in philosophy, religion, psychology, music, architecture, and painting.

Interpretation of Visual Sources

1. Study the illustration entitled *Guernica* on page 1115 of the textbook. Describe the event and then describe how Picasso used expressionism, cubism, and surrealism in this painting.

2. Study the photo of "Falling Water" on page 1114 of the textbook. Describe the house and its architect in terms of the new architecture of the age. What makes this building different from other architectural forms?

Understanding History Through the Arts

1. What can we learn about the age of anxiety from the novels of the period? The message of existentialist philosophy is movingly told in Albert Camus's *The Myth of Sisyphus,** and the Paris Gertrude Stein claimed was "where the twentieth century was" is the subject of Ernest Hemingway's *A Moveable Feast** and Janet Flanner's *Paris Was Yesterday** (1972). The text bibliography lists a number of excellent books, including several on life during the depression. George Orwell's *Animal Farm** and *1984** are classics for good reason, and his *Road to Wigan Pier** is a view of British working-class life in the era of the Great Depression.

2. What are the distinguishing characteristics of modern architecture? Functionalism in architecture (including the Chicago school) is treated in N. Pevsner, *Pioneers of Modern Design** (1960). The international style and the Bauhaus leader who made Chicago the most important architectural center in America are the subjects of P. Blacke, *Mies van der Rohe: Architecture and Structure** (1964), and more recently, F. Schulze, *Mies van der Rohe, A Critical Biography* (1985). An important Dutch movement in design is covered in C. Blotkamp, et al., *De Stijl: The Formative Years** (1986, 1990). An excellent review of Le Corbusier's buildings and his writings is found in S. von Moos, *Le Corbusier** (1985), and the aims and achievements of the German Bauhaus movement are examined in H. Wingler, *Bauhaus: Weimar, Dessau, Berlin, Chicago** (1978), and in two books by G. Naylor: *The Bauhaus** (1968) and *The Bauhaus Re-assessed** (1985). A revolution in photography is covered in E. Marzona and R. Fricke, eds., *Bauhaus Photography* (1987). For a more critical view, perhaps the most famous and most outspoken critic of modern functionalist architecture and urban planning is the Prince of Wales, whose book on the subject is *A Vision of Britain: A Personal View of Architecture* (1989).

3. How was film used for propaganda in this period? One of the most chilling examples of the use of film for the ideological transformation of a country is Leni Riefenstahl's documentary *The Triumph of the Will*, showing the 1934 Nazi party rally at Nuremburg.

*Available in paperback.

It reveals a great deal about what Nazis wanted to believe about themselves and their leader, Adolf Hitler. It is available on video film.

Problems for Further Investigation

1. How did events following the First World War lead to the Second World War? Those interested in the complexities of interwar economic history will find B. W. E. Alford, *Depression and Recovery: British Economic Growth, 1918–1939** (1972), a short and readable discussion of a number of interpretations of the British economy. The Versailles treaty is dealt with in the Problems in European History book *The Versailles Settlement** (1960), ed. I. J. Lederer.

2. What was daily life like in this period? The dramatic changes in domestic life, sport, amusement, politics, sex, and other aspects of life in the twenty-one-year period between the two great wars make a stimulating subject for student research. Begin your investigation with R. Graves and A. Hodge, *The Long Week End: A Social History of Great Britain, 1918–1939** (1940, 1963). For two aspects of the so-called sex revolution of the interwar era, see R. Bridenthal, "Something Old, Something New: Women Between the Two World Wars," in R. Bridenthal, C. Koonz, and S. Stuard, eds., *Becoming Visible: Women in European History* (1987), and J. Steakley, *The Homosexual Emancipation Movement in Germany* (1975).

*Available in paperback.

CHAPTER 35

Dictatorships and the Second World War

Chapter Questions

After reading and studying this chapter, you should be able to answer the following questions:

What are the characteristics of the twentieth-century totalitarian state? How did the totalitarian state affect ordinary people, and how did it lead to another war? How did the Grand Alliance defeat Germany and its allies? What were the strengths and weaknesses of this alliance?

Chapter Summary

The anxiety and crisis that followed the First World War contributed to the rise of powerful dictatorships in parts of Europe, and, unfortunately, to an even more horrible Second World War. Some of these dictatorships were old-fashioned and conservative, but there were new totalitarian dictatorships as well, notably in Soviet Russia and Nazi Germany. This chapter examines the different kinds of dictatorship in a general way and then looks at Stalin's Russia and Hitler's Germany in detail. It goes on to describe the Second World War and why and how the great coalition of the Soviet Union, Britain, and the United States defeated Germany and its allies.

In Soviet Russia, Lenin relaxed rigid state controls in 1921 after the civil war in order to revive the economy. After defeating Trotsky in a struggle for power, Stalin established a harsh totalitarian dictatorship, which demanded great sacrifices from the people. Soviet Russia built up its industry while peasants lost their land and a radically new socialist society came into being. Mussolini's government in Italy was much less radical and totalitarian.

This chapter then examines Adolf Hitler and the totalitarian government of the Nazis in Germany. The roots of Nazism are found in racism, extreme nationalism, and violent irrationality, all of which drove Hitler relentlessly. Hitler was also a master politician, and this helped him gain power legally. His government was popular, especially because it appeared to solve the economic problems of the Great Depression. Hitler also had the support of many of the German people because of his success in foreign affairs. He used bullying and fears of communism in Britain and France to rearm and expand, until finally war broke out over Poland in 1939. By 1942, Hitler and the Nazis had temporarily forged a great empire and were putting their anti-Jewish racism into operation.

The Grand Alliance, consisting of the Soviet Union, Britain, and the United States, was able to wage a successful war against Hitler partly because it postponed political questions and adopted the principle of unconditional surrender of Germany and Japan, and partly because of the great and heroic contributions of the British and Soviet peoples and American resources. The beginning of the end for Germany came in 1942, when its offensive into the Soviet Union was turned into a retreat, and the end became certain in 1944, when the American and British forces began to push into Hitler's empire from the west.

Study Outline

Use this outline to preview the chapter before you read a particular section in your textbook and then as a self-check to test your reading comprehension after you have read the chapter section.

I. Authoritarianism and totalitarianism in Europe after the First World War
   A. Conservative authoritarianism
      1. Conservative authoritarianism had deep roots in European history and led to an antidemocratic form of government that believed in avoiding change but was limited in its power and objectives.
      2. Conservative authoritarianism revived after the First World War in eastern Europe, Spain, and Portugal.
         a. These countries lacked a strong tradition of self-government.
         b. Many were torn by ethnic conflicts.
         c. Large landowners and the church looked to dictators to save them from land reform.
      3. The new authoritarian governments were more concerned with maintaining the status quo than with forcing society into rapid change.
   B. Modern totalitarianism
      1. Modern totalitarianism emerged from the First World War and the Russian civil war, when individual liberties were subordinated to a total war effort.
      2. Nothing was outside of the control of the totalitarian state: it was a dictatorship that used modern technology and communications to try to control the political, economic, social, intellectual, and cultural components of its subjects' lives.
      3. Unlike old-fashioned authoritarianism, which was based on elites, modern totalitarianism was based on the masses.
      4. Totalitarian regimes believed in mobilizing society toward some great goal.

C. Totalitarianism of the left and right
1. In Stalinist Russia, the leftists prevailed; private property was taken over by the state, and the middle class lost its status and power.
2. In Nazi Germany, private property was maintained.

II. Stalin's Russia
A. From Lenin to Stalin
1. By 1921, the economy of Russia had been destroyed.
2. In 1921, Lenin's New Economic Policy (NEP) re-established limited economic freedom in an attempt to rebuild agriculture and industry.
   a. Peasants bought and sold goods on the free market.
   b. Agricultural production grew, and industrial production surpassed the prewar level.
3. Economic recovery and Lenin's death in 1924 brought a struggle for power between Stalin and Trotsky, which Stalin won.
   a. Stalin met the ethnic demands for independence within the multinational Soviet state by granting minority groups limited freedoms.
   b. Stalin's theory of "socialism in one country," or Russia building its own socialist society, was more attractive to many Communists than Trotsky's theory of "permanent revolution," or the overthrow of other European states.
4. By 1927, Stalin had crushed all opposition and was ready to launch an economic-social revolution.
B. The five-year plans
1. The first five-year plan (1928) to increase industrial and agricultural production was extremely ambitious, but Stalin wanted to erase the NEP, spur the economy, and catch up with the West.
2. Stalin waged a preventive war against the better-off peasants, the kulaks, to bring them and their land under state control.
   a. Collectivization of the peasants' land—forcible consolidation of individual peasant farms into large, state-controlled enterprises—resulted in disaster for agriculture and unparalled human tragedy.
   b. But it was a political victory for Stalin and the Communist party, as the peasants were eliminated as a potential threat.
3. The five-year plans brought about a spectacular growth of heavy industry, especially with the aid of government control of the workers and foreign technological experts.
4. Massive investment in heavy industry, however, meant low standards of living for workers.
C. Life in Stalinist society
1. The Communists wanted to create a new kind of society and human personality.
2. Stalin's reign of terror and mass purges created fear and eliminated any opposition.
3. Propaganda and indoctrination were common features of life, and even art and literature became highly political.

4. Life was hard, but people were often inspired by socialist ideals and did gain some social benefits and the possibility of personal advancement through education.

D. Women in Soviet Russia
1. Women were given much greater opportunities in industry and education.
   a. The 1917 revolution proclaimed complete equality of rights for women.
   b. In the 1920s, divorce and abortion were made easy, and women were urged to work outside the home and liberate themselves sexually.
2. Medicine and other professions were opened to them.
3. Most women had to work to help support their families in addition to caring for the home and the children.

III. Mussolini's Italy
A. The fascist seizure of power
1. The First World War and postwar problems ended the move toward democracy in Italy.
2. By 1922, most Italians were opposed to liberal, parliamentary government.
3. Mussolini's Fascists opposed the "Socialist threat" with physical force (the Black Shirts).
4. Mussolini marched on Rome in 1922 and forced the king to name him head of the government.
B. The regime in action
1. Mussolini's Fascists manipulated elections and killed the Socialist leader Matteotti.
2. Between 1924 and 1926, Mussolini built a one-party Fascist dictatorship but did not establish a fully totalitarian state.
   a. Much of the old power structure remained, particularly the conservatives, who controlled the army, economy, and state.
   b. The Catholic church supported Mussolini because he recognized the Vatican as an independent state and gave the church heavy financial support.
   c. Women were repressed, but Jews were not persecuted until late in the Second World War.

IV. Hitler's Germany
A. The roots of Nazism
1. Hitler became a fanatical nationalist while in Vienna, where he absorbed anti-Semitic and racist ideas.
2. He believed that Jews and Marxists lost the First World War for Germany.
3. By 1921, he had reshaped the tiny extremist German Workers' group into the Nazi party using the mass rally as a particularly effective tool of propaganda.
   a. The party grew rapidly.
   b. Hitler and the party attempted to overthrow the Weimar government, but he was defeated and sent to jail (1923).

B. Hitler's road to power
1. The trial after Hitler's attempted coup brought him much publicity, but the Nazi party remained small until 1929.
2. Written in jail, his autobiography, *Mein Kampf*, was an outline of his desire to achieve German racial supremacy and domination of Europe, under the leadership of a dictator (Führer).
3. The depression made the Nazi party attractive to the lower middle class and to young people, who were seized by panic as unemployment soared and Communists made election gains.
4. By 1932, the Nazi party was the largest in the Reichstag.
5. The Weimar government's orthodox economic policies intensified the economic collapse and convinced the middle class that its leaders were incompetent; hence, they welcomed Hitler's attacks on the republican system.
6. The Communists refused to ally with the Social Democrats to block Hitler.
7. Hitler was a skilled politician, a master of propaganda and mass psychology who generated enormous emotional support with his speeches.
8. Hitler was legally appointed chancellor in 1933.
C. The Nazi state and society
1. The Enabling Act of March 1933 gave Hitler absolute dictatorial power.
2. Nazis took over every aspect of German life—political, social, economic, cultural, and intellectual.
   a. Germany became a one-party state—only the Nazi party was legal.
   b. Strikes were forbidden and labor unions abolished.
   c. Publishing houses and universities were brought under Nazi control, and life became violently anti-intellectual.
3. Hitler took over total control of the military by purging the storm troopers.
4. The Gestapo, or secret police, used terror and purges to strengthen Hitler's hold on power.
5. Hitler set out to eliminate the Jews.
   a. The Nuremberg Laws (1935) deprived Jews of their citizenship.
   b. Jews were constant victims of violence and outrages.
D. Hitler's popularity
1. Hitler promised and delivered economic recovery through public works projects and military spending.
2. Hitler reduced Germany's traditional class distinctions.
3. He appealed to Germans for nationalistic reasons.
4. Communists, trade unionists, and some Christians opposed Hitler; many who opposed him were executed.

V. Nazi expansion and the Second World War
A. Aggression and appeasement (1933–1939)
1. Hitler's main goal was territorial expansion for the superior German race.
   a. He withdrew from the League of Nations in 1933.
   b. An Anglo-German naval agreement in 1935 broke Germany's isolation.
   c. In violation of the Treaty of Versailles, Hitler occupied the demilitarized Rhineland in 1936.

2. The British policy of appeasement, motivated by both guilt and pacifism, lasted far into 1939.
3. Mussolini attacked Ethiopia in 1935 and joined Germany in supporting the fascists in Spain.
4. Germany, Italy, and Japan formed an alliance.
5. Hitler annexed Austria and demanded part of Czechoslovakia in 1938.
6. Chamberlain flew to Munich to appease Hitler and agree to his territorial demands.
7. Hitler accelerated his aggression and occupied all of Czechoslovakia in 1939.
8. In 1939, Hitler and Stalin signed a public nonaggression pact and a secret pact that divided eastern Europe into German and Russian zones.
9. Germany attacked Poland, and Britain and France declared war on Germany (1939).

B. Hitler's empire (1939–1942)
1. The key to Hitler's military success was speed and force (the blitzkrieg).
2. He crushed Poland quickly and then France; by July 1940 the Nazis ruled nearly all of Europe except Britain.
3. He bombed British cities in an attempt to break British morale but did not succeed.
4. In 1941, Hitler's forces invaded Russia and conquered the Ukraine and got as far as Leningrad and Moscow until stopped by the severe winter weather.
5. After Japan attacked Pearl Harbor (1941), Hitler also declared war on the United States.
6. Hitler began building a New Order based on racial imperialism.
   a. Nordic peoples were treated with preference; the French were heavily taxed; the Slavs were treated as "subhumans."
   b. The S.S. evacuated Polish peasants to create a German "settlement space."
   c. Polish workers and Russian prisoners of war did most of the heavy labor.
   d. Jews, gypsies, Jehovah's Witnesses, and Communists were condemned to death—six million Jews were murdered in concentration camps.

C. The Grand Alliance
1. The allies had three policies that led them to victory.
   a. The United States concentrated on European victory first, then on victory over Japan.
   b. The Americans and British put military needs before political questions, thus avoiding conflict over postwar settlements.
   c. The Allies adopted the principle of "unconditional surrender" of Germany and Japan, denying Hitler the possibility of dividing his foes.
2. American aid to Britain and the Soviets, along with the heroic support of the British and Soviet peoples and the assistance of resistance groups throughout Europe, contributed to the eventual victory.

D. The tide of battle
1. The Germans were defeated at Stalingrad at the end of 1942, and from there on the Soviets took the offensive.
2. At the same time American, British, and Australian victories in the Pacific put Japan on the defensive.

    a. The Battle of the Coral Sea (1942) stopped the Japanese advance.

    b. The Battle of Midway Island (1942) established American naval superiority in the Pacific.

3. The British defeat of Rommel at the Battle of El Alamein (1942) helped drive the Axis powers from North Africa in 1943.

4. Italy surrendered in 1943, but fighting continued as the Germans seized Rome and northern Italy.

5. Bombing of Germany and Hitler's brutal elimination of opposition caused the Germans to fight on.

6. The British and Americans invaded German-held France in June 1944, but did not cross into Germany until March 1945.

    a. The Soviets pushed from the east, crossing the Elbe and meeting the Americans on the other side on April 26, 1945; Hitler committed suicide, and Germany surrendered on May 7, 1945.

    b. The United States dropped two atomic bombs on Japan in August 1945, and it too surrendered.

Review Questions

Check your understanding of this chapter by answering the following questions.

1. Why did conservative authoritarian governments develop in Poland, Hungary, Yugoslavia, and Portugal?

2. What are the characteristics of modern totalitarianism? How does it differ from conservative authoritarianism?

3. What was the purpose of Lenin's New Economic Policy?

4. How successful was Stalin's program of five-year plans for the industrialization of Soviet Russia? What were its strengths and weaknesses?

5. How does one explain that despite a falling standard of living, many Russians in the 1920s and 1930s willingly worked harder and were happy?

6. Generally, did women gain or lose status and power in the new Stalinist Russian state?

7. What were the circumstances under which Mussolini rose to power in Italy? What were his goals and tactics?

8. Many Germans in the 1920s and 1930s viewed Hitler as a reformer. What were his ideas about the problems and the future of Germany?

9. How did the Great Depression affect German political life?

10. What was the role of mass propaganda and psychology in Hitler's rise to power?

11. Why did Hitler acquire such a mass appeal? Did he improve German life?

12. Describe the Munich Conference of 1938 and Chamberlain's policy of appeasement. Why were so many British willing to appease Hitler? What was the result of the Munich Conference?

13. What was Hitler's foreign and military policy up to 1938? Was there enough evidence of aggression to convince the world that Hitler was dangerous?

14. What was the "final solution of the Jewish question"?

15. Describe German-Soviet relations between 1939 and 1941. Was war between the two inevitable?

16. What were the strengths of the Grand Alliance?

17. How did the Allies finally defeat Hitler?

Study-Review Exercises

Define the following key concepts and terms.

Hitler's final solution

modern totalitarianism

"socialism in one country"

appeasement

fascism

anti-Semitism

Identify and explain the significance of the following people and terms.

Weimar Republic

National Socialist German Workers' party

Benito Mussolini

Leon Trotsky

General Paul Hindenburg

Neville Chamberlain

kulaks

Nazi Storm Troopers (the SA)

Joseph Goebbels

German Social Democrats

Explain what the following events were, who participated in them, and why they were important.

Stalin's collectivization program

Lenin's New Economic Policy (1921)

Mussolini's march on Rome (1922)

Hitler's Munich plot (1923)

Great Depression in Germany (1929–1933)

Munich Conference (1938)

Russo-German ("Nazi-Soviet") nonaggression pact (1939)

Stalin's five-year plans

Grand Alliance

Battle of Stalingrad, 1942

Battle of El Alamein, 1942

Battle of the Coral Sea, 1942

Normandy invasion, June 6, 1944

Hiroshima and Nagasaki

Test your understanding of the chapter by providing the correct answers.

1. Unlike his rival, Trotsky, Stalin *favored/opposed* the policy of "socialism in one country."

2. In Germany, the Communists *agreed/refused* to cooperate with the Social Democrats in opposition to Hitler.

3. Stalin's forced collectivization of peasant farms was a political *victory/failure* and an economic *success/disaster*.

4. Hitler's Nazi party ruled a modern totalitarian state of the *right/left*.

5. Totalitarian states of the right usually *do/do not* advocate state takeover of private property.

6. He was an antisocialist and the leader of the Italian Black Shirts.

———————————

7. Lenin's New Economic Policy *was/was not* a return to capitalism.

8. He was legally appointed chancellor of Germany in 1933. _____

9. The standard of living of the average Russian worker in the 1930s *improved/declined* as a result of Stalin's five-year plans.

10. The foreign policy of Prime Minister Chamberlain of Britain tended to be *pro-German/anti-German*.

11. Mussolini's Italy *did/did not* have all the characteristics of a modern totalitarian state.

Multiple-Choice Questions

1. The Nuremberg laws related to
    a. antidepression programs.
    b. the Versailles treaty.
    c. the elimination of the fascists.
    d. Jewish citizenship.

2. The Vichy government of 1940 was established in
    a. Poland.
    b. Germany.
    c. Czechoslovakia.
    d. France.

3. Which of the following was *not* a modern totalitarian state in the 1930s?
    a. Germany
    b. Italy
    c. Russia
    d. France

4. The two countries in which modern totalitarianism reached its most complete form in the 1930s were
    a. Russia and Germany.
    b. Italy and France.
    c. Germany and Italy.
    d. Russia and Italy.

5. Before the modern totalitarian state, the traditional form of antidemocratic government in Europe was
   a. conservative authoritarianism.
   b. absolutism.
   c. republicanism.
   d. military government.

6. The modern totalitarian state is
   a. lethargic in its approach.
   b. built on elite groups.
   c. concerned only with survival.
   d. characterized by rapid and profound changes.

7. Lenin's New Economic Policy of 1921
   a. nationalized industries.
   b. called for the collectivization of agriculture.
   c. restored limited economic freedom.
   d. set five-year goals.

8. Before Lenin died, he named which of the following as his successor?
   a. Stalin
   b. Trotsky
   c. No one
   d. Dzhugashvili

9. Stalin became Lenin's successor because he
   a. was chosen by Lenin.
   b. was able to work outside the party.
   c. successfully related Russian realities to Marxist teachings.
   d. devised a system whereby minorities enjoyed total freedom.

10. Stalin's plans for rapid industrialization were based on
    a. importing coal from Japan.
    b. factories staffed exclusively by party members.
    c. depriving peasants in order to feed workers.
    d. a huge domestic market for consumer goods.

11. Under Stalin, women's greatest real benefits were
    a. sexual liberation and abortion.
    b. easy divorce and day-care centers.
    c. work freedom and accessible education.
    d. easier work than in the past and freedom from family worries.

12. Most Germans reacted to Hitler's purge of Jews with
    a. hostility and anger.
    b. protests and demonstrations.
    c. apathy and indifference.
    d. joy and celebration.

13. Which of the following characterized Stalinist society?
    a. Very slow economic and industrial growth
    b. The encouragement of religion
    c. The politicization of art and literature
    d. Large-scale discrimination against women in the job market

14. For Italian women, the fascist regime of Mussolini meant
    a. no improvement and a probable decline in status.
    b. considerable gains, especially in finding new careers in industry.
    c. more birth control and better-paying jobs.
    d. greater political participation and legal rights.

15. The social class within German society to whom Hitler appealed most was the
    a. industrial working class.
    b. poor.
    c. Jewish banking class.
    d. middle class.

16. Which of the following would have most likely supported Hitler?
    a. Communists
    b. Social Democrats
    c. Conservatives
    d. Nationalists

17. Conservative authoritarianism differed from modern totalitarianism in that it
    a. did not result in dictatorships.
    b. allowed popular participation in government.
    c. was more concerned with maintaining the status quo than with rapid change or war.
    d. did not persecute liberals or socialists.

18. Which of the following countries experienced a revival of conservative authoritarianism in the 1920s?
    a. Hungary
    b. Russia
    c. France
    d. Germany

19. In essence, the totalitarian state was
    a. a form of liberalism.
    b. an extension of the dictatorial state.
    c. a rigid, conservative society rooted in tradition.
    d. a form of government built on the power of the elite.

20. One major reason for British appeasement of Hitler was that
    a. he was seen as a way to block German capitalist expansion.
    b. he was seen as the bulwark against communism.
    c. the British government was prosocialist.
    d. Britain wanted time to prepare for war.

21. The Russians defeated the Germans at
    a. Leningrad.
    b. Brest-Litovsk.
    c. Stalingrad.
    d. El Alamein.

22. Prior to June 1944, most of the fighting against Germany on the Continent was carried out by
    a. France.
    b. Britain.
    c. the Soviet Union.
    d. the United States.

23. American policy during the Second World War can be best described as
    a. a conditional war against Germany.
    b. massive use of American troops on the eastern front.
    c. "Europe first" and the war in the Pacific second.
    d. pursue political goals first, military goals second.

24. The turning point in the North African war was the British defeat of the Germans in the Battle of
    a. the Coral Sea.
    b. Kursk.
    c. El Alamein.
    d. Leningrad.

25. It appears that rapid industrialization in the Soviet Union under Stalin was accompanied by
    a. a significant rise in the standard of living.
    b. a strengthening of trade unionism.
    c. an overall rise in real wages.
    d. a fall in the standard of living.

Major Political Ideas

Define totalitarianism. What are its fundamental characteristics and its origins? What is the difference between totalitarianism of the left and totalitarianism of the right? Compare totalitarianism to liberalism.

Issues for Essays and Discussion

1. The 1920s and the 1930s witnessed the rise of totalitarian states in Europe. How did this totalitarianism differ from authoritarian regimes of the past, and what were the goals and motives of the totalitarian state? In your answers, refer to the Soviet Union, Germany, and Italy.

2. Was the Second World War and the accompanying Holocaust the fault of the German people or the product of the evil mind of Adolf Hitler? Discuss this by describing the roots of Nazism and the reason for German expansionism.

Interpretation of Visual Sources

Study the photographs in your textbook labeled "Nazi Mass Rally, 1936" and "Hitler, Our Last Hope," on pages 1135 and 1152, respectively. What do the Hitler propagandists mean by the phrase "our last hope"? Do the people in the photo seem to fit the poster? How does this photograph help explain the photograph entitled "Nazi Mass Rally"? Contrast the portrayal of the individual in the two photos.

Geography

On Outline Map 35.2 provided, and using Maps 35.1 and 35.2 in the textbook for reference, mark the following: Germany in 1933, the step-by-step growth of Nazi Germany through September 1939 (shade in each area taken and give the date of acquisition), the extent of German penetration into the Soviet Union, Leningrad, Moscow, the Elbe River, the Ruhr, Poland, Austria, the Rhine, East Prussia, Czechoslovakia, Sudetenland, Munich, the Rhineland, Danzig, the Normandy beachhead. (Remember that duplicate maps for class use are at the back of this book.)

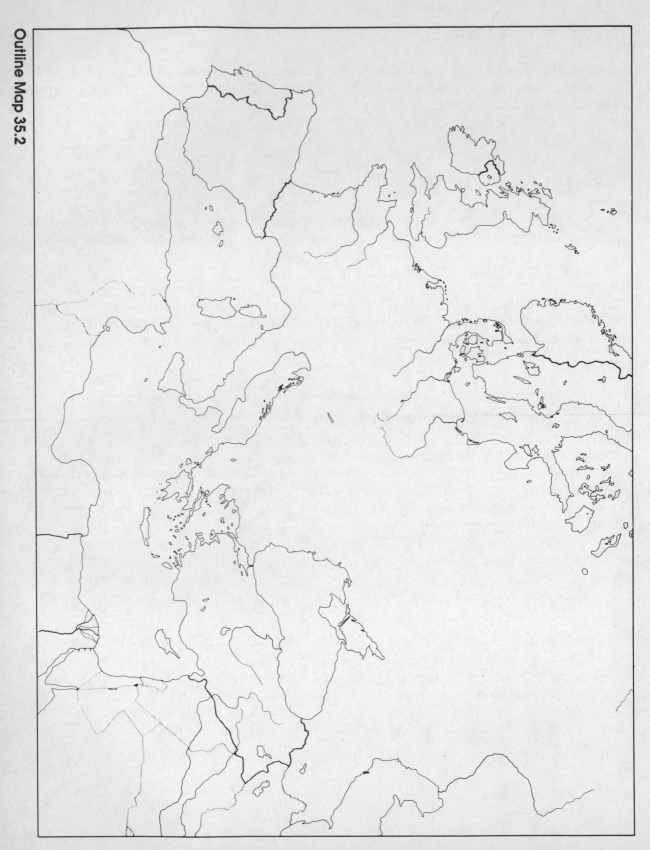

Understanding History Through the Arts

1. What role did architecture play in the Nazi German plan to build a new society? Begin your investigation into this subject with A. Speer, *Inside the Third Reich** (1971); Speer was an architect who became Hitler's chief war planner and one of the people closest to Hitler. His picture of Hitler's view of architecture is revealing in many ways.

2. What can we learn from films of the period? A large number of first-rank films have been made about Europe in the 1930s. *The Shop on Main Street* (1966) is a drama of a man living under Nazi occupation in Czechoslovakia who is sent to take over a button shop from an old Jewish woman. Similarly moving is *The Diary of Anne Frank* (1959), which is about a Jewish family hiding in an attic in Amsterdam in World War II. John Gielgud and Irene Worth narrate a French documentary about the Spanish Civil War entitled *To Die in Madrid* (1965). The film *Night and Fog,* by Renais, is a chilling documentary of the Nazi concentration camps.

Problems for Further Investigation

The period considered in this chapter is constantly undergoing reinterpretation, and new material appears each year. Helpful is A. Funk, et al., *A Select Bibliography of Books on the Second World War** (1975), a bibliography of books published from 1966 to 1975.

1. How did the Second World War begin? The problem of the origins of the Second World War is the subject of K. Eubank, *The Origins of World War II* (1990), and W. L. Kleine-Ahlbrandt, ed., *Appeasement of the Dictators* (1970).

2. How did Hitler, Mussolini, and Stalin gain power? Those interested in examining the tangle of views on the life and motives of Hitler should begin with R. G. L. Waite, ed., *Hitler and Nazi Germany* (1965), and A. Bullock, *Hitler: A Study in Tyranny* (revised, 1962). For Hitler's impact on German society, see D. G. Williamson, *The Third Reich* (1984). A scholarly account of Hitler's appeal to the German people is R. Hamilton, *Who Voted for Hitler?* (1982). About the Italian dictator, the student should read D. M. Smith, *Mussolini* (1982). Stalin's contribution to history has been the subject of much debate. The best overall summary of this debate is M. McCauley, *Stalin and Stalinism** (1983), while the chilling horrors of one aspect of Stalin's reign is dealt with (including photographs) in I. Deutscher and D. King, *The Great Purges* (1985). A good short discussion of the origins and motives of the political extremes of the decades between the two world wars is D. Smith, *Left and Right in Twentieth-Century Europe** (1970). And the issue of work and working life in the Soviet Union is dealt with in V. Andrle, *Workers in Stalin's Russia: Industrialization and Social Change in a Planned Economy* (1988).

*Available in paperback.

3. Few subjects in this period are as bloody and hate-filled as that of the civil war in Spain from 1936–1939. What happened and why? These and many other questions are examined in P. Preston, *The Spanish Civil War* (1986).

4. How can we begin to understand the Nazi treatment of the Jews? There has been a burst of literature on the Holocaust in recent years. One of the most readable books is L. S. Davidowicz, *The War Against the Jews, 1933–1945* (1975). Davidowicz writes about the German "final solution"—a chilling story, but one that needs to be told to every generation. The relationship between anti-Semitism and German fascism is further examined in Y. Bauer, *A History of the Holocaust* (1982), and the motives of a concentration camp commandant are evaluated in G. Sereny, *Into That Darkness* (1974, 1982). The least-known of the Nazi atrocities is dealt with in F. Rector, *The Nazi Extermination of Homosexuals* (1981).

5. What was the impact of totalitarian society on women? Did their position in society change in any significant ways? Was life for women in totalitarian Germany much different than for women in totalitarian Russia? Begin your investigation with two essays, R. Stites, "Women in the Revolutionary Process in Russia," and C. Koonz, "The Fascist Solution to the Women Question in Italy and Germany," in R. Bridenthal, C. Koonz, and S. Stuard, *Becoming Visible: Women in European History* (1987).

6. How did the Second World War affect civilian populations? What was it like to be a child in wartime Britain? See the interesting book *Children of the Blitz—Memories of Wartime Childhood* (1987), by R. Westall.

*Available in paperback.

CHAPTER 36

Recovery and Crisis in Europe and the Americas

Chapter Questions

After reading and studying this chapter, you should be able to answer the following questions:

How did Europe recover from the Second World War? What were the causes of the cold war? How did economic nationalism transform Latin America? How and why did European empires collapse and Asian and African peoples gain political independence?

Chapter Summary

This chapter discusses the main political and economic trends in the Western world since the dark days of the Second World War. It shows how Europe, especially western Europe, recovered from the destruction of 1945, how the cold war split the Continent into communist and noncommunist blocs, how European empires came to an end as the peoples of Africa and Asia achieved national independence, and how North and South America also revived and evolved in the postwar era.

The chapter begins by examining why the Grand Alliance of Britain, the Soviet Union, and the United States failed to hold together after it succeeded in defeating Nazi Germany. Military decisions, ideological differences, and disputes over eastern Europe were key factors in the origins of the cold war. By 1950, the Iron Curtain was in place, and western and eastern Europe were going their separate ways. Battered western Europe rebuilt quickly and successfully, helped by new leaders and attitudes, American aid, and the creation of the Common Market. Developments in east European countries closely followed those in Soviet Russia. Stalin reimposed a harsh dictatorship after the war, which Khrushchev relaxed but which Brezhnev tightened once again. The so-called "Gorbachev era" changed all of this. Perestroika and glasnost brought democratization and then, in 1989, a virtual revolution in Europe as the Soviets allowed the Berlin Wall to be dismantled and Germany reunited, and then watched as the Soviet Union itself was dissolved.

European empires in Asia and Africa went out of business after the Second World War. India led the way to national independence right after the war, and other British, French, and Dutch territories followed. Most countries gained independence peacefully, but there were bitter colonial wars in Vietnam and Algeria. Western influence lives on in Asia and Africa, since most of the newly independent countries have retained Western nationalism and either communism or democracy as guiding ideas.

Study Outline

Use this outline to preview the chapter before you read a particular section in your textbook and then as a self-check to test your reading comprehension after you have read the chapter section.

I. The cold war (1942–1953)
    A. The origins of the cold war
        1. The Allied decision to postpone political questions such as the makeup of postwar Europe strengthened the Soviets.
        2. The decision of the Big Three at Teheran (1943) to launch an American-British invasion of Hitler's empire via France meant that American-British and Russian troops would meet along a north-south line in Germany, and only Soviet Russia would liberate eastern Europe.
        3. At the Yalta Conference (1945) the Allies decided to divide Germany into occupation zones.
            a. It was agreed that Germany would pay heavy reparations to Russia.
            b. Stalin agreed to declare war on Japan after Germany was defeated and to join the United Nations.
        4. The Yalta Compromise over eastern Europe broke down almost immediately.
        5. At the Potsdam Conference (1945) Truman demanded free elections throughout eastern Europe, but Stalin refused.
            a. Stalin believed that only communist states could be loyal allies.
            b. He feared that free elections would result in possibly hostile governments on his western border.
        6. Short of war, the Western Allies could not really influence developments in eastern Europe.
    B. West versus East
        1. Truman cut off aid to Russia because of Stalin's insistence on having communist governments in eastern Europe.
        2. By 1947, many Americans believed that Stalin was trying to export communist revolution throughout Europe and the world.
        3. The Marshall Plan was established to help European economic recovery; the Truman Doctrine was meant to ward off communist subversion with military aid.
        4. The Soviet blockade of Berlin led to a successful Allied airlift.

5. In 1949, the United States formed an anti-Soviet military alliance of Western governments, the North Atlantic Treaty Organization (NATO); in return, Stalin united his satellites in the Warsaw Pact.
6. In 1949, the communists won in China.
7. In 1950, when communist North Korea invaded the south, American-led UN troops intervened.
8. The Western attempt to check Stalin probably came too late and may have encouraged Russian aggression.

II. The western European renaissance
   A. The postwar challenge
      1. The war left Europe physically devastated and in a state of economic and moral crisis.
         a. Food rationing was necessary.
         b. Russia's border had been pushed west, as was Poland's; thus, many Germans were forced to resettle in a greatly reduced Germany.
         c. All the Allies treated Germany harshly.
      2. New leaders and new parties, especially the Catholic Christian Democrats, emerged in Italy, France, and Germany, and provided effective leadership and needed reforms.
      3. In many countries, such as Britain, France, and Italy, Socialists and Communists emerged from the war with considerable power and a strong desire for social reform.
      4. The Marshall Plan aided in economic recovery and led to the Organization for European Economic Cooperation (OEEC); military protection was provided through NATO.
   B. Economic "miracles"
      1. Led by West Germany, a European economic miracle was under way by 1963.
         a. American aid helped get the process off to a fast start.
         b. European nations coordinated the distribution of American aid, so barriers to European trade and cooperation were quickly dropped.
      2. A free-market economy—with a social welfare network—brought rapid growth to Germany.
      3. Flexible planning and a mixed state and private economy brought rapid growth to France.
      4. A skilled labor pool, new markets for consumer products, and the Common Market stimulated economic development in western Europe.
   C. Toward European unity
      1. Democratic republics were re-established in France, West Germany, and Italy.
      2. The Christian Democrats were committed to a unified Europe, but economic unity proved to be more realistic than political unity.
      3. The six-nation Coal and Steel Community marked the beginning of a movement toward European unity and led to further technical and economic cooperation.

4. The Treaty of Rome (1957) created the European Economic Community (EEC, or Common Market), whose immediate goal was to create a free-trade area by reducing tariffs.
5. However, regenerated hopes for political union in Europe were frustrated by a resurgence of nationalism in the 1960s.
    a. de Gaulle, a romantic nationalist, wanted France to lead the Common Market.
    b. He withdrew from NATO and vetoed British attempts to join the Common Market.

D. Decolonization of Asia and Africa
1. The causes of imperial decline
    a. Nationalism brought demands for political self-determination in colonial areas after the First World War.
    b. The Second World War reduced European power and destroyed the Western sense of moral superiority.
2. Britain under the Labour party gave up India, but France tried to re-establish colonial rule in Indochina, Vietnam, and Algeria.
3. African states gained independence, but many increased economic and cultural ties with their former European rulers.
    a. Britain's colonies entered the British Commonwealth of Nations.
    b. Most of France's colonies chose to remain tied to France.
4. As a result, a renewed economic subordination (or neocolonialism) was imposed on Africa by western Europe and the United States.

E. The changing class structure of Europe
1. Economic/technological change led to a breakdown in class distinctions.
    a. Managers and experts replaced traditional property owners as the bosses of the middle class.
    b. Big corporations replaced family businesses with a new class of managers and technocrats.
    c. The industrial working class became smaller.
2. Government reduced class tensions.
    a. Britain's Labour government established a National Health Service; others followed.
    b. Most governments provided new social services.
3. A rising standard of living occurred.

F. Political upheaval in the late 1960s
1. Student unrest in Europe signaled the end of the era of postwar recovery.
    a. Many students rejected materialism.
    b. They saw the Vietnam War as immoral.
    c. They criticized their university curriculum.
    d. Student revolt in France in 1968 led to a general strike and a challenge to de Gaulle.
2. Economic problems of the 1970s did not cause Europe to return to economic nationalism; instead, more nations joined the Common Market and the movement toward European unity.

3. Democracy was strengthened as Spain, Portugal, and Greece turned toward democratic rule, and as the Italian and French Communist parties participated in democratic governments.

G. The troubled economy in recent times
1. Economic crisis in the 1970s grew out of an unstable American gold supply and an energy crisis.
   a. American abandonment of gold sales led to a decline in the dollar and abandonment of fixed rates of exchange.
   b. OPEC increased oil prices—a shock to the oil companies and the West.
   c. This led to a great recession and a second oil shock in 1979 due to the Iranian revolution.
   d. By 1985, unemployment in Europe was at its highest level since the Great Depression.
2. The postwar welfare state contributed to political and social stability.
   a. State social services continued.
   b. The European Common Market expanded as Denmark, Iceland, and Britain joined, followed by Portugal, Spain, and Greece.
   c. The Common Market set 1992 as the year for total European economic and social integration.

III. Soviet eastern Europe
A. Stalin's last years
1. The national unity of the war period ended in rigid dictatorship again.
2. Stalin began a new series of purges and enforced cultural conformity.
   a. Soviet citizens living outside Russia were forced to return, and nearly a million of them, plus other Russians, died in labor camps.
   b. Culture, art, and the Jewish religion were attacked.
3. Five-year plans were reintroduced; heavy and military industry were given top priority, while consumer goods, housing, and agriculture were neglected.
4. Stalin's system was exported to eastern Europe.
   a. Only Tito in Yugoslavia was able to build an east European communist state free from Stalinist control.
   b. Tito's success led Stalin to purge the Communist parties of eastern Europe in an attempt to increase their obedience to him.
B. Reform and de-Stalinization
1. Khrushchev and fellow reformers won the leadership of Russia over the conservatives, who wanted to make as few changes as possible in the Stalinist system.
2. Khrushchev denounced Stalin at the Twentieth Party Congress in 1956 and began a policy of liberalization.
   a. The Soviet standard of living was improved, and greater intellectual freedom was allowed.
   b. Nevertheless, Pasternak was not allowed to accept the Nobel Prize in 1958 for *Doctor Zhivago*.
   c. Solzhenitsyn's book on life in a Stalinist camp, *One Day in the Life of Ivan Denisovich*, caused an uproar when it was published in Russia in 1962.

   d. Khrushchev pushed for "peaceful coexistence" with the West and a relaxation of cold war tensions.

  3. De-Stalinization caused revolution in eastern Europe in 1956.

   a. Poland under Gomulka won greater autonomy.

   b. Hungary expelled Soviet troops in 1956 and declared its neutrality but was invaded by Russia and defeated.

C. Brezhnev and stagnation

  1. Re-Stalinization began with Khrushchev's fall (1964).

   a. Khrushchev's policy of de-Stalinization was opposed by conservatives, who saw it as a threat to the whole communist system.

   b. Khrushchev's erratic foreign policy was also an issue—he was successful in building the Berlin Wall but was forced to back down on the installation of missiles in Cuba.

   c. Brezhnev stressed Stalin's good points and launched a massive arms buildup.

  2. Under Dubček, the Czech communist party instituted reforms that stressed socialism with freedom and democracy.

   a. The reforms were popular but frightened entrenched powers.

   b. The Soviet and other East bloc leaders feared Czech nationalism or even pro-Western policy.

   c. The Soviets responded in August 1968 with brutal repression.

   d. The Czech leaders backed down; reforms were canceled.

   e. Later, the Brezhnev Doctrine was announced, declaring that the Soviet Union had the right to intervene in any socialist country.

   f. Western Europe stood by without responding because it believed in the sphere-of-influence principle.

  3. In the Soviet Union the Czech crisis caused a step backward toward Stalinization.

   a. However, the standard of living continued to improve.

   b. Russian national pride contributed to stability.

   c. The Great Russians feared demands for autonomy from east European and non-Russian nationalists.

   d. Art and culture were re-Stalinized.

   e. But urban growth, a rise in managerial and science jobs, and growth in educational and job freedom led to a silent political revolution that set the stage for the Gorbachev era.

D. Gorbachev era

  1. A new era of fundamental change began under Gorbachev in 1985.

   a. By 1982, economic decline was worsened by mass apathy and lack of personal initiative.

   b. Andropov tried to reinvigorate the system after Brezhnev's death, with little success.

   c. Gorbachev set forth a series of reforms to restructure the economy (perestroika) largely centering on a freer market economy, but the economy stalled midway between central planning and free-market mechanisms.

        d. He instituted glasnost, or openness in society and politics, leading to much more freedom of speech.

        e. Democratization of the Soviet state was begun; free elections were held in 1989 for the first time since 1917.

    2. Democratization encouraged demands for autonomy by non-Russian minorities.

    3. Gorbachev withdrew troops from Afghanistan and encouraged reform in eastern Europe, repudiating the Brezhnev Doctrine.

  E. The revolutions of 1989

    1. In Poland, Solidarity was again legalized and won overwhelmingly in free elections.

    2. Popular resistance and Communist liberalization in Hungary led to the end of one-party rule and free elections in 1990.

        a. A multiparty democracy was established.

        b. Borders between Hungary and East Germany were opened.

    3. Growing economic dislocation brought revolution in East Berlin.

        a. The Berlin Wall was opened.

        b. Communist leaders were swept out of power.

        c. East and West Germany moved rapidly toward unification.

    4. The people of Czechoslovakia ousted the Communist bosses.

    5. Only in Romania was the revolution violent and bloody.

        a. Ceauşescu was executed.

        b. Romania's political prospects remained uncertain.

IV. The Western Hemisphere

  A. Postwar prosperity in the United States

    1. Conversion to a peacetime economy went smoothly, and the well-being of Americans increased dramatically.

    2. Until the 1960s, domestic politics consisted largely of consolidating the New Deal and maintaining the status quo.

        a. True innovations were rejected in the 1950s.

        b. In 1960, Kennedy was elected amid hopes he would revitalize the country.

  B. The civil rights revolution

    1. School segregation was declared unconstitutional by the Supreme Court in 1954.

    2. Blacks used militant nonviolence and growing political power to gain reforms in the 1960s.

        a. The Civil Rights Act of 1964 prohibited discrimination in public services and on the job.

        b. The Voting Rights Act of 1965 guaranteed all blacks the right to vote.

    3. The United States became more of a welfare state in the 1960s, as a surge of liberal social legislation was passed.

  C. The Vietnam trauma and beyond

    1. U.S. involvement in Vietnam grew out of its fear of communism.

        a. The United States refused to allow free elections in Vietnam, and it deposed uncooperative leaders.

      b. President Johnson vowed not to "lose" Vietnam and carried out a massive military buildup and bombing, but without achieving victory.
2. Public criticism of the war brought about Johnson's withdrawal from the presidential race and the election of Nixon in 1968.
      a. Nixon cut war costs and brought many troops home, but the war continued for another four years.
      b. Nixon's illegal activities led to the Watergate crisis and his resignation.
3. Vietnam became unified, and the United States was left divided and uncertain about its world policy.
4. The policy of détente resulted in an East-West agreement at Helsinki guaranteeing frontiers and human rights.
      a. But Soviet involvement in Afghanistan and elsewhere convinced some Americans that the Soviets were violating the spirit of détente.
      b. President Reagan undertook a U.S. arms buildup and sought to overthrow pro-Marxist governments.

D. Economic nationalism in Latin America
1. Beginning with the Great Depression, more popularly based governments encouraged the development of national industry to reduce their dependence on raw-materials production and foreign markets.
2. In Mexico the revolution of 1910 opened a new era of economic nationalism, social reform, and industrialization.
      a. President Cárdenas nationalized the petroleum industry in 1938.
      b. The Mexican state successfully promoted industrialization from the early 1940s to the late 1960s.
3. Under the strongman Vargas, Brazil also embraced economic nationalism and moderate social reform.

E. The Cuban Revolution
1. Cuba was relatively rich but suffered from dictatorship, corruption, and a tradition of American intervention.
2. The magnetic Fidel Castro led a successful revolution in 1958, which had major consequences.
      a. Castro repelled an American-supported invasion by Cuban exiles (the Bay of Pigs invasion), thereby winning great prestige.
      b. He established a typical communist dictatorship.
      c. The Cuban Revolution brought the cold war to Latin America.
      d. In 1961, the United States helped create the Alliance for Progress to promote long-term economic development and social reform.

F. Authoritarianism and democracy in Latin America
1. Democratic government has been in retreat in Latin America since the Cuban Revolution, and the gap between rich and poor has widened.
2. In Brazil and Argentina the military has generally ruled since 1964, with the support of conservatives and most of the middle class.
3. In Chile the army overturned a leftist government and imposed a harsh dictatorship.
4. The new authoritarians oppose communism, but they are also determined modernizers, committed to national independence and industrialization.

5. In the 1980s, Peru, Bolivia, and Ecuador re-established elected governments, and in Argentina military defeat led to democratic and antimilitary action.
6. Brazil's government was turned over to civilian rule.
7. In Nicaragua in 1979 the Sandinista reform government overthrew the U.S.-supported Somoza dictatorship—to the dismay of the Reagan government in the United States.
    a. The Nicaraguan economy collapsed.
    b. Free elections led to the replacement of the Sandinistas by Chamorro's government.

Review Questions

Check your understanding of this chapter by answering the following questions.

1. Describe the dispute between the United States and Russia at the end of the Second World War. How and why did it escalate into a cold war?

2. Why were the Teheran and Yalta conferences important in shaping the map of postwar Europe?

3. What were the sources of the Soviet Union's paranoia about Germany and vice versa?

4. How did Europe accomplish economic recovery after the war? What factors contributed to its growth?

5. Which approach toward European unity was most successful, the political or the economic? Why?

6. Describe the steps taken toward European economic unity. What impact does this unity have on the European and world economy?

7. Was nationalism completely dead in postwar Europe? Who was Charles de Gaulle and what was his ambition?

8. What impact did the Second World War have on peoples' opinions about imperialism and European empires?

9. Evaluate Stalin's postwar policy and actions. Why were many Russian nationalists disappointed in them? How would you judge Stalin's place in Soviet history?

10. Describe the circumstances surrounding Khrushchev's famous Twentieth Party Congress speech in 1956. What were the results of his policy?

11. What were the reasons for Khrushchev's fall from power and the beginning of the re-Stalinization of Russia in 1964?

12. Describe life in the Soviet Union after 1964. What were the positive and negative features of the Soviet state in the Brezhnev era?

13. "Postwar domestic politics in the United States consisted largely of making modest adjustments to the status quo." Why was this so?

14. What were the milestones in the civil rights revolution?

15. What are some of the key components of economic nationalism? How and why did it arise in Latin America?

16. How did Mexico and Brazil fare in the postwar period?

17. What were the causes and the consequences of the Cuban Revolution?

18. What are Gorbachev's motives and methods? What impact has he had on Soviet society? On eastern Europe?

Study-Review Exercises

Define the following key concepts and terms.

European Steel and Coal Community

cold war

de-Stalinization

decolonization

economic nationalism

Identify and explain the significance of the following people and terms.

NATO

British Labour party

Alliance for Progress

Marshall Plan

Warsaw Pact

Organization of European Economic Cooperation

Common Market (EEC)

Taft-Hartley Act

Franklin D. Roosevelt

Josip Tito

Nikita Khrushchev

Lázaro Cárdenas

Clement Atlee

Charles de Gaulle

Fidel Castro

Winston Churchill

Leonid Brezhnev

Getulio Vargas

Yevgeny Yevtushenko

Explain what happened at the following wartime conferences of the Big Three and what impact each one had on the postwar world.

Casablanca (January 1943)

Teheran (November 1943)

Yalta (February 1945)

Potsdam (July 1945)

Explain what the following events were, who participated in them, and why they were important.

Berlin Airlift of 1948

Schuman Plan (1950)

Twentieth Party Congress of the Soviets (1956)

Bay of Pigs invasion (1961)

Nicaragua Revolution (1979)

Multiple-Choice Questions

1. French economic recovery following the Second World War centered on
   a. free-market capitalism alone.
   b. socialism.
   c. a mixed state and private economy.
   d. trade unionism.

2. Stalin's successor, Khrushchev
   a. denounced Stalinist policies and Stalin himself.
   b. carried on the Stalinist traditions.
   c. opposed reconciliation with the West.
   d. placed restrictions on cultural freedom.

3. The Soviet writer and poet who was forced by Khrushchev to refuse the Nobel Prize in 1958 was
   a. Pasternak.
   b. Solzhenitsyn.
   c. Gomulka.
   d. Beria.

4. The only eastern European communist leader to build an independent communist state free from Stalinist control was
   a. Nagy.
   b. Tito.
   c. Dubček.
   d. Schuman.

5. In Italy, the leading political party in the immediate postwar elections was the
   a. Communists.
   b. Catholic Center.
   c. Socialists.
   d. Christian Democrats.

6. American-Soviet conflict in the post–Second World War era first centered on the problem of the future of
   a. France.
   b. East Germany.
   c. Yugoslavia.
   d. Poland.

7. In recent times, Latin American countries have demonstrated an increase in
   a. foreign control of industry.
   b. capital investment by foreign nations.
   c. economic nationalism.
   d. dependence on foreign markets and products.

8. Which of the following statements describes a policy of Stalin after the Second World War?
   a. He allowed Soviets abroad to remain in political asylum.
   b. He insisted on political conformity but allowed cultural freedom.
   c. He relaxed Soviet control of east European states.
   d. He revived forced-labor camps.

9. In Mexico, the Cárdenas presidency resulted in
   a. a counterrevolution that returned power to the landed elite.
   b. a return to the cultural connections between Mexico and Europe.
   c. the de-nationalization of the petroleum industry.
   d. the division of large estates among small farmers.

10. During and after the Second World War, American leaders were most concerned that the east European countries would
    a. become American allies.
    b. be friendly toward Russia.
    c. have freely elected governments.
    d. reject German fascism.

11. The Frenchman who came to symbolize the resurgence of European nationalism was
    a. Jean Monnet.
    b. Charles de Gaulle.
    c. Robert Schuman.
    d. André Malraux.

12. Since the Second World War, communist participation in west European governments has
    a. decreased.
    b. disappeared entirely.
    c. been outlawed in most countries.
    d. increased.

13. The only east European communist country able to remain free of Stalin's control was
    a. Poland.
    b. Yugoslavia.
    c. East Germany.
    d. the Ukraine.

14. The country that blocked British entry into the Common Market and withdrew its forces from NATO was
    a. Belgium.
    b. West Germany.
    c. Italy.
    d. France.

15. Under Stalin, top priority in production in the Soviet Union was given to
    a. consumer goods.
    b. military goods.
    c. aid for rebuilding East Germany.
    d. building new housing.

16. After the Second World War, Stalin's chief policy goal was
    a. an extension of civil liberties.
    b. Russian domination of eastern Europe.
    c. the elimination of anti-Semitism in Russia.
    d. relaxing prohibitions against capitalism.

17. The Allied nations of the Second World War included all of the following *except*
    a. the Soviet Union.
    b. the United States.
    c. Austria.
    d. Britain.

18. Khruschev's de-Stalinization led to revolts in
    a. Italy and Turkey.
    b. Poland and Hungary.
    c. Volgograd and Leningrad.
    d. Yugoslavia.

19. All the following phrases characterize the views of the French government under Charles de Gaulle *except*
    a. "anti-British."
    b. "anti-American."
    c. "willing to compromise French goals for European security."
    d. "anti-NATO and a reluctant participant in the Common Market."

20. Economic nationalism came to Brazil in 1930 with
    a. the establishment of a broad-based democracy.
    b. the Vargas dictatorship.
    c. the growth of regional centers of power.
    d. Kubitschek's "Fifty Years' Progress in Five" program.

21. The 1954 Supreme Court decision on segregation was based on the principle that
    a. separate but equal facilities are constitutional.
    b. separate educational facilities are unequal, hence unconstitutional.
    c. sit-ins and demonstrations are unconstitutional.
    d. the southern school system should remain unchanged.

22. The new leader of Poland in 1956 was
    a. Wladyslaw Gomulka.
    b. Nikita Khrushchev.
    c. Josip Tito.
    d. Boris Pasternak.

23. The six original members of the new coal and steel community, which eventually became the Common Market, were
    a. Britain, France, West Germany, Italy, Belgium, the Netherlands.
    b. Britain, France, West Germany, Italy, the Netherlands, Sweden.
    c. France, West Germany, Italy, Belgium, the Netherlands, Luxembourg.
    d. France, West Germany, Italy, Belgium, Luxembourg, Sweden.

24. *Détente* means
    a. European cooperation.
    b. relaxation of cold war tensions.
    c. a "blocked society."
    d. "decolonization."

Major Political Ideas

1. Define the concept of European unity and trace its origins. Who belonged to this movement, what forms did it take, and why were people so willing to replace nationalism with a common Europe?

2. Define economic nationalism. Why did it emerge, and what form did it take?

3. Glasnost and democratization have both had a profound effect on Soviet and east European society. Define each and provide examples of how it has been implemented.

Issues for Essays and Discussion

1. What were the most important developments in Europe in the decades following 1945? Make particular reference to western and eastern Europe, the cold war, the process of decolonization, and changes in class structure and the economy.

2. With the defeat of Germany in 1945 there arose a new war, a cold war between the United States and the Soviet Union. What were the causes of this war? Could the United States have blocked the Soviet takeover of eastern Europe? Was the conflict a result more of Soviet strength or of American weakness?

Interpretation of Visual Sources

Study the reproduction of the painting by Diego Rivera on page 1204 of your textbook. What events in Mexican history can you identify in this mural? What beliefs about Mexico's past does this artist set forth in this work? Would you regard this painting as support for revolutionary ideas?

Geography

On Outline Map 36.2 provided, and using Maps 36.1 and 36.2 in your textbook as references, mark the following:

1. The location of the Iron Curtain that divided Europe after the Second World War, the territory lost by Germany after the Second World War (should East Germany be considered "lost" territory?), the territory gained by the Soviet Union after the Second World War (did Poland gain anything in return for its losses to the Soviet Union?), the original members of the Common Market, the countries that joined in later years, Berlin, Brussels, Paris, London, Warsaw, Rome, Belgrade, Moscow, Bonn, Prague.

2. Identify the various republics that made up the Soviet Union. Which of these make up the areas of the so-called Great Russians? What impact has democratization and glasnost had on the political cohesion of the Soviet Union?

Remember that duplicate maps for class use appear at the back of this book.

Outline Map 36.2

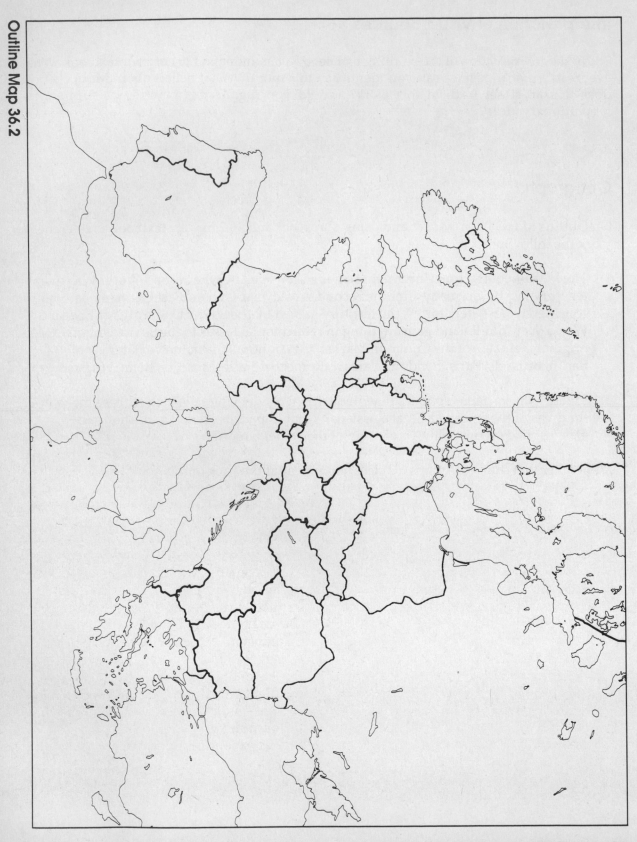

Understanding History Through the Arts

1. What literature did the cold war era produce? Alexander Solzhenitsyn's *One Day in the Life of Ivan Denisovich** (1963) is a powerful and moving story of one human being in a postwar prison camp in Stalinist Russia.

2. What do the songs of Edith Piaf tell us? The release from Nazi occupation gave an enormous boost to popular song throughout Europe. Nowhere were songwriters and young artists as inspired as in France, and no one was as loved by the French people as Edith Piaf. Piaf was a nightclub singer who sang *chansons réalistes*—songs about the joys, frustrations, and sorrows of the people of the streets. She made her first recording in 1936. Her first recording after the war, *Les Trois Cloches*, was described as "the folklore of the future." She died in 1963 after a full and sometimes tragic life. Many recordings of her performances are available.

3. How did the experiences of the Latin American nations mix with European influences to form a powerful and indigenous art? This is the subject of D. Ades, ed., *Art in Latin America* (1989). The politically committed mural art of Diego Rivera and others is discussed in *Art in Latin America* (1989).

Problems for Further Investigation

1. Who shaped the great postwar alliance among Europe, the United States, and Japan? What were the key events and ideas behind this alliance? Based on interviews, memoirs, and documents, the key figures of the postwar era—Eisenhower, De Gaulle, Kennedy, Schmidt, MacArthur, and others—come alive in R. Barnet, *The Alliance* (1983).

2. How did the cold war begin? Those interested in the military history of the Second World War and the postwar era will want to begin with P. Paret, *Makers of Modern Strategy, from Machiavelli to the Nuclear Age** (1986). The origins of the cold war, according to its earliest interpreters, were rooted in the conflict between communist aggression and American benevolence. Preoccupied with the task of defeating the Axis powers, the United States misjudged the intentions of the Soviet Union and, unknowingly, opened the door to communist expansion. American policymakers then adopted policies designed to "contain" Russian aggression. For example, see G. F. Kennan, *American Diplomacy, 1900–1950* (1951). One of the best books on the cold war is L. Halle, *The Cold War as History* (1967). The turbulent sixties, which were characterized by a reappraisal of American truths, led some historians to re-examine the origins of the cold war. One such revisionist, W. Lafeber, *America, Russia and the Cold War, 1945–1975** (1976), emphasized American economic expansion as a major reason for the

*Available in paperback.

confrontation between East and West. For a good brief survey of cold war literature, see the pamphlet by B. Tierney, et al., *The Cold War—Who Is to Blame?** (1967).

3. Why did the Berlin Wall fall? Two scholars have written accounts of Germany's bloodless revolution of 1989–90. These are R. Darnton, *Berlin Journal, 1989–90* (1991), and J. Borneman, *After the Wall, East Meets West in the New Berlin* (1991).

*Available in paperback.

PRIMARY SOURCES
The Vietnam War

The Vietnam War was extremely complex and evolved over a long period of time. The historian thus faces the task of uncovering the motives of all sides involved, including the French, who dominated Vietnam from the late nineteenth century until their expulsion in 1954, the Vietnamese people and their leaders, and the American government. The following two documents represent conflicting views: that of Ho Chi Minh, the nationalist leader of Vietnam (who was a communist), and Dwight Eisenhower, the president of the United States, who sets forth here what was to become a very popular American view of the world and justification for American engagement in Vietnam.

How did each use the past to analyze the present and to shape his view of the future? How did each see the role of Vietnam in world events? What appears to be the motives of each? Keep in mind that between 1945, when Ho's *Declaration* was made, and 1954, when Eisenhower made his statement, China became a communist state (1949) and imperialist France was on the verge of losing its hold on Vietnam.

The Declaration of Independence of Vietnam, September 2, 1945*

"All men are created equal. They are endowed by their Creator with certain inalienable rights; among these are Life, Liberty, and the pursuit of Happiness."

This immortal statement was made in the Declaration of Independence of the United States of America in 1776. In a broader sense, this means: All the peoples on the earth are equal from birth, all the peoples have a right to live, to be happy and free.

The Declaration of the French Revolution made in 1791 on the Rights of Man and the Citizen also states: "All men are born free and with equal rights, and must always remain free and have equal rights."

Those are undeniable truths.

Source: Ho Chi Minh, *Selected Works,* 4 vols. (Hanoi: Foreign Languages Publishing House, 1960–1962), 17–21.

Nevertheless, for more than eighty years, the French imperialists, abusing the standard of Liberty, Equality, and Fraternity, have violated our Fatherland and oppressed our fellow-citizens. They have acted contrary to the ideals of humanity and justice.

In the field of politics, they have deprived our people of every democratic liberty.

They have enforced inhuman laws; they have set up three distinct political regimes in the North, the Center and the South Vietnam in order to wreck our national unity and prevent our people from being united.

They have built more prisons than schools. They have mercilessly slain our patriots; they have drowned our uprising in rivers of blood.

They have fettered public opinion; they have practised obscurantism against our people.

To weaken our race they have forced us to use opium and alcohol.

In the field of economics, they have fleeced us to the backbone, impoverished our people, and devastated our land.

They have robbed us of our rice fields, our mines, our forests, and our raw materials. They have monopolized the issuing of bank-notes and the export trade.

They have invented numerous unjustifiable taxes and reduced our people, especially our peasantry, to a state of extreme poverty.

They have hampered the prospering of our national bourgeoisie; they have mercilessly exploited our workers.

In the autumn of 1940, when the Japanese Fascists violated Indochina's territory to establish new bases in their fight against the Allies, the French imperialists went down on their bended knees and handed over our country to them.

Thus, from that date, our people were subjected to the double yoke of the French and Japanese. Their sufferings and miseries increased. The result was that from the end of last year to the beginning of this year, from Quang Tri province to the North of Vietnam, more than two million of our fellow-citizens died from starvation. On March 9, the French troops were disarmed by the Japanese. The French colonialists either fled or surrendered showing that not only were they incapable of "protecting" us, but that, in the span of five years, they had twice sold our country to the Japanese.

On several occasions before March 9, the Vietminh League urged the French to ally themselves with it against the Japanese. Instead of agreeing to this proposal, the French colonialists so intensified their terrorist activities against the Vietminh members that before fleeing they massacred a great number of our political prisoners detained at Yen Bay and Caobang.

Notwithstanding all this, our fellow-citizens have always manifested toward the French a tolerant and humane attitude. Even after the Japanese putsch of March 1945, the Vietminh League helped many Frenchmen to cross the frontier, rescued some of them from Japanese jails, and protected French lives and property.

From the autumn of 1940, our country had in fact ceased to be a French colony and had become a Japanese possession.

After the Japanese had surrendered to the Allies, our whole people rose to regain our national sovereignty and to found the Democratic Republic of Vietnam.

The truth is that we have wrested our independence from the Japanese and not from the French.

The French have fled, the Japanese have capitulated, Emperor Bao Dai has abdicated. Our people have broken the chains which for nearly a century have fettered them and have won independence for the Fatherland. Our people at the same time have overthrown the monarchic regime that has reigned supreme for dozens of centuries. In its place has been established the present Democratic Republic.

For these reasons, we, members of the Democratic Provisional Government, representing the whole Vietnamese people, declare that from now on we break off all relations of a colonial character with France; we repeal all the international obligation that France has so far subscribed to on behalf of Vietnam and we abolish all the special rights the French have unlawfully acquired in our Fatherland.

The whole Vietnamese people, animated by a common purpose, are determined to fight to the bitter end against any attempt by the French colonialists to reconquer their country.

We are convinced that the Allied nations which at Tehran and San Francisco have acknowledged the principles of self-determination and equality of nations, will not refuse to acknowledge the independence of Vietnam.

A people who have courageously opposed French domination for more than eighty years, a people who have fought side by side with the Allies against the Fascists during these last years, such a people must be free and independent.

For these reasons, we, members of the Provisional Government of the Republic of Vietnam, solemnly declare to the world that Vietnam has the right to be a free and independent country—and in fact is so already. The entire Vietnamese people are determined to mobilize all their physical and mental strengths, to sacrifice their lives and property in order to safeguard their independence and liberty.

The American Domino Theory: President Eisenhower's Press Conference of April 7, 1954*

Q: Robert Richards, Copley Press: Mr. President, would you mind commenting on the strategic importance of Indochina to[1] to the free world? I think there has been, across the country, some lack of understanding of just what it means to us.

THE PRESIDENT: You have, of course, both the specific and the general when you talk about such things.

First of all, you have the specific value of a locality in its production of materials that the world needs.

Then you have the possibility that many human beings pass under a dictatorship that is inimical to the free world.

Finally, you have broader considerations that might follow what you would call the "falling domino" principle. You have a row of dominoes set up, you knock over the first one, and what will happen to the last one is the certainty that it will go over very quickly. So you could have a beginning of a disintegration that would have the most profound influences.

---

*Source: Dwight D. Eisenhower, "The President's News Conference of April 7, 1954," No. 73, *Public Papers of Presidents of the United States: Dwight D. Eisenhower, 1954* (Washington, D.C., GPO, 1960), 83.
[1]Vietnam was part of the old French colony of Indochina.

Now, with respect to the first one, two of the items from this particular area that the world uses are tin and tungsten. They are very important. There are others, of course, the rubber plantations and so on.

Then with respect to more people passing under this domination, Asia, after all, has already lost some 450 million of its peoples to the Communist dictatorship, and we simply can't afford greater losses.

But when we come to the possible sequence of events, the loss of Indochina, of Burma, of Thailand, of the Peninsula, and Indonesia following, now you begin to talk about areas that not only multiply the disadvantages that you would suffer through loss of materials, sources of materials, but now you are talking really about millions and millions and millions of people.

Finally, the geographical position achieved thereby does many things. It turns the so-called island defensive chain of Japan, Formosa, of the Philippines and to the southward; it moves in to threaten Australia and New Zealand.

It takes away, in its economic aspects, that region that Japan must have as a trading area or Japan, in turn, will have only one place in the world to go—that is, toward the Communist areas in order to live.

So, the possible consequences of the loss are just incalculable to the free world. . . .

CHAPTER 37

Asia and Africa in the Contemporary World

Chapter Questions

After reading and studying this chapter, you should be able to answer the following questions:

How did Asian and African countries reassert or establish their political independence in the postwar era? How in the postindependence world did leading states face up to the enormous challenges of nation building, challenges that were all the more difficult after the 1960s?

Chapter Summary

A turning point in modern world history has been the resurgence and political self-assertion of Asian and African peoples since 1945. Under Mao Tse-tung, China transformed itself from a weak nation to a major world power. The Communist victory of 1949 was due to the Communists' strong guerrilla army, their program of land redistribution, and the failure of the Nationalists to gain peasant support. At first Mao followed the Soviet model and stressed the development of heavy industry and totalitarian social controls. Then, with the Great Leap Forward, China turned its back on Russia by placing emphasis on peasant communal agriculture. This was followed by a cultural revolution, reconciliation with the United States, and, more recently, a "second revolution" that has resulted in a return to peasant family agriculture, as opposed to communal agriculture.

While China looked to communism, Japan turned to a mix of traditionalism, capitalism, and democratic liberalism to induce national recovery. Here a sweeping American revolution brought demilitarization and a liberal constitution, but it was largely the characteristic Japanese stress on social cooperation that brought about the economic miracle. In India independence was accompanied by a hate-filled and bloody struggle between Hindu and Muslim, and then a population explosion that threatened economic development and parliamentary democracy. The old British India was divided (in 1947) into two (and then three) different states. More recently, another religious-cultural group, the Sikhs, has fought for an independent state. One outcome of this was a bloody struggle in which Indira Gandhi, the prime minister, was killed. Ethnic conflict followed independence in Malaya as well, while in the Philippines the democratic system of twenty years fell to a dictatorship, as did the experiment in democracy in Indonesia, but with more brutal consequences. One of the most violent struggles for independence was in Vietnam, where the French refusal to grant independence led to a bitter war in which the Communists emerged as the champions of the nationalistic cause.

In the Muslim world, anti-Western nationalism has been the dominant political force. Here change and bewildering conflict have prevailed, including war over Palestine, revolution in Egypt and Iran, and war in Algeria. Arab opposition to Israel has been the most important factor in unifying the Arab states. Most recently, an Arab-Persian conflict (which is a Shi'ite-Sunni conflict as well) has taken place in the form of the bloody Iran-Iraq war.

By 1900, black Africa was bound to a somewhat uniform imperialist system of bureaucratic rule, a world economy, and few social services. But within this pattern there were numerous variations. In British Ghana and French Senegal, for example, a black elite benefited from imperialist rule, whereas in Kenya, South Africa, and the Congo, a system of indirect slave labor and rigorous segregation prevailed. When the Europeans carved out their African states, they did so without regard to ethnic and tribal boundaries—a fact that has both fostered and hindered African unity and national development.

African nationalism was encouraged by the idea of African unity and wartime promises of self-determination. The Great Depression and the Second World War, however, encouraged black nationalism the most. Following the example of radical mass politics in Ghana, most of Africa was free of foreign control by the mid-1960s, although Algeria (like the Belgian Congo) won its independence only after a bitter struggle. Unfortunately, by the late 1960s, the tendency toward democratic government slipped into reverse gear, and a trend toward one-party or military government emerged. Nigeria illustrates a number of these patterns of nationalist development: a lack of ethnic/tribal homogeneity, civil war, and military rule. South Africa remains the exception to African nationalism, because its white minority succeeded in implementing a sophisticated and harsh system of apartheid. In South Africa, where the white minority system reserves the best jobs and housing and most political power for itself, black opposition centers in the African National Congress. Over the years Afrikaner constitutional reform has given some power to nonwhites, but none to the black majority. The Afrikaners, in 1985 and 1986, increasingly turned to ruling through hard-line military power and press censorship.

Study Outline

Use this outline to preview the chapter before you read a particular section of your textbook and then as a self-check of your reading comprehension after you have read the chapter section.

I. The resurgence of East Asia
    A. The Communist victory in China
        1. The triumph of communism was the result of two forces.
            a. First was Mao's strong communist guerrilla movement, based on peasant interests.
            b. Second was war with Japan, which weakened the Nationalists and resulted in 3 million dead or wounded.
        2. After Japan surrendered, civil war between the Nationalists and the Communists resumed.
            a. The Communists were a smaller force but were better led.
            b. Chiang Kai-shek and 1 million Chinese fled to the island of Taiwan in 1949.
        3. The Communists transformed China.
            a. Land was redistributed to the poor peasants as collective farms.
            b. They liquidated many "class enemies."
            c. They used re-education, self-criticism sessions, and other means to eliminate their opposition.
            d. They created a strong, unified, and centralized state.
        4. The American threat to China during the Korean War caused the people of China to rally to the Communist government.
    B. Mao's China
        1. At first, China followed the Soviet model and allied itself with Stalin's Soviet Union.
            a. Soviet aid and Soviet-type five-year plans brought about industrialization and attention to the sciences.
            b. Soviet totalitarian techniques were used to control culture and thought.
            c. Prostitution and drug abuse were eliminated, and women were given equality and new opportunities.
        2. In 1958, Mao led China in an independent Great Leap Forward.
            a. Economic growth via small-scale peasant economy was planned.
            b. A new socialist personality was to be sought by all.
            c. The Great Leap ended in economic disaster and hostility between Russia and China.
        3. To save his position and his revolution, Mao launched the Great Proletarian Cultural Revolution.
            a. His goal was to eliminate the bureaucrats and recapture the fervor of the revolution.
            b. He also sought to eliminate revisionism and Russian influence.
        4. The Cultural Revolution was an important youth movement carried out by the Red Guards.
            a. They were encouraged to practice rebellion.
            b. They intended to purge China of feudal and bourgeois culture and thought.
            c. The Cultural Revolution mobilized the masses, shook up the party, and created greater social equality, but it also caused chaos and resentment among officials and others.

C. Limits of reform
   1. After Mao's death in 1976 and the defeat of the Gang of Four, a moderate counterattack, led by Deng Xiaoping, took place.
   2. Called the "second revolution," this counterattack opened the door to reconciliation between China and the United States (1971).
      a. Major reforms were initiated (the "four modernizations")—the most important being a switch from communal to a free-market peasant family agriculture.
      b. Communist party control over politics and family size led to university student protest demonstrations in 1986.
      c. New demonstrations in 1989 led to the massacre of students in Tiananmen Square—and thus a victory for authoritarian rule.
D. Japan's American revolution
   1. After the war, power in Japan resided in the hands of the American occupiers.
      a. General Douglas MacArthur and his advisers exercised almost absolute authority.
      b. The Americans carried out a plan of demilitarization and radical reform.
      c. MacArthur wisely allowed the emperor to remain as figurehead.
      d. A new constitution created a popular government with a bill of rights and also abolished the armed forces.
   2. A powerful Japanese bureaucracy pushed reforms through the Diet.
      a. A labor movement was promoted.
      b. American-style antitrust laws broke the old zaibatsu firms.
      c. Women were liberated, and education was reformed and democratized.
      d. Land reform made the peasants supporters of democracy.
   3. The cold war and American fears of communism influenced the United States to push Japan in a more conservative direction.
      a. Left-wingers were purged.
      b. Labor and antitrust reforms were dropped.
   4. Occupation ended in 1952; Japan became independent but remained a military protectorate of the United States.
E. "Japan, Inc."—the rebuilding of the country
   1. Slow economic recovery turned into a great economic burst between 1950 and 1970, so that by 1986 per capita income exceeded that in the United States.
   2. Japan's success brought both foreign imitation and foreign criticism.
   3. Japan's economic success is related to its history and national character.
      a. Its geography contributed to political unity and cultural homogeneity.
      b. Traditionally, Japanese society puts the needs of the group before those of the individual.
   4. Government and big business shared leading roles in bringing about economic growth.
      a. As during the Meiji era, government supported and encouraged big business.
      b. In return for lifetime job guarantees, workers and unions are loyal to their companies.
      c. Distance between workers and managers is less than in the West.

      d. Workers are quickly retrained, and efficiency, quality, and quantity are stressed.

   5. Japan's emphasis on cooperation and compromise led to a decrease in crime and solutions to pollution and energy resources problems.

II. New nations in South Asia and the Muslim world
  A. The Indian subcontinent
    1. The Second World War accelerated India's desire for independence and worsened Indian-British relations.
    2. The Muslim League demanded the division of India to allow for a Muslim state.
      a. The Muslim leader Jinnah feared Hindu political and cultural domination.
      b. Gandhi opposed the division of India.
    3. The British promise of independence led to clashes between Hindu and Muslim.
      a. Jinnah and the Muslim League would not accept a proposed federal constitution.
      b. The partition of 1947 led to massacres, and Gandhi was assassinated.
      c. War between India and Pakistan took place in 1948–49, 1965–66, and 1971.
  B. Pakistan
    1. Although an authoritarian state, Pakistan did not remain unified.
    2. East Pakistan's Bengalis constituted the majority but were neglected by the ruling elite in West Pakistan.
    3. In 1971 a Bengali revolt led to an independent Bangladesh.
  C. India
    1. After 1947 India was ruled by Jawaharlal Nehru.
      a. Nehru and the Congress party initiated major social reforms.
      b. Women were granted new rights.
      c. The untouchable caste classification was abolished.
    2. India's population growth canceled out much of its economic growth, and poverty increased.
    3. Indira Gandhi took on the task of population control.
      a. She subverted parliamentary democracy and carried out a campaign of mass sterilization.
      b. She won a great election victory, but conflict between Punjab Sikhs and the government led to her assassination in 1984.
      c. Her son, Rajiv Gandhi, was elected prime minister but was voted out of office in 1989—illustrating that free elections still play a role in Indian life.
  D. Southeast Asia
    1. Sri Lanka (Ceylon) gained independence quickly and smoothly.
    2. Independence in Malaya led to warfare between the Islamic Malays and the Chinese minority.
      a. A federated Malaysia was formed.
      b. In 1965, the largely Chinese city of Singapore was pushed out of the federation.

3. Philippine independence was granted in 1946.
    a. President Marcos subverted the constitution and ruled as a dictator.
    b. In 1986, Corazon Aquino led a successful campaign to oust Marcos, but the gap between the rich elite and the poor remains enormous.
4. The Netherlands East Indies became the independent Indonesia.
    a. The anti-Western Sukarno attempted to forge a "guided democracy."
    b. Supposed communist influence led to Sukarno's downfall and a military regime.
5. France's attempt to re-impose its rule in Vietnam led to an independence movement led by the nationalist Ho Chi Minh.
    a. Despite American help, the French were defeated in 1954.
    b. The agreed-on elections to unify Vietnam were never held.
    c. Civil war between communists and anticommunists led, eventually, to a communist victory and a defeat for the United States.
E. The Muslim world
  1. Arab nationalism has two faces.
    a. The practical side has concentrated on nation building.
    b. The idealistic side has concentrated on Arab unification.
    c. Arab nationalism is unified on anticolonial and anti-Jewish levels, but regional and ideological rivalry has hurt the pan-Arab dream.
  2. After the Second World War, conflict over Jewish immigration led to conflict between the Jews and the Palestinian Arabs and the Arab League states.
F. Palestine and Israel
  1. In 1947, the United Nations proposed that Palestine be divided into Jewish and Arab states.
    a. The Jews accepted, but the Arabs rejected the proposal.
    b. War between the two sides led to an Israeli victory.
    c. While the Israelis conquered more territory, 900,000 Arab refugees left old Palestine.
  2. The Palestine Liberation Organization (PLO) was formed after the war to continue the opposition to Israel.
G. Egypt
  1. The Arab humiliation triggered a nationalist revolution, led by Nasser.
    a. Nasser drove out the pro-Western King Farouk in 1952.
    b. Nasser instituted radical land reform.
  2. Nasser's Egypt sought neutrality and took aid from Russia.
    a. The United States canceled its offer to build a great new dam on the Nile.
    b. Nasser retaliated by nationalizing the Suez Canal Company.
    c. In turn, the British, French, and Israelis invaded Egypt.
    d. The United States and Russia forced the invaders to withdraw.
    e. Although Arab victory encouraged anti-Western radicalism in the Arab world, the Arabs remained divided.
  3. War recurred in 1967 and 1973.

    4. Sadat of Egypt, with the help of President Carter, engineered a settlement between Israel and Egypt.

       a. Other Arab leaders continued their opposition to Israel and their support of the PLO.

       b. With Sadat's assassination, Egypt-Israeli relations deteriorated over the issue of the West Bank settlement.

       c. Egypt stood by as Israel occupied Lebanon in 1982 in an effort to destroy the PLO.

II. An independence movement in the French colony of Algeria resulted in the Algerian war.

    1. Tunisia and Morocco had won independence from France in 1956.

    2. The 1 million French-Europeans in Algeria were determined to prevent a Muslim nationalist state in Algeria.

    3. A military coup in Algeria brought General de Gaulle to power in France.

    4. However, de Gaulle accepted the idea of Algerian independence.

I. Turkey, Iran, and Iraq

    1. Turkey followed Atatürk's vision of a modern, secularized, and Europeanized state.

    2. As in 1939, Iran tried to follow Turkey's example.

       a. Shah Muhammad Reza Pahlavi angered Iranian nationalists because he courted the West.

       b. The shah nationalized Iranian oil, but the West retaliated with a boycott that hurt the economy.

       c. In 1953, Mosaddeq forced the shah to flee, but the Americans supported both his return and his harsh dictatorship.

       d. After an Islamic revolution (led by Ayatollah Khomeini) in 1978, the shah fled and U.S. diplomats were imprisoned.

       e. Fearing the Iranian Shi'ites, Iraq began a long and bloody war against Iran.

III. Imperialism and nationalism in black Africa

    A. All but two areas of black Africa—Portugal's territory and South Africa—won political independence after the Second World War.

    B. The imperial system (1900–1930)

       1. By 1900, most of black Africa had been taken by the Europeans.

          a. Trade in raw materials replaced trade in human beings.

          b. Imperialism shattered the existing black society.

          c. This society had consisted of thousands of political units and hundreds of languages.

          d. The imperialists themselves ruled differently, and the number of settlers varied.

       2. The British and French goal was "good government."

          a. In reality this meant maintaining law and order by military force.

          b. The imperialists spent little on social services and feared that education would encourage revolt.

3. The economic goal was to draw raw materials out of the interior.
   a. Railroads and roads were built from coast to interior to move raw materials out and manufactured goods in.
   b. Railroads and roads enabled the imperialists to put down rebellions quickly, and they provided wage jobs for former peasants.
   c. Forced labor was widespread until about 1920.
   d. Agricultural self-sufficiency gave way to export production for the world market.
C. Ghana and Kenya illustrate the variations of the impact of imperialism.
   1. Precolonial Ghana was the powerful and economically vigorous kingdom of Ashanti.
   2. The British made Ashanti into a crown colony (the Gold Coast), which set the pace for West Africa's Westernization.
      a. They introduced large-scale cocoa bean production.
      b. Much of the economic success in cocoa was due to native, not British, entrepreneurship.
      c. A black elite participated in colonial government.
   3. British-controlled Kenya experienced a more harsh colonial rule.
      a. These East African peoples were less numerous and less interested in commerce.
      b. Indian and white settlers exploited the territory.
      c. The British imposed a rigorous system of segregation on the blacks and Indians.
D. The growth of African nationalism
   1. Western imperialism caused the rise of African nationalism, but it differed from the nationalist movements evidenced in other parts of the world.
      a. Imperialism and Western ideas came later to Africa.
      b. A multiplicity of ethnic groups and arbitrary boundaries complicated political nationalism.
   2. The impetus for black nationalism came from the United States and the British West Indies.
      a. W. E. B. Du Bois was the most influential of the black nationalists.
      b. Based on Wilson's idea of self-determination, Du Bois's Pan-African Congress called for the union of all African peoples.
      c. A minority of blacks in Senegal favored union with France.
      d. The Senegal poet and leader Senghor articulated the idea of joy and pride in "blackness," or *négritude*.
      e. In British West Africa, the Westernized blacks pushed for moderate steps toward greater self-government.
   3. With the Great Depression, African nationalism became more radical.
      a. The black elite became hostile to the system.
      b. Like Azikiwe in Nigeria, they became the leaders who spread nationalist ideas.
      c. The depression resulted in cooperative "holdups" by farmers and a racial interpretation of economic conflict.

E. Achieving independence with new leaders
    1. The Second World War speeded up the nationalist movement.
        a. The growth of towns and the shortages of goods increased discontent.
        b. The wartime experiences and antiracist ideals of blacks encouraged nationalism.
        c. The British and French began to push for economic and social improvement.
        d. Wartime ideals encouraged adoption of the principle of self-determination.
    2. New leaders like Nkrumah, Azikiwe, and Touré succeeded in bringing independence to Africa.
        a. The postwar leaders were of humble social origins and were influenced by Western thought.
        b. They accepted the prevailing colonial territorial boundaries.
        c. They channeled the hopes and discontent of the masses into organized politics.
F. Ghana showed the way to African independence.
    1. Under Nkrumah, Ghana became the first independent African state.
        a. Nkrumah was influenced by European socialists and the "Back to Africa" movement of Marcus Garvey.
        b. Garvey preached the idea of "Africa for the Africans."
    2. Nkrumah's independence movement followed the Second World War.
        a. Economic discontent turned into anti-imperialist rioting.
        b. The British encouraged constitutional reform.
        c. Nkrumah built a radical mass party that demanded "self-government now."
        d. In and out of prison, Nkrumah led his radical nationalist party to victory over all rivals.
        e. Ghana's independence encouraged speedy independence for other African states.
    3. In some areas, white settlers tried to retain their privileged position.
        a. Eventually the blacks of Southern Rhodesia won over the whites and renamed their country Zimbabwe.
        b. In Zambia and East Africa, the whites were too few to block black nationalism for long.
G. Nationalism in French-speaking regions of Africa
    1. With some black support, France under de Gaulle developed an alternative to independence.
        a. French West Africa and French Equatorial Africa were formed into a federation and participated in French government.
        b. The black elite, led by Senghor, wanted to retain ties with France.
        c. Under Touré's leadership, Guinea rejected the French plan and won independence.
        d. Other French territories followed, although many retained close ties with France.

2. Belgium's harsh rule in its Congo colony ended with civil war and tribal conflict, an exception to the general African experience.

IV. Black Africa since 1960
   A. In the years since independence, democracy has given way to one-party rule or military dictatorship.
      1. Corruption is widespread and dictatorship common.
      2. White racist rule in South Africa represents a ticking time bomb for Africa.
      3. Some developments have proved beneficial.
         a. Imperialism has been thrown off.
         b. Some degree of unity and modernization has been created.
   B. Building national unity
      1. Imperialism affected Africa in several positive ways.
         a. About forty states were created.
         b. Some modernization and urbanization took place.
         c. A modern, diversified social structure was established.
      2. Other features of imperialism were negative.
         a. Disruption of traditional life caused suffering and unfulfilled expectations.
         b. The economy was geared for export and was under foreign control.
         c. Artificial boundaries did not consider ethnic-cultural groupings, and hence many states were faced with multi-ethnic problems.
      3. Western-style democracy and political systems have not worked well.
         a. Parties based on ethnic or regional lines encouraged conflict.
         b. Leaders turned to tough measures to hold countries together.
      4. For example, Nkrumah built a "revolutionary" one-party state in Ghana.
         a. He used communist and totalitarian models.
         b. His grandiose projects failed, and he was deposed by the army in 1966.
      5. Also, French-speaking Mali and Guinea adopted one-party governments, whereas Senegal and the Ivory Coast remained moderate.
      6. Military takeovers have been common in Africa.
         a. Some military governments, like that in Amin's Uganda, have terrorized the people.
         b. Others, such as Ethiopia in the late 1970s, had redeeming qualities: they held the country together and were committed to modernization.
         c. Military leaders often believe in the ultimate goal of free democratic government.
   C. Nigeria, Africa's giant, illustrates the difficulties of nation building.
      1. Nigeria contains many religious, regional, and tribal groups.
      2. Modern Nigeria was a creation of the British consolidation of two administrative districts.
         a. The key issue in preindependence years was the relationship between central government and the regions.
         b. A federal system was worked out that shared power with the three state governments.

    3. Ethnic rivalry in 1964 led to violence, a military coup, and civil war.
       a. A military council killed many politicians and officers and abolished regional governments.
       b. Ibo domination led to civil war and the creation of an independent Ibo state of Biafra.
       c. After three years of bloodshed, Biafra was forced to remain in Nigeria.
    4. A new Nigerian federal government was formed, with nineteen states.
       a. Iboland was rebuilt as oil revenues soared.
       b. An elected civilian government took over in 1979.
       c. However, military rule returned in 1983, followed by a more liberal military coup in 1985.
  D. The struggle in southern Africa
    1. Black nationalist guerrillas moved Portugal and the white population out of Angola and Mozambique.
    2. The roots of racial conflict in the Republic of South Africa are complex.
       a. After conquest, Britain allowed the Dutch settlers self-rule.
       b. Britain also allowed the whites (Afrikaners) to limit landownership.
       c. The black land reserves were a pool for indirect forced labor.
    3. The Afrikaner racist-totalitarian system is the efficient and well-organized system of apartheid (meaning "separation" or "segregation").
       a. The population is divided into four legally unequal racial groups.
       b. Whites control the economy and enjoy the wealth.
       c. Despite poverty and exploitation, a distinct black urban culture has emerged.
    4. Black nationalist protest has a long history.
       a. Peaceful civil disobedience has existed since the 1950s but has not worked.
       b. The moderate nationalists were destroyed, and a more radical African National Congress movement took their place.
       c. A new parliamentary reform made no provision for black representation.
       d. Despite internal and foreign protest, the white government moved closer toward dictatorship for all—until 1989.
       e. The United States and the Common Market imposed economic sanctions on South Africa.
    5. A major step forward came in 1989 when black nationalist leader Nelson Mandela was freed and the ANC was legalized.
       a. Mandela subsequently suspended the ANC's armed struggle.
       b. The prospects for a multiracial democratic state in South Africa seem considerably improved.

Review Questions

1. Explain why Mao's Communists were victorious against the Nationalists. Why did the Communists appeal to many peasants?

2. How did the Soviet Union influence China during the early years of Communist rule?

3. Describe the cultural and economic policies of Chairman Mao. How successful was he in transforming China into a country based on modernization and equality?

4. Compare the cultural and economic goals of China during Mao's Cultural Revolution to those following his death.

5. Describe Japan's "American revolution." In what ways did the United States influence postwar Japan?

6. What are the reasons for the Japanese economic miracle?

7. What role has big business played in the Japanese economy? How does this differ from the relationships among labor, big business, and government in the United States?

8. Explain Japan's group-centered and cooperative ideals. Give examples of how these have contributed to Japan's economic and social success.

9. What effect did the coming of national independence have on Hindu and Muslim relations in India? What was the outcome? Could it have been avoided?

10. Explain the reason for the Bangladesh revolt of 1971.

11. How successful was Indira Gandhi in solving India's problems and preserving democracy in India?

12. What were the results—in terms of political order and social reform—when Malaya and the Philippines gained their independence?

13. What were the goals of the Vietnamese nationalists? Describe the process and the outcome of the nationalist struggle.

14. What were the reasons for the Jewish-Arab conflict? What was its outcome?

15. What were the goals and the achievements of Nasser and Sadat?

16. Why did the Iranian revolution of 1978 occur? Explain by making reference to the shah, U.S. interests, the Iranian nationalists, and how this revolution affected Iran-Iraq relations.

17. What key ideas influenced and emerged out of the black nationalist movements? Pay particular attention to the ideas of Du Bois, Senghor, Garvey, Nkrumah, and Touré.

18. In what sense was Nkrumah's movement in Ghana a mass movement based on radical nationalism?

19. Describe de Gaulle's plan to keep French Africans within the French empire. What were the results, and what was Touré's role?

20. Why did Belgium's rule in the Congo come to such a violent end? How did Belgium's colonial policy differ from that of France and Britain?

21. How did European imperialism affect black Africa in terms of human life and economic arrangements?

22. What were the objectives of the French and British rulers in black Africa, and how did they achieve these objectives?

23. What social and economic rearrangements took place in Ghana and Kenya as a result of British colonial rule?

24. How did imperialism affect Africa in both positive and negative ways?

25. Why hasn't the Western-style political system worked well in Africa? Use Ghana and Nigeria as examples.

26. In what ways does Nigeria illustrate the difficulties of nation building in Africa? Why did the Biafran war take place, and what was its outcome?

27. How does apartheid work, and how has it affected the blacks in South Africa?

Study-Review Exercises

Define the following key concepts and terms.

pan-Africanists/"black Frenchmen"

French ideology of assimilation

négritude

apartheid

Shi'ite Muslims/Sunni Muslims

Identify and explain the significance of the following people and terms.
Mao's Great Proletarian Cultural Revolution

Mao's Great Leap Forward

Red Guards

Deng's "second revolution"

Japan's Democratic Liberal party

Battle of Dien Bien Phu

General Douglas MacArthur

Jawaharlal Nehru

Ho Chi Minh

Punjab Sikhs

Indira Gandhi

Rajiv Gandhi

Achmed Sukarno

Ferdinand Marcos

Muhammad Ali Jinnah

Muslim League

Bengali Hindus

Bengali revolt of 1971

Gamal Abdel Nasser

Arab League

Suez Crisis of 1956

Palestine Liberation Organization (PLO)

Ayatollah Khomeini

Anwar Sadat

W. E. B. Du Bois

"Back to Africa" movement

Lord Louis Mountbatten

Kwame Nkrumah

Marcus Garvey

Nnamdi Azikiwe

Léopold Senghor

Afrikaner

South African Native Land Act of 1913

Nelson Mandela

African Nationalist Congress (ANC)

Frederik W. de Klerk

Explain when, how, and from whom each of the following colonial states received its independence.
Palestine

India

Pakistan

Malaya

Philippine Islands

Vietnam

Nigeria

South Africa

Ghana

Test your understanding of the chapter by providing the correct answers.

1. U.S. military movement across the thirty-eighth parallel eventually *weakened/strengthened* the Chinese Communist position.

2. Mao's Great Leap Forward *did/did not* improve relations between China and Russia.

3. The U.S. general who exercised great power in postwar Japan. _____

4. Japan's economic success after the Second World War *is/is not* related to its history and national character.

5. Compared to the United States, the relationship between worker and employer in Japan is *more combative/based more on cooperation*.

6. Led by the Muslim leader _____ , India's Muslims were given a

   separate homeland called _____ . The eastern part of this new country was eventually given its own independence and named itself

   _____ .

7. The Philippine experiment with U.S.-style government *did/did not* bring true democracy and constitutionalism to that country.

8. The South African Native Land Act of 1913 was an important step in *limiting/expanding* the land-use rights of blacks.

9. The nationalist leader of Indonesia whose authoritarian and anti-Western regime was

   toppled by the army in 1965. _____

10. The ANC leader in South Africa who was freed in 1989. _____

Multiple-Choice Questions

1. After its victory in 1949, the early Communist regime under Mao
   a. was unwilling to carry out land reform.
   b. was greatly influenced by the Soviet model of five-year plans.
   c. completely divorced itself from Soviet influence.
   d. turned to the capitalist West for its economic ideas.

2. Compared to the Russian land redistribution of the 1930s, Mao's land redistribution program and the creation of the collectives
   a. was rapid, brutal, and unsuccessful.
   b. was opposed by the masses.
   c. was gradual and less brutally carried out.
   d. did not affect the holdings of the old landlords and the rich peasants.

3. Mao's Great Leap Forward was intended to
   a. bypass the Russians to arrive at true communism.
   b. jump from communism to bureaucratic capitalism.
   c. prepare China for the Olympics.
   d. make the family the basis of communist society.

4. U.S. occupation of Japan
   a. left Japan's powerful bureaucracy intact.
   b. resulted in the elimination of the emperor.
   c. restored the military.
   d. all of the above.

5. The "reverse course" that U.S. policy toward Japan took as a result of the cold war refers to a(n)
   a. U.S. decision to withdraw from Japanese affairs.
   b. economic war between Japan and the United States.
   c. purge of the left wing in Japanese politics.
   d. return of all land to the big landlords.

6. The Muslim leader Jinnah pushed the British for
   a. an independent Pakistan.
   b. continued British presence in India.
   c. a unified federal India for Muslim and Hindu.
   d. none of the above.

7. According to Indira Gandhi's government, improvement of living standards could be obtained only after
   a. the British paid reparations to the Indians.
   b. India was reunited with Pakistan.
   c. heavy industry was developed.
   d. the rate of population growth was greatly reduced.

8. The U.S. black nationalist whose goals were solidarity among blacks everywhere and eventually a union of all African peoples was
   a. Léopold Senghor.
   b. W. E. B. Du Bois.
   c. Kwame Nkrumah.
   d. Sekou Touré.

9. The Great Depression of the 1930s
   a. had little if any effect on black Africa.
   b. hurt only the elite Westernized blacks.
   c. did not affect agricultural production.
   d. produced extreme hardship and discontent among the African masses.

10. Nkrumah's independence movement was based on
    a. support of the demands of tribal leaders.
    b. moderate and gradual transition to independence.
    c. immediate self-government.
    d. independence through elite leadership rather than mass participation.

11. The Belgian policy toward its Congo colony was different than that of France toward its colonies in that it
    a. discouraged the development of an educated population.
    b. supported a plan of imperial federation.
    c. welcomed the idea of self-determination for Africans.
    d. none of the above.

12. The South African Native Land Act of 1913
    a. limited the landownership of the white population.
    b. turned the land over to anyone who could prove ownership.
    c. brought about wide-scale British ownership.
    d. greatly limited black ownership of land.

13. The largest barrier to Nigerian unity has been
    a. British reluctance to grant independence.
    b. regional and tribal rivalries.
    c. lack of natural resources.
    d. white supremacy.

14. Indira Gandhi's defeat at the polls and much of her unpopularity were due to her
    a. refusal to call for free elections.
    b. failure to attack dishonest officials and black marketeers.
    c. mass sterilization campaign.
    d. foreign policy.

15. In the end, the war with Japan
    a. weakened the Chinese Communists.
    b. weakened the Chinese Nationalists.
    c. weakened Mao's appeal to the peasants.
    d. allowed the Nationalists to eliminate the Communists in China.

16. To save China from "revisionist" influence and to recover his lost influence after the failure of the Great Leap Forward, Mao
    a. gave more power to the party bureaucrats.
    b. reinstituted some capitalist practices in China.
    c. strengthened China's relations with Russia.
    d. launched a cultural revolution.

17. Which of the following is true of postwar Japan?
    a. It was allowed to remilitarize.
    b. It rid itself of the emperor.
    c. It rejected a constitution.
    d. It became a military protectorate of the United States.

18. Which of the following is true of the black nationalist movement?
    a. The Great Depression and the Second World War made it less radical.
    b. It was influenced by the ideas of Marcus Garvey.
    c. It proceeded most rapidly and peacefully in the Belgian Congo.
    d. It rejected the ideas of W. E. B. Du Bois.

19. The city of Singapore was pushed out of the Malaysia Federation because it
    a. refused to agree to federation.
    b. was dominated by the communists.
    c. was dominated by the Chinese.
    d. was too large.

20. Mao's radical cadres of young people who were encouraged to denounce their teachers and practice rebellion were known as the
    a. Red Guards.
    b. Student Youth Movement.
    c. Revolutionary Youth Corps.
    d. Red Terror.

21. The leader who fled to Taiwan with his Nationalist followers was
    a. Emperor Hirohito.
    b. Chiang Kai-shek.
    c. Deng Xiao-ping.
    d. Mao Tse-tung.

22. The first black African state to gain independence from its colonial overlord was
    a. Kenya.
    b. Ghana.
    c. Guinea.
    d. the Congo.

23. The successor to Ferdinand Marcos as president of the Philippines was
    a. Indira Gandhi.
    b. Ho Chi Minh.
    c. Achmed Sukarno.
    d. Corazón Aquino.

24. The successful leader of the black nationalist movement in Ghana was
    a. Sekou Touré.
    b. Léopold Senghor.
    c. Kwame Nkrumah.
    d. Nnamdi Azikiwe.

25. The Egyptian president who signed a peace settlement with Israel was
    a. Anwar Sadat.
    b. Gamal Abdel Nasser.
    c. Menachem Begin.
    d. Muhammad Reza Pahlavi.

26. The European leader who accepted the principle of self-determination for Algeria in 1959 was
    a. Charles de Gaulle.
    b. Winston Churchill.
    c. Helmut Schmidt.
    d. Leonid Brezhnev.

27. The battle of Dien Bien Phu in 1954 marked the end of French control of
    a. Algeria.
    b. Indochina.
    c. South Sudan.
    d. Teheran.

28. The British, French, and Israelis were forced to withdraw from Egypt by
    a. Egypt and Syria.
    b. Russia and Egypt.
    c. the United States and Russia.
    d. the Palestinians and Libya.

Major Political Ideas

Communism is often thought of as a political system, although it has economic and social origins as well as goals. What were the social and economic motives behind the communist revolution in China? Did the communist plan succeed?

Issues for Essays and Discussion

How did Asian and African countries reassert or establish their political independence in the postwar era? Answer this question by making specific reference to China, Japan, India, and Ghana.

Geography

On Outline Map 37.2 provided show the locations of the following black African states: Ghana, Kenya, Senegal, Zambia, Zimbabwe, Guinea, Zaire, Mali, and the Ivory Coast. Next, briefly describe to what European power each had been attached, and compare and contrast the process of achieving independence (such as peacefully, through war, or through revolution). Which of the imperialist countries—France, Britain, or Belgium—provided the smoothest and least violent transition to independence? (Remember that duplicate maps for class use are at the back of this book.)

Outline Map 37.2

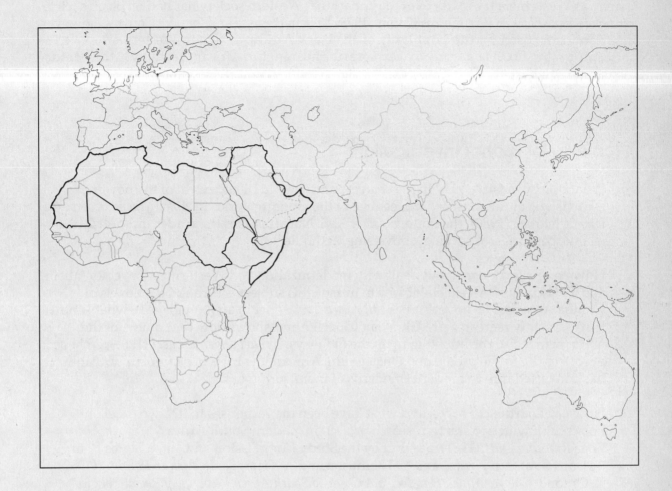

Understanding History Through the Arts

How has African art influenced the West? The study of black Africa has been largely a one-way street, as Westerners try to uncover the impact that Western society has had on black society. In *Image of the Black in Western Art* (2 vols., 1979) by Jean Devisse and Jean M. Courtes, however, attention is focused on the popularity of the black African image in Western art since the fifteenth century B.C. For a study that explores the full range of African creativity in this century see Susan Vogel et al., *Africa Explores: Twentieth Century African Art* (1991).

Problems for Further Investigation

1. What role does Islam play in the contemporary world? The revival of the power of Islam is one of the most salient features of the modern world. In *Among the Believers: An Islamic Journey* (1980), the famous writer V. S. Naipaul takes the reader through four Islamic countries, observing, conversing, and reflecting.

2. How have Africans met and dealt with modernization and Westernization, colonialism and Christianity? An excellent way to pursue this subject is through the novels of Chinua Achebe. His novel *Things Fall Apart** (1959), set in an Ibo village in what is now Biafra, vividly recreates pre-Christian tribal life and shows how the coming of the white man led to the breaking up of the old ways. In *No Longer at Ease** (1960), Achebe describes the tragic predicament of a young African idealist whose foreign education has converted him to modern standards of moral judgment.

3. How did apartheid evolve, and what have been the responses to it? Two excellent books with which to start a research project on modern South Africa are *South Africa: Time Running Out** (1981), a report by the Study Commission on United States Policy Toward Southern Africa, and L. Thompson and A. Prior, *South African Politics** (1982). R. Omond, *The Apartheid Handbook: A Guide to South Africa's Everyday Racial Policies** (1985), uses specific examples to show exactly how the apartheid system works today, and T. Lodge, *Black Politics in South Africa Since 1945** (1983), is an excellent history of the development of mass protest movements in South Africa since 1945.

4. What can be learned from biographies of key figures in African history? Those interested in the use of biography as history will want to read the biography of the first secretary of the African National Congress, a man whose life included childhood on a German mission station, work in the diamond town of Kimberley, and experience in journalism and political activism. The book is *Sol Plaatje** (1984) by B. William.

*Available in paperback.

CHAPTER 38

Life in the Third World

Chapter Questions

After reading and studying this chapter, you should be able to answer the following questions:

How have the emerging nations of the Third World sought to escape from poverty? Have their efforts been successful? What has caused the prodigious growth of Third World cities, and what does this growth mean for their inhabitants? How do Third World thinkers and artists interpret their world and modern life before, during, and after foreign domination?

Chapter Summary

This chapter examines one of the most vexing and complex problems facing the world today—that of improvement of life in the Third World. Despite the enormous strides the Third World has made in industrializing and modernizing, its progress has been uneven, has left serious imbalances, and has widened the gap between rich and poor. The term *Third World* is appropriate because it denotes a group of countries with certain common characteristics: all experienced foreign domination and a nationalist reaction, all are dominated by agricultural economies, and all are aware of their common poverty. As the chapter proceeds, it becomes clear that the Third World is united by the problems of how to successfully industrialize, control urbanization, and stop the population explosion.

It is difficult to understand the true dimensions of Third World poverty. Income statistics tend to overstate poverty levels because they do not account for the cheapness of basic necessities or the widespread reliance on noncash transactions. Hence poverty is best understood by looking at accounts of diet, housing, and public health services. Most Third World countries cannot provide minimal daily caloric requirements or meet the average diet of the rich nations of the Northern Hemisphere. In addition, a medical revolution that dramatically lowered the mortality rate caused by certain diseases but did little to lower the birthrate has brought on a population explosion of an unprecedented magnitude. The Third World population, which numbered about 1.7 billion in 1950, is expected to reach 5.2 billion by the year 2000. Thus, much of the progress made toward modernization and industrialization has been canceled by population increase.

Most Third World leaders saw industrialization as the way to modernize. In many ways, the Third World's first industrialization drive was a success: industry grew and per capita income increased at record rates. The most popular route of those who dreamed of industrial greatness was that of a "mixed economy"—part socialist and part capitalist. India exemplifies this general trend, but it is in capitalist Taiwan and South Korea and in communist China that success is most notable. In South Korea and Taiwan, radical land reform, government encouragement of business, and considerable U.S. aid and multinational investment have laid the foundation for a growing and competitive market economy. China's land reform has been a major factor in its success in working out a balance between agriculture and industry.

Most Third World countries, however, made a drastic mistake by neglecting to improve and modernize agriculture. Agricultural development was avoided because it didn't hold the promise (or prestige) of industrialization and because the prerequisite land reform was unpopular with ruling elites. Besides, cheap food from America made paying attention to agriculture seem unnecessary. By the late 1960s it was clear that Third World industrialization had not solved the puzzle of large-scale poverty, population explosion, and the need for agricultural self-sufficiency. A food crisis in India made real the world's nightmare visions of starvation and wars for survival. The Green Revolution changed all of this. The dramatic increase in agricultural production that followed made food self-sufficiency possible—although it appears that the Green Revolution works only in areas where peasants, and not big landlords, own the land. But like the medical revolution and industrialization, the Green Revolution has not lifted the landless peasants out of poverty.

It is the problem of urbanization without industrialization that has most affected the masses of the Third World. Half the world's city dwellers now live in Third World cities, which teem with makeshift squatter shantytowns. Runaway urban growth is an ever-present feature of Third World life. Rural poverty has pushed millions of people into already crowded cities. Although most leaders and advisers either avoid them or hope to eliminate the shantytowns, overcrowding points to the fact that the gap between rich and poor in the Third World is monumental. There is no evidence, however, that any particular ideology—socialist, revolutionary, or capitalist—produces any more or less income inequality.

The great majority of urban dwellers are employed in low-paying and irregular industries, such as street selling and handicraft trades. Equally important, urban migration of men has fostered a new and more independent life for women, who have been left alone in the countryside. Meanwhile, education and mass communication have changed the ideas and aspirations of the masses. Unfortunately, although it is a path to government jobs and politics, education has failed to fulfill the hopes of the masses because it neglects the technical training that would allow them to move into modern agriculture and industry. At the same time, mass communication propagates the modern lifestyle and challenges old values. In this atmosphere of rootlessness, rising expectations, and poverty, members of a new school of writers point to the richness of Third World culture, hoping above all to reduce the loneliness and homelessness of its uprooted people.

Study Outline

Use this outline to preview the chapter before you read a particular section in your textbook and then as a self-check of your reading comprehension after you have read the chapter section.

I. Defining the Third World
   A. Despite some limitations, the concept of a "Third World" is valid.
      1. All Third World countries have experienced foreign domination and a struggle for independence and have a common consciousness.
      2. Most people in Third World countries live in the countryside and depend on agriculture.
      3. Third World countries are united by an awareness of their poverty.
   B. Not everyone in the Third World is poor, but the average standard of living is low.

II. Economic and social challenges in the Third World
   A. Third World peoples and leaders hoped that, with independence, they could fulfill the promises of a brighter future.
      1. At first it was thought that the answer to rural poverty was rapid industrialization and "modernization."
      2. By the late 1960s, the failure of this program caused a shift in emphasis to rural development.
   B. From the late 1960s on, the Third World became less unified and more complex.
   C. Understanding the poverty of the Third World is not easy.
      1. A comparison of national income statistics often exaggerates Third World poverty.
      2. Basic necessities are less costly in the Third World.
      3. The statistics are often incomplete and do not account for noncash transactions.
   D. "Poverty" means lack of food, unbalanced diet, poor housing, ill health, and scanty education.

III. The medical revolution and the population explosion
   A. A spectacular and ongoing medical revolution came with the independence most Third World nations achieved after the Second World War.
      1. Modern methods of immunology and public health were adopted.
      2. The number of hospitals, doctors, and nurses increased.
      3. The recent trend is toward medical services for the countryside.
   B. This revolution lowered the death rate and lengthened life expectancy.
      1. Infant and juvenile mortality declined.
      2. By 1980, life expectancy was between 40 and 64, whereas in developed countries it was about 71.
   C. This has accelerated population growth.
      1. The birthrate did not fall correspondingly.
      2. Malthus's conclusions have been revived and updated.

3. Birth control and family planning are hindered by religious and cultural attitudes.

IV. The race to industrialize (1950–1970)
   A. Most Third World countries adopted the theory that European-style industrialization was the answer to their development.
      1. Much reliance was placed on state action and enterprise.
      2. The result for most was a "mixed economy"—part socialist, part capitalist.
      3. Heavy industry was promoted at the expense of agriculture.
      4. India's concentration on state planning of industry exemplifies these trends—including a neglect of agriculture and land reform.
   B. Nevertheless, the drive to industrialize the Third World was a success in many ways.
      1. Industrial growth exceeded population growth, and its pace was as rapid as in pre-1914 United States.
      2. Industrialization stimulated an unprecedented growth in per capita income.
      3. The fastest growth was in the capitalist economies of South Korea, Taiwan, the Ivory Coast, Hong Kong, and Singapore.
   C. South Korea and Taiwan changed from typically underdeveloped nations into economic powers for several reasons.
      1. "Capitalist" land reform drew farmers into a market economy.
      2. Government encouraged business enterprise.
      3. U.S. aid and the multinationals encouraged growth.
      4. Some traditional culture was preserved, and political stability was maintained, but democracy suffered.
   D. By the late 1960s it was clear that, for most countries, an economic miracle had not occurred and that industrialization had failed in important areas.
      1. The economic gap between rich and poor nations had widened.
      2. The main beneficiaries were not the rural masses.
      3. Industrialization failed to provide enough jobs.

V. Agriculture and village life
   A. Since the late 1960s, the limitations of industrialization have forced attention toward rural development and rural life.
   B. Third World governments avoided agricultural issues in the 1950s and 1960s for a variety of reasons.
      1. Some saw agriculture as a mark of colonial servitude.
      2. Few understood how to improve peasant farming.
      3. Land reform was an unpopular issue in countries where powerful landlords prevailed.
      4. Free food from the West discouraged serious internal reform.
   C. Following the Indian food crisis of 1966–67, however, fears of famine caused a shift of interest to Third World agriculture.
      1. The Green Revolution began in Mexico and then transformed agriculture in the Philippines, followed by India and China.
      2. Countries such as India could feed their entire populations.

3. This revolution appears to have brought profits to both large and small landowners.
4. However, the landless or nearly landless people gained only slightly.
5. The Green Revolution works best in countries where the peasants own land.
6. The Green Revolution has not been successful in Africa and, with the exception of Mexico, it has not worked in Latin America because of lack of peasant landownership.
D. The Green Revolution, like the revolution in medicine and advances in industrialization, has not benefited the poorest groups in the Third World.

VI. The growth of cities
A. Urbanization in the Third World
1. Runaway urban growth is a feature of the Third World.
a. Cities have grown rapidly, and the proportion of the total population living in the city has increased.
b. Half the world's city dwellers live in Third World cities, which will be of staggering size by the year 2000.
2. Cities have grown for many reasons.
a. The rural population explosion and the restrictive pattern of landowner- ship (particularly in Latin America) have pushed masses of people toward the cities.
b. Many are drawn to the city by the hope of industrial employment.
c. City life offers services and opportunities to break away from traditional rural society.
B. Overcrowding and shantytowns
1. Inadequate social services have made urban life difficult.
2. Some governments have sought to limit and/or reverse migration to urban areas.
3. Overcrowding, as in Singapore, has reached staggering proportions.
a. Makeshift squatter settlements have sprung up overnight.
b. These shantytowns house up to two-fifths of the urban populations.
4. A debate exists over the worth of the shantytown environment.
a. The "pessimists" stress the miseries of squatter life.
b. The "optimists" point to worthwhile kinship ties and self-help fostered in the shantytown.
c. Some advise the government to help the squatters help themselves.
C. Rich and poor
1. The gap between rich and poor is monumental.
a. Income distribution figures show inequality similar to that in pre-1914 Europe.
b. The problem is not related to a country's ideological inclinations.
2. The gap is greatest in urban areas.
a. It is best seen in differences in housing: slums versus mansions with servants.
b. A "modern"—Western—lifestyle is the byword of the urban elite.

   c. Education distinguishes the wealthy from the masses and is the road to government positions.

   d. The middle class is small and includes factory workers.

   e. The great urban majority work in traditional, low-paying, and irregular trades such as street selling.

  D. Migration and the family

   1. In Asia and Africa the great majority of migrants to the city are young men.

    a. This has had a great impact on traditional family life and the women left behind.

    b. Reasons for this pattern include the seasonal and temporary nature of urban work for many males.

    c. Also, kinship ties between city and original village encourage temporary migration by males.

   2. The consequences of this male out-migration have been mixed.

    a. African and Asian women, once subordinates, have become heads of households and have embarked on the path of liberation.

    b. Only children remain to help with the work.

   3. In Latin America, permanent migration of whole families is more typical.

 VII. Mass culture and contemporary thought in the Third World

  A. Education and mass communication

   1. Third World leaders and people view education as the avenue to jobs and economic development.

    a. The number of young people in school has increased.

    b. Still, compared to the rich countries, the percentage of children in school is low and the quality of education is mediocre.

    c. The universities lack courses in technical education.

    d. Because of "brain drain," many countries lose their best-educated people to the rich countries.

    e. The educational system does not serve the needs of rural society.

   2. Mass communication propagates modern lifestyles and challenges traditional values.

  B. Interpreting the experiences of the emerging world

   1. Intellectuals and writers have responded differently to the search for meaning.

    a. Some have merely followed a Western-style Marxist or capitalist line.

    b. Others have broken with Western thought and values.

   2. Fanon argued that imperialist exploitation remains after independence and that the Third World provided Europe with its wealth.

   3. Achebe argues that Africans must recognize and identify their native culture; he is critical of Third World leaders.

   4. Naipaul also criticizes Third World leaders and points to the plight of uprooted people.

   5. These varying opinions reflect the intellectual maturity and independence of many Third World writers.

Review Questions

Check your understanding of this chapter by answering the following questions.

1. Describe the level of poverty in the Third World. How well do statistics help us understand poverty?

2. What benefits and ill consequences did the so-called medical revolution bring to the Third World? Why did this revolution occur after independence was achieved?

3. Was European-style industrialization the solution for Third World underdevelopment? Discuss the strengths and weaknesses of Third World industrialization.

4. Describe the economic miracles in South Korea and Taiwan. Why did they occur in those two countries?

5. What is a "mixed economy"? Why was it an attractive idea to Third World countries?

6. Why did complacency with regard to Third World agriculture turn into a concern for agricultural reform? Where and under what circumstances has the Green Revolution worked best?

7. In what ways can it be said that, overall, the Green Revolution, the medical revolution, and industrialization represent large but uneven and unbalanced steps forward for the Third World?

8. How does agricultural change in those regions with peasant landownership compare with change in those without peasant landownership?

9. Compared to the Western world, how rapidly are Third World cities growing? Why have Third World cities grown?

10. What are the two sides in the debate over the worth of the shantytowns?

11. How wide is the gap between the Third World rich and poor? How is this gap evidenced in contemporary Third World life?

12. How has urbanization affected family patterns and female roles in Asia, Africa, and Latin America?

13. What has been the impact of education and mass communication on Third World life?

14. What are the weaknesses of the Third World educational systems?

15. What are the principal ideas of Fanon, Achebe, and Naipaul?

Study-Review Exercises

Define the following key concepts and terms.
neo-Malthusian theory

Third World

medical revolution

mixed economy

Green Revolution

out-migration

"modern" lifestyle

"brain drain"

"bazaar economy"

shantytowns

Explain how each of the following have interpreted the Third World experience.
Frantz Fanon

Chinua Achebe

V. S. Naipaul

Test your understanding of the chapter by providing the correct answers.

1. The Third World *has/has not* been very successful in lowering its death rate.

2. Most Third World countries are characterized by populations that are overwhelmingly concentrated in *the countryside/the cities*.

3. The birthrate in the Third World has *declined/not declined*.

4. In the 1960s most Third World countries adopted the idea of a _____ economy, which was part socialist and part capitalist.

5. For the most part, economic progress based on European-style industrialization *has/has not* worked for Third World countries.

6. Industrialization in the Third World *provided more jobs than there were workers to fill them/was seen as more desirable than agricultural development*.

7. The Green Revolution works best in countries where *there is a small number of big landowners/most of the land is peasant-owned*.

8. Unlike in Asia and Africa, the migration pattern in Latin America *has/has not* encouraged the women's liberation movement.

9. Recent advice from the "optimists" to Third World politicians is that the shantytowns should be *eliminated/supported*.

10. In general, the educational system of the Third World lays primary stress on a *technical/liberal arts* curriculum.

Multiple-Choice Questions

1. Since independence, Third World countries' populations have
   a. increased dramatically.
   b. increased only slightly.
   c. decreased.
   d. not changed.

2. National income statistics, such as those collected by the United Nations to compare the standard of living of rich and poor nations, are
   a. misleading and promote distorted comparisons.
   b. reliable and helpful.
   c. reliable to estimate food and clothing only.
   d. the best indicator of poverty.

3. The health status of people in the Third World has been the lowest in
   a. Asia.
   b. Latin America.
   c. tropical Africa.
   d. India.

4. The main beneficiaries of Third World economic growth were the
   a. rural masses.
   b. poor.
   c. peasants.
   d. businessmen and the skilled and professional workers.

5. South Korea and Taiwan engineered an economic miracle by emphasizing
   a. socialist economic principles.
   b. isolation from the world economy.
   c. dynamic capitalism.
   d. none of the above.

6. The Green Revolution
   a. works best in economies where land is held by a few big landowners.
   b. made many countries, such as India, food-sufficient.
   c. failed in Mexico but succeeded in Bangladesh.
   d. brought no benefits to small landowners.

7. Fears of famine and food crises in the Third World were partly a result of
   a. the Green Revolution.
   b. starvation in Mexico.
   c. the failure of agricultural growth in Communist China.
   d. near famine in India in 1966–67.

8. By the late 1960s it was clear to most Third World countries that
   a. industrialization had solved the problems of underdevelopment.
   b. only a "mixed economy" would bring about industrialization.
   c. industrialization had left them vulnerable to food shortages.
   d. industrialization had brought benefits to all segments of society.

9. In Asia and Africa, the majority of the migrants to the cities have been
   a. young men.
   b. women.
   c. families.
   d. all of the above.

10. The major problem with Third World university education is that
    a. it lacks students.
    b. education is not recognized as important.
    c. it does not have enough good teachers.
    d. it fails to stress technical education.

11. Frantz Fanon sees Western influence in the Third World as
    a. beneficial but short-lived.
    b. exploitative even after independence.
    c. important and beneficial because of its economic contributions.
    d. irrelevant.

12. Achebe argues that
    a. European culture must be taught in Africa.
    b. European culture is the key to African identity.
    c. African culture was born out of European imperialism.
    d. African culture existed prior to the European invasions.

13. Compared to the rich nations, the percentage of Third World children in school is
    a. about the same.
    b. higher.
    c. lower.
    d. higher in Asia, but lower in Latin America.

14. The great majority of urban workers in the Third World work in
    a. factories.
    b. irregular trades such as street selling.
    c. professions.
    d. construction.

15. The underlying message of Third World writers such as Achebe, Fanon, and Naipaul is that
    a. European domination brought benefits as well as damage.
    b. the colonial experience was a good way to break with tradition.
    c. real independence requires a break with Western culture.
    d. freedom can come only with industrialization.

16. In the Third World, the gap between rich and poor
    a. is much less than in the industrialized West.
    b. has become much less since independence.
    c. is considerable and is similar to that in pre-1914 Europe.
    d. is about the same as that in the industrialized West.

17. Which of the following statements about Third World countries is true?
    a. Few have experienced foreign domination.
    b. All have experienced a decline in health services since independence.
    c. All have populations that are heavily rural.
    d. All are unaware of their poverty.

18. The growth in Third World cities has been due to
    a. a rural population explosion.
    b. plentiful job opportunities in urban industry.
    c. rural people wanting to break away from traditional rural society.
    d. massive influxes of people from industrialized nations.

19. Which of the following Third World countries is considered an "economic miracle"?
    a. Kenya
    b. Brazil
    c. India
    d. South Korea

20. Paul Ehrlich, in his 1968 best-seller *The Population Bomb*, predicted that
    a. the Third World would rise to destroy the West.
    b. world death rates would increase dramatically.
    c. Third World countries would catch up to industrialized nations by the year 2000.
    d. massive immigration from the Third World to the West would occur.

21. Probably the most substantial success in the Third World in the past thirty years is
    a. the medical revolution.
    b. stable political organization.
    c. industrialization.
    d. agricultural reform.

22. The spraying of DDT in Southeast Asia has lowered the number of deaths caused by
    a. smallpox.
    b. cholera.
    c. bubonic plague.
    d. malaria.

23. The decline in the death rate of the Third World
    a. has lengthened life expectancy.
    b. accompanied a decline in the birthrate.
    c. did not include a decline in infant mortality.
    d. was not influenced by the medical revolution.

24. Most Third World economies are
    a. capitalist.
    b. mixed.
    c. socialist.
    d. barter.

25. The trend in the Third World since the late 1960s has been to
    a. deindustrialize.
    b. institute massive land reforms.
    c. coordinate rural development with industrialization.
    d. deurbanize.

26. The Green Revolution has been due in great part to
    a. the work of Western plant scientists.
    b. plentiful rainfall.
    c. shifting global weather patterns.
    d. the greenhouse effect.

27. The Green Revolution's greatest successes have occurred in
    a. Asia.
    b. Latin America.
    c. Africa.
    d. Bangladesh.

28. The "brain drain" affecting the Third World refers to
    a. poor educational systems.
    b. the disillusionment that rural workers have for education.
    c. a lack of technical schools.
    d. professionals educated in the West who do not return to their native countries.

Major Political Ideas

In the Third World the era after political emancipation became the era of industrial expansion. What is the relationship between industrialization and politics in the Third World? What have been the benefits? The associated failures and problems? Why have many become disillusioned with industrialization?

Issues for Essays and Discussion

How successful have Third World leaders and peoples been in improving their nations' well-being and ending the problems of poverty? Discuss this in terms of medicine, population growth, education, industrialization, and agriculture. What problems are left to be solved?

Interpretation of Visual Sources

Study the photograph "Peasant Farming in Ecuador" on page 1264 of the textbook. What does this tell us about agricultural methods? About life for women in the Third World?

Geography

Examine Map 38.1 in the textbook. What parts of the world have the highest population density? How do you explain this?

Problems for Further Investigation

1. Has land reform really helped the poor in the Third World? For the impact of land reform and agricultural policies on Third World countries, see J. Powelson and R. Stock, *The Peasant Betrayal: Agriculture and Land Reform in the Third World* (1987), and on the issue of Third World poverty and food supply, begin with F. M. Lappé and J. Collins, *Food First: Beyond the Myth of Scarcity** (1977).

2. What has been the relationship between the Third World and the industrialized West and Japan? Those who are interested in this subject will want to read Jean-Jacques Servan-Schreiber's book *The World Challenge* (1982). Servan-Schreiber argues that the world's industrialized countries have a moral obligation to transfer their knowledge of advanced technology to the underdeveloped Third World.

3. What are the implications of continuing population growth? A good place to begin, if you are interested in investigating the problem of population growth and how it relates to resources and production, is C. M. Cipolla, *The Economic History of World Population* (1974). This book has an excellent bibliography.

*Available in paperback.

4. What is life like in the shantytowns? The lowliest and poorest are hardly ever written about. A unique opportunity to understand life in the squalid shantytowns of Brazil (the *favelas*) is available in Carlina Maria De Jesus's book *Child of the Dark* (1962). Written on scraps of paper picked from gutters, this is a raw, primitive diary of a woman in the slums of São Paulo who fought daily for her survival and that of her three illegitimate children.

CHAPTER 39

One Small Planet

Chapter Objectives

After reading and studying this chapter, you should be able to answer the following questions:

How has the planet been organized politically, and will competing nation-states continue to dominate world politics? How does the human race use its resources to meet its material needs? What key ideas are guiding human behavior as our planet moves toward an uncertain future?

Chapter Summary

The purpose of this chapter is to show how the modern world has become increasingly interdependent—at the very time when the global economic order generates a measure of animosity and the global political system threatens to destroy us all. The problem is that our great technological achievements have not been matched by any corresponding change in the way we humans govern ourselves. Hence the triumph of nationalism is one of the tragic results of human history. The United Nations has not been able to establish a global authority that transcends the sovereign and quarrelsome national states. The Security Council's ability to police the world remains theoretical and severely restricted. Instead, the United Nations affirms and reinforces the primacy of the national state. Until the Persian Gulf war of 1991, the Security Council had succeeded only in quieting conflict between smaller states. The important question is whether the Security Council will continue the role it adopted in 1990–91. The General Assembly, on the other hand, has become the sounding board for the Third World. The U.N. has made its greatest contribution in the area of its specialized agencies, such as world health, labor, trade, and industrial development—responding to the Third World majority's successful expansion of the U.N.'s world mission.

The most striking and dangerous characteristics of our planet are its political complexity and its violence. Until the collapse of Soviet power and the re-unification of Germany in

1989–90, the old cold war hostilities remain very much alive. Now the East-West blocs are less solid than they were. With the rise of middle, or regional, powers such as Brazil, Nigeria, Iran, and India, which are intent on dominating their regions, the world is becoming increasingly multipolar. Hence we see not only a new plague of war, but a massive refugee problem that has left tens of millions homeless. Meanwhile, the East-West and multipolar drift to militarism has caused nuclear weapons to proliferate, although the recent Soviet–United States agreement signals that a new era may be in sight.

Ironically, alongside violence and political competition is a trend toward global interdependence—particularly in vital resources such as oil, air, and sea, and in capital and technology. Here we see two major problems. First, a rapid growth in world population has placed great pressures on resources; second, an unequal distribution of world wealth threatens relations between the rich North and the poor South. Out of this, and encouraged by the OPEC oil coup, the Third World has gone some distance toward the establishment of a "new international economic order" based on a more equitable distribution of the world's wealth. The chapter states that our future lies in global collective bargaining, as the case of the international debt crisis in 1981 suggests, and not in international class war. To be sure, despite the harmful consequences brought on by the multinational corporations, the multinationals are a striking feature of global economic interdependence.

The ideas by which the human race lives have taken on a global unity as well. Europe's secular ideologies of liberalism, nationalism, Marxian socialism, and democracy have come to be shared by the rest of the world. Marxism and the concept of "modernization" in particular have come under attack and have undergone revision by intellectuals, such as Djilas and Solzhenitsyn. Christianity has come under the spell of fundamentalism, as has the Islamic faith. At the same time, a whirlwind of mystical cults has accompanied a general global drift toward nonrational thought in popular literature and life.

Study Outline

Use this outline to preview the chapter before you read a particular section of your textbook and then as a self-check of your reading comprehension after you have read the chapter section.

I. World politics
   A. The human race has not matched its technological achievements with an effective global political organization—sovereign states still reign supreme.
   B. Nation-states and the United Nations
      1. Many Europeans and Americans have expressed disillusionment with the nation-state system; Toynbee believed that nationalism upset the balance between humans and their habitat.
      2. The United Nations was founded in 1945 to maintain international peace and security.
         a. A twelve-member Security Council was given the responsibility of maintaining world peace.

      b. In practice, the Security Council's power is limited by the veto power of the Big Five.

      c. The U.N. has reinforced the primacy of the national state.

      d. The General Assembly is more of a Third World debating society than a lawmaking body.

   3. The U.N. also exists to solve international problems and promote human rights.

   4. Through the 1980s, cold war politics deadlocked the Security Council.

      a. The General Assembly has assumed greater authority.

      b. The Third World majority has stressed anti-Western issues.

      c. The U.N. is often ignored, and most people identify with their own nation.

      d. Yet the U.N. has established powerful international agencies—such as those promoting world health, agriculture, and industrial growth—to deal with global issues.

   5. The U.N. took almost unprecedented action in 1990 when it imposed sanctions on Iraq and passed resolutions against Saddam Hussein that were enforced by the United States and its allies.

      a. This was possible only because China and the Soviet Union agreed to take action against Iraq.

      b. Only once before, in the Korean War, had the United States and its allies fought with U.N. authorization.

C. Complexity and violence

   1. The old East-West cold war still raged in the 1980s.

   2. Tensions within the East-West blocs weakened the superpowers—the U.S.S.R. and the United States.

      a. China and Poland challenged Soviet hegemony.

      b. Western Europe differed with the United States.

      c. The unification of Germany in 1989 signaled the end of the cold war.

   3. A "third force" of nonaligned nations was formed in 1955, leading to Latin American, African, and Asian nations working together at the U.N.

   4. World politics has become multipolar.

      a. New "middle powers"—such as Brazil, Mexico, Nigeria, Egypt, Israel, and Iran—have emerged.

      b. Multipolar politics is regionalist, highly competitive, and violent.

      c. Regional wars, such as in Lebanon and Kampuchea, have destroyed entire communities.

      d. A multitude of regional wars has created a serious world refugee problem.

D. The arms race and nuclear proliferation

   1. Multipolar politics has encouraged militarism in countries like Israel, South Africa, and Vietnam.

   2. Many countries are developing nuclear weapons capability.

   3. Despite U.S. hopes for international control of atomic weapons, the Soviets built an atomic bomb in 1949.

4. Popular concern over nuclear fallout led to test ban and nonproliferation treaties.
   a. France, China, and India have disregarded the nonproliferation treaty.
   b. Part of this disregard was due to U.S. and Soviet failures to move toward disarmament.
   c. The Soviet–U.S. nuclear arms race continued after the failure of the United States to ratify the SALT II agreement in 1980.
   d. Fear of its neighbors has led powers such as India to develop nuclear weapons.
   e. It is possible that Israel, Iraq, South Africa, and Pakistan also have the bomb.
5. New hopes emerged with Soviet-American cooperation to reduce nuclear arsenals, and with German renunication of nuclear weapons in 1990.

II. Global interdependence
   A. Although political and military competition between nations continues, nations find themselves increasingly dependent on one another in economic affairs, a fact that should promote peaceful cooperation.
   B. Pressure on vital resources
      1. Predictions of a shortage of resources have led to doubts about unlimited growth.
         a. The 1970s pointed to the problems of population explosion, resource shortages, and pollution of the biosphere.
         b. The OPEC price increases of 1973 caused widespread panic.
         c. Increased world demands have depleted Third World resources and land—for example, overuse of land has caused the Sahara to advance southward.
         d. Many claim that the biosphere and the oceans are becoming poisoned.
      2. The greatest pressure on world resources comes from population growth.
         a. Fortunately, birthrates have begun to fall in many Third World countries.
         b. Decline in child mortality, better living conditions, urbanization, and education encourage women to limit childbearing.
         c. Some state-run birth control programs, such as that in China, have succeeded.
         d. Elsewhere, as in India, the Muslim world, and the Americas, birth control is controversial and thus less successful.
         e. The prediction is that the present world population of 4 billion will not stabilize until it has hit 10 to 12 billion in about 2050.
         f. Some optimists argue that the earth can support this population.
   C. North-South relations
      1. Many in the Third World (the "South") argue that the present international system is exploitive and needs to be reformed.
         a. They demand that a "new international economic order" be established.
         b. The "theory of dependency" argument claims that Third World "underdevelopment" is deliberate and permanent.

2. The OPEC oil coup brought hope of greater world interdependence.
   a. The 1973–74 coup brought the end to economic boom, and a massive global transfer of wealth occurred.
   b. The U.N. followed with a call for a "new international economic order."
   c. The Program for Action and the Common Fund exist to give Third World countries greater control over their resources, to improve terms of exchange, and to reduce Third World debt.
   d. The United States and other nations have refused to agree to the new Law of the Sea.
   e. There are still sharp distinctions in terms of wealth and income.
   f. In reality, change will come through bargaining, not international class war.
3. The international debt crisis illustrates North-South dependency.
   a. World recession has caused many Third World states to overborrow.
   b. U.S. banks have rescued Mexico and others from financial crisis.
D. The multinational corporations
1. Multinationals are huge business firms that operate on a global, not national, basis.
   a. Supporters claim that multinationals will bring economic and technological unity to the world.
   b. Critics argue that multinationals are replacing nations.
2. The multinationals emerged with the postwar economic revival.
   a. These firms applied new technologies and marketing techniques to industry.
   b. Since the late nineteenth century, the United States has pioneered in mass production of standardized goods and developed advanced and innovative products.
3. U.S. oil and machinery firms led the way.
   a. This was known as "the American challenge" in Europe.
   b. They invested in Third World raw materials as well.
   c. By the 1970s, the Japanese and European multinationals pushed into the game, and Japan's new economic power caused fear in the United States.
   d. By 1989, Japan and Europe had invested considerably more in the United States than the United States had invested in Japan.
4. The social consequences of the multinationals are great.
   a. They have created islands of wealth and consumerism in the Third World.
   b. Critics claim that multinationals, as they take over Third World industries, are part of a growing neocolonialism, and many of their products are harmful to Third World people and society.
   c. However, Third World governments have learned how to control and manipulate the multinationals.

III. Patterns of thought
  A. Secular ideologies
    1. Most secular ideologies, such as liberalism and nationalism, evolved out of the Enlightenment and nineteenth-century Europe.
      a. The spread of secular ideology testifies to our global interdependence.
      b. These ideas develop and change as global dialogue takes place.
    2. Since 1945, Marxist ideology has been revised and criticized.
      a. New concepts, such as the idea of peasant revolution, have been injected into Marxism by Third World intellectuals.
      b. Yugoslavs claim that the Leninists and Stalinists have created a "new class" in history.
      c. Revel argued that communism has brought about totalitarianism rather than progressive socialism.
    3. Alternatives to traditional secular creeds have emerged.
      a. Sakharov advocates welfare capitalism and democratic socialism.
      b. Others argue that the best solution to human problems is internationalism.
      c. Solzhenitsyn, Heilbroner, and Schumacher typify the call for a return to a more simple life and alternative technologies.
  B. Religious belief: Christianity and Islam
    1. Pope John Paul II exemplifies the surge of popular Christianity.
      a. He preaches a liberal social gospel along with conservative religious doctrines.
      b. Poland illustrates the strength of spiritualism in a communist country.
    2. Islam has also experienced a powerful resurgence.
      a. The trend among Muslim intellectuals after 1945 was to modernize Islam.
      b. Recently the swing has been a return to strict fundamentalism.
      c. Iran's revolution was in part an Islamic fundamentalist reaction to modernization.
      d. The Ayatollah Khomeini's Islamic Republic seeks a return to rule by the laws of the Qur'an.
      e. This antimodernism is based on Shi'ite Islamic beliefs.
      f. Fundamentalism has found popularity in every Muslim country.
  C. Searching for mystical experience
    1. Meditation, mysticism, and a turn to the supernatural have become popular in industrialized societies.
    2. This illustrates the intellectual challenge from the non-Western world.
      a. More people today are receptive to mysticism.
      b. Heilbroner suggests that postindustrial people stress inner exploration rather than material accomplishment.
      c. Thompson and others contend that the search for spiritualism will humanize our technological world.

Review Questions

Check your understanding of this chapter by answering the following questions.

1. Why have some observers expressed disillusionment with nationalism and the nation-state system?

2. Describe the workings of the United Nations. Has it met its goals, and what have been its successes and weaknesses?

3. How and why has multipolar politics made world affairs more complex and more violent?

4. Why has the world been thrown into a renewal of the arms race? What or who is to blame?

5. Why have countries such as India spent valuable resources on nuclear arms development?

6. How does the problem of resource shortages illustrate the interdependence of rich and poor nations?

7. How successful has been the worldwide attempt to limit population growth? Is overpopulation a serious problem?

8. Many people of the Third World argue that they are being exploited by the rich northern nations. What is the basis of their argument? What do they seek with the so-called new international economic order?

9. Cite an argument for and an argument against the multinationals. Why did they emerge, and what have been the social consequences of their presence in Third World countries?

10. What is meant by the term *secular ideologies*? How has Marxism been revised and criticized in recent times?

11. What is religious fundamentalism, and how has it reinterpreted Christianity and Islam?

12. People today are more receptive to mysticism. Why? What forms does this take?

13. What effect has the Shi'ite Islamic faith had on Iranian society? On all of the Middle East?

Study-Review Exercises

Define the following key concepts and terms.

world population explosion

multipolar politics

proliferation of nuclear weapons

theory of dependency

new international economic order

Law of the Sea

religious fundamentalism

global interdependence

rich nations/poor nations

multinational corporations

Identify and explain the significance of the following people and terms.

OPEC

U.N. Security Council

United Nations

Afghanistan, 1978–79

Vietnam's "boat people"

Somalia-Ethiopia War

Strategic Arms Limitation Treaty

international debt crisis of the 1980s

Andrei Sakharov

Milovan Djilas

United Nations Common Fund

Ayatollah Khomeini

Pope John Paul II

1968 Treaty on the Non-Proliferation of Nuclear Weapons

Persian Gulf war

Explain the basic ideas of each of the following.
Solzhenitsyn's "return to the earth" doctrine

Islamic fundamentalism

modern search for mystical experience

Sakharov's "convergence school"

Djilas's interpretation of modern communism

Revel's idea of "phony" communist revolution

Limits to Growth study of 1972

Test your understanding of the chapter by providing the correct answers.

1. The trend in world politics has been toward *lesser/greater* gravitation of nations to the U.S. or Soviet camp.

2. The _____ of the United Nations has the responsibility of maintaining

   world peace, whereas the _____ has become an expression of Third World interests.

3. Since the early 1980s, population growth in the developed countries has *speeded up/slowed down*, while in poorer countries the birthrate has *speeded up/slowed down*.

4. It appears that Third World governments *have/have not* learned how to control and manipulate multinational corporations.

5. The trend in today's world is *toward/away from* nonrational, mystical experience.

6. The movement in global politics has been toward *East-West alignments/multipolar alignments*.

Multiple-Choice Questions

1. The goal of the "third force" or "middle powers," which are making the world increasingly multipolar, is to
   a. increase their political and military prowess to the level of a Great Power.
   b. achieve economic independence for their region.
   c. dominate their region.
   d. form regional alliances strong enough to oppose the Great Powers.

2. The world's vast refugee problem has been aggravated largely by
   a. famine.
   b. disease epidemics.
   c. local wars and civil conflicts.
   d. natural disasters.

3. The first and second largest armies in the world are the Soviet and Chinese, respectively. Which of the following nations is in third place?
   a. United States
   b. Great Britain
   c. Vietnam
   d. France

4. Treaties have failed to halt the spread of nuclear weapons because
   a. the United States and Russia have ignored the treaties.
   b. smaller powers have been anxious to develop their own nuclear weapons.
   c. nations have feared their enemies more than nuclear weapons.
   d. all of the above.

5. The chapter suggests that world population will stabilize in the mid-twentieth-first century at
   a. 10 to 12 billion.
   b. 6 to 8 billion.
   c. 15 billion.
   d. none of the above.

6. Steps toward the establishment of the Third World's "new international economic order" are most likely to include
   a. military action.
   b. tariff wars.
   c. global collective bargaining.
   d. "soak the rich" taxes.

7. It may be generally said of the Third World's debt to the West that
   a. most of it can never be repaid.
   b. additional loans are needed to prevent default.
   c. its level has dropped in recent years.
   d. most nations are able to back their payments with gold.

8. The trend among multinational corporations in Third World countries is for them to
   a. behave exactly as they please.
   b. treat natives as inferiors.
   c. increasingly submit to local control.
   d. become nationalized.

9. Most of the more recent contributions to Marxist thought have come from
   a. the Soviet Union.
   b. the Third World.
   c. eastern Europe.
   d. intellectuals in western Europe.

10. The Law of the Sea Treaty drawn up in the early 1980s
    a. has been universally adopted.
    b. is opposed by the Third World.
    c. is supported by the Soviet bloc.
    d. was opposed by the U.S. government.

11. Most of the secular ideologies such as liberalism
    a. are revivals of ancient ideas.
    b. were products of twentieth-century thought.
    c. originated in eighteenth- and nineteenth-century Europe.
    d. are becoming less popular today.

12. Internationalists are
    a. believers in the United Nations.
    b. unpatriotic individuals.
    c. in favor of world government.
    d. in favor of creeping socialism.

13. Muslim fundamentalists believe
    a. the Qur'an should be adapted to modern life.
    b. the Qur'an should be taken literally.
    c. in strict separation of church and state.
    d. none of the above.

14. It may be said of the communist states that
    a. they are still firmly under Soviet control.
    b. there are real tensions among them.
    c. the bloc is less solid than formerly.
    d. both b and c

15. Many developing nations see defense spending as a way to
    a. dominate their region.
    b. induce economic development.
    c. reduce unemployment.
    d. spend surplus oil revenues.

16. European contributions to modern Marxist thought have been largely
    a. economic theories.
    b. agricultural models.
    c. criticisms.
    d. ignored.

17. Andrei Sakharov envisions the East and West meeting in some ideological middle ground. This is called
    a. the cooperation theory.
    b. the convergence school.
    c. détente.
    d. none of the above.

18. William Thompson describes the search for mystical experiences as a
    a. rejection of traditional religion.
    b. mere fad.
    c. defeat for scientific thought.
    d. desire to humanize technology.

19. The Russian novelist Alexander Solzhenitsyn called on Soviet leaders to
    a. renounce Western technology.
    b. adopt population controls.
    c. adopt Western-style modernization and consumerism.
    d. renounce communism.

20. Ayatollah Khomeini's Islamic reform movement is founded on
    a. Westernization of Iran.
    b. support of the shah.
    c. separation of church and state.
    d. religious fundamentalism.

21. British historian Arnold Toynbee argued in his book *Mankind and Mother Earth* that
    a. the national state is the truest form of government.
    b. global government is necessary to maintain peace on earth.
    c. overpopulation is inevitable.
    d. man is inherently evil.

22. What fraction of the earth's people are Muslim?
    a. One-half
    b. One-seventh
    c. One-twentieth
    d. One-fiftieth

23. Milovan Djilas has argued that
    a. Lenin contributed the most to Marxist thought.
    b. Trotsky was an ineffectual idealist.
    c. Stalin-type communism created a new class.
    d. the Marxist dialectic has lost its value.

24. Which of the following is considered a "middle power"?
    a. Burma
    b. Ecuador
    c. Brazil
    d. Botswana

25. The second Strategic Arms Limitation Treaty
    a. failed to reduce the number of warheads.
    b. was never ratified by the U.S. Senate.
    c. called for reductions in stockpiles.
    d. succeeded in reducing the number of short-range missiles.

26. In China, abortion is
    a. free on demand.
    b. outlawed because it is subversive to the state.
    c. legal but expensive.
    d. available but discouraged.

27. Birthrates have remained much higher in Africa and South America than in Asia in
    recent years because in part
    a. Asians are less virile.
    b. Asian women are less fertile.
    c. the sexual revolution never reached Asia.
    d. contraception and abortion are controversial in Africa and South America.

Major Political Ideas

1. Why have Marxism and the faith in industrialization and modernism recently come
   under attack? Discuss this and give examples.

2. What are the political ideas and motives behind the "third force" of nonaligned nations
   and the idea of Third World solidarity?

Issues for Essays and Discussion

Discuss and describe the present organization of the planet in terms of the success and failures of nationalism and internationalism. Which has prevailed, and what are the current trends? Support your arguments with as much evidence as possible.

Interpretation of Visual Sources

Study Figure 39.1, "Total Investment by American Corporations in Foreign Subsidiaries," on page 1302 of the textbook. When did the most significant increase take place? What does this mean? Is foreign investment in the United States of any significance?

Geography

Study Map 39.4 in the textbook, "Estimated GNP per Capita Income in the Early 1980s," and then answer the following questions.

1. What are the various "classes" of nations in terms of wealth and income? Is there a north-south divide?

2. What characteristics distinguish each "class"? Is the trend toward greater or lesser interdependence?

Problems for Further Investigation

1. What are the most important research topics relating to the recent past and the present? Many research topics are suggested in two excellent periodicals. They are *Current History* and *History Today*, both of which specialize in looking at current world events from a historical perspective.

2. Is nuclear war likely? Those interested in pursuing the issue of the arms race and the possibility of nuclear war will want to begin with D. Halloway, *The Soviet Union and the Arms Race* * (1984), and G. Kennan, *The Nuclear Delusion: Soviet-American Relations in the Atomic Age* * (1982). A provocative look at the business of nuclear strategy in the 1950s and 1960s is *The Wizards of Armageddon* * (1983) by F. Kaplan. An excellent way to

*Available in paperback.

pursue this chapter's look into the complexities of Polish-Soviet relations is to begin with *The Polish August: The Self-Limiting Revolution** (1982) by N. Ascherson.

3. What have Russian intellectuals written about their own society? This chapter has discussed the views of a number of important Soviet writers. You can find further discussion of Sakharov's views in his book, *Progress, Coexistence, and Intellectual Freedom* (1970 edition), and Djilas's criticism of how the Marxist system works is found in his book, *The New Class** (1957).

4. What is the human prospect? In two of his books the renowned biologist René Dubos discusses how humans are shaped by their environment, and how we need to control the forces of urbanization and technology. His famous slogan "think globally, act locally" could well serve as a blueprint for balance in nature and nations alike. The books are *So Human an Animal* (1970) and *Celebrations of Life** (1981).

*Available in paperback.

Answers to Objective Questions

Chapter 14

Study-Review Exercises

Test your understanding.

1. *Unam Sanctam*	6. Sicily	11. Hanseatic League	16. England, France
2. Exchequer	7. Magna Carta	12. Peter Abelard	17. economic
3. Frederick Barbarossa	8. Scholastic	13. Thomas Becket	
4. *Domesday Book*	9. Romanesque	14. did not	
5. England	10. *summa*	15. bad	

Place the following events in chronological order.

1. 2	4. 5	7. 8
2. 7	5. 1	8. 4
3. 3	6. 6	

Multiple-Choice Questions

1. b	8. a	15. a	22. a
2. b	9. a	16. c	23. b
3. b	10. c	17. a	24. c
4. d	11. a	18. d	25. c
5. b	12. c	19. d	26. d
6. c	13. d	20. c	27. d
7. d	14. c	21. d	

Chapter 15

Study-Review Exercises

Test your understanding.

1. south
2. Five
3. Phoenicians
4. Sundiata
5. Mansa Musa
6. Timbuktu
7. Portuguese

Multiple-Choice Questions

1. c	8. b	15. a	22. a
2. a	9. b	16. d	23. d
3. c	10. d	17. d	24. a
4. c	11. d	18. c	25. d
5. c	12. d	19. c	26. a
6. b	13. c	20. a	
7. c	14. c	21. d	

Chapter 16

Study-Review Exercises

Test your understanding.

1. Andes
2. Amazon
3. Huitzilopochtli
4. Aztecs
5. Toltec
6. Manco Capac

Multiple-Choice Questions

1. b	6. d	11. d	16. b
2. d	7. a	12. c	17. a
3. c	8. b	13. a	
4. a	9. d	14. a	
5. c	10. b	15. c	

Chapter 17

Study-Review Exercises

Test your understanding.

1. Niccolò Machiavelli
2. less
3. increased
4. Thomas More
5. declined
6. is not
7. did
8. king
9. political
10. Alexander VI

Multiple-Choice Questions

1. d	8. b	15. d	22. c
2. b	9. b	16. b	23. b
3. b	10. b	17. a	24. c
4. d	11. a	18. c	25. b
5. d	12. d	19. a	
6. c	13. a	20. b	
7. b	14. b	21. d	

Chapter 18

Study-Review Exercises

Test your understanding.

1. Thirty Years' War	5. Gustavus Adolphus	7. Amsterdam	11. Concordat of
2. Cortés	6. the United	8. Elizabeth I	Bologna
3. Edict of Nantes	Provinces of the	9. skepticism	12. Portugal
4. sixteenth	Netherlands	10. Charles V	

Multiple-Choice Questions

1. a	9. a	17. b	25. c
2. b	10. c	18. d	26. d
3. d	11. a	19. d	27. a
4. d	12. b	20. c	28. b
5. d	13. c	21. d	
6. b	14. c	22. b	
7. a	15. b	23. c	
8. b	16. b	24. a	

Chapter 19

Study-Review Exercises

Test your understanding.

1. stadholder	5. John Churchill	9. increased	12. Frederick II
2. Colbert	6. Laud	10. Suleiman the	(the Great)
3. entered	7. Calvin	Magnificent	
4. disaster	8. Peter the Great	11. maintained	

Multiple-Choice Questions

1. b	9. d	17. d	25. b
2. d	10. b	18. d	26. b
3. a	11. b	19. a	27. a
4. d	12. a	20. c	28. b
5. d	13. a	21. a	29. a
6. d	14. c	22. b	
7. b	15. c	23. a	
8. c	16. a	24. b	

Chapter 20

Study-Review Exercises

Test your understanding.

1. water, earth	4. universal gravitation	7. was not	10. Newton
2. did not	5. philosophy	8. did not	11. failed
3. motion	6. Portugal	9. skeptic	

Place the following events in chronological order.

1. 4	3. 5	5. 3
2. 1	4. 2	

Multiple-Choice Questions

1. a	8. d	15. a	22. a
2. b	9. d	16. c	23. c
3. c	10. b	17. b	24. c
4. d	11. a	18. d	25. a
5. d	12. a	19. c	
6. c	13. a	20. d	
7. b	14. b	21. a	

Chapter 21

Study-Review Exercises

Test your understanding.

1. limited	4. potato	7. the common people
2. was not	5. longer	8. Wesley
3. did	6. cowpox	

Multiple-Choice Questions

1. b	8. d	15. b	22. d
2. d	9. b	16. c	23. c
3. b	10. c	17. d	24. a
4. c	11. c	18. a	25. c
5. c	12. d	19. d	
6. b	13. a	20. b	
7. a	14. d	21. d	

Chapter 22

Study-Review Exercises

Test your understanding.

1. Swahili	3. Songhay	5. England	7. varied
2. homogeneous	4. Portuguese	6. did	

Multiple-Choice Questions

1. b	6. c	11. c	16. a
2. b	7. b	12. b	17. d
3. b	8. c	13. a	18. b
4. c	9. d	14. c	19. d
5. a	10. d	15. c	

Chapter 23

Multiple-Choice Questions

1. b	7. b	13. a	19. d
2. a	8. d	14. c	20. a
3. a	9. a	15. b	
4. b	10. c	16. d	
5. a	11. a	17. d	
6. d	12. b	18. d	

Chapter 24

Study-Review Exercises

Test your understanding.

1. Hung Wu
2. increased, more
3. was
4. was
5. growth

Multiple-Choice Questions

1. d	8. a	15. b	22. b
2. b	9. a	16. c	23. a
3. c	10. b	17. b	24. c
4. c	11. b	18. a	25. c
5. a	12. a	19. b	26. b
6. b	13. b	20. d	27. c
7. a	14. d	21. a	

Chapter 25

Study-Review Exercises

Test your understanding.

1. Trafalgar
2. an important
3. Thomas Paine
4. a great deal of
5. victory
6. a military ruler

Multiple-Choice Questions

1. c	8. a	15. a	22. a
2. d	9. d	16. a	23. d
3. d	10. c	17. a	24. d
4. a	11. d	18. b	25. b
5. d	12. d	19. b	
6. c	13. a	20. d	
7. c	14. c	21. d	

Chapter 26

Study-Review Exercises

Test your understanding.

1. 1780/textile
2. increased
3. James Watt
4. iron
5. Liverpool-Manchester, *Rocket*
6. decrease
7. Crystal Palace
8. decreased
9. greater
10. Zollverein
11. decreased
12. Factory, decrease

Multiple-Choice Questions

1. d
2. a
3. d
4. a
5. a
6. b
7. b
8. b
9. b
10. d
11. b
12. a
13. b
14. a
15. a
16. c
17. a
18. d
19. d
20. a
21. c
22. a
23. d
24. b
25. d
26. d

Chapter 27

Study-Review Exercises

Test your understanding.

1. defeat
2. Louis Napoleon
3. Eugène Delacroix
4. should not
5. Austrian
6. Johann Herder
7. Louis Blanc
8. competition/victory

Multiple-Choice Questions

1. a
2. a
3. b
4. c
5. c
6. a
7. c
8. c
9. b
10. d
11. a
12. d
13. b
14. d
15. c
16. b
17. c
18. a
19. d
20. c
21. b
22. d
23. a
24. d
25. a

Chapter 28

Study-Review Exercises

Test your understanding.

1. decreased
2. Bentham
3. antiseptic
4. 1890
5. improved
6. no change
7. labor aristocracy
8. rose
9. music halls
10. love
11. stronger
12. more
13. decreased

Multiple-Choice Questions

1. a
2. b
3. a
4. c
5. a
6. d
7. a
8. d
9. c
10. b
11. a
12. c
13. a
14. c
15. d
16. c
17. d
18. c
19. b
20. b
21. c
22. b
23. a
24. b
25. a

Chapter 29

Study-Review Exercises

Test your understanding.

1. approved
2. middle
3. defeat, freedom
4. opposed
5. fell
6. Protestant, against
7. France

Multiple-Choice Questions

1. b
2. b
3. c
4. d
5. b
6. c
7. a
8. c
9. c
10. b
11. c
12. b
13. c
14. d
15. a
16. b
17. d
18. b
19. b
20. c
21. a
22. d
23. a
24. d
25. c

Chapter 30

Study-Review Exercises

Test your understanding.
1. Lord Kitchener
2. Khedive Ismail
3. H. M. Stanley
4. Evelyn Baring
5. Walter Bagehot
6. Commodore Perry
7. Sun Yat-sen
8. Tzu Hsi

Multiple-Choice Questions

1. c	8. d	15. a	22. a
2. c	9. b	16. b	23. c
3. b	10. a	17. c	24. c
4. a	11. a	18. a	25. d
5. b	12. b	19. a	
6. b	13. c	20. a	
7. c	14. b	21. d	

Chapter 31

Study-Review Exercises

Test your understanding.
1. Creoles, peninsulares
2. encouraged
3. more
4. Creoles
5. unfavorable
6. the United States, Britain
7. long, rare
8. only slaves in rebel states
9. two
10. Jacob Riis
11. did

Multiple-Choice Questions

1. b	10. b	19. c	28. a
2. a	11. c	20. d	29. c
3. b	12. a	21. d	30. c
4. d	13. d	22. b	31. c
5. a	14. b	23. a	32. b
6. c	15. b	24. b	
7. b	16. d	25. d	
8. b	17. b	26. b	
9. d	18. b	27. b	

Chapter 32

Study-Review Exercises

Test your understanding.

1. Belgium
2. Vladimir Lenin
3. Georges Clemenceau
4. Leon Trotsky
5. Rasputin
6. Schleiffen
7. June 28, 1914
8. Alexander Kerensky
9. soviets
10. T. E. Lawrence
11. Brest-Litovsky
12. Bismarck
13. Black Hand
14. Russia
15. Duma

Place the following events in chronological order.

1. 1
2. 4
3. 3
4. 2
5. 5
6. 7
7. 6

Multiple-Choice Questions

1. a
2. a
3. c
4. c
5. b
6. c
7. b
8. c
9. d
10. c
11. d
12. b
13. a
14. c
15. a
16. a
17. a
18. b
19. a
20. d
21. d
22. a
23. d
24. c
25. b
26. d

Chapter 33

Study-Review Exercises

Test your understanding.

1. mandates
2. support for its Arab subjects
3. accepted
4. in favor of
5. France, Christian
6. kibbutz
7. less
8. included in, excluded from

Multiple-Choice Questions

1. d
2. b
3. a
4. b
5. a
6. a
7. c
8. a
9. b
10. d
11. b
12. b
13. d
14. c
15. d
16. c
17. d
18. a
19. a
20. b
21. c
22. b
23. a
24. b
25. c
26. d
27. d
28. b

Chapter 34

Study-Review Exercises

Test your understanding.

1. were not	2. Germany, Britain, France, the United States	3. Paul Valéry 4. discard 5. challenge	6. J. M. Keynes

Multiple-Choice Questions

1. a	8. d	15. c	22. c
2. b	9. c	16. c	23. d
3. c	10. a	17. d	24. c
4. c	11. c	18. d	25. b
5. c	12. a	19. c	
6. a	13. a	20. b	
7. a	14. d	21. b	

Chapter 35

Study-Review Exercises

Test your understanding.

1. favored	4. right	7. was	10. pro-German
2. refused	5. do not	8. Adolf Hitler	11. did not
3. victory, disaster	6. Benito Mussolini	9. declined	

Multiple-Choice Questions

1. d	8. c	15. d	22. c
2. d	9. c	16. d	23. c
3. d	10. c	17. c	24. c
4. a	11. c	18. a	25. d
5. a	12. c	19. b	
6. d	13. c	20. b	
7. c	14. a	21. c	

Chapter 36

Multiple-Choice Questions

1. c	8. d	15. b	22. a
2. a	9. d	16. b	23. c
3. a	10. b	17. c	24. b
4. b	11. b	18. b	
5. d	12. d	19. c	
6. d	13. b	20. b	
7. c	14. d	21. b	

Chapter 37

Study-Review Exercises

Test your understanding.

1. strengthened
2. did not
3. Douglas MacArthur
4. is
5. based more on cooperation
6. Jinnah, Pakistan, Bangladesh
7. did not
8. limiting
9. Achmed Sukarno
10. Mandela

Multiple-Choice Questions

1. b	9. d	17. d	25. a
2. c	10. c	18. b	26. a
3. a	11. a	19. c	27. b
4. a	12. d	20. a	28. c
5. c	13. b	21. b	
6. a	14. c	22. b	
7. d	15. b	23. d	
8. b	16. d	24. c	

Chapter 38

Study-Review Exercises

Test your understanding.

1. has
2. the cities
3. declined
4. mixed
5. has not
6. provided more jobs than there were workers to fill them
7. most of the land is peasant-owned
8. has
9. supported
10. liberal arts

Multiple-Choice Questions

1. a	9. a	17. c	25. c
2. a	10. d	18. a	26. a
3. c	11. b	19. d	27. a
4. d	12. d	20. b	28. d
5. c	13. c	21. a	
6. b	14. b	22. d	
7. d	15. c	23. a	
8. c	16. c	24. b	

Chapter 39

Study-Review Exercises

Test your understanding.

1. lesser
2. Security Council, General Assembly
3. slowed down, speeded up
4. have
5. toward
6. multipolar alignments

Multiple-Choice Questions

1. c	8. c	15. b	22. b
2. c	9. b	16. c	23. c
3. c	10. d	17. b	24. c
4. d	11. c	18. d	25. b
5. a	12. c	19. a	26. a
6. c	13. b	20. d	27. d
7. b	14. d	21. b	

Outline Map 14.2

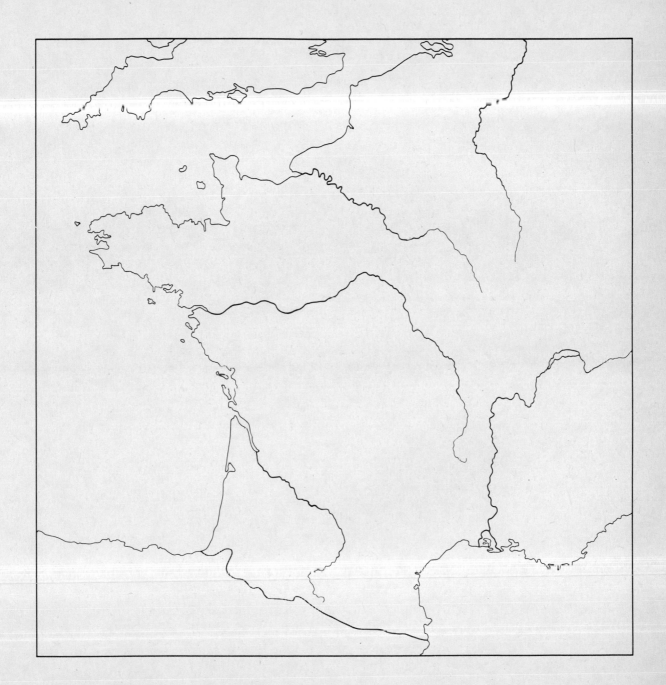

Outline Map 15.1

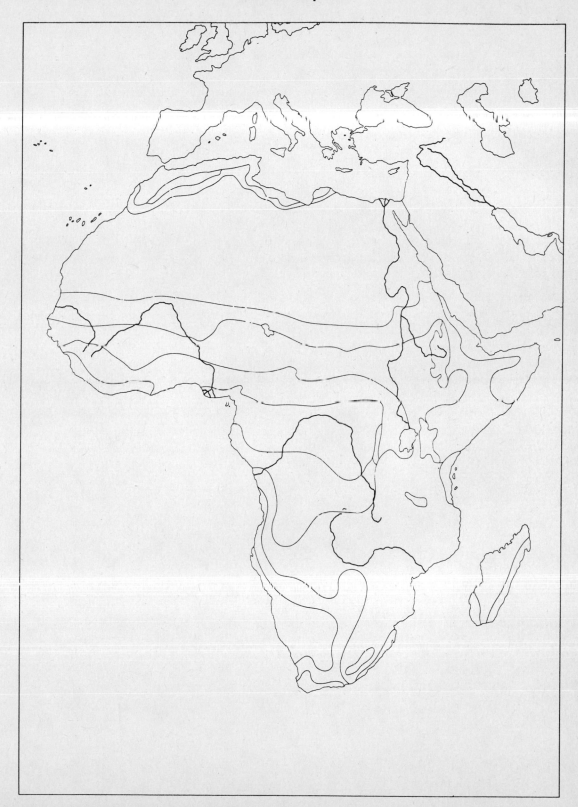

Outline Map 16.4

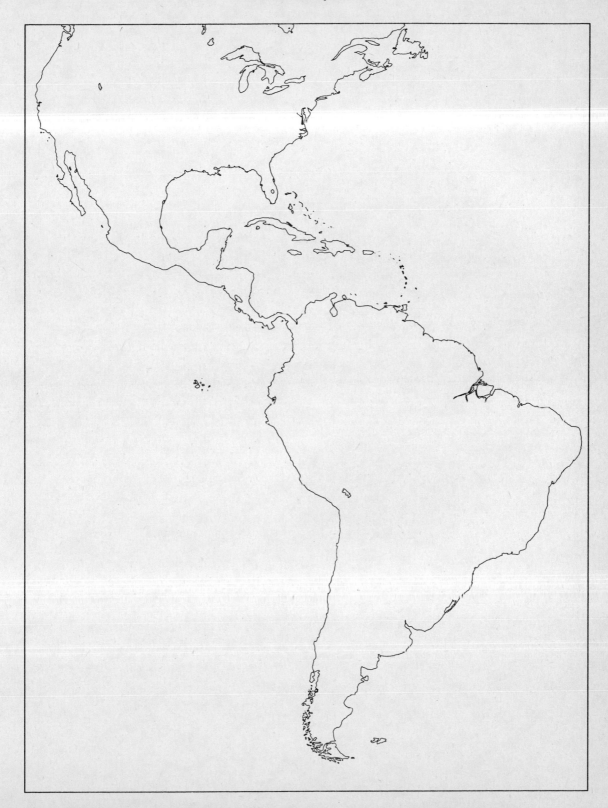

Outline Map 17.1

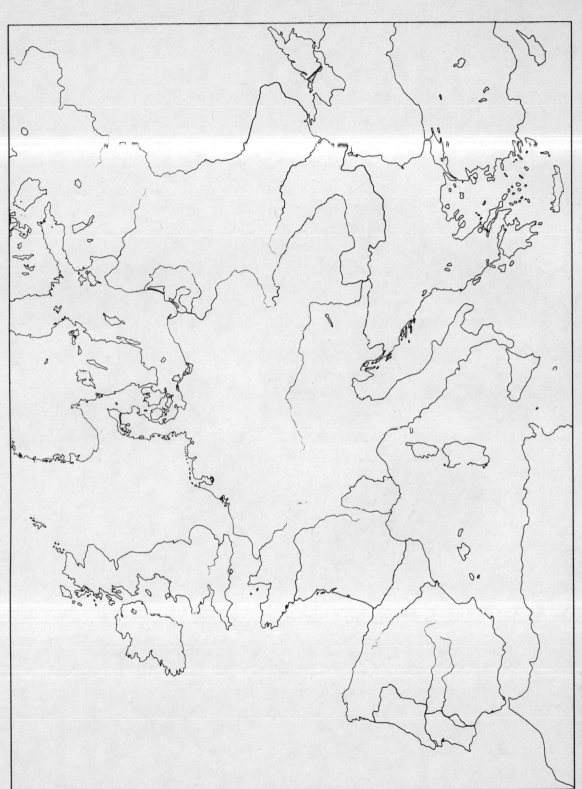

Outline Map 17.4

Outline Map 18.1

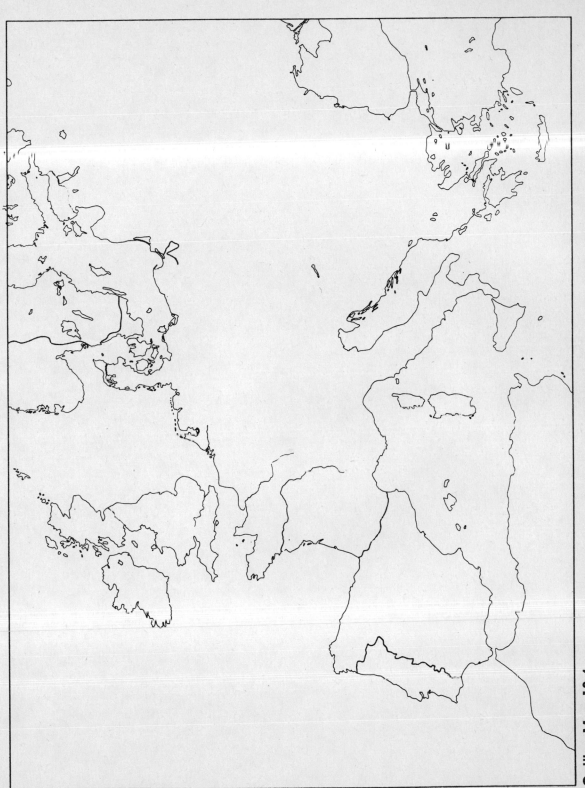

Outline Map 18.4

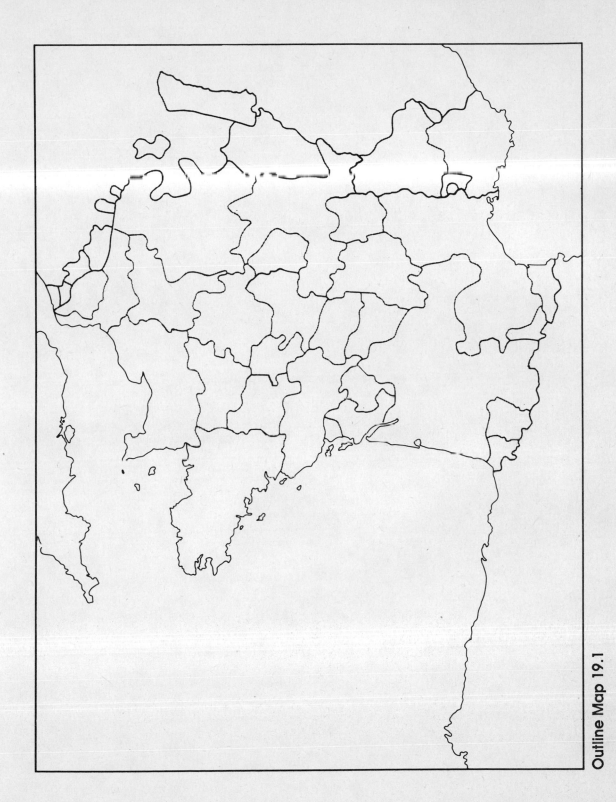

Outline Map 19.1

Outline Map 19.4

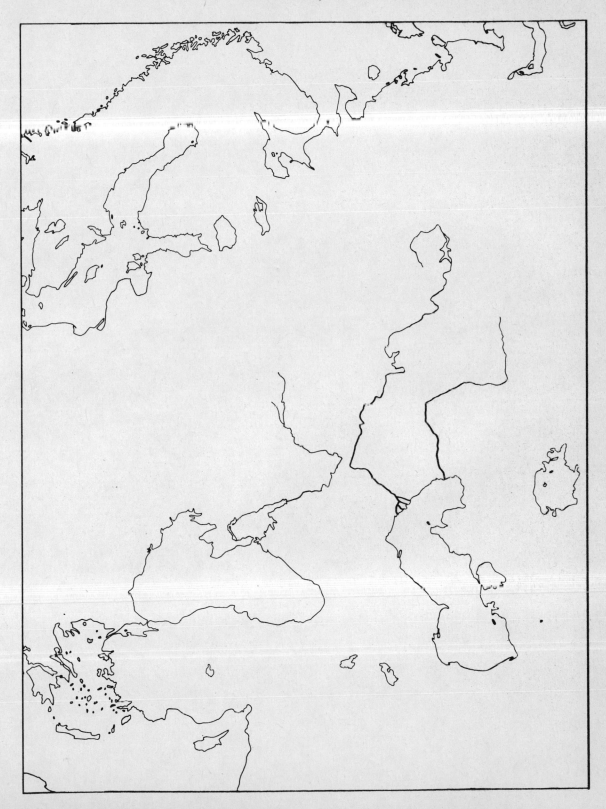

Outline Map 22.3

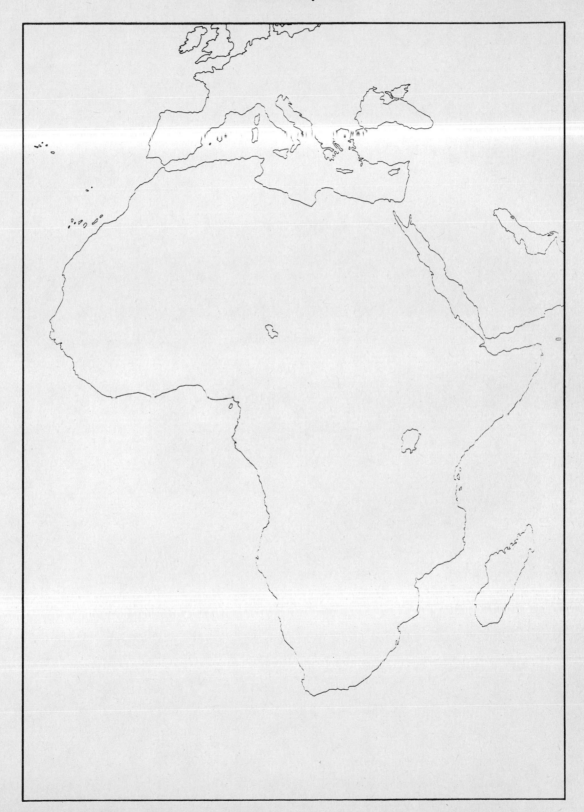

Outline Map 23.1

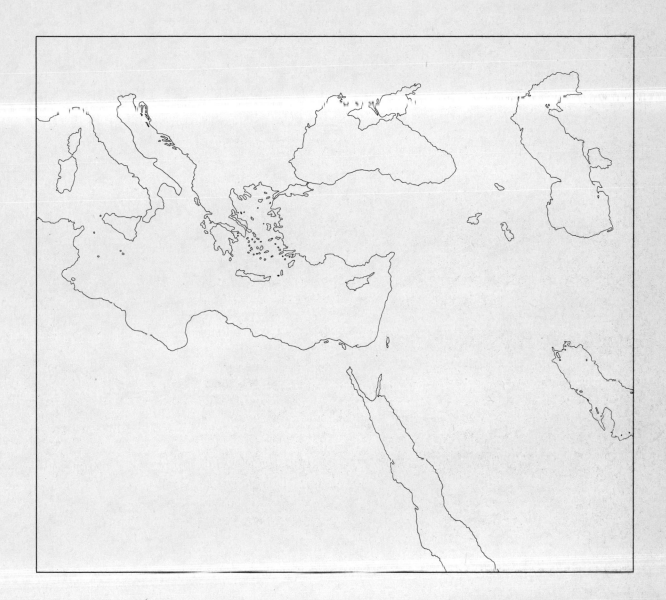

Outline Map 24.1

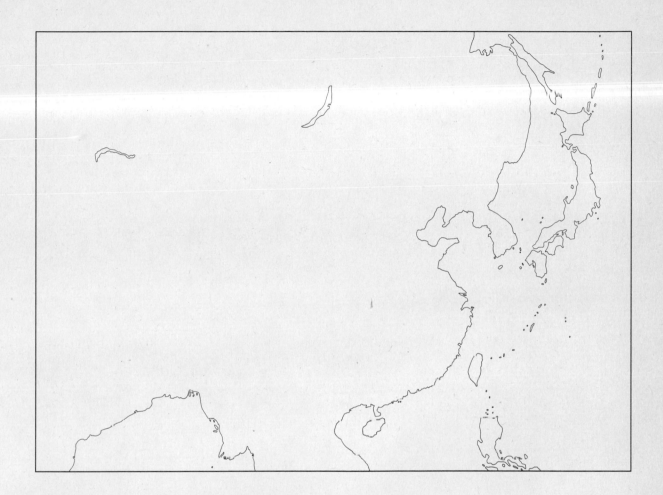

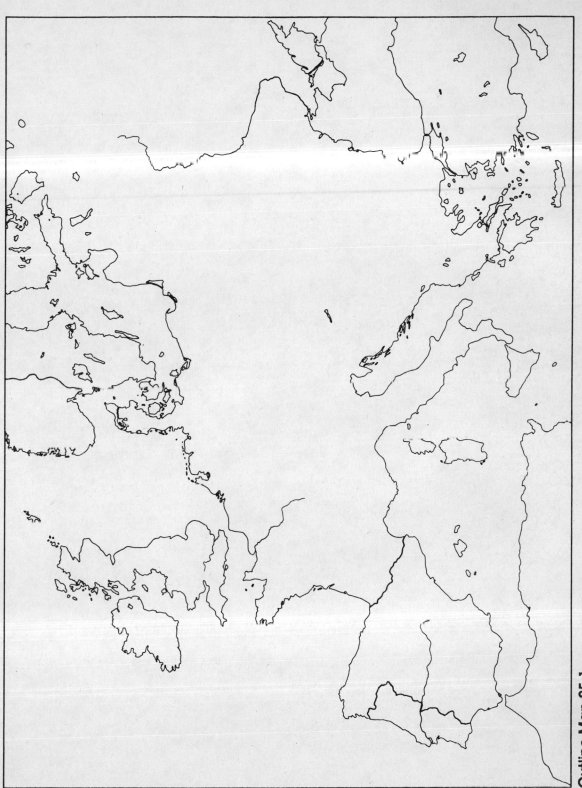

Outline Map 25.1

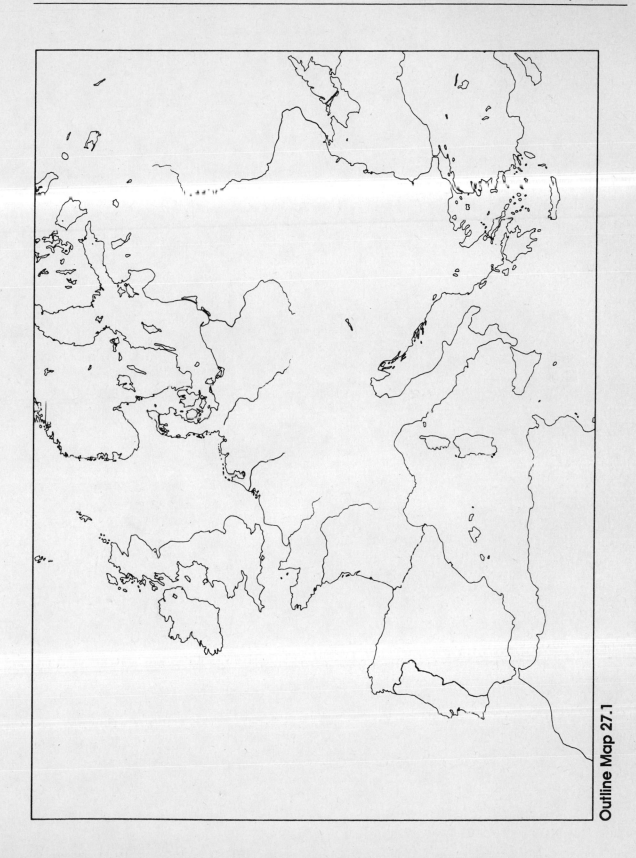

Outline Map 27.1

Outline Map 29.2

Outline Map 30.2

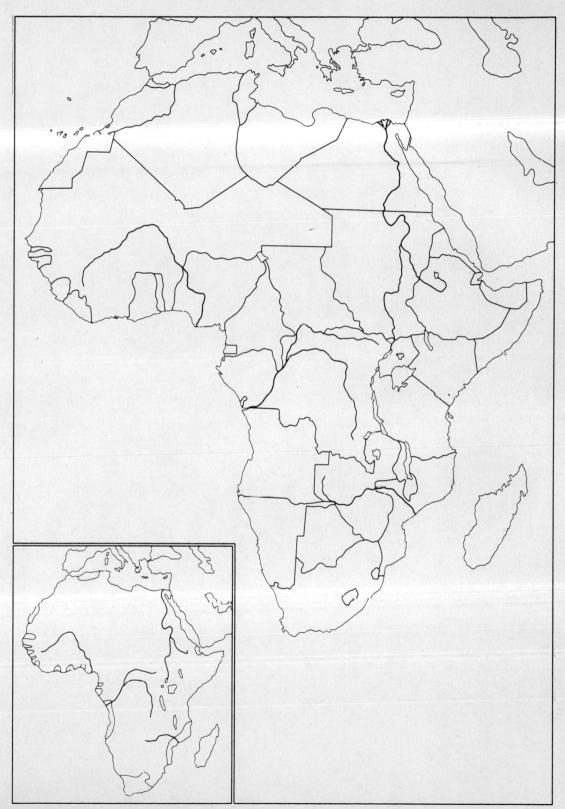

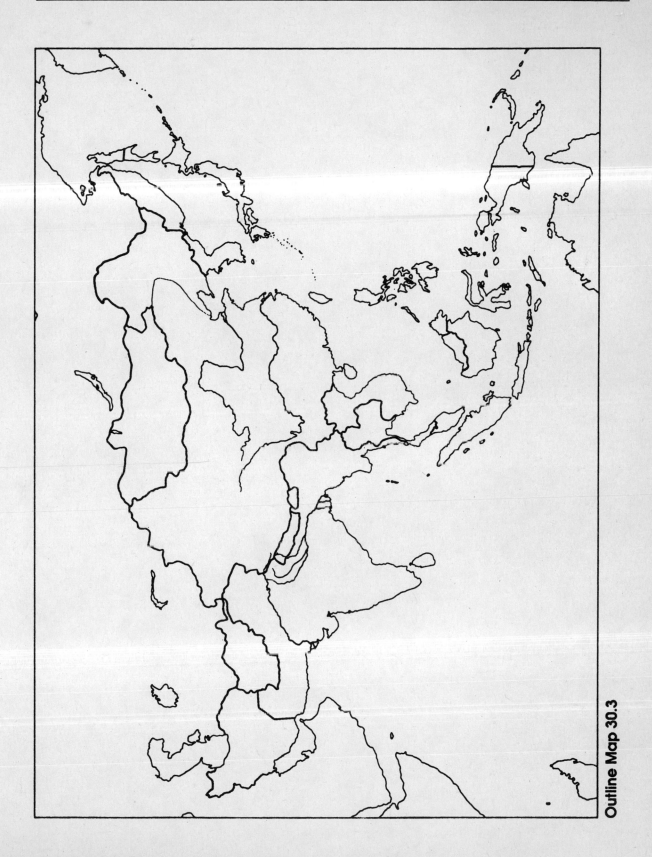

Outline Map 30.3

Outline Map 31.2

Outline Map 32.4

Outline Map 33.1

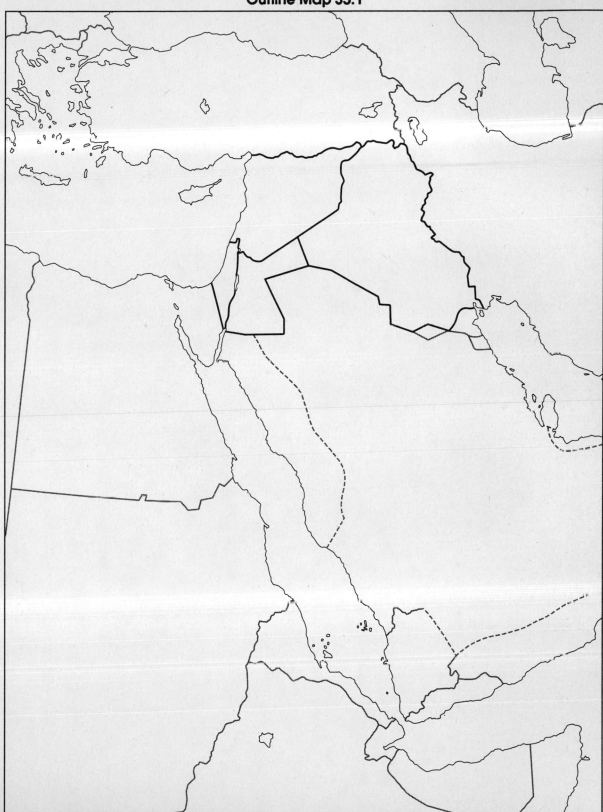

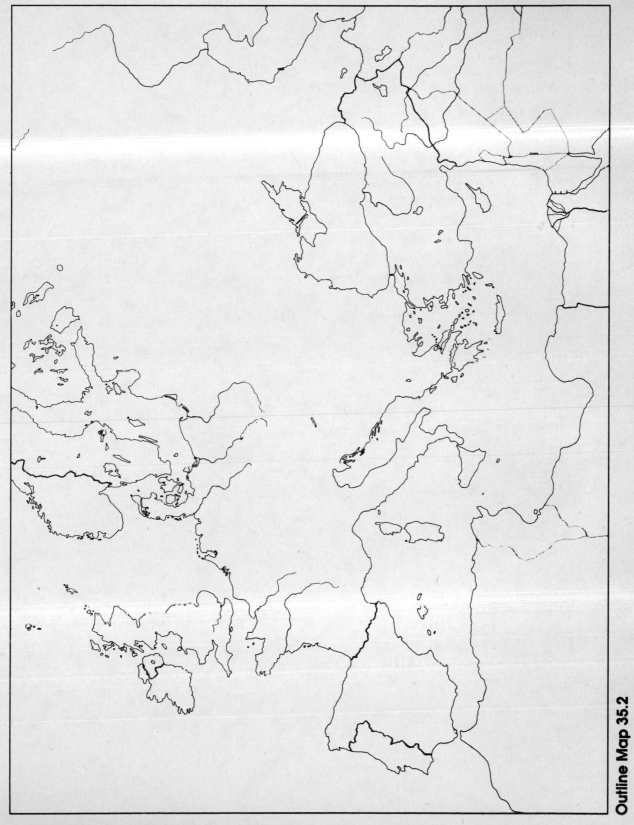

Outline Map 35.2

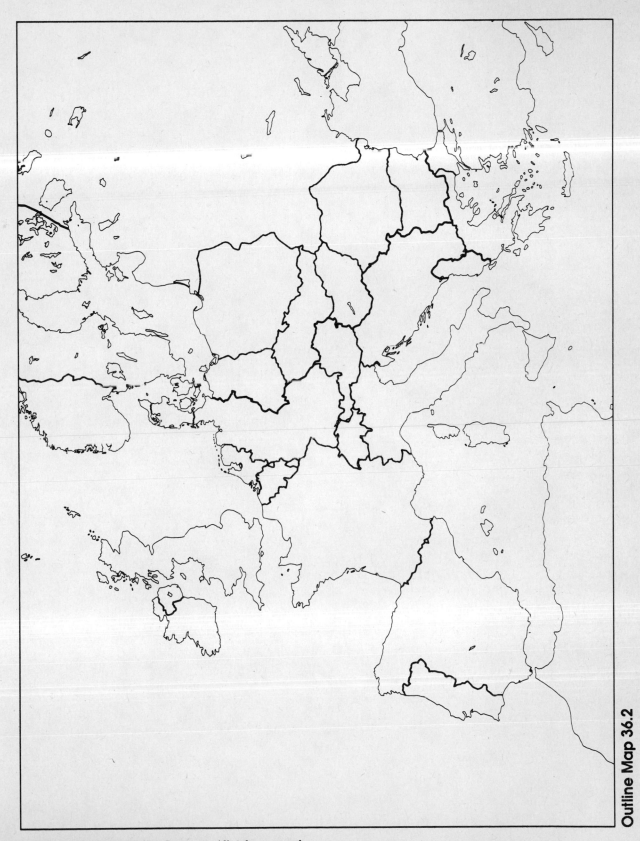

Outline Map 36.2

Outline Map 37.2

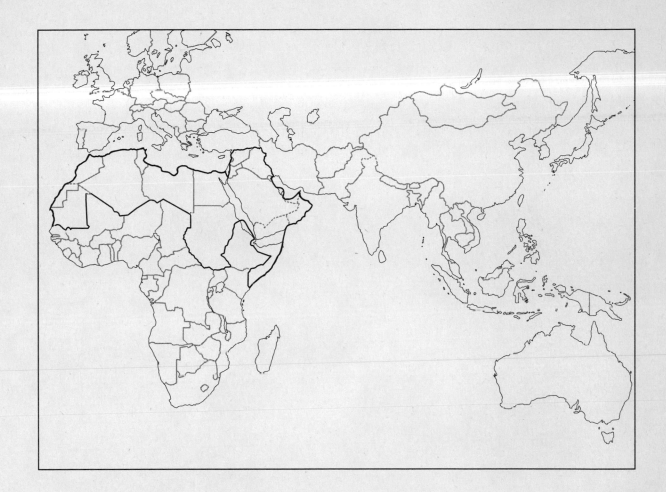